Ho Chi Minh City (Saigon)

Mason Florence
Robert Storey

LONELY PLANET PUBLICATIONS
Melbourne • Oakland • London • Paris

Ho Chi Minh City (Saigon)
2nd edition – January 2001
First published – October 1995

Published by
Lonely Planet Publications Pty Ltd ABN 36 005 607 983
90 Maribyrnong St, Footscray, Victoria 3011, Australia

Lonely Planet Offices
Australia Locked Bag 1, Footscray, Victoria 3011
USA 150 Linden St, Oakland, CA 94607
UK 10a Spring Place, London NW5 3BH
France 1 rue du Dahomey, 75011 Paris

Photographs
All of the images in this guide are available for licensing from Lonely Planet Images.
email: lpi@lonelyplanet.com.au

Front cover photograph
Billboard detail (Bethune Carmichael)

ISBN 0 86442 614 3

Printed by SNP Offset (M) Sdn Bhd

RICHARD I'ANSON

The ubiquitous Uncle Ho: a statue of Ho Chi Minh with typical raised-right-hand gesture, Cantho.

JOHN BANAGAN

A boy poses before Le Van Duyet Temple.

PHIL WEYMOUTH

Two-wheeled traffic on DL Le Duan

ANDERS BLOMQVIST

French-colonial splendour: the Hotel de Ville, now home to the People's Committee

RICHARD I'ANSON

Billboards and skyscrapers (seen from the Saigon River) are tangible evidence of 'new thinking'.

Contents – Text

Contents – Maps

THINGS TO SEE & DO

EXCURSIONS

COLOUR MAPS

The Authors

Mason Florence

Mason gave up his budding career as a rodeo cowboy in 1990, traded in his boots and spurs for a Nikon and a laptop, and relocated from Colorado to Japan. Now a Kyoto-based photo-journalist, he spends half the year on the road in South-East Asia, and free moments in Japan restoring a 300-year-old thatched-roof farmhouse in rural Shikoku. Since his first arrival in Vietnam in 1991, Mason has returned dozens of times. He has travelled the length of the country by every conceivable means of transport; from motorbike to water buffalo to basket boat.

In addition to this guide, Mason has worked on LP's *South-East Asia*, *Vietnam*, *Hanoi*, *Japan*, *Kyoto*, *Hiking in Japan* and *Rocky Mountain States*. His travel articles have been printed in publications around the world, and his photographs, notably those of Vietnam's colourful ethnic minorities, appear all over the country as *'Postcards from the Edge'*.

From Mason Florence I'd like to express my gratitude to all who shared their knowledge and tips. Special thanks to Sinh and Tram, my Saigon lifeline, and to Richard Craik and Peter Murray for their tireless advice (and for putting up with the countless questions).

Robert Storey

Robert has had a number of distinguished careers, including monkeykeeper at a zoo and slot-machine repairman in a Las Vegas casino. It was during this era that he produced his first book, *How to Do Your Own Divorce in Nevada*, which sold nearly 200 copies. Since this wasn't enough to keep him in the manner to which he was accustomed, Robert decided to skip the country and sought his fortune in Taiwan as an English teacher. But writing was in his blood, and he was soon flooding the Taiwanese market with various books.

Robert's *Taiwan On Your Own* attracted the attention of Lonely Planet, and was rehashed to become LP's *Taiwan*. Since then, Robert has been involved in over a dozen LP projects, all to do with East Asian countries. His latest scheme – still a work in progress – is his first novel, *Life in the Fast Lane*.

This Book

FROM THE PUBLISHER

This (long-overdue) second edition of Ho Chi Minh City was authored and revised by our man in Shikoku, Mason Florence. Robert Storey authored the first edition.

The book was produced in LP's Melbourne office. Along the way, it passed through many willing hands. Among these were the hands of Kristin Odijk, Martin Heng and Jocelyn Harewood, supervising editors, Lucy Williams, manuscript assessor, Michael Day, editor, Pablo Gastar, book designer and inimitable illustrator of our frog-in-a-cyclo chapter ends, Margaret Jung, who designed this cover and that of its joined-at-the-hip twin, *Hanoi*, Chris Love, supervising designer, Neb Milic, Jack Gavran and Kusnandar, designer/cartographers, Quentin Frayne, who put together the Language chapter, Glenn Beanland, photos and images person, Matt King, illustrations coordinator, Tim Uden, layout and software solutions go-to guy, Jane Hart, design-checking person.

THANKS

Many thanks to the travellers who used the last edition and wrote to us with helpful hints, useful advice and interesting anecdotes:

Bettina Holl, Cecil F Bowes, Gayle De Gregori, Haroon Akram-Lodhi, Jamie Uhrig, Joan Rivs Illop, John Pracy, Kwong, Lim Seng, MA Childers, Mark Robinson, Mary Guthrie, Michael Moeller, Nadia Lafrate, Patricia Vo, Ray Coe, Richard Johnson, Robert Graham, Tara Brayshaw

Foreword

ABOUT LONELY PLANET GUIDEBOOKS

The story begins with a classic travel adventure: Tony and Maureen Wheeler's 1972 journey across Europe and Asia to Australia. Useful information about the overland trail did not exist at that time, so Tony and Maureen published the first Lonely Planet guidebook to meet a growing need.

From a kitchen table, then from a tiny office in Melbourne (Australia), Lonely Planet has become the largest independent travel publisher in the world, an international company with offices in Melbourne, Oakland (USA), London (UK) and Paris (France).

Today Lonely Planet guidebooks cover the globe. There is an ever-growing list of books and there's information in a variety of forms and media. Some things haven't changed. The main aim is still to help make it possible for adventurous travellers to get out there – to explore and better understand the world.

At Lonely Planet we believe travellers can make a positive contribution to the countries they visit – if they respect their host communities and spend their money wisely. Since 1986 a percentage of the income from each book has been donated to aid projects and human rights campaigns.

Updates Lonely Planet thoroughly updates each guidebook as often as possible. This usually means there are around two years between editions, although for more unusual or more stable destinations the gap can be longer. Check the imprint page (following the colour map at the beginning of the book) for publication dates.

Between editions up-to-date information is available in two free newsletters – the paper *Planet Talk* and email *Comet* (to subscribe, contact any Lonely Planet office) – and on our Web site at www.lonelyplanet.com. The *Upgrades* section of the Web site covers a number of important and volatile destinations and is regularly updated by Lonely Planet authors. *Scoop* covers news and current affairs relevant to travellers. And, lastly, the *Thorn Tree* bulletin board and *Postcards* section of the site carry unverified, but fascinating, reports from travellers.

Correspondence The process of creating new editions begins with the letters, postcards and emails received from travellers. This correspondence often includes suggestions, criticisms and comments about the current editions. Interesting excerpts are immediately passed on via newsletters and the Web site, and everything goes to our authors to be verified when they're researching on the road. We're keen to get more feedback from organisations or individuals who represent communities visited by travellers.

Lonely Planet gathers information for everyone who's curious about the planet – and especially for those who explore it first-hand. Through guidebooks, phrasebooks, activity guides, maps, literature, newsletters, image library, TV series and Web site we act as an information exchange for a worldwide community of travellers.

Research Authors aim to gather sufficient practical information to enable travellers to make informed choices and to make the mechanics of a journey run smoothly. They also research historical and cultural background to help enrich the travel experience and allow travellers to understand and respond appropriately to cultural and environmental issues.

Authors don't stay in every hotel because that would mean spending a couple of months in each medium-sized city and, no, they don't eat at every restaurant because that would mean stretching belts beyond capacity. They do visit hotels and restaurants to check standards and prices, but feedback based on readers' direct experiences can be very helpful.

Many of our authors work undercover, others aren't so secretive. None of them accept freebies in exchange for positive write-ups. And none of our guidebooks contain any advertising.

Production Authors submit their raw manuscripts and maps to offices in Australia, USA, UK or France. Editors and cartographers – all experienced travellers themselves – then begin the process of assembling the pieces. When the book finally hits the shops, some things are already out of date, we start getting feedback from readers and the process begins again …

WARNING & REQUEST

Things change – prices go up, schedules change, good places go bad and bad places go bankrupt – nothing stays the same. So, if you find things better or worse, recently opened or long since closed, please tell us and help make the next edition even more accurate and useful. We genuinely value all the feedback we receive. Julie Young coordinates a well travelled team that reads and acknowledges every letter, postcard and email and ensures that every morsel of information finds its way to the appropriate authors, editors and cartographers for verification.

Everyone who writes to us will find their name in the next edition of the appropriate guidebook. They will also receive the latest issue of *Planet Talk*, our quarterly printed newsletter, or *Comet*, our monthly email newsletter. Subscriptions to both newsletters are free. The very best contributions will be rewarded with a free guidebook.

Excerpts from your correspondence may appear in new editions of Lonely Planet guidebooks, the Lonely Planet Web site, *Planet Talk* or *Comet*, so please let us know if you *don't* want your letter published or your name acknowledged.

Send all correspondence to the Lonely Planet office closest to you:

Australia: Locked Bag 1, Footscray, Victoria 3011
USA: 150 Linden St, Oakland, CA 94607
UK: 10A Spring Place, London NW5 3BH
France: 1 rue du Dahomey, 75011 Paris

Or email us at: talk2us@lonelyplanet.com.au

For news, views and updates see our Web site: www.lonelyplanet.com

HOW TO USE A LONELY PLANET GUIDEBOOK

The best way to use a Lonely Planet guidebook is any way you choose. At Lonely Planet we believe the most memorable travel experiences are often those that are unexpected, and the finest discoveries are those you make yourself. Guidebooks are not intended to be used as if they provide a detailed set of infallible instructions!

Contents All Lonely Planet guidebooks follow roughly the same format. The Facts about the Destination chapters or sections give background information ranging from history to weather. Facts for the Visitor gives practical information on issues like visas and health. Getting There & Away gives a brief starting point for researching travel to and from the destination. Getting Around gives an overview of the transport options when you arrive.

The peculiar demands of each destination determine how subsequent chapters are broken up, but some things remain constant. We always start with background, then proceed to sights, places to stay, places to eat, entertainment, getting there and away, and getting around information – in that order.

Heading Hierarchy Lonely Planet headings are used in a strict hierarchical structure that can be visualised as a set of Russian dolls. Each heading (and its following text) is encompassed by any preceding heading that is higher on the hierarchical ladder.

Entry Points We do not assume guidebooks will be read from beginning to end, but that people will dip into them. The traditional entry points are the list of contents and the index. In addition, however, some books have a complete list of maps and an index map illustrating map coverage.

There may also be a colour map that shows highlights. These highlights are dealt with in greater detail in the Facts for the Visitor chapter, along with planning questions and suggested itineraries. Each chapter covering a geographical region usually begins with a locator map and another list of highlights. Once you find something of interest in a list of highlights, turn to the index.

Maps Maps play a crucial role in Lonely Planet guidebooks and include a huge amount of information. A legend is printed on the back page. We seek to have complete consistency between maps and text, and to have every important place in the text captured on a map. Map key numbers usually start in the top left corner.

Although inclusion in a guidebook usually implies a recommendation we cannot list every good place. Exclusion does not necessarily imply criticism. In fact there are a number of reasons why we might exclude a place – sometimes it is simply inappropriate to encourage an influx of travellers.

Introduction

The name Saigon has for decades etched itself onto the Western consciousness. For the French, it was the capital of colonial Indochina, the tropical 'Paris of the Orient'. In 1950, Norman Lewis, author of *A Dragon Apparent*, described Saigon thus:

> Its inspiration has been purely commercial and it is therefore without folly, fervour or much ostentation…a pleasant, colourless and characterless French provincial city.

Since WWII Saigon has had three masters. The French got the boot in 1954 and the Americans had a go at running the place for about 15 years, as the capital of the Republic of Vietnam (see History in the Facts about Ho Chi Minh City chapter). In 1975, Saigon fell to advancing North Vietnamese forces. The Communists renamed the place Ho Chi Minh City (Than Pho Ho Chi Minh) and set about remodelling it in fact as well as in name. Little did they realise that the city they had hoped to change would eventually change them.

While Hanoi can claim the title of national capital, Ho Chi Minh City is still Vietnam's heart and soul: the nation's largest city, economic capital and cultural trendsetter. And with 'new thinking' in Hanoi slowly remaking the economic life of the whole country in the mould of pre-reunification Saigon, people have remarked that, in the end, Saigon really won the war.

For the Vietnamese, Ho Chi Minh City exerts a magnetic pull, an irresistible force that sucks people in and rarely lets them go. During the war, the city's population increased enormously as civilians sought refuge from the fighting in the countryside. When the war ended, the former rural peasants decided that they would rather stay put. The government's efforts to persuade them to leave proved fruitless. Attempts to forcibly move them back to their rural homes failed – the urban pioneers simply snuck back into the city at the first opportunity. And although the nation has been at peace for over a quarter of a century, the 'rural refugees' keep coming. They come not to escape war, but to seek their fortunes.

Many do not find the proverbial pot of gold at the end of the rainbow and wind up sleeping on the pavement. Yet very few Vietnamese who come to live in Ho Chi Minh City ever leave it. For better or worse, it is the place to be. Oddly enough, they are now being joined by a small but steady trickle of foreigners who feel the same way. Some get discouraged and soon leave, but there is an emerging community of long-term expats. A few learn to speak Vietnamese, set up a business, marry, have children and try to blend in with their exotic new surroundings. It takes a special sort of person to do that – but increasingly, such people are finding their way to Ho Chi Minh City.

Interestingly enough, some of the most enthusiastic foreign tourists, investors and expatriates are Vietnam's former enemies, the French and the Americans. Even the veterans come back: to see old battlefields, find old friends, relive old experiences and wonder why such tragic wars ever happened. Also returning are Overseas Vietnamese *(Viet Kieu)*, many of whom risked their lives in flimsy boats to flee their homeland. Some come to visit family, others come as tourists and investors, but a surprising number are staying on.

Images of the exotic and mundane are everywhere: the street markets, where bargains are struck and deals are done; pavement cafes, whose stereo speakers fill the surrounding streets with a melodious thumping beat; and sleek new pubs, where tourists chat over beer, peanuts, coffee and croissants. A young female office worker donning a graceful *a˜ dai* (the national dress for Vietnamese women) manoeuvres her Honda through rush hour traffic, long hair flowing, high heels working the brake pedal. A sweating Chinese businessman chats on his cellular telephone, cursing his necktie which is so absurdly dysfunctional in the tropical heat.

Explosive growth is making its mark everywhere, in new high-rise buildings, joint-venture hotels and colourful shops. The downside is the sharp increase in traffic, pollution and other urban ills. Against this, Ho Chi Minh City's neoclassical and international-style buildings and its pavement kiosks selling French rolls and pâté still give certain neighbourhoods an attractive, vaguely French atmosphere.

The Americans left their mark on the city too, such as the pillboxes and bomb-proof retaining walls of Tan Son Nhat Airport. The occasional balcony protected with iron bars or lined with barbed wire and broken glass makes you wonder if the war is still on. Of course, there is a war going on – between the haves and the have-nots. With so much poverty surrounding so much plenty, it's not hard to understand why.

Ho Chi Minh City hums and buzzes with the tenacious will of human beings to survive and improve their lot. There is something reassuring about this, and perhaps something frightening too. It is in Ho Chi Minh City that the economic changes sweeping Vietnam – and their negative social implications – are most evident.

The traffic roars. The jackhammers of progress pound the past into pulp to make way for the new. The city churns, ferments, bubbles and fumes. Yet beneath the teeming metropolis are three centuries of history, timeless tradition and the beauty of an ancient culture. There are pagodas, where monks pray and incense burns. In workshops artists create their masterpieces on canvas or in carved wood, while in parks puppeteers entertain children. In back alleys, where tourists seldom venture, acupuncturists poke needles into patients and students learn to play the violin.

Beyond the metropolis is another world, where canoes ply the canals of the Mekong Delta and young boys harvest coconuts. Within easy reach of the city is the Dong Tam Snake Farm, where one can watch cobras from a respectful distance or pet a giant python; the Caodai Holy See, a unique, otherworldly temple; and the tropical beaches at Long Hai, where commercial tourism on a mass scale has yet to wash ashore.

Politically and economically, Vietnam's situation is far from settled. Despite official pronouncements and bureaucratic 'five-year plans', no one is quite sure what the future will bring. There is no doubt, however, that Ho Chi Minh City is poised to emerge as one of Asia's great cities.

Facts about Ho Chi Minh City

HISTORY

In the Beginning

From the 1st to the 6th centuries AD, the south of what is now Vietnam was part of the Indianised kingdom of Funan, renowned for its refined art and architecture. The Funanese constructed an elaborate system of canals which crisscrossed the Mekong Delta and may have extended to the site of present-day Ho Chi Minh City. The canals were used for both transportation and the irrigation of wet rice agriculture. The principal port of Funan was Oc-Eo, close to what is now the city of Rach Gia, in the Mekong Delta.

In the mid-6th century, Funan was attacked by the Khmer kingdom of Chenla, which gradually absorbed the territory of Funan into its own (the Khmer are thought to have originally moved southwards from China some time before 200 BC).

Throughout the 17th and 18th centuries, Vietnam was divided between the Trinh lords of the north and the Nguyen lords of the south. The Nguyeh expanded their territories into the Khmer (Cambodian) regions of the Mekong Delta, including the site of present-day Ho Chi Minh City, and in the mid-17th century Cambodia was forced to accept Vietnamese suzerainty. Vietnamese settlers moved into the area and founded the city of Saigon on an ancient Khmer site.

About 700,000 Khmer people remain in Vietnam to this day, most now living in the Mekong Delta. A look at the map still reveals a large finger of Cambodia (called the 'Parrot's Beak' because of its shape) that extends very close to the border of present-day Ho Chi Minh City. Resentment over Vietnam's historical annexation of ancient Khmer territory was the excuse given by the Khmer Rouge when they massacred Vietnamese villagers living near the Cambodian border, triggering a war with Vietnam in late 1978.

French Era

Saigon was captured by the French in 1859 and was made the capital of the French colony of Cochinchina (southern Vietnam) a few years later. In 1887, the French expanded their colony to include all of Indochina (present-day Vietnam, Laos and Cambodia), with Saigon as its capital.

The French tried to mould Saigon in their own image and succeeded to the extent of installing wide boulevards and some beautiful French architecture, and converting a sizeable minority of the locals to Catholicism.

The French colonial authorities carried out ambitious public works, constructing the Saigon-Hanoi railway as well as ports, extensive irrigation and drainage systems and improved dikes. The administration also established various public services and set up research institutes.

Where the French failed was in winning the hearts and minds of the locals. Indochina was ruthlessly run as a money-making enterprise, and the Vietnamese watched in dismay as their incomes fell while the French became wealthy. The government heavily taxed the peasants, devastating the traditional rural economy. The colonial administration also ran alcohol, salt and opium monopolies for the purpose of raising revenue. In Saigon, they produced a quick-burning type of opium which helped increase addiction and thus earned hefty profits.

French capital was invested for quick returns in mining, and in tea, coffee and rubber plantations, all of which became notorious for the abysmal wages they paid and the inhuman treatment to which their Vietnamese workers were subjected. Farmers lost their land and became little more than itinerant labourers.

It was a stage set for rebellion. The French colonial administration spent much of its time putting down one small revolt after another, and often publicly guillotined the perpetrators.

Ultimately, the Communists proved to be the most successful of the anti-colonial groups. Communist successes in the late

1920s included major strikes by urban workers. A 1940 uprising in the south was brutally suppressed, however, seriously damaging the party's infrastructure. French prisons, filled with cadres, were turned by the captives into revolutionary 'universities' where the curriculum was Marxist-Leninist theory.

WWII

When France fell to Nazi Germany in 1940, the Indochinese government of Vichy-appointed Admiral Jean Decoux agreeed to accept the presence of Japanese troops in Vietnam. For their own convenience, the Japanese, who sought to exploit the area's

Ho Chi Minh

SIMON BORG

Ho Chi Minh is the best known of some 50 aliases assumed over the course of a long career by Nguyen Tat Thanh (1890–1969), founder of the Vietnamese Communist Party and President of the Democratic Republic of Vietnam from 1946 until his death. The son of a fiercely nationalistic scholar-official of humble means, he was educated in the Quoc Hoc Secondary School in Hué before working briefly as a teacher in Phan Thiet. In 1911, he signed on as a cook's apprentice on a French ship, sailing to North America, Africa and Europe. He disembarked in Europe where, while working as a gardener, snow sweeper, waiter, photo retoucher and stoker, his political consciousness and ideas began to take shape.

After living briefly in London, Ho Chi Minh moved to Paris, where he adopted the name Nguyen Ai Quoc (Nguyen the Patriot). During this period, he mastered a number of languages (including English, French, German and Mandarin) and began to write about and debate the issue of Indochinese independence. During the 1919 Versailles Peace Conference, he tried to present an independence plan for Vietnam to US president Woodrow Wilson.

Ho was a founding member of the French Communist Party, which was established in 1920. In 1923, he was summoned to Moscow for training by the Communist International, which later sent him to Guangzhou (Canton), where he founded the Revolutionary Youth League of Vietnam, a precursor to the Indochinese Communist Party and the Vietnamese Communist Party.

After spending time in a Hong Kong jail in the early 1930s, and more time in the USSR and China, Ho Chi Minh returned to Vietnam in 1941 – for the first time in 30 years. That same year, at the age of 51, he helped found the Viet Minh Front, the goal of which was the liberation of Vietnam from French colonial rule and Japanese occupation. In 1942, he was arrested and held for a year by the Nationalist Chinese. As Japan prepared to surrender in August 1945, Ho Chi Minh led the August Revolution, which took control of much of the country. He composed Vietnam's Declaration of Independence (modelled in part on the American Declaration of Independence) and read it publicly very near the eventual site of his mausoleum in Hanoi.

The return of the French shortly thereafter forced Ho Chi Minh and the Viet Minh to flee Hanoi and take up armed resistance. Ho spent eight years conducting a guerrilla war, until the Viet Minh's victory against the French at Dien Bien Phu in 1954. He led North Vietnam until his death in September 1969 – he never lived to see the North's victory over the South. Ho Chi Minh is affectionately referred to as Uncle Ho (Bac Ho) by his admirers.

Uncle Ho may have been the father of his country, but he wasn't the father of any children, at least none that are known. Like his erstwhile nemesis, South Vietnamese President Ngo Dinh Diem, Ho Chi Minh never married.

strategic location and its natural resources left the French administration in charge of the day-to-day running of the country.

In 1941, Ho Chi Minh (see boxed text, opposite) formed the League for the Independence of Vietnam (Viet Nam Doc Lap Dong Minh Hoi), better known as the Viet Minh, which resisted the Japanese occupation (and thus received Chinese and US aid) and carried out extensive political organising during WWII. Despite its broad nationalist program and claims to the contrary, the Viet Minh was, from its inception, dominated by Ho's Communists.

Vietnam (American) War

With the defeat of the Japanese in 1945, the Vietnamese had high hopes of achieving true independence. But France had different ideas, and tried to reassert control over all Indochina. The Franco-Viet Minh War started in 1946 and culminated in the dramatic French defeat at Dien Bien Phu (north-western Vietnam) in 1954.

A peace agreement between France and the Viet Minh was negotiated in Geneva. The Geneva Accords provided for the temporary division of Vietnam into two zones (thus creating North and South Vietnam) and the holding of nationwide elections on 20 July 1956.

After the signing of the Geneva Accords, the South was ruled by a government led by Ngo Dinh Diem, a fiercely anti-Communist Catholic. His power base was significantly strengthened by some 900,000 refugees who fled the Communist North.

In 1955, Diem, convinced that if elections were held Ho Chi Minh would win, refused to implement the Geneva Accords; instead, he held a rigged referendum on his continued rule. Diem declared himself president of the Republic of Vietnam, and Saigon became its capital in 1956.

In December 1960, Hanoi announced the formation of the National Liberation Front (NLF), whose aim was to 'liberate' the South through all means (including military) and reunify the country. In the South, the NLF came to be known as the Viet Cong or just the VC; both are abbreviations for Viet Nam Cong San, which means Vietnamese Communist. The Viet Cong were also joined by regular troops from the North Vietnamese Army (NVA).

Diem's tyrannical rule earned him many enemies. In the early 1960s, Saigon was rocked by anti-Diem unrest led by university students and Buddhist clergy, including several self-immolations by monks (see the boxed text Human Sacrifice in the Things to See & Do chapter). These acts, combined with the indifference shown to them by Diem's sister-in-law, Tran Le Xuan, shocked the world. In November 1963, Diem was assassinated by his own troops in Saigon.

The first American soldiers to die in the Vietnam War were killed at Bien Hoa (30km from Saigon) in 1959, at a time when about 700 US military personnel were in Vietnam. As the military position of the South Vietnamese government continued to deteriorate, the US sent more and more military advisors and troops to Vietnam. In April 1969, the number of US soldiers in Vietnam reached an all-time high of 543,400.

In order to extract itself from this guerilla war without end, the US began a policy of 'Vietnamisation' in which the Army of the Republic of Vietnam (ARVN) was equipped and trained to do the fighting without direct US involvement. US troops were slowly withdrawn while the US pursued peace negotiations with the North Vietnamese.

The Paris Agreements, signed by the warring parties on 27 January 1973, provided for a cease-fire, the total withdrawal of US combat forces and, on the VC side, the release of 590 American POWs.

In March 1975, the NVA quickly occupied a strategic section of South Vietnam's Central Highlands in a surprise attack. In the absence of US military support or advice, South Vietnamese President Nguyen Van Thieu personally decided on a strategy of tactical withdrawal to more defensible positions. This proved to be a spectacular military blunder. The totally unplanned withdrawal turned into a rout, as panicked ARVN soldiers deserted en masse, in order to try to save their families.

President Thieu, in power since 1967, resigned on 21 April 1975 and fled the country.

He was replaced by Vice President Tran Van Huong, who quit a week later, turning the presidency over to General Duong Van Minh. He, in turn, lost his post after less than 43 hours in office, surrendering on the morning of 30 April 1975 in Saigon's Independence Palace (now Reunification Palace). The first official act of the North Vietnamese was to change the name of Saigon and its surrounds to Ho Chi Minh City.

Since Reunification

Whatever else can be said, the North Vietnamese troops *(bo doi)* were well disciplined. Saigon residents had feared that their enemy would engage in an orgy of rape, murder and looting, but this never happened. Not that revenge for the war was not on the agenda – it would come later – but during the first three weeks of occupation, the NVA behaved impeccably. Indeed, the only incidents of theft were those committed by the South Vietnamese. The bo doi were treated as country bumpkins by the arrogant Saigonese. Unfortunately, these country bumpkins had AK-47s.

By the third week, the crackdown on crime began. Suspected thieves were simply rounded up and shot. But even this was only the beginning of a harsh new reality. Reunification (officially called 'liberation') was accompanied by large-scale political repression that destroyed whatever trust and goodwill the South might have felt towards the North. Despite promises to the contrary, hundreds of thousands of people who had ties to the previous regime came under suspicion. Their property, which the Northerners viewed as having been gained through capitalist exploitation, was confiscated, and they were subsequently rounded up and imprisoned without trial in forced labour camps or 're-education camps'. Others simply fled abroad. However, many of the prisoners were released in 1979.

The purges were aimed, not only former opponents of the Communists, but also at their descendants. More than a decade after the war, the children of former 'counter-revolutionaries' were still treated as if they had some hereditary disease and were thus prevented from receiving an education or employment. This desire to take revenge against the children of the former regime has now saddled Ho Chi Minh City with a huge new set of social problems – it may take decades to eradicate the resultant poverty, illiteracy and crime.

Opening the Door

After reunification, Vietnam set up an economic system modelled on that of the former Soviet Union. The economy shrank and billions of roubles of Soviet aid were needed to stave off economic collapse. When the Soviet Union itself collapsed in 1991, Vietnam had little choice but to seek reconciliation with the West.

The decision to experiment with capitalistic reforms quickly revived the fortunes of Ho Chi Minh City. Indeed, bureaucrats from Hanoi have come south to seek out their former capitalist enemies and learn the art of doing business from them.

GEOGRAPHY

Ho Chi Minh City is an enormous municipality covering an area of 2056 sq km. It lies between 106°E and 186°E longitude and between 10°N and 11°N latitude, just 50km inland from the South China Sea, and stretches north-west, almost to the Cambodian border. This vast territory is overwhelmingly rural, dotted with villages and groups of houses set amidst rice paddies.

Rural regions comprise around 90% of the land area of greater Ho Chi Minh City and hold around 25% of the city's population. The other 75% of the population is crammed into the 10% that constitutes the urban centre. Today, the city is experiencing an increasing urban sprawl into the outskirts, as city planners grapple with how to accommodate the continuing influx of people from the country and a rising birth rate.

The word 'city' is of course English, and the official name in Vietnamese is Thanh Pho Ho Chi Minh. This is often abbreviated as TP Ho Chi Minh or TP HCM. Politically, Ho Chi Minh City is divided into 16 urban districts *(quan*, derived from the French *quartier)* and five rural districts *(huyen)*.

Ho Chi Minh City rests on very flat terrain at an elevation between 10m and 30m above sea level. Of the thousands of rivers and ditches flowing in the city, the largest are the Saigon River (Song Saigon), covering a distance of 106km, and the Dong Nai River. They are the chief geographical features in Ho Chi Minh City. The largest but least populated district of Ho Chi Minh City is Can Gio, a vast mangrove swamp near the sea.

Interesting displays detailing the physical geography of the city, including the river and canal systems, flora and fauna, climate and vegetation cover, are well represented at the Museum of Ho Chi Minh City (see the Museums entry in the Things to See & Do chapter).

GEOLOGY

Ho Chi Minh City was formed by old sediment deposited by the flow of the Mekong River during the Pleistocene era. As the region around Tay Ninh Province (Dong Nai Bo) and Cambodia's Dau Khau Range rose, the southern Mekong Delta region (including present-day Ho Chi Minh City) submerged. At the time the city was founded, just three centuries ago, it was little more than a wild mangrove swamp. The ground today is a mix of alum, old grey earth alluvium and salty soil.

CLIMATE

Being only 10.5° north of the equator and 5m to 10m above sea level, Ho Chi Minh City has a tropical climate. There are two main seasons: wet and dry. The wet season (summer) lasts from May to November (June to August are the wettest months). During this time, there are heavy but short-lived downpours almost daily, usually in the afternoon. The dry season (winter) runs from December to April. Late February through May are the hottest months, when it's also very humid, but things cool down slightly when the summer rainy season begins.

Between July and November, violent and unpredictable typhoons often develop over the ocean east of Vietnam, hitting central and northern Vietnam with devastating results. Fortunately, Ho Chi Minh City is so far south that it is spared most of the damage, but these big storms can still generate several days of heavy rain.

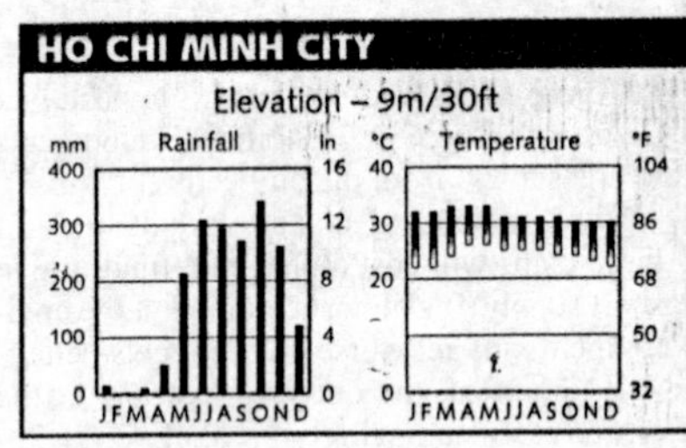

Temperatures vary little with the seasons, averaging 26°C in January and 28°C in July. Summer daily highs are usually in the low 30s, while in January the overnight lows are about 21°C. Average humidity is 80%. Annual rainfall averages 1979mm, most of which occurs during summer. The coldest temperature ever recorded in Ho Chi Minh City was 14°C.

ECOLOGY & ENVIRONMENT

As in much of the world, economic development gets priority over environmental protection in Ho Chi Minh City. Recent economic growth has worsened the situation considerably as the newly affluent purchase polluting motorcycles and automobiles. As in the rest of Vietnam, littering is indiscriminate, and throwaway plastic containers and other detritus are finding their way into the city's once charming canals, which are already choked by raw sewage. The rapidly increasing population puts further strains on the city's environment.

While there seems little doubt that cleaning up the environment of Ho Chi Minh City will be a considerable challenge, the situation is not hopeless. There is a surprisingly high level of awareness of what the problems are and what should be done about them. The local newspapers continually rail against plans to put up new high-rise buildings that will spoil the skyline, and engineers have undertaken a study of the feasibility of building a mass-transit system to alleviate the city's traffic problems. The city plans to put the sewage canals into underground pipes and install a modern sewage treatment plant. Furthermore, the government wants to push factories and other new economic developments to areas away from the city centre.

The problem, of course, is that most of these plans will cost money and funds are in short supply. It's almost certain that the environment will get worse before it gets better.

By contrast, the outlying districts of the city are still amazingly rural. Even a 30-minute drive from busy central Saigon can bring one to areas of surprisingly rural charm and tranquillity.

FLORA & FAUNA

Considering the low level of environmental awareness in Vietnam, Ho Chi Minh City boasts a healthy number of trees and flowers lining the city's streets and filling its parks and gardens.

Vietnam is home to 273 species of mammal, over 800 species of bird, 180 species of reptile, 80 species of amphibian, hundreds of species of fish and thousands of kinds of invertebrate. Unfortunately, however, most of Ho Chi Minh City's animal population has been severely degraded.

The city's birds fight an uphill battle against human encroachments, though during migration periods a fair variety of bird life can still be seen in Ho Chi Minh City's parks and gardens.

On the outskirts of Ho Chi Minh City are several areas popular with bird-watchers, including the Go Cong Hamlet stork sanctuary (see the Excursions chapter). There is also an expanding array of national parks and nature reserves in Vietnam, many within a day's journey of the city. Some areas are demonstrating potential for ecotourism and, in addition to being a great escape from the city, have the added appeal of being protected, in the sense that tourists are rarely, if ever, hassled to buy anything.

Highly recommended by bird-watchers is Nam Cat Tien National Park, in the Central Highlands. The park is easily reached from Ho Chi Minh City by car or motorcycle, and also offers great hiking and camping. Inquire at the cafes in the Pham Ngu Lao area about organising a trip.

GOVERNMENT & POLITICS

Vietnam is ruled by the 1.8 million-member Communist Party, centred in Hanoi, whose influence is felt at every level of the country's social and political life.

Nevertheless, the party has a relatively decentralised structure that allows local leaders considerable leeway for initiative. All of Vietnam's 50 provinces and three municipalities, including Ho Chi Minh City, is headed by a people's committee. Most of the people's committees are dominated by cadres from northern Vietnam, a hangover from the Vietnam War which still causes resentment. Nevertheless, it can be said that the people's committee of Ho Chi Minh City is more enterprising and forward-looking than almost any other local government in the country.

Candidates to the municipal people's committee are elected to office. The voting age is 18. Everyone of voting age is required to vote, though proxy voting is allowed (and is very common). This permits the government to boast that elections produce 100% voter participation, thus conferring legitimacy on the process.

Elections are held with great fanfare and it all appears very democratic – on the surface. In practice, most Vietnamese are cynical about their 'democracy'. Usually, election results are decided before the voting takes place. Only party-approved candidates are permitted to run and opposition parties are prohibited. Some 'independents' have appeared on the slate in Ho Chi Minh City (and nowhere else), but they must have the government's approval to run. During elections, the number of candidates running in a given constituency usually exceeds the number of contested seats by 20% to 30%.

With the national government based in Hanoi, visitors wishing to talk to officials may have to go there. However, some possible government contacts in Ho Chi Minh City are given under Useful Organisations in the Facts for the Visitor chapter.

ECONOMY

Ho Chi Minh City is the industrial and commercial heart of Vietnam, accounting for 30% of the country's manufacturing output and

25% of its retail trade. Incomes here are three times the national average. It is to Ho Chi Minh City that the vast majority of foreign businesspeople come to invest and trade. It is to Ho Chi Minh City that ambitious young people and bureaucrats – from the north and south – gravitate to make a go of it.

Long before it was called Ho Chi Minh City, Saigon was by far the most prosperous place in Vietnam. The city reached its economic zenith during the Vietnam War, when US aid poured into the country. US assistance was not only economic and military, but also technical. The Vietnamese proved to be fast learners, absorbing everything from engineering to cost accounting.

The sudden success of the 1975 North Vietnamese offensive surprised the North almost as much as it did the South. As a result, Hanoi had not prepared specific plans to deal with integrating the two parts of the country, whose social and economic systems could hardly have been more different.

Until the formal reunification of Vietnam in July 1976, the South was nominally ruled by a Provisional Revolutionary Government (PRG). One thing the PRG did was to cancel South Vietnam's currency and issue a new PRG banknote, at a swap rate of 500:1 in favour of the new money. This instantly wiped out the savings of millions of South Vietnamese and sent the economy into a tailspin. In an attempt to implement a rapid transition to socialism, an anti-capitalist campaign was launched in March 1978, during which most private property and businesses were seized. The goal was to set up a centrally planned economy based on the Soviet model. The economy plunged into an abyss and Vietnam became one of the poorest countries in the world. Famine was averted only by massive assistance from the Soviet Union.

Vietnam's efforts to restructure the economy really got started with the Sixth Party Congress, held in December 1986. Immediately upon the legalisation of limited private enterprise, family businesses began popping up all over the country. But it was in Ho Chi Minh City, with its previous experience of capitalism, that the entrepreneurial skills and managerial dynamism needed to effect the reforms were to be found.

Privatisation of large state industries has not yet begun but is being considered. As we went to press, Vietnam had no stock market – establishing one would be a prerequisite for any moves toward privatisation. In 1995, the government promised to open a capital market by year's end.

The government is intent on limiting Vietnam's restructuring *(doi moi)* to the economic sphere, keeping ideas such as pluralism and democracy from undermining the present power structure.

Foreign investors say that their biggest obstacles include the formidable bureaucracy, official incompetence, corruption, nepotism, the high rents that foreigners must pay and the ever-changing rules and regulations. On paper, intellectual property rights are protected, but enforcement is lax – patents, copyrights and trademarks are openly pirated. Tax rates and government fees are frequently revised.

POPULATION & PEOPLE

Officially, Ho Chi Minh City claims a population of 4½ million people. In reality, six to seven million is closer. The wide discrepancy is explained by the fact that census-takers only count those who have official residence permits, but probably one-third of the population lives here illegally. Many of the illegal residents actually lived legally in Saigon prior to 1975 but their residence permits were transferred to rural re-education camps after reunification. Not surprisingly, these people (and now their children and grandchildren) have simply snuck back into the city, though without a residence permit they cannot own property or a business.

People

Ethnic Vietnamese The Vietnamese people (called Annamites by the French) developed as a distinct ethnic group between 200 BC and AD 200 through the fusion of a people of Indonesian stock with Viet and Thai immigrants and with Chinese, who moved into and ruled the north of Vietnam from the 2nd century AD.

Swords into Market Shares

The word is out – it's time to put away the guns and beat the swords into ploughshares. Yes, the battle for market share is on in earnest and everyone wants a piece of the action. Joint-venture capitalists from Japan, Korea, Taiwan, France, Germany, the UK and Australia have been flocking to Vietnam since the beginning of the 1990s.

MASON FLORENCE

The most recent arrivals in town have been the Americans and they bring with them several competitive advantages. Amongst the Vietnamese, there is a strange nostalgia for doing business with those who just yesterday were Vietnam's enemies. Anyway, the fact is that Vietnamese love anything American, be it Mickey Mouse or Britney Spears. Long prohibited from doing business in Vietnam by a US-imposed embargo (lifted in 1994), American companies are making up for lost time.

As in much of the rest of Asia, consumerism is rampant in Vietnam, at least among the relatively affluent. Being called a member of the upper crust (once defined as a lot of crumbs held together by dough) is no longer an insult. Making money is a good thing. And so is spending it. It's this consumer boom that keeps foreign investors awake at night.

American companies have already splashed ashore. Computers sporting the label 'Intel inside' are on display in newly opened hi-tech electronic shops. Chrysler has formed a joint venture to produce its gas-guzzling Jeep Cherokee in Vietnam. Motorola pagers can be heard beeping in the pockets and handbags of Saigon's well-to-do. Pepsi was the first American soft drink vendor to return to Vietnam, but Coke was not far behind. American fast food, such as McDonalds, should find a ready market among Vietnam's trendy urban elite. That is, of course, if people can tell the real thing from the clones. Already, Ho Chi Minh City has seen several fake 7-Elevens come and go.

The Americans, for their part, are displeased with the lack of Vietnamese protection for intellectual property rights (despite the recent signing of pacts with the US). Trademarks, patents and copyrights continue to be violated with impunity by the Vietnamese. The proliferation of pirated music tapes and fake Rolex watches are potential bones of contention. Nothing is sacred – even downsized copies of the Statue of Liberty have popped up in Vietnam's newest avant-garde cafes. Vietnamese who know their history point out that the original Statue of Liberty was a gift to America from France – 'Why', they ask, 'shouldn't we have one too?'

On the other hand, the Vietnamese government has so far refused anyone permission to capitalise on Ho Chi Minh's name. A proposal to open an American joint venture called Uncle Ho's Hamburgers went down like a lead balloon. Nor were the Vietnamese persuaded when the American business reps pointed out that Ho Chi Minh does vaguely resemble Colonel Sanders. 'No,' said the frowning Vietnamese, 'Ho Chi Minh was a general.'

From the time of the Chinese arrival, Vietnamese civilisation was profoundly influenced by China and, via the Khmers and the kingdom of Champa, India. However, the fact that the Vietnamese were never absorbed by China indicates that a strong local culture existed prior to the 700 years of Chinese rule, which ended in 938 AD.

Over a period of two millennia, the ethnic Vietnamese slowly pushed southward along Vietnmam's narrow coastal strip, first defeating the Chams in the 15th century and then, in the late-17th century, taking over the Mekong Delta (including the site of present-day Ho Chi Minh City) from the Khmers.

Ethnic Chinese The ethnic Chinese (Hoa) constitute the largest single minority group in Vietnam. Most of Ho Chi Minh City's ethnic Chinese live in and around District 5, an area officially called Cholon before 1975, and still referred to by most as such. Cholon rose to prominence after Chinese merchants began settling there in 1778 and, despite the ethnic Chinese leaving in droves after 1975, still constitutes the largest ethnic Chinese community in Vietnam.

The Chinese have organised themselves into communities, known as congregations *(bang)*, according to their ancestors' province of origin and dialect. Important congregations include Fujian (Phuoc Kien in Vietnamese), Cantonese (Quang Dong in Vietnamese or Guangdong in Mandarin Chinese), Hainan (Hai Nam), Chaozhou (Tieu Chau) and Hakka (Nuoc Hue in Vietnamese or Kejia in Mandarin).

Indians Almost all of South Vietnam's population of Indians, most of whose roots were in southern India, left in 1975. The remaining community in Ho Chi Minh City worship at the Mariamman Hindu temple and the Central Mosque.

Khmers The number of Khmers (ethnic Cambodians) is estimated at about 700,000 in Vietnam, but most live south of Ho Chi Minh City in the Mekong Delta region. They practise Hinayana (Theravada) Buddhism.

Chams Vietnam's 60,000 Chams are the remnant of the once-vigorous Indianised kingdom of Champa, which flourished from the 2nd to the 15th centuries but was destroyed as the Vietnamese moved southward. Most live along the coast between Nha Trang and Phan Thiet, and in the Mekong Delta province of An Giang. The Chams were influenced by both Hinduism and Buddhism, but most are now Muslims.

The Chams are best known for the many brick sanctuaries (known as 'Cham towers') they constructed all over the southern part of the country. In Ho Chi Minh City, you can see a downsized reproduction of a Cham tower in Cong Vien Van Hoa Park.

Hill Tribes Most of the country's minority groups occupy the highlands of Vietnam. Many are distantly or directly related to hill tribes in neighbouring Laos, Cambodia and China, as well as in Thailand and Myanmar (Burma). Of the 54 distinct ethnic groups in Vietnam, about 20 different minorities reside in and around Ho Chi Minh City. Most, however, are very difficult to distinguish from ethnic Vietnamese.

You may occasionally encounter hill tribe people in Ho Chi Minh City, but mostly they are rural inhabitants. The French called them *montagnards* (which means highlanders), a term they still use themselves. The Vietnamese often refer to the hill tribe people as *moi*, a derogatory word meaning savages that unfortunately reflects all-too-common popular attitudes. The present government prefers the term 'ethnic minorities' and has been making efforts in recent times to celebrate the country's racial diversity.

EDUCATION

Compared with other developing countries, Vietnam's population is very well educated. Although university education is out of reach for most Vietnamese, the literacy rate is estimated at 88.6%, although official figures put it even higher (95%). Before the colonial period, the majority of the population possessed some degree of literacy, but by 1939 only 15% of school-age children were receiving any kind of instruction and 80% of the population was illiterate. Unlike in many other poor countries, women generally receive the same access to education as men.

During the late 19th century, one of the few things that French colonial officials and Vietnamese nationalists agreed on was that the traditional Confucian educational system, on which the mandarin civil service was based, was in desperate need of reform. Examinations for the mandarinate were held in Tonkin until WWI and in Annam until the war's end. Many of Indochina's independence leaders were educated in elite French-language secondary schools, such as Ho Chi Minh City's Lyc Chasseloup.

Although the children of foreign residents can theoretically attend Vietnamese schools, the majority go to expensive private academies (see the Facts for the Visitor chapter for a list of schools).

ARTS

Music & Dance

Each of Vietnam's ethnic minorities has its own musical and dance traditions, which often include colourful costumes and instruments such as reed flutes, lithophones (similar to xylophones), bamboo whistles, gongs and stringed instruments made from gourds. Ho Chi Minh City has a music conservatory teaching both traditional Vietnamese and Western classical music.

Bizarrely, much Vietnamese pop music originates in California, the home of numerous Overseas Vietnamese. One reason why Vietnam itself produces so few local singers is because all music tapes are instantly pirated, thus depriving the singing stars of the revenue they would need to survive.

Cinema

One of Vietnam's first cinematographic efforts was a newsreel of Ho Chi Minh's 1945 proclamation of independence. After Dien Bien Phu (see History in this chapter), parts of the battle were restaged for the benefit of movie cameras.

Prior to reunification, the South Vietnamese movie industry concentrated on producing sensational, low-budget flicks. Until recently, most North Vietnamese film-making efforts have been dedicated to 'the mobilisation of the masses for economic reconstruction, the building of socialism and the struggle for national reunification'. Predictable themes include 'workers devoted to socialist industrialisation', 'old mothers who continuously risk their lives to help the people's army' and 'children who are ready to face any danger'.

The relaxation of ideological censorship of the arts has proceeded in fits and starts, but the last few years has seen a gradual easing of restrictions. However, paranoia about evil foreign influence means the government still keeps the film industry on a tight leash. One film worth seeing that has been successful overseas is *The Scent of Green Papaya.*

Theatre & Puppetry

There are many kinds of Vietnamese theatre and performing arts.

Classical Theatre Classical theatre is known in the south as *hat boi* (literally, songs with show dress). Northerners call it *hat truong*. It is based on Chinese opera, and was probably brought to Vietnam by the 13th century Mongol invaders eventually chased out by Tran Hung Dao. Hat boi is very formalistic, employing gestures and scenery similar to Chinese theatre. The accompanying orchestra, which is dominated by the drum, usually has six musicians. Often, the audience have a drum so they too can comment on the on-stage action. Hat boi has a limited cast of characters whose identities are established by means of stylised make-up and dress that the audience easily recognises. For instance, red face paint represents courage, loyalty and faithfulness. Traitors and cruel people have white faces. Lowlanders are given green faces; highlanders have black ones. Horizontal eyebrows represent honesty, erect eyebrows symbolise cruelty and lowered eyebrows belong to characters with a cowardly nature. A male character can express emotions (pensiveness, worry, anger etc) by fingering his beard in various ways.

Popular Theatre Popular theatre *(hat cheo)*, though a typically northern Vietnamese art form, can occasionally be seen in Ho Chi Minh City. It often engages in social protest through satire. The singing and declamation are in everyday language and include many proverbs and sayings. Many of the melodies are of peasant origin.

Modern Theatre Modern theatre *(cai luong)* originated in the south in the early 20th century and shows strong Western influences. In recent years this form has also gained popularity in the north.

Spoken Drama Spoken drama *(kich noi* or *kich)*, with its western roots, appeared in the 1920s. It is a popular form with students and intellectuals.

Puppetry Conventional puppetry *(roi can)* and that uniquely Vietnamese art form, water puppetry *(roi nuoc)*, draw their plots from the same legendary and historical sources as other forms of traditional theatre.

Lacquered wooden puppets, around 50cm in height, are manipulated by rods to make them appear to be walking on the water surface. It is thought that water puppetry developed when determined puppeteers in the Red River Delta (northern Vietnam) managed to carry on with the show despite flooding. Often shows were performed in village ponds, which greatly enhanced their magical effect. In Ho Chi Minh City, water puppetry can be seen at the War Remnants Museum and the History Museum (see the Things to See & Do chapter).

Architecture

The Vietnamese have not been great builders – unlike their predecessors, the Chams, whose brick towers grace many parts of the southern half of the country. Most Vietnamese architecture used wood and other materials that proved highly vulnerable in the tropical climate.

Plenty of pagodas and temples founded hundreds of years ago are still functioning, but they have usually been rebuilt many times, with little concern for making the upgraded structure an exact copy of the original. As a result, modern elements have been casually introduced into pagoda architecture; neon haloes for statues of the Buddha are only the most glaring example of this.

Because of the Vietnamese custom of ancestor worship, many graves from previous centuries are still extant. These include temples erected in memory of high-ranking mandarins, members of the royal family, emperors and, most recently, Ho Chi Minh.

To coincide with the 300 year anniversary of Saigon in 1998, many of the city's great buildings were treated to a major facelift, including the thoughtfully restored Municipal Theatre.

Sculpture

Traditionally, Vietnamese sculpture had a religious function as an adjunct to architecture, especially to pagodas, temples and tombs. Many inscribed stelae, erected hundreds of years ago to commemorate important local or national events, remain today.

Lacquerware

The art of making lacquerware was brought to Vietnam from China in the mid-15th century. Previously, the Vietnamese had used lacquer solely for sealing things and making them watertight. Designs are created on the lacquer by engraving in low relief; by painting; or by inlaying mother-of-pearl, eggshell, silver or even gold.

Ceramics

The production of ceramics has a long history in Vietnam. In ancient times, ceramic objects were made by coating a wicker mould with clay and baking it. Later, ceramics production became very refined, and each dynastic period is known for its particular techniques and motifs.

Painting

Traditional Painting on frame-mounted silk dates from the 13th century. Silk painting was at one time the preserve of scholar-calligraphers, who also painted scenes from nature. Before the advent of photography, realistic portraits for use in ancestor worship were produced. Some of these portraits – usually of former head monks – can still be seen in Buddhist pagodas.

Modern During this century, Vietnamese painting has been influenced by Western trends. Much of the recent work done in Vietnam has had political rather than aesthetic or artistic motives. According to an official account, the fighting of the Vietnam War provided painters with:

> ...rich human material: people's army combatants facing the jets, peasant and factory women in the militia who handled guns as well as they did their production work, young volunteers who repaired roads in record time...old mothers offering tea to anti-aircraft gunners...

There's lots of this stuff at the Art Museum in Ho Chi Minh City.

Recent economic liberalisation has convinced many young artists to abandon the revolutionary themes and concentrate on producing commercially saleable paintings. Some have gone back to traditional silk painting, while others are experimenting with new subjects. Nudes are popular, which might indicate either an attempt to appeal to Western tastes or an expression of long-suppressed desires.

The cheaper stuff (US$10 to US$30) gets spun off to gift shops and street markets. Higher-standard works are put on display in both private and government-run art galleries (see the Shopping chapter). Typical prices are in the US$30 to US$100 range, though the artists may ask 10 times that. It's important to know that there are quite a few forgeries around – just because you spot a painting by a 'famous Vietnamese artist' does not mean that it's an original, though it may still be an attractive work of art.

SOCIETY & CONDUCT

Traditional Culture

Dress The graceful national dress of Vietnamese women is known as the *ao dai* (pronounced 'ow-yai'). The ao dai consists of a close-fitting blouse with long panels in the front and back that is worn over loose black or white trousers.

Ao dais have been around a long time, and in the beginning they were anything but revealing. But in the past few years the partially see-through ao dai has become all the rage – it's doubtful many Western women would wear something so provocative.

Traditionally, men also wore ao dai, but today this generally only occurs in the theatre or at traditional music performances.

Beauty Concepts The Vietnamese have traditionally considered pale skin to be beautiful. On sunny days, trendy Vietnamese women can often be seen strolling under the shade of an umbrella in order to keep from tanning. As in 19th-century Europe, peasants get tanned and those who can afford not to don't. Women who work in the fields will go to great lengths to preserve their pale skin by wearing long-sleeved shirts, gloves, a conical hat and wrapping their face in a towel.

Geomancy Geomancy is the art (or science if you prefer) of manipulating or judging the environment. If you want to build a house or find a suitable site for a grave, then you call in a geomancer. The orientation of houses, communal meeting halls, tombs and pagodas is determined by geomancers, which is why cemeteries have tombstones turned every which way. The location of an ancestor's grave is an especially serious matter – if the grave is in the wrong spot or facing the wrong way, then there is no telling what trouble the spirit may cause.

Businesses that are failing call in a geomancer. Sometimes the solution is to move the door or a window. If this doesn't do the trick, it might be necessary to move an ancestor's grave. Distraught spirits may have to be placated with payments of cash (donated to a temple), especially if one wishes to erect a building or other structure which blocks the spirits' view.

The concept of geomancy is believed to have originated with the Chinese. Although the Communists (both Chinese and Vietnamese) have disparaged geomancy as superstition, it still has an influence on people's behaviour.

Lunar Calendar The Vietnamese lunar calendar closely resembles the Chinese one, though there are some minor variations. Year 1 of the Vietnamese lunar calendar corresponds to 2637 BC, and each lunar month has 29 or 30 days, resulting in years with 355 days.

Approximately every third year is a leap year; an extra month is added between the third and fourth months to keep the lunar year in sync with the solar year. If this weren't done, you'd end up having the seasons gradually rotate around the lunar year, playing havoc with all elements of life linked to the agricultural seasons. To find out the Gregorian (solar) date corresponding to a lunar date, check any Vietnamese or Chinese calendar.

Instead of reckoning time in centuries, the Vietnamese calendar uses units of 60 years called *hoi*. Each hoi consists of six 10-year cycles *(can)* and five twelve year cycles *(ky)*, which run simultaneously. The name of each year the cycle consists of the can (heavenly stem) name followed by the chi (zodiacal stem) name, a system which never produces the same combination twice in any hoi.

The 10 stems of the can cycle are:

giap	water in nature
at	water in the home
binh	lighted fire
dinh	latent fire
mau	wood
ky	wood prepared for burning
canh	metal
tan	wrought metal
nham	virgin land
quy	cultivated land

The 12 zodiacal stems of the chi cycle are:

tý	rat
suu	water buffalo
dan	tiger
mao	cat
thin	dragon
ty	snake
ngo	horse
mui	goat
than	monkey
dau	rooster
tuat	dog
hoi	pig

Thus, in 2000 the Vietnamese year is Canh Thin (dragon), in 2001 it's Tan Ty (snake), in 2002 it's Nham Ngo (horse) and in 2003 it's Quy Mui (goat).

Dos & Don'ts

Name Cards Name cards are very popular in Ho Chi Minh City and, like elsewhere in East Asia, exchanging business cards is an important part of even the smallest transaction or business contact. Get some printed before you arrive in Vietnam and hand them out like confetti.

Deadly Chopsticks Leaving a pair of chopsticks sticking vertically in a rice bowl looks very similar to the incense sticks which are burned for the dead. This is a powerful death sign and is not appreciated anywhere in Asia.

Mean Feet It's rude to let the bottom of your feet point towards other people except maybe with close friends. When sitting on the floor, you should fold your legs into the lotus position so you're not pointing your soles at others. And most importantly, never point your feet towards anything sacred, such as figures of the Buddha.

In formal situations, when sitting on a chair do not cross your legs.

Keep Your Hat in Your Hand As a form of respect to the elderly or other people regarded with respect (monks etc), take off your hat and bow your head politely when addressing them.

Pity the Unmarried Telling the Vietnamese that you are single or divorced and enjoying a life without children will disturb them greatly. Not having a family is regarded as bad luck, and such people are to be pitied, not envied. Almost every Vietnamese will ask if you are married and have children. If you are young and single, simply say you are 'not yet married' and that will be accepted. If you are not so young (over 30) and unmarried, it's better to lie. Divorce is scandalous.

Also, don't be too inquisitive about other people's family problems such as divorce or death (even if they are inquisitive about yours). Failure in family life is a major loss of face, and loss of family members through death is the ultimate tragedy. The discussion of such tragedies is to be avoided.

Face Having 'big face' is synonymous with prestige, and prestige is important in Asia. All families, even poor ones, are expected to have big wedding parties and throw money around like water in order to gain face. This is often ruinously expensive, but the fact that the wedding may result in bankruptcy for the young couple is far less important than losing face.

A certain amount of generosity would also be expected of foreigners in a business context, such as giving small gifts or holding banquets – though gratuitous displays of largesse would not be appreciated.

Smile Asians say that Westerners tend to speak too frankly and are rude and inconsiderate of the feelings of others. Perhaps this is unfair criticism, but you can certainly find Westerners flying off the handle when things go wrong (as they inevitably do) when travelling in Vietnam.

In most of Asia, including Vietnam, people put much value on being pleasant and smiling a lot. Gruff criticism and complaints are to be avoided. Be sure that you don't make others lose face. If you want to criticise someone, do it in a joking manner to avoid confrontation. Expect delays – build them into your schedule. And never show anger. Getting visibly upset is not only rude – it will cause you to lose face.

Finally, don't act as though you deserve service from someone. If you do, it's likely that you will be delayed.

Treatment of Animals

Vietnam, particularly by Western standards, has a very low level of awareness when it comes to treatment of animals.

For an interesting read on one foreign visitor's encounter with the illegal monkey trade, look for Karen Muller's *Hitchhiking in Vietnam* (1998). A film was made of the book; the website of the film is at www.pbs.org/hitchhikingvietnam/.

RELIGION

Three great philosophies and religions, Confucianism, Taoism and Buddhism, have fused with Vietnamese animism and popular Chinese beliefs such as ancestor worship to form what is known collectively as the Triple Religion, or Tam Giao. About 90% of the population subscribe to Tam Giao. The pagodas in Ho Chi Minh City thus contain a mixture of deities, with Chinese gods and the various manifestations of the Buddha predominating.

Today, Vietnam has the highest percentage of Catholics in Asia (8% to 10% of the population) outside the Philippines. There is also a small minority of Protestants.

The Hoa Hao sect, which is strictly Buddhist, constitutes 2% of the population. Caodaism is an indigenous Vietnamese sect. It also claims roughly 2% of the population.

Muslims – mostly ethnic Khmers and Chams – constitute about 0.5% of the population. Champa was profoundly influenced by Hinduism, but after the fall of Champa in the 15th century most Chams who remained in Vietnam became Muslims. However, they continue to practise various Brahmanic (high-caste Hindu) rituals and customs.

Facts for the Visitor

WHEN TO GO

There is really no bad season to visit Ho Chi Minh City. The city offers countless attractions that can be visited year-round, and aside from some hot spells and variable weather patterns, the climate is generally pleasant.

The foreign tourist high season runs from late June through August, tapering off in September, and picking up again from October until Tet – the colourful Lunar New Year celebration, which falls in late January or early February.

Things quieten down again from late February through late April, when the start of summer and the domestic tourist season kicks into high gear. Be aware that public transport can get very busy with large domestic group bookings.

Visitors should allow for the fact that during Tet, public transportation into, out of and around Vietnam can be booked solid. Tet, however, is a fascinating time to be in Ho Chi Minh City, with lots of colourful festivals and ceremonies in the city and surrounding villages (see the Festivals section later in this chapter).

ORIENTATION

Ho Chi Minh City is divided into 16 urban districts *(quan,* derived from the French *quartier)* and five rural districts *(huyen)*. The urban districts are as follows: Districts 1 to 8, Districts 10, 11 and 12, Binh Thanh, Go Vap, Phu Nhuan, Thu Duc and Tan Binh. The five rural districts are Binh Chanh, Can Gio, Cu Chi, Hoc Mon and Nha Be.

The downtown section of Ho Chi Minh City, now officially called District 1, is still known as Saigon. In the south, most people use the terms Saigon and Ho Chi Minh City interchangeably. In the north, people toe the official line and people may correct you if you say Saigon. Since most government officials are from the north, you'd be wise to say Ho Chi Minh City whenever dealing with them. District 1 – Saigon – is where most of the city's attractions and life-support facilities are located. The largest concentration of places to stay, eat and shop are in the budget travellers' Pham Ngu Lao area and the Dong Khoi area, downtown.

To the west of the centre is District 5, the old Chinese city of Cholon, which some people will tell you means Chinatown. In fact, Cholon means Big Market in Vietnamese, though its Chinese name, *Di an,* means Embankment. Cholon rose to prominence after Chinese merchants began settling there in 1778. These days it's also known as Ho Chi Minh City's copy centre, the source of pirated videos and counterfeit Swiss watches.

Most of Ho Chi Minh City's streets are labelled as *duong* (abbreviated in this book as Đ), while wider boulevards are generally called *dai lo* (abbreviated as ĐL).

Urban orienteering is very easy in Ho Chi Minh City, as Vietnamese is written with a Latin-based alphabet. Street names are sometimes abbreviated on street signs to just the initials (DBP for ĐL Dien Bien Phu etc). Unfortunately, the numbering can be a problem. In some places, consecutive buildings are numbered 15A, 15B, 15C and so forth, while elsewhere, consecutive addresses read 15D, 17D, 19D etc. Most streets have even numbers on one side and odd numbers on the other, but number 75 can be three blocks down the street from number 76. Often, two numbering systems – the old confusing one and the new confusing one – are in use simultaneously, so that an address may read 1743/697. In some cases several streets, numbered separately, have been run together under one name so that as you walk along, the numbers go from one into the hundreds (or thousands) and then start over again.

An oddity found in Ho Chi Minh City is streets named after momentous historical dates. For example, ĐL 3 Thang 2 (usually written ĐL 3/2) refers to 3 February, the anniversary of the founding of the Vietnamese Communist Party.

Many restaurants are named after their street addresses. For example, Nha Hang 51 Nguyen Hue (*nha hang* means restaurant) would be at No 51 ĐL Nguyen Hue.

MAPS

Reasonably detailed colour tourist maps of Ho Chi Minh City are cheap and readily available. At tourist shops or from street vendors the going rate is US$1, but at most private and government book shops (see the Shopping chapter) the price is around US$0.50. One popular map with travellers features Ho Chi Minh City on one side, and the Mekong Delta on the flip side.

If you're heading into the countryside, Lonely Planet's *Thailand, Vietnam, Laos & Cambodia Road Atlas* is a boon to hikers and cyclists. It gives an in-depth view of towns, highways and topographic features.

Gecase Company (a government agency) produces highly detailed topographical maps, but you'll need special permission to purchase them. The Vietnamese government treats them like military secrets – ridiculous in this age of satellite photos – and typically requires proof of how you plan to use them, and/or reassurance by a local that the maps will not leave the country.

If you can obtain the necessary special permission, the place to buy these (US$3 each, but you may be forced to purchase a minimum of 10) is Gecase Company (☎ 845 2670, fax 842 4216, 28 Đ Nguyen Van Troi, Phu Nhuan District) which is very close to Vinh Nghiem Pagoda.

RESPONSIBLE TOURISM

The effects of the recent arrival of mass tourism, both positive and negative, are being felt in Vietnam. While positive contributions may include US dollars flowing into the local economy, the creation of jobs and a growing sense of globalisation, it is important for travellers to recognise and try to minimise the potentially damaging costs of their visit.

Negative effects of tourism, both domestic and international, can be markedly reduced by responsible travel and a general respect for local culture and customs. By minimising their negative impacts, each visitor can make a difference.

In Asia, the prevalence of prostitution is unfortunate but real. As part of the social evils campaign, the government regularly cracks down on the sex industry with heavy penalties, but the problem still remains. Avoid patronising bars and clubs that offer sex as the main service, such as the 'bar oms', and never buy sexual services.

The sexual exploitation of children is another significant problem in Asia. As a direct response to this child abuse a number of countries, including Australia, New Zealand, Germany, Sweden, Norway, France and the USA, now prosecute and punish citizens for paedophiliac offences committed abroad.

Many Vietnamese still have a low level of environmental awareness and responsibility, and many remain unaware of the implications of littering. Try to raise awareness by example.

Vietnam's animal populations are under considerable threat from domestic consumption and the illegal international trade in animal products. Though it may be exotic to try wild meats such as muntjac, bat, frog, deer, sea horse, shark fin and snake wine etc – or to buy products made from endangered plants and animals – it will indicate your support and acceptance of such practices and add to the demand for them.

Similarly, forest products such as rattan, orchids, medicinal herbs etc are under threat. Some of these products can be grown domestically, earning local people additional income while natural areas are protected from exploitation and degradation. However, the majority are still collected directly from Vietnam's dwindling forests.

Finally, do not remove or buy souvenirs that have been taken from historical sites and natural areas.

TOURIST OFFICES

Local Tourist Offices

Vietnam's tourist offices are not like those found in other countries. If you were to visit a government-run tourist office in Australia, Western Europe or Japan you'd get lots of free, colourful, glossy brochures, maps and helpful advice on transport, places to stay where to book tours and so on. Such tourist offices make no profit – instead they are typically supported by a tax on travel agencies or hotels which benefit from the tourist office's services.

Vietnam's tourist offices operate on a different philosophy. They are not really in the business of promoting Vietnam as a tourist destination. Rather, they are state-run enterprises that masquerade as tourist offices, and their primary interests are booking tours and earning a profit. In fact, these tourist offices are little more than travel agencies, but they are among the most profitable hard currency cash cows the Vietnamese government has. There has been talk of creating not-for-profit tourist information offices, as well a tourist police force, but these are yet to materialise.

Perhaps the best sources of independent travel information in Ho Chi Minh City are the budget tour agencies. Staff should be willing to part with useful travel information, especially if you approach them in a friendly manner. They will of course also be happy to sell you their tours as well. Some of these places also have message boards where travellers post the latest travel tips, praise, gripes, warnings etc.

For a listing of local tour operators, see the Organised Tours section in the Getting Around chapter.

Tourist Offices Abroad

France

Vietnam Tourism: (☎ 01 42 86 86 37, fax 01 42 60 43 32) 4 rue Cherubini, 75002 Paris

Saigon Tourist: (☎ 01 40 51 03 02, fax 01 43 25 05 70) 24 rue des Bernadins, 75005 Paris

Germany

Saigon Tourist: (☎ 030-786 5056, fax 786 5596) 24 Dudenstrasse 78 W, 1000 Berlin 61

Japan

Saigon Tourist: (☎ 03-3258 5931, fax 3253 6819) IDI 6th floor, Crystal Building, 1-2 Kanda Awaji-cho, Chiyoda-ku, Tokyo 101

Singapore

Vietnam Tourism: (☎ 532 3130, fax 532 2952, pager 601 3914) 101 Upper Cross St, No 02-44 People's Park Centre, Singapore 0105

Saigon Tourist: (☎ 735 1433, fax 735 1508) 131 Tanglin Rd, Tudor Court, Singapore 1024

DOCUMENTS

Visas

While Vietnamese red tape is legendary, completing the necessary paperwork to obtain a visa is not all that daunting. The only problem is that it tends to be quite expensive and unnecessarily time-consuming.

In most cases, getting your visa from a travel agent rather than directly through the Vietnamese embassy can save time and headaches. The travel agency doing your visa usually needs a photocopy of your passport and two or three photos.

Fortunately, passing through Vietnamese immigration at Ho Chi Minh City's Tan Son Nhat Airport has become far easier and smoother than in past years. However, many entering overland still face hassles. Immigration authorities at overland border checks are notorious for extorting extra fees from travellers.

Always have some photos with you because immigration police have been known to inexplicably give travellers more forms to fill out and attached photos are required. Of course, there is a photographer right there at the airport to serve you – for a substantial fee.

See the Internet Resources section later in this chapter for details of Lonely Planet's Web site, which has hot links to the most up-to-date visa information.

Tourist Visas Tourist visas are valid only for a single 30-day stay. The visa specifies the exact date of arrival and departure, thus you must solidify your travel plans well in advance. You cannot arrive even one day earlier than your visa specifies. And if you change your plans and postpone your trip by two weeks, then you'll only have 16 days remaining on your visa instead of 30 days.

Prices for single-entry tourist visas are around US$45 to US$60. In Bangkok they can be issued in about four days, in Hong Kong five days, but in other places (eg, Taiwan) it can take as long as 10 working days. Many travel agencies offer package deals with visa and air ticket included.

Visa Extensions If you've got the dollars, they've got the rubber stamp. In Ho Chi

Minh City, visa extensions cost around US$30; they are granted for 15 days at a time and you can get extensions up to a maximum stay of three months. You should probably go to a hotel, cafe or travel agency to get this taken care of. Some hotels have a sign on the front desk indicating that they have a visa extension service.

For what it's worth, there's also the Immigration Police Office, or Phong Quan Ly Nguoi Nuoc Ngoai (☎ 839 2221), at 254 Đ Nguyen Trai, District 1. It's open from 8 to 11 am and from 1 to 4 pm. Fronting up at the immigration police yourself usually doesn't work – most probably, you will be turned away and told to use the services of a private agency. Moreover, the cost may range for any number of mysterious and ineluctable reasons.

One popular agency handling visa extensions is Ben Thanh Tourist (☎ 886 0365, fax 836 1953) at 45 Đ Bui Vien, District 1. The procedure typically takes three working days and one or two photos are needed. You can apply for your extension several weeks before it's necessary.

Re-entry Visas It's possible to enter Cambodia, Laos or China from Vietnam and then re-enter on your original single-entry Vietnamese visa. However, you must apply for a re-entry visa *before* you leave Vietnam. If you do not have a re-entry visa, then you will have to go through the whole expensive and time-consuming procedure of applying for a new Vietnamese visa. Re-entry visas are easy enough to arrange in Ho Chi Minh City, but you will almost certainly have to ask a travel agent to do the paperwork for you. They charge about US$25 for this service and can complete the procedure in three days.

If you already have a valid visa which allows you multiple entries for Vietnam, you do not need a re-entry visa.

Business Visas There are several advantages in having a business visa: such visas are usually valid for three or six months, can be issued for multiple-entry journeys and will look more impressive when you have to deal with bureaucratic authorities. Also, you are permitted to work if you have a business visa.

Business visas can be prearranged through a local sponsor in Vietnam (in most cases a company). If approved, you must receive confirmation from the sponsor, and then go to pick up the visa from a Vietnamese embassy abroad. This usually costs around US$90.

It is also possible to arrive on a tourist visa and make arrangements locally for a business visa.

Student Visas A student visa is something you usually arrange after arrival. It's acceptable to enter Vietnam on a tourist visa, enrol in a Vietnamese language course and then apply through the immigration police for a change in status. Of course, you do have to pay tuition and are expected to attend class. A minimum of 10 hours of study per week is needed to qualify for student status.

Resident Visas Only a few foreigners can qualify for a resident visa. Probably the easiest way to do this is to marry a local, though anyone contemplating doing this had best be prepared for the mountains of paperwork. Spouses of Vietnamese nationals gain a few other advantages besides a resident visa – eg, they can own 50% of the couple's property (including real estate).

Travel Insurance

Although you may have medical insurance in your own country, it may not be valid in Vietnam. A travel insurance policy is a very good idea – it can protect you against cancellation penalties on advance purchase flights, medical costs through illness or injury, theft or loss of possessions and the cost of additional air tickets if you get really sick and have to fly home.

If you do have to undergo medical treatment, be sure to collect all receipts and copies of your medical report – in your native language if possible – for your insurance company. If you get robbed, you'll need to get a police report if you want to claim from your insurance company.

Many student travel organisations offer insurance policies. Some of these are very cheap, but only offer very minimal coverage. Be sure to read the small print carefully to avoid being caught out by exclusions.

Driving Licence & Permits

If you plan to drive in Vietnam, get an International Driver's Licence from your local automobile association or motor vehicle department before you leave. You must carry a valid driving licence from your home country, together with this licence. Make sure your licence states that it is valid for motorcycles if you plan to ride one.

Student & Youth Cards

Full-time students coming from the USA, Australia and Europe can often get some good discounts on international (not domestic) air tickets with the help of an International Student Identity Card (ISIC). To get this card, inquire at your campus. Student Travel Australia (STA) issues STA Youth Cards, which have some of the same benefits, to persons aged between 13 and 26 years. However no place in Ho Chi Minh City issues these cards, nor are they of any use within Vietnam.

International Health Card

A useful (though not essential) document is an International Health Certificate to record any vaccinations you've had. These can also be issued in Vietnam.

Other Documents

Losing your passport is very bad news indeed. Getting a new one takes time and money. It's wise to have a driving licence, student card, ID card or something else with your photo on it – some embassies want to see a picture ID before issuing a replacement passport. Keeping the original of an old expired passport is also very useful for this purpose.

If you're travelling with your spouse, a photocopy of your marriage certificate might come in handy should you become involved with the law, hospitals or government authorities.

If you're planning on working or studying in Vietnam, it could be helpful to bring copies of transcripts, diplomas, letters of reference and other relevant professional qualifications.

Copies

It certainly helps to keep a separate record of the number and issue date of your passport, as well as a photocopy of it or your birth certificate. While you're compiling that information, add the serial number of your travellers cheques, credit card numbers, travel insurance details, and about US$50 or so in emergency cash (better hotels have a safe for these valuables).

If police stop you on the street and ask for your passport, give them a photocopy and explain your hotel has the original. Trusting anyone with your documents always makes you very vulnerable.

Photocopy shops – signposted in English – are never far away and easy to spot.

EMBASSIES & CONSULATES

It's important to realise what your own embassy – the embassy of the country of which you are a citizen – can and can't do to help you if you get into trouble.

Generally speaking, it won't be much help in emergencies if the trouble you're in is remotely your own fault. Remember that you are bound by the laws of the country you are in. Your embassy will not be sympathetic if you end up in jail after committing a crime locally, even if such actions are legal in your own country.

In genuine emergencies you might get some assistance, but only if other channels have been exhausted.

Vietnamese Embassies & Consulates

The following addresses are for Vietnamese embassies abroad; consulates are also listed (and indicated) as appropriate:

Australia
Embassy: (☎ 02-6286 6059, fax 6286 4534) 6 Timbarra Crescent, O'Malley, Canberra, ACT 2603
Consulate: (☎ 02-9327 2539, fax 9328 1653) 489 New South Head Rd, Double Bay, NSW 2028

Cambodia (☎ 05-1881 1804, fax 236 2314) 436 Blvd Preach, Monivong, Phnom Penh
Canada (☎ 613-236 0772, fax 236 2704) 226 Maclaren St, Ottawa, Ontario K2P 0L9
China
Embassy: (☎ 010-532 1125, fax 532 5720) 32 Guanghua Lu, Jianguomenwai, Beijing
Consulate: (☎ 020-652 7908, fax 652 7808) Jin Yanf Hotel, 92 Huanshi Western Rd, Guangzhou
Consulate: (☎ 22-591 4510, fax 591 4524) 15th floor, Great Smart Tower Bldg, 230 Wanchai Rd, Hong Kong
France (☎ 10 44 14 64 00, fax 10 45 24 39 48) 62–66 Rue Boileau, Paris 75016
Germany (☎ 228-357021, fax 351866) Konstantinstrasse 37, 5300 Bonn 2
Italy (☎ 06-854 3223, fax 854 8501) 34 Via Clituno, 00198 Rome
Japan
Embassy: (☎ 03-3446 3311, fax 3466 3312) 50-11 Moto Yoyogi-cho, Shibuya-ku, Tokyo 151
Consulate: (☎ 06-263 600, fax 263 1770) 10th floor, Estate Bakurocho Bldg, 4-10 Bakurocho 1-chome, Chuo-ku, Osaka
Laos
Embassy: (☎ 214-13409) 1 Thap Luang Rd, Vientiane
Consulate: (☎ 412-12739, fax 12182) 418 Sisavang Vong, Savannakhet
Philippines (☎ 2-500 364, 508 101) 54 Victor Cruz, Malate, Metro Manila
Thailand (☎ 2-251 7201, 251 5836) 83/1 Wireless Rd, Bangkok
UK (☎ 020-7937 1912 fax 7937 6108) 12–14 Victoria Rd, London W8 5RD
USA (☎ 202-861 073-, fax 861 0917) 1233 20th St NW, Washington, DC 20036

Consulates in Ho Chi Minh City

If you are staying a long time in Vietnam you should register your passport at your embassy or consulate. This is particularly useful if you later need them to issue a new one, should your original be lost or stolen. Also consider registering with them if you intend travelling to more remote areas. They can help you obtain a ballot for absentee voting or provide forms for filing income tax returns.

Embassies and consulates can advise businesspeople, and are are good source of local information. They will also sometimes intervene in trade disputes.

The following is a list of the addresses of some foreign consulates:

Australia (☎ 829 6035, fax 829 6031) Landmark Building, 5B Đ Ton Duc Thang, District 1
Cambodia (☎ 829 2751, fax 829 2744) 41 Đ Phung Khac Khoan, District 1
Canada (☎ 825 5025, fax 829 4528) 235 Đ Kong Khoi, 10th floor, District 1
China (☎ 829 2457, fax 829 5009) 39 Đ Nguyen Thi Minh Khai, District 3
France (☎ 829 7231, 829 1675) corner of ĐL Hai Ba Trung & ĐL Le Duan, District 1
Germany (☎ 829 1967, fax 823 1919) 126 Đ Nguyen Dinh Chieu, District 3
Japan (☎ 822 2600, fax 822 5316) 13–17 ĐL Nguyen Hue, District 1
Laos (☎ 829 7667) 181 ĐL Hai Ba Trung, District 3
Netherlands (☎ 823 5932, fax 823 5934) Saigon Tower, 29 Đ Le Duan, District 1
New Zealand (☎ 822 6907, fax 822 6905) Fifth floor, Yoko Bldg, 41 D Nguyen Thi Minh Khai, District 1
Thailand (☎ 822 2637, fax 829 1002) 25 Đ Tran Quoc Thao, District 3
UK (☎ 829 8433, fax 822 1971) 25 ĐL Le Duan, District 1
USA (☎ 822 9433, fax 822 9434) 4 ĐL Le Duan, District 1

CUSTOMS

Travellers occasionally report trouble with Vietnamese customs. Several years back some have even had their Lonely Planet books seized or sections torn out! Ditto for video tapes. It's best to keep such dangerous items buried deep down in your luggage or in your coat pocket.

You are not permitted to take antiques or other 'cultural treasures' out of the country. If you purchase fake antiques, be sure that you have a receipt and a customs clearance form from the seller. Suspected antiques will be seized, or else you'll have to pay a fine, or bribe.

If you enter Vietnam by air, the customs inspection is usually fast and cursory. However, if you enter overland, you may be subjected to a rigorous search.

You are permitted to bring in a duty-free allowance of 200 cigarettes, 50 cigars or 250g of tobacco; 2L of liquor; gifts worth up to US$50; and a reasonable quantity of luggage and personal effects. Items that you cannot bring into Vietnam include opium, weapons, explosives and 'cultural materials' which the government deems 'unsuitable to Vietnamese society'.

Tourists can bring an unlimited amount of foreign currency into Vietnam, but they are required to declare it on their customs form upon arrival. Theoretically, when you leave the country you should have exchange receipts for all the foreign currency you have spent, but in practice the authorities really don't care.

When entering Vietnam, visitors must also declare all precious metals, jewellery, cameras and electronic devices in their possession. Theoretically, declaring your goods means that when you leave, you will have no hassles taking these items out with you. It also means that you could be asked to show these items so that customs officials know you didn't sell them on the black market, though in practice you will seldom be troubled unless you bring in an unreasonable amount of goods or something of great value.

The import and export of Vietnamese currency and live animals is forbidden.

MONEY

Currency

The currency of Vietnam is the dong (abbreviated as a 'd' following the amount). The banknotes come in denominations of 200d, 500d, 1000d, 2000d, 5000d, 10,000d, 20,000d and 50,000d.

Now that Ho Chi Minh has been canonised (against his wishes), you'll find his picture on *every* banknote. There are no coins currently in use in Vietnam, though the dong used to be subdivided into 10 hao and 100 xu. All dong-denominated prices in this book are from a time when US$1 was worth 14,098d.

The US dollar acts virtually as a second local currency: hotels, airlines and travel agencies all normally quote their prices in dollars. This is in part because Vietnamese prices are so unwieldy, since US$100 is well over one million dong! For this reason, we also quote prices in US dollars. However, realise that you can, and should, pay dong. Indeed, Vietnamese law requires that all transactions be in dong, though in practice many people will accept dollars.

It's advisable to bring a small pocket calculator with you for converting currency, unless of course you are the sort of person who can nonchalantly multiply US$33.50 by 14,098d (and add 10% tax) in your head.

Exchange Rates

The following table shows exchange rates:

country	unit		dong
Australia	A$1	=	8270
Canada	C$1	=	9470
China	Y1	=	1703
euro	€1	=	12,795
France	10FF	=	1951
Germany	DM1	=	6542
Japan	¥100	=	130
New Zealand	NZ$1	=	6440
Thailand	B1	=	347
UK	£1	=	21,212
USA	US$1	=	14,098

Exchanging Money

The dong has certainly experienced its ups and downs. Past attempts by the government to solve the country's debt problems with the printing press led to devastating inflation and frequent devaluations. More recently, the Asian economic crisis, which has wreaked havoc on the Thai, Korean and Indonesian currencies, caused the dong to lose about 15% of its US dollar value.

Although you can at least technically convert French francs, German marks, British pounds sterling, Japanese yen and other major currencies, the reality is that US dollars are still much preferred.

Once in Vietnam, beware of counterfeit cash, especially the 20,000d and 50,000d notes. There shouldn't be any problem if you've changed money in a bank, but out in the free market it's a different story.

Vietcombank is another name for the state-owned Bank for Foreign Trade of Vietnam (Ngan Hang Ngoai Thuong Viet Nam). Banking hours are normally from 8 am to 3 pm Monday to Friday and from 8 am to noon Saturday; most banks also close for 1½ hours during lunchtime and all day Sunday and public holidays.

You can reconvert reasonable amounts of dong back into dollars on departure without an official receipt, though the definition of 'reasonable' is questionable. Most visitors have had no problem, but having an official receipt should settle any arguments that arise. You cannot legally take the dong out with you.

For cashing travellers cheques or taking a credit card cash advance, you are required to show your passport as ID.

Cash Large-denomination bills (US$100) are preferred when changing into dong, but a small supply (say US$20 worth) of ones and fives may prove useful. Be *very* careful with your money – travellers cheques and large-denomination cash belong in a concealed money belt or a hotel safe.

Travellers Cheques Travellers cheques can be exchanged only at authorised foreign exchange banks. Major foreign exchange banks can cash travellers cheques, but private moneychangers will not. The foreign exchange counter at the airport also changes travellers cheques. Banks usually charge a 2% commission to change US dollar travellers cheques into US dollars cash (other banks may charge more). Vietcombank charges no commission if you exchange travellers cheques for dong.

If your travellers cheques are denominated in currencies other than US dollars, you may find them difficult to exchange. If you insist, the banks may exchange non-US dollar cheques for dong, but they will charge a hefty commission to protect themselves against any possible exchange rate fluctuations.

Foreign exchange banks observe all major public holidays. If you arrive during the Lunar New Year, the banks may be closed for three or four days in a row. Try not to get caught short.

ATMs ANZ Bank (near the riverfront at Me Linh Square) has a 24-hour automated teller machine (ATM) that dispenses dong if you have an internationally accepted Visa, MasterCard or Cirrus card. There is no service fee levied.

HSBC (in the New World Hotel Annexe) also has a 24 hour ATM hooked up to Plus/Cirrus networks; withdrawals using cards connected to the Global Access Network are free; Visa and MasterCard are free in Vietnamese dong. From either ATM, you may only draw a daily maximum of two million dong. New regulations no longer allow US dollar withdrawals from ATMs.

Credit Cards Visa, MasterCard, American Express (AmEx) and JCB cards are now accepted at many places in Ho Chi Minh City, typically mid-range and top end hotels, restaurants and shops. Some places (in particular travel agents) may charge up to 4% commission each time you use a credit card, so ask first.

Getting a cash advance is possible at Vietcombank and Sacombank, but you'll be charged a 3% commission.

Banks There is a bank just outside the airport exit which gives the official exchange rate. However, be sure to have sufficient US dollar notes in small denominations to get yourself into the city, in case it is closed.

Vietcombank (☎ 829 7245, fax 823 0310) occupies two adjacent buildings at the intersection of Đ Ben Chuong and Đ Pasteur, District 1. The east building is for foreign exchange and it's worth a visit even if you don't change money – the ornate interior is absolutely stunning! It's open from 7 to 11.30 am and from 1.30 to 3.30 pm daily except Saturday afternoon and the last day of the month. Besides US dollars, accepted hard currencies include Australian dollars, British pounds sterling, Canadian dollars, Deutschmarks, French francs, Hong Kong dollars, Japanese yen, Singapore dollars, Swiss francs and Thai baht. Travellers cheques in US dollars can be changed for US dollars cash for a 2% commission.

In the city centre there is a smaller branch of Vietcombank (☎ 823 0214), at 132 Đ Dong Khoi, District 1, adjacent to the Continental Hotel. It's open from 8 to 11.30 am and from 1 to 4 pm.

In the Pham Ngu Lao area, Vietcombank has a money changing desk in the Fiditourist office at 195 Đ Pham Ngu Lao, District 1, on the corner of Đ De Tham. It's open from 7.30 am to 9 pm Monday to Saturday and is a good place to change money after normal working hours. Also popular in the budget travellers' zone is Sacombank, at 211 Đ Nguyen Thai Hoc, District 1, on the corner of Đ Pham Ngu Lao. Both of these are popular places to change cash and travellers cheques and to get advances on credit cards.

Vietnam-Eximbank's foreign currency exchange desk 59 (☎ 823 1316), at 15A Le Loi, District 1, handles cash, travellers cheques and Visa/MasterCard cash advances, and is open from 7 am to 9 pm. One traveller reported being short-changed there, so beware.

Other state-run banks that can change a wide variety of foreign currencies include the Phuong Dong Bank (☎ 822 0961), at 45 ĐL Le Duan, District 1 and the Bank for Investment & Development (☎ 823 0123), at 134 Đ Nguyen Cong Tru, District 1.

There are several foreign-owned banks in Ho Chi Minh City, but they are often compelled by law to impose higher fees than Vietnam's state-owned banks. ANZ Bank and HSBC are both highly popular for their ATMs (see the ATM entry earlier in this section) and telegraphic transfers. Some of the more notable foreign banks include:

ANZ Bank (☎ 829 9319, fax 829 9316)
11 Me Linh Square, District 1
Bangkok Bank (☎ 822 3416, fax 822 3421)
117 Đ Nguyen Hue, District 1
Bank of America (☎ 829 9928, fax 829 9942)
1 Đ Phung Khac Khoan, District 1
Banque Nationale de Paris (☎ 829 9504, fax 829 9486) 2 Đ Thi Sach, District 1
Crédit Lyonnais (☎ 829 9226, fax 829 6465)
4th floor, 65 Đ Nguyen Du, District 1
Deutsche Bank (☎ 822 2747, fax 822 2760)
174 Đ Nguyen Dinh Chieu, District 3
HSBC (☎ 829 2288, fax 823 0530) 75 Đ Pham Hong Thai, District 1
Thai Military Bank (☎ 822 2218, fax 823 0045) 11 Đ Ben Chuong, District 1

All the major tourist hotels can change money easily, legally and well after business hours; however, they offer rates around 5% lower than the bank rate.

International Transfers Money can be cabled into Vietnam quickly and cheaply and the recipient can be paid in US dollars or Vietnamese dong. Vietcombank is authorised to handle wire transfers. Money should be cabled to Vietcombank Ho Chi Minh City (see the Banks entry earlier for its address). The cable needs to include the recipient's name and passport number. Vietcombank's telex number in Ho Chi Minh City is 811.234 VCB.VT or 811.235 VCB.VT.

Black Market The black market is Vietnam's unofficial banking system. How to find it? Well, it's almost everywhere. Perhaps the term black market is really too strong since it implies some cloak and dagger operation. It's in fact very open. Private individuals and some shops (jewellery stores, travel agencies) will exchange US dollars for dong and vice versa. While the practice is supposedly illegal, enforcement is virtually nonexistent. But it's important to realise that black market exchange rates can be *worse* than the official exchange rates.

If people approach you on the street with offers to change money at rates better than the official bank rate, then you can rest assured that you are being set up for a rip-off. Don't even think about trying it. Remember, if an offer seems too good to be true, that's because it is.

Security

Ho Chi Minh City boasts some of the craftiest street criminals in South-East Asia. In the eyes of the city's expert pickpockets and bands of street children, you will no doubt be eyed as a potential target. Rather than lose your precious cash and travellers cheques (not to mention your passport), large amounts of money and other valuables should be kept far from sticky fingers.

Various devices to thwart pickpockets include pockets sewn on the inside of your trousers, Velcro tabs to seal pocket openings, a moneybelt under your clothes or a pouch under your shirt. A vest (waistcoat) worn under your outer jacket will do very nicely, but only in the colder seasons. Simply put, do not have anything dangling off of your body (this includes bags, jewellery, sunglasses etc) that you are not willing to part with.

Fortunately, crimes against foreigners rarely involve any physical threat, but it is imperative to take the necessary precautions against common theft and *stay on guard*.

Should you need the services of the police, travellers have reported the large police station at 73 Đ Yersin, at the western terminus of Đ Nguyen Thai Binh (a short walk from the Ben Thanh Market) is the best place to go. Arrive well dressed (not in shorts and sandals). If you need to file a police report, you'll need to furnish a passport photo.

Costs

Foreigners are frequently overcharged, particularly when buying souvenirs and occasionally in restaurants. However, don't assume that everyone is trying to rip you off – despite being poor, many Vietnamese will only ask the local price for most goods and services.

The cost of staying in Ho Chi Minh City depends on your tastes and susceptibility to luxuries. Ascetics can get by on US$10 a day while most backpackers can live very well on US$20 to US$25.

Bare-bones private hotel rooms come as cheap as US$6, but for around US$10 to US$15 you can get something decent with an attached bath and air-con. Once you pass the US$20 limit, expect to be spoiled with satellite TV, IDD phones etc.

If you were to dine exclusively at local Vietnamese places and travellers' cafes, it is theoretically possible to eat in Ho Chi Minh City on about US$2 to US$4 per day. Most budget travellers, however, would require something closer to US$10 for three square meals, and sampling some of the city's finer fare could push this over US$20 in no time.

Transportation expenses can be kept down by walking (which Ho Chi Minh City is fairly well suited to). For reaching areas out of walking distance, travelling by rented bicycle (about US$1 per day) can also save a considerable sum.

Tipping & Bargaining

Tipping according to a percentage of the bill is not expected but it's enormously appreciated. For a person who earns US$50 per month, a US$1 tip is about half a day's wages. Government-run hotels and restaurants that specifically cater to tourists usually have an automatic 10% service charge – whether much of this (if any) actually goes to the low-paid staff is questionable.

In general, if you stay a couple of days in the same hotel it's not a bad idea to tip the staff who clean your room – US$0.50 to US$1 should be enough. You should also tip drivers and guides, especially on trips out of the city.

Men you deal with will also greatly appreciate small gifts such as a pack of cigarettes (women almost never smoke). But make sure it's a foreign brand of cigarettes; people will be insulted if you give Vietnamese cigarettes. The 555 brand (said to be Ho Chi Minh's favourite) is popular, as are most US brands. Most of the usual kinds of gifts (chocolates and sweets, coffee-table books etc) are acceptable, as long as they are foreign-made.

It is considered proper to make a small donation at the end of a visit to a pagoda, especially if the monk has shown you around; most pagodas have contribution boxes for this purpose.

Many foreigners just assume that every Vietnamese person is out to rip them off. That just isn't true – you needn't bargain for everything, but there are times when bargaining is essential. In touristy areas, postcard vendors have a reputation for charging about five times the going rate. Many cyclo and motorcycle drivers also try to grossly overcharge foreigners – try to find out the correct rate in advance and then bargain accordingly. Bargaining is common – even with the police if you are fined!

Remember, the concept of 'face' is important in Asia. Bargaining should be good-natured – smile, don't raise your voice and don't get argumentative.

Some seem to take bargaining too seriously, and take it personally if they don't get the goods for less than half the original asking price. By publically venting their frustration, people just end up looking foolish. Don't let yourself get angry. Once the money is accepted, the deal is done – if you harbour hard feelings because you later find out that someone else got it cheaper, the only one you are hurting is yourself.

Taxes & Refunds

After years on the drawing board, Vietnam introduced a controversial Value Added Tax (VAT) on 1 January 1999. The VAT technically applies to all consumer goods and, depending on which sector of the economy it is applied to, is levied at four rates: 0%, 5%, 10% or 20%.

So far, VAT has created nothing but confusion, stemming from a lack of public understanding of how to interpret the tax and how it will actually be implemented. The government has gone so far as to air a special TV program aimed at clarifying the situation, but to date the public remains largely perplexed.

On many goods you pay for, the marked or stated price includes any relevant taxes. Only in some hotels, restaurants and shops do people actually add the VAT separately.

The issue of paying income tax is totally flaky. Expatriates working in Vietnam for six months or more every year are subject to tax on their total income (including worldwide income earned outside Vietnam, which they are supposed to declare). Tax brackets range from 10% to 50%, depending on how much you earn. Vietnam's arbitrary income tax laws change when the moon is full and the tides are high, so don't consider the aforementioned to be the final word. If you are planning to work in Vietnam, enquire about tax at the Ho Chi Minh City Tax Office.

POST & COMMUNICATIONS

Ho Chi Minh City's French-style Central Post Office, Buu Dien Thanh Pho Ho Chi Minh (☎ 829 6555), occupies a full city block, at 2 Đ Cong Xa Paris, District 1, facing Notre Dame Cathedral. The structure was built between 1886 and 1891 and is by far the largest post office in Vietnam. It's open from 6.30 am to 8 pm.

The entrance in the middle of the block leads to the postal services windows, where you can send letters, pick up domestic packages and purchase philatelic items, all under the benevolent gaze of Uncle Ho. The staff at the information desks in the postal services section speak English.

The same entrance in the middle of the block leads to the telex, telegram and telephone/fax office. Telex and telephone services are available from 6.30 am to 8 pm; telegrams can be sent 24 hours a day. To your right as you enter the building is poste restante, which is labelled Delivery of Mail – Mail to Be Called For. Pens, envelopes, aerograms, postcards and stamp collections are on sale at the counter to the right of the entrance, and outside the CPO along Đ Nguyen Du.

Every district and sub-district in Ho Chi Minh City has some sort of post office; all are sign-posted with the words Buu Dien. Most smaller post offices in town also keep long hours, from about 6 am to 8 pm including weekends and public holidays.

Postal Rates

Domestic postal rates are sinfully cheap; a domestic letter costs just US$0.04 to mail.

International postal rates are similar to those levied in European countries, ie postcards to Europe or the USA cost about US$0.50 to send. While these rates might not seem expensive by Western standards, the tariffs are so out of line with most salaries that locals literally cannot afford to send letters to their friends and relatives abroad. If you would like to correspond with Vietnamese whom you meet during your visit, try leaving them enough stamps to cover postage for several letters, explaining that the stamps were extras you didn't use and would be of no value to you at home. Or buy a bunch of Vietnamese stamps to take home with you and when you write to Vietnamese friends place a few stamps in the envelope for their replies.

Sending Mail

Foreigners sending parcels out of Vietnam sometimes have to deal with time-consuming inspections of the contents, but happily this is happening less frequently. The most important thing is to keep your parcel small. If it's documents only, you should be OK. However, sending out video tapes and the like can be problematic.

Vietnamese stamps often have insufficient gum on them; use the paste provided in little pots at post offices. If practicable, ensure that the clerk cancels them, as some travellers have reported that someone (for whom the stamps were probably worth a day's salary) had soaked the stamps off and thrown their letters away.

Airmail service from Ho Chi Minh City takes approximately 10 days to most Western countries. Express Mail Service (EMS) is available to most developed countries and a few of the less developed ones. It's perhaps twice as fast as regular airmail, but a bigger advantage is that the letter or small parcel will be registered. The EMS office (☎ 824 4666), at 80D Đ Nguyen Du, District 1, is located on the south side of the CPO. There is also reasonably priced domestic EMS between Ho Chi Minh City and Hanoi (and other major cities in Vietnam) promising next-day delivery.

Private Couriers For a price, private couriers can deliver both international and domestic small parcels or documents.

Airborne Express (☎ 829 2976, fax 829 2961) 80C Đ Nguyen Du, District 1. Opening hours are from 7 am to 7 pm Monday to Saturday and from 8 am to noon Sunday. Airborne Express also has a representative office (☎ 848 5369) near the airport, at 2E Đ Tien Giang.

DHL Worldwide Express (☎ 823 1525, fax 845 6841) Offers express document delivery from the CPO and from its main office (☎ 844 6203, fax 844 5387) at 4 Đ Phan Thuc Duyen, Tan Binh District. It's open from 6.30 am to 9 pm Monday to Saturday and from 8 am to 4 pm Sunday.

Federal Express (☎ 825 6257) 141 ĐL Nguyen Hue, District 1. Most prefer to use the Fed-Ex branch (☎ 829 0995, fax 829 0477) attached to Rex Hotel, at 146 Đ Pasteur (on the corner of Đ Le Thanh Ton). Opening hours for the Rex Hotel branch are from 7 am to 8 pm Monday to Saturday and from 9 am to 5 pm Sunday. Outside Ho Chi Minh City you can call Federal Express on its toll-free number (☎ 018-829 0747).

TNT Express Worldwide (☎ 844 6460, fax 844 6592) 56 Đ Truong Son, Ward 2, Tan Binh District

United Parcel Service (☎ 824 3597, fax 824 3596) 80 Đ Nguyen Du, District 1 (attached to the CPO)

Freight Forwarders Planning on shipping home Vietnamese furniture or a used car? Or will you move your entire household and belongings to Vietnam for a long stay? For these you need the services of an international mover or freight forwarder.

Much of this business goes to Saigon Van (☎ 829 3502) at 76 Đ Ngo Duc Ke, District 1. This company is associated with the international company, Atlas Van Lines. Other moving companies to consider include Transpo Vietnam (☎ 829 4886), at 1A Me Linh Square, District 1 and Vietrade Removal Services (☎ 825 3328), at 6–8 Đ Doan Van Bo.

Freight forwarding shipping agents in Ho Chi Minh City include:

JNE Crie (☎ 842 9441, fax 842 9442) 5 Đ Cong Ha, Tan Binh District

Maersk (☎ 824 3252, fax 823 1395) Block B, 28 Đ Phung Khac Khoan, District 1

Saigon Express – Viconship Saigon (☎ 825 3328) 6–8 Đ Doan Van Bo, District 4

Sealand (☎ 822 5324) 5–7 ĐL Nguyen Hue, District 1

Receiving Mail

Mail delivery is mostly reliable and fast. However, this reliability becomes questionable if your envelope or package contains something worth stealing. Normal letters and postcards should be fine. Letters and parcels airmailed from abroad to Vietnam can be delivered in as little as four days or as long as 10 months! Prolonged delays are almost certainly due to the Vietnamese security apparatus inspecting any documents that have been deemed 'suspicious'. Reliability is greatly enhanced if your envelope or package contains nothing that somebody would want to steal.

The poste restante windows at city post offices work well. It is possible to receive mail at any post office, but the sender will need to specify when addressing the envelope or package. Generally speaking, the CPO is the best bet. Foreigners have to pay a US$0.04 service charge for each letter they pick up from poste restante.

Receiving even a small package from abroad can cause a headache and large ones may produce a migraine. If you're lucky, customs will clear the package and the clerks at the post office will simply let you take it away. If you're unlucky, customs will demand an inspection at which you must be present and pay some small fees. In that case, the post office will give you a written notice which you take to the customs office along with your passport. The customs office for incoming parcels is at the rear of the CPO building.

Procedures from this point on can be very tedious; and if you are particularly unlucky, you may have to pay import duty. If your parcel contains books, documents, video tapes, computer disks or other 'dangerous' goods, it's possible that a further inspection will be required by the Ministry of Culture. This could take anywhere from a few days to a few weeks.

Telephone

International and domestic long-distance calls can be booked at many hotels, but this is expensive.

It's somewhat less expensive to book long-distance phone calls from the post office. For operator-assisted calls, you will be charged for three minutes even if you only talk for one minute, plus the rate per minute will be higher. As in most countries, the cheapest way to make a long-distance call is to dial direct.

Ho Chi Minh City's area code is ☎ 08.

Domestic Calls Except for some special numbers (eg, fire brigade and directory assistance), all phone numbers in Ho Chi Minh City have seven digits.

Local calls can usually be made from any hotel or restaurant phone and are often free – the exception is calling a mobile phone (mobile telephone numbers begin with ☎ 090 and are followed by six more digits).

Domestic long-distance calls are reasonably priced and are cheaper if you dial direct. Calls between Ho Chi Minh City and Hanoi at the full daytime rate will cost US$0.45 per minute. An operator-assisted call is US$0.82 per minute, though there is a three-minute minimum charge time. You can save up to 20% if you call between 10 pm and 5 am.

To make domestic direct-dial calls outside the Ho Chi Minh City area code (08), dial the area code followed by the local number. For example, to call Hanoi (area code 04) you would dial ☎ 04-123 4567. Area codes in Vietnam are assigned according to province, and the current dispensation is as follows:

province	capital city	area code
An Giang	Long Xuyen	☎ 76
Bac Can	Bac Can	☎ 281
Bac Giang	Bac Giang	☎ 240
Bac Lieu	Bac Lieu	☎ 781
Bac Ninh	Bac Ninh	☎ 241
Ba Ria	Vung Tau	☎ 64
Ben Tre	Ben Tre	☎ 75
Binh Dinh	Quia Nhon	☎ 56
Binh Duong	Thu Dau Mot	☎ 65
Binh Phuoc	Dong Xuoi	☎ 65
Binh Thuan	Phan Thiet	☎ 62
Camau	Camau	☎ 780
Cantho	Can Tho	☎ 71
Cao Bang	Cao Báng	☎ 26
Dac Lac	Buon Ma Thuot	☎ 50
Dong Nai	Bien Hoa	☎ 61
Dóng Thap	Cao Lanh	☎ 67
Gia Lai	Pleiku	☎ 59
Ha Giang	Ha Giang	☎ 19
Hai Duong	Hai Duong	☎ 32
Ha Nam	Ha Nam	☎ 351
Ha Tay	Ha Dong	☎ 34
Ha Tinh	Ha Tinh	☎ 39
Hoa Binh	Hoa Binh	☎ 18
Hung Yen	Hung Yen	☎ 32
Khanh Hoa	Nha Trang	☎ 58
Kien Giang	Rach Gia	☎ 77
Kon Tum	Kon Tum	☎ 60
Lai Chau	Dien Bien Phu	☎ 23

province	capital city	area code
Lam Dong	Dalat	☎ 63
Lang Son	Lang Son	☎ 25
Lao Cai	Lao Cai	☎ 20
Long An	Tan An	☎ 72
Nam Dinh	Nam Dinh	☎ 350
Nghe An	Vinh	☎ 38
Ninh Binh	Ninh Binh	☎ 30
Ninh Thuan	Phan Rang	☎ 68
Phu Tho	Viet Tri	☎ 21
Phu Yen	Tuy Hoa	☎ 57
Quang Binh	Dong Hoi	☎ 52
Quang Nam	Tam Ky	☎ 510
Quang Ngai	Quang Ngai	☎ 55
Quang Ninh	Halong City	☎ 33
Quang Tri	Dong Ha	☎ 53
Soc Trang	Soc Trang	☎ 79
Son La	Son La	☎ 22
Tay Ninh	Tay Ninh	☎ 66
Thai Binh	Thai Binh	☎ 36
Thai Nguyen	Thai Nguyen	☎ 280
Thanh Hoa	Thanh Hoa	☎ 37
Thua Thien	Hué	☎ 54
Tien Giang	Mytho	☎ 73
Tra Vinh	Tra Vinh	☎ 74
Tuyen Quang	Tuyen Quang	☎ 27
Vinh Long	Vinh Long	☎ 70
Vinh Phuc	Vinh Yen	☎ 211
Yen Bai	Yen Bai	☎ 29

municipality	area code
Da Nang	☎ 511
Hai Phong	☎ 31
Hanoi	☎ 4
Ho Chi Minh City	☎ 8

International Calls International calls from Vietnam are ridiculously expensive and, outside major cities, unreliable. To be fair, the phone company has lowered rates slightly in the past two years, but its international rates are easily two to five times higher than in Western countries. The monopoly enjoyed by the Directorate General of Posts & Telecommunications (DGPT) means that price decreases will come slowly and grudgingly.

Perhaps the most obnoxious example of the greed of the DGPT is the fact that foreigners are not permitted to make international reverse-charge (collect) calls. However, Vietnamese nationals can. Why? Because the DGPT earns considerably less from a reverse-charge call than from calls paid for in Vietnam. However, since most Vietnamese cannot possibly afford to pay for an international call, they are permitted to call collect to their overseas relatives (the assumption being that those relatives will probably send them money).

Calling from most countries to Vietnam will be at least 50% cheaper than calling from Vietnam to abroad. So if you plan to talk more than a few minutes, it's best to make a very brief call abroad and ask the other party to call you back.

The cheapest and simplest way by far to make an international direct-dial (IDD) call is to buy a telephone card, known as a UniphoneKad. They are on sale at the telephone company. UniphoneKads can only be used in special telephones, usually found in the lobbies of major hotels. The cards are issued in four denominations: 30,000d (US$2.50), 60,000d (US$5), 150,000d (US$12) and 300,000d (US$24). The 30,000d and 60,000d cards will work only for domestic calls.

To make an IDD call, you must first dial the international prefix ☎ 00 followed by the country code, area code (if any) and the local number. Note that for many countries (eg, Australia) area codes start with a zero, but this zero must not be dialled when calling internationally. So to call Melbourne (area code ☎ 03) in Australia (country code ☎ 61) from Vietnam, you would dial ☎ 00-61-3-9123 4567. Some useful country codes include:

country	country code
Australia	☎ 61
Belgium	☎ 32
Canada	☎ 1
Denmark	☎ 45
France	☎ 33
Germany	☎ 49
Hong Kong	☎ 852
Italy	☎ 39
Japan	☎ 81
Korea (South)	☎ 82
Malaysia	☎ 60
Netherlands	☎ 31
New Zealand	☎ 64
Norway	☎ 47

country	country code
Philippines	☎ 63
Singapore	☎ 65
Spain	☎ 34
Sweden	☎ 46
Switzerland	☎ 41
Taiwan	☎ 886
Thailand	☎ 66
UK	☎ 44
USA	☎ 1
Vietnam	☎ 84

Calls are charged by one-minute increments; any fraction of a minute is charged as a full minute. But many travellers find that international calls cost more than the advertised rate (is there some sort of hidden tax?) – this applies even when you use a phone card. There is only a 10% discount for calls placed between 11 pm and 7 am.

Useful Telephone Numbers Ho Chi Minh City produces its own version of the Yellow Pages in which you can look up services by subject. For example, to find the phone numbers of hotels look under *khach san*. You can find telephone books at most hotel reception desks, and you can also purchase these directories from the phone company offices.

The following free phone services are available, but don't be surprised if the person answering only speaks Vietnamese:

Ambulance	☎ 115
Fire brigade	☎ 114
International operator	☎ 110
International prefix	☎ 00
Local directory assistance	☎ 116
Police	☎ 113
Time	☎ 117

Kudos to Vietnam's ☎ 1080 information service, a source of an amazing array of facts, figures and trivia. For a mere US$0.03 per minute, you can ask the operator everything from phone numbers to train and plane timetables, to exchange rates and the latest football scores. We have used ☎ 1080 to confirm historical dates, economic statistics, and receive a morning wake-up call. You can even order up a bedtime story for your child (told in a sweet voice)! Most of the time it is possible to be connected to an operator who speaks English or French.

Pagers Aside from the convenience they offer, using a pager is more economical than having a telephone installed. Pagers also solve the problem posed if you are forced to move. At least if you have to move, the pager goes with you.

There are currently several paging companies operating in Ho Chi Minh City. For additional information, try contacting any of the following:

Di Dong MCC (☎ 829 0117) 125 ĐL Hai Ba Trung, District 1

PhoneLink (☎ 824 3038, fax 822 3997) 146–150 Đ Pasteur, District 1
(☎ 825 1368) 230 ĐL Hai Ba Trung, District 1
(☎ 835 1070, fax 835 1062) 180 ĐL Tran Hung Dao B, District 5

Saigon ABC Paging Centre (☎ 824 1338, fax 824 1340) 125 ĐL Hai Ba Trung, District 1

Cellular Phones Like many other developing countries, Vietnam is pouring a lot of money into the cellular network and more and more locals and expats are depending on the portability and convenience of mobile phones.

The place to look for mobile phones and all the trendy accessories required to outcool your friends is along ĐL Hai Ba Trung, running north from the back side of the CPO. Companies offering cellular sales, rental and service in Ho Chi Minh City include VinaPhone (☎ 824 5168), at 80 Đ Nguyen Du, District 1 and VMS Mobi-Fone (☎ 822 8171), at 123 ĐL Hai Ba Trung, District 1.

Amy Limited (☎ 844 8813), located at 46D Đ Nguyen Van Troi, Phu Nhuan District, offers mobile phone rentals and will even deliver to your home or hotel. They have a contact number in the US if you want to prearrange a mobile phone rental – call ☎ 215-592 4632.

Fax

Most of Ho Chi Minh City's post offices and tourist hotels offer relatively cheap domestic and international fax services, as well as telegraph and telex.

Faxes can be sent to you at the CPO (fax 829 8540, 829 8546) and these will be delivered to your hotel for a small charge. In order for this to work, the fax should clearly indicate your name, hotel phone number and the address of the hotel (including your room number). The cost for receiving a fax is about US$0.80.

Top-end hotels also have business centres, many of which operate 24 hours a day. You can send and receive fax and email messages at these places. You do not have to be a guest at these hotels to take advantage of these services, but hotels will generally charge more than the post office.

Email & Internet Access

Access to online services is available through cybercafes and a growing number of hotels. Most people staying long term sign up with one of Ho Chi Minh City's three main Internet service providers.

If you have an established email account with a non-Vietnamese service provider, access from Vietnam will require you to download your mail through a Web-based service such as Hotmail. Unfortunately, other popular international email service providers such as CompuServe, America Online and Asia Online do *not* have local nodes in Vietnam.

The cost for Web access in Ho Chi Minh City ranges from about US$0.01 to US$0.08 per minute – the going rate in the budget travellers' ghetto is just 250 dong (US$0.03) per minute. While this is indeed cheap, connections can be painfully slow, so you'll need to figure in some extra time and patience. Printing typically costs between US$0.08 and US$0.16 per page.

There is a rapidly expanding number of places offering Internet access, mostly concentrated in the Pham Ngu Lao area. Of the 20 or more easy-to-spot places for sending/receiving email in this area, Saigon Net (☎ 837 2573, ⓔ tiendat@Saigonnet.vn) at 220 Đ De Tham, District 1. It is one of the better ones and keeps long hours (from 6 am to midnight). There's a smaller branch of Saigon Net adjacent to the Pham Ngu Lao post office, at 199–205 Đ Nguyen Thai Hoc, District 1.

Viet Quang Office Systems (☎ 830 0317, fax 830 0741, ⓔ vmax.110@hcm.vnn.vn), at 110 Đ Bui Thi Xuan, District 1, is about a 10-minute walk from the cafes around Đ Pham Ngu Lao. You can surf your socks off in clean, air-con, smoke-free rooms, plus play an array of computer games. It's open from 8 am to 9 pm. Viet Quang has a second branch (☎ 837 1938) at 271 Đ Pham Ngu Lao, District 1, closer to the heart of backpacker central, but less comfortable.

An alternative closer to the centre of town is the Tin Cafe (☎ 822 9786, ⓔ PQHOI@bdvn.vnmail.vnd.net) at 2A ĐL Le Duan, District 1. It's a pleasant place to check your mail or surf the Net while sipping a cappuccino. It's open from 7.30 am to 10.30 pm.

INTERNET RESOURCES

The World Wide Web is a rich resource for travellers. You can research your trip, hunt down bargain air fares, book hotels, check weather conditions or chat with locals and other travellers about the best places to visit (or avoid).

There's no better place to start your Web explorations than the Lonely Planet Web site (www.lonelyplanet.com). Here you'll find succinct summaries on travelling to most places on earth, postcards from other travellers and the Thorn Tree bulletin board, where you can ask questions before you go or dispense advice when you get back. You can also find travel news and updates to many of our most popular guidebooks, and the subWWWay section links you to the most useful travel resources elsewhere on the Web.

One of the best all-round sites on contemporary Vietnam is Destination Vietnam (www.destinationvietnam.com), a one-stop Vietnam information zone that covers travel, art, history, government and culture, and even adoption.

Another place to begin is Vietnam Adventures Online (www.vietnamadventures.com). It is full of practical travel information and features monthly adventures and special travel deals.

Vietnam Online (www.vietnamonline .com) is loaded with useful travel lore and boasts good coverage on employment and business opportunities in the country. Very useful if you plan to stay on a while.

The Vietnam Arts & Culture Channel (www.namviet.net/arts_1.html) is another excellent site to check out..

BOOKS

An increasing variety of English and French books are now available in Ho Chi Minh City. For a listing of local bookshops, see the Bookshops section of the Shopping chapter later in this book.

Lonely Planet

Lonely Planet's *Vietnam* covers the entire country inside-out, from boating in the Mekong Delta to trekking along the Chinese border. Those travelling further afield should consider taking along LP's *South-East Asia on a shoestring*.

Cyclists, hikers and other back-country explorers may want to score a copy of LP's *Vietnam travel atlas*. Our *Vietnamese phrasebook* is not only educational and practical, but will also give you something to do on a rainy day. And if you'd like the latest details on the ins and outs of Hanoi, there is the *Hanoi* city guide.

Guidebooks

The book you hold in your hands is the most detailed English-language travel guide to Ho Chi Minh City.

The state-run The Gioi Publishers puts out several books on Ho Chi Minh City and Vietnam. Though published in 1994 and as such rather out of date, you might look for *Saigon: 20 Years After Liberation*.

Some of Ho Chi Minh City's museums publish small books or pamphlets on their collections. Worth picking up at the History Museum for US$2 is *The Museum of Vietnamese History* (1996). The book provides detailed information on most of the museum's exhibits and includes several pages of colour photographs.

Travel

A Dragon Apparent is about author Norman Lewis' fascinating journeys through Vietnam, Laos and Cambodia in 1950. This classic travelogue is now available as a reprint from Eland in London and Hippocrene in New York.

Sparring with Charlie: Motorbiking down the Ho Chi Minh Trail by Christopher Hunt is a light-hearted travelogue about modern Vietnam.

Another effort in this direction is *Ten Years After* by Tim Page. This impressive book boasts '12 months worth of photos taken 10 years after the war'. Page also returned to Vietnam to write *Derailed in Uncle Ho's Victory Garden*.

History & Politics

The Fall of Saigon by David Butler (1985) is one of the best researched and most readable accounts of the Communist takeover of the city in 1975.

Vietnam: Politics, Economics and Society by Melanie Beresford (1988) gives a good overview of the aspects of post-reunification Vietnam mentioned in its title.

The Birth of Vietnam by Keith Weller Taylor tackles the country's early history.

The Vietnamese Gulag is a harrowing account by Doan Van Toai. It tells of one man's experiences in the post-reunification re-education camps.

For a very readable account of Vietnamese history from prehistoric times until the fall of Saigon, try Stanley Karnow's *Vietnam: A History*, which was published as a companion volume to the American Public Broadcasting System series *Vietnam: A Television History*.

A number of biographies of Ho Chi Minh have been written, including *Ho Chi Minh: A Political Biography* by Jean Lacouture, and *Ho* by David Halberstam.

An excellent reference work is *Vietnam's Famous Ancient Pagodas (Viet Nam Danh Lam Co Tu)*, which is written in Vietnamese, English, French and Chinese. The publisher is the Social Sciences Publishing House and you should be able to find copies in Ho Chi Minh City.

Franco–Viet Minh War Worthwhile books covering this topic include Peter M Dunn's *The First Vietnam War* and two works by Bernard B Fall – *Street Without Joy: Indochina at War 1946-54* (1961) and *Hell in a Very Small Place: The Siege of Dien Bien Phu* (1967).

Vietnam (American) War The earliest days of US involvement in Indochina – when the US Office of Strategic Services (OSS, predecessor of the CIA) was providing funding and weapons to Ho Chi Minh at the end of WWII – are recounted in *Why Vietnam?*, a riveting work by Archimedes L Patti. Patti was the head of the OSS team in Vietnam and was at Ho Chi Minh's side when he declared Vietnam independent in 1945.

Three of the finest essays on the war are collected in *The Real War* by Jonathan Schell. An overview of the conflict is provided by George C Herring's *America's Longest War*.

An excellent autobiographical account of the war by a Vietnamese woman is Le Ly Hayslip's *When Heaven and Earth Changed Places*.

A highly acclaimed biographical account of the US war effort is *A Bright Shining Lie* by Neil Sheehan. It won both the Pulitzer Prize and the National Book Award, and was also made into a major motion picture under the same name.

Another fine biography is Tim Bowden's *One Crowded Hour* which details the life of Australian film journalist Neil Davis.

Some of the horror that American POWs endured comes through in *Chained Eagle* by Everett Alvarez Jr, a US pilot who was imprisoned in North Vietnam for 8½ years.

Viet Cong Memoir by Truong Nhu Tang is the autobiography of a Viet Cong cadre who later became disenchanted with post-1975 Vietnam.

One of the finest books about the war written by a Vietnamese is *The Sorrow of War* by Bao Ninh. A new English-language edition has become available in the US and Australia.

General

Graham Greene's 1954 novel *The Quiet American*, which is set during the last days of French rule, is probably the most famous Western work of fiction on Vietnam. Much of the action takes place at Saigon's Continental Hotel and at the Caodai complex in Tay Ninh.

The Lover by Marguerite Duras is a fictional love story set in Saigon during the 1930s. The book has been made into a major motion picture.

Saigon by Anthony Grey (Pan Books), is your standard blockbuster by the author of *Peking*. Not bad.

Passport Vietnam by Jeffrey Curry & Jim Chinh Nguyen may be of interest to business travellers.

CD ROM

The classic choice here is *Passage to Vietnam*, a collection of beautiful photos and narrative. This CD was produced by Rick Smolan, who created the famed *Day in the Life* series. The same photos also appear in a lavish coffee-table book.

NEWSPAPERS & MAGAZINES

Vietnam has no equivalent to the sleaze circus that characterises the Western tabloid press. Basically, it's self-congratulatory rhetoric and sombre financial news.

The *Vietnam News* is an English-language newspaper published daily. If you're desperate for some news of the outside world, it will do in a pinch. It's also good for wrapping ceramics and other souvenirs.

The best locally made English-language magazine is the monthly *Vietnam Economic Times*. *VET*'s free insert, *The Guide*, is an excellent source of leisure information. The supplement can be picked up in most hotels, and some bars and restaurants.

The weekly *Vietnam Investment Review* is a weekly broadsheet economic newspaper. *VIR*'s free supplement, *Time Out*, is also useful for finding what's going on in town.

Imported newspapers and magazines are available in most large bookshops and hotels.

RADIO & TV

Radio

The Voice of Vietnam broadcasts on short wave, AM and FM for about 18 hours a day. The broadcasts consist mostly of music, but there are also news bulletins in Vietnamese, English, French and Russian. Don't worry if you miss one bulletin – the same edition is broadcast throughout the day and a text version is printed in the daily *Vietnam News*.

Visitors wishing to keep up on events in the rest of the world – and in Vietnam itself – may want to bring along a small shortwave receiver. News, music and features programs such as BBC World Service and Voice of America can easily be picked up, especially at night.

Vietnamese TV

Vietnamese TV began broadcasting in 1970 and it's fair to say that the content has improved little since then. There are currently three main channels in Ho Chi Minh City and Hanoi, and two channels elsewhere. Broadcast hours are from 9 to 11.30 am and from 7 to 11 pm Monday to Saturday. On Sunday there is an extra broadcast from 3 to 4 pm. English-language news follows the last broadcast some time after 10 pm. Sometimes soccer or other sports come on at strange hours like 1.30 am.

Satellite TV

Satellite TV is now widely available, which is a boon for foreign visitors. You're most likely to find it in the better hotels and some pubs. Hong Kong's Star TV is the most popular station, along with CNN, Sports Channel, Asia Business News (ABN) and Channel V (an MTV station).

VIDEO SYSTEMS

It's hard to know what Vietnam's official video standard is. That's because most new TVs and VCRs sold in Vietnam are multistandard: PAL, NTSC and SECAM.

PHOTOGRAPHY & VIDEO

Film & Equipment

Colour film is widely available. Look for well-frequented shops and check the expiry date printed on the box. Don't buy film from outdoor stalls – it may have been cooking in the sun for months. Negative film prices are perfectly reasonable and you won't save much by bringing film from abroad.

Colour slide film and B&W film is mostly found in speciality shops. If you really need it then you'd best bring a supply from abroad.

Photo processing shops have become ubiquitous in places where tourists congregate. There are several good places along ĐL Nguyen Hue (near the Rex Hotel), and a handful in the Pham Ngu Lao area – Photo Nhu (☎ 836 8093), at 231 Đ Pham Ngu Lao, District 1, is very good, though the others nearby should be fine as well. Most of these shops are equipped with the latest one-hour, colour printing equipment. Printing costs about US$5 per roll, depending on the print size you choose. The quality tends to be quite good. Be sure to specify if you want glossy or mat finish on your prints.

Colour slide film can be developed quickly (the standard being three hours). Processing costs about US$5 per roll, but most shops do not mount the slides unless you request and pay for it. We've personally had (and heard of) several bad experiences with slide film coming back scratched, fingerprinted and dusty, so unless you have no choice, it is recommended to take slide and B&W film outside Vietnam to a proper photo lab.

Plastic laminating is cheap. Just look for the signs saying Ep Plastic.

Cameras are fairly expensive in Vietnam and the selection is limited – bring one from abroad. Happily, lithium batteries (needed by many of today's point-and-shoot cameras) are widely available.

Restrictions

The Vietnamese police usually don't care what you photograph, but on occasion they get pernickety. Obviously, don't photograph something militarily sensitive (airports, military bases, border checkpoints etc). Photography from aircraft is permitted. Many museums, however, have restrictions. Taking pictures inside pagodas and temples is *usually* all right, but it's always better to ask permission first from the monks.

Some touristy sites charge a camera fee of about US$0.50, or a video fee of US$2 to US$5. If the staff refuse to issue a receipt for the camera fee, then you should refuse to pay – the fee in that case is likely to go into their pockets.

Photographing People

Photographing people demands the utmost respect for local customs. The beauty and colour of Vietnamese society and the surrounding landscape provides ample opportunity for photography, but it is important to remember you are a guest in Vietnam and that not only might your actions be interpreted as rude or offensive, but you might also spoil things for future visitors.

Airport Security

The dreaded X-ray machines at Tan Son Nhat Airport have been upgraded and are now film-safe. At least it says so on the machines. The old Soviet-made microwave ovens had a habit of frying your film, but they've been replaced with modern, film-safe equipment imported from Germany. Don't attempt to film the airport security procedures: the film will most likely be ripped out of your camera.

The great stumbling block at Tan Son Nhat appears to be what the authorities like to call cultural materials. Video tapes are deemed to be cultural materials which may be screened in advance by 'experts' from the Department of Culture.

TIME

Ho Chi Minh City (like Bangkok) is seven hours ahead of GMT/UTC. Daylight saving (summer time) is *not* observed. When it's noon in Ho Chi Minh City it is 10 pm the previous day in San Francisco, 1 am in New York, 5 am in London, 1 pm in Perth and 3 pm in Sydney. When Western countries are on daylight saving time, subtract one hour from the times listed for the previous cities.

ELECTRICITY

Voltages & Cycles

Electric current in Vietnam is mostly 220V at 50Hz (cycles), but often you'll still find 110V (also at 50Hz).

Plugs & Sockets

Looking at the shape of the outlet on the wall gives no clue as to what voltage is flowing through the wires. If the voltage is not marked on the socket try finding a light bulb or appliance with the voltage written on it. In Ho Chi Minh City, most outlets are US-style flat pins but you'll also see Russian-inspired round pins. All sockets are two-prong only – in no case will you find a third wire for ground (earth).

Vietnam's electrical power is often unstable. Sudden voltage drops can cause computers to crash, meaning you'll have to shut it down and restart. Even worse is a high-voltage surge, which can actually damage the sensitive electronics. A voltage surge suppressor can help solve this problem – many portable computers already come with these built into the power supply.

WEIGHTS & MEASURES

The Vietnamese use the international metric system (see the back of this book for a metric conversion table). In addition, two weight measurements have been borrowed from the Chinese: the *tael* and the *catty*. A catty equals 0.6kg (1.32lb). There are 16 taels to the catty, so one tael equals 37.5g (1.32oz). Gold is always sold by the tael.

LAUNDRY

Almost every hotel does laundry, though it is prudent to politely check the cost to avoid surprises when you go to pay the bill.

At budget hotels, it is usually easy to find a hotel attendant who will get your laundry spotlessly clean for the equivalent of US$1 or slightly more. The best prices are in the Pham Ngu Lao area, where some places charge by weight (usually about US$0.80 or US$1 per kg). Like the rest of the world, the more expensive the hotel, the more you pay for such services. Larger hotels might display a price list.

Budget hotels do not have clothes dryers – they rely on the sunshine – so allow at least a day and a half for washing and drying, especially during the wet season.

If you have a backpack full of dirties and a little time, Hong Chau (☎ 843 6649), at

221 Đ Tran Quang Khai, District 1, is a good self-service laundrette.

TOILETS

Better hotels will have the more familiar Western-style sit-down toilets, but squat toilets still exist in cheaper hotels and public places such as restaurants and bus stations.

The scarcity of public toilets seems to be a greater problem for women than for men. Vietnamese males (and children) are often seen urinating in public, but this appears to be socially unacceptable for women. It is not very clear how Vietnamese women handle this situation, but about the best advice one can give is not to drink too much.

Toilet paper is seldom provided in the toilets at bus and train stations or in other public buildings, though hotels usually supply it. If you don't want to go Asian-style, you'd be wise to keep a stash of your own with you at all times while touring the city.

LEFT LUGGAGE

You may find baggage storage at some train and bus stations, but in general these are not reliable. Hotels or budget cafes are a better bet, though it never hurts to padlock your bag.

HEALTH

Travel health depends on your predeparture preparations, your daily health care while travelling and how you handle any medical problem that does develop. While the potential dangers can seem quite frightening, in reality few travellers experience anything more than an upset stomach.

Vaccinations

Plan ahead for getting your vaccinations: some of them require more than one injection, while some should not be given together. Note that some vaccinations should not be given during pregnancy or to people with allergies – discuss this with your doctor. It is recommended you seek medical advice at least six weeks before travel. Be aware that young children and pregnant woment generally run a greater risk of disease when travelling.

Poisonous Wind

In Ho Chi Minh City (and more so in the Vietnamese countryside), you will no doubt see Vietnamese covered with long bands of red welts on their necks and backs. This is not some kind of horrid skin disease, but a treatment. In traditional Vietnamese folk medicine, many illnesses are attributed to 'poisonous wind' *(trung gio)*. Poisonous wind can be released by scraping the skin with spoons, coins etc, thus raising the welts you see. The results aren't pretty, but the locals say this treatment is good for what ails you. Try it at your own peril.

Another way to fight poisonous wind is a technique – borrowed from the Chinese – that employs suction cups made of bamboo placed on the patient's skin. A burning piece of alcohol-soaked cotton is briefly put inside the cup to drive out the air before it is applied. As the cup cools, a partial vacuum is produced, leaving a nasty-looking but harmless red circular mark on the skin.

PHIL WEYMOUTH

FACTS FOR THE VISITOR

Carry proof of your vaccinations. A yellow fever vaccination certificate is required only if travellers are coming from an infected area – this is occasionally needed to enter Vietnam. There is no risk of yellow fever in South-East Asia.

Discuss your requirements with your doctor, but vaccinations you should consider for this trip include the following:

Diphtheria & Tetanus Vaccinations for these two diseases are usually combined and are recommended for everyone. After an initial course of three injections (usually given in childhood), boosters are necessary every 10 years.

Polio Everyone should keep up to date with this vaccination, which is normally given in childhood. A booster every 10 years maintains immunity.

Hepatitis A Hepatitis A vaccine (eg, Avaxim, Havrix 1440 or VAQTA) provides long-term immunity (possibly more than 10 years) after an initial injection and a booster at six to 12 months.

Alternatively, an injection of gamma globulin can provide short-term protection against hepatitis A – from two to six months, depending on the dose given. It is not a vaccine, but is ready-made antibody collected from blood donations. It is reasonably effective and, unlike the vaccine, its prophylactic effect is immediate, but because it is a blood product, there are current concerns about its long-term safety.

Hepatitis A vaccine is also available in a combined form, Twinrix, with hepatitis B vaccine. Three injections over a six-month period are required, the first two providing substantial protection against hepatitis A.

Hepatitis B Travellers to Ho Chi Minh City should consider vaccination against hepatitis B if they plan to go journeying farther afield in the countryside, where blood transfusions may not be adequately screened. Hep' B is always a risk where sexual contact or needle sharing occurs. Vaccination involves three injections, with a booster at 12 months. More rapid courses are available if necessary.

Malaria Medication

Antimalarial drugs do not prevent you from being infected but kill the malaria parasites during a stage in their development and may significantly reduce the risk of becoming very ill or dying. Expert advice on medication should be sought, as there are many factors to consider, including the area to be visited, the risk of exposure to malaria-carrying mosquitoes, the side effects of medication, your medical history and whether you are a child or pregnant.

There is minimal risk of malarial infection in Ho Chi Minh City, however there remains a risk of malaria year-round in rural areas of Vietnam, so travellers should take the appropriate precautions as necessary (discuss this with your doctor). Note that many medical professionals *do not* recommend taking malarial prophylactics, though they may recommend carrying a treatment dose of medication for use if symptoms occur.

Health Insurance

Make sure that you have adequate health insurance. See Travel Insurance under Documents earlier in this chapter for details.

Travel Health Guides

If you are planning to be away or travelling in remote areas for a long period of time, you may like to consider taking a more detailed health guide.

Healthy Travel Asia & India by Dr Isabelle Young. Lonely Planet's guide to keeping healthy on the road. Geared specifically to the independent traveller.

CDC's Complete Guide to Healthy Travel by the US Centers for Disease Control & Prevention. Recommendations for international travel.

Staying Healthy in Asia, Africa & Latin America by Dirk Schroeder. A handy all-round guide – detailed and well organised.

Travellers' Health by Dr Richard Dawood. Comprehensive, easy to read, authoritative and highly recommended, although it's rather large to lug around.

Where There Is No Doctor by David Werner. A very detailed guide intended for someone, such as a Peace Corps worker, going to work in a developing country.

Travel with Children by Maureen Wheeler. Has advice on travel health for younger children.

There are also a number of excellent travel health sites available on the Web. From Lonely Planet's home page there are links at www.lonelyplanet.com/weblinks/wlheal.htm to the World Health Organization and the US Centers for Disease Control & Prevention.

Other Preparations

Make sure you're healthy before you travel. If you are going on a long trip make sure your teeth are OK. If you wear glasses take a spare pair and your prescription.

If you require a particular medication take an adequate supply, as it may not be available locally. Take part of the packaging showing the generic name rather than the brand, which will make getting replacements easier. It's a good idea to have a legible prescription or letter from your doctor to show that you legally use the medication to avoid any problems.

Sunburn can be more than just uncomfortable – it can lead to skin cancer in later years. Bring sunscreen (UV) lotion and wear something to cover your head. Protect your eyes with decent sunglasses.

Food & Water

Food There is an old colonial adage that says: 'If you can cook it, boil it or peel it you can eat it…otherwise forget it.' Vegetables and fruit should be washed with purified water or peeled where possible. Beware of ice cream that is sold in the street or anywhere it might have been melted and refrozen; if there's any doubt (eg, a power cut in the last day or two), steer well clear. Beware of undercooked meat, particularly in the form of mince. Shellfish such as mussels, oysters and clams should be avoided as well. Steaming does not make shellfish safe for eating.

If a place looks clean and well run and the vendor also looks clean and healthy, then the food is probably safe. In general, places that are packed with travellers or locals will be fine, while empty restaurants may be questionable. The food in busy restaurants is cooked and eaten quite quickly with little standing around and is probably not reheated. You may want to consider carrying your own set of chopsticks with you, at least this way you know exactly how clean they are. Chopsticks can be bought very cheaply on arrival in Vietnam.

Water The number one rule is *be careful of the water* and especially ice. If you don't know for certain that the water is safe, assume the worst. Reputable brands of bottled water or soft drinks are generally fine, although in some places bottles may be refilled with tap water. Only use water from containers with a serrated seal – not tops or corks. Take care with fruit juice, particularly if water may have been added.

In Ho Chi Minh City, tap water is not too bad (it's chlorinated) but it's still recommended that you boil it before drinking. In the nearby countryside, the water varies from pretty safe to downright dangerous. After a typhoon and subsequent flooding, there is a problem with sewers overflowing into reservoirs. Do not even brush your teeth with unboiled water after flooding.

Bottled water or soft drinks are generally fine. Milk should be treated with suspicion as it is often unpasteurised or kept unrefrigerated. Yoghurt should be OK if it's been kept refrigerated and is not too old. Tea and coffee should both be OK since the water should have been boiled.

While boiling will kill nasty microbes, freezing will not. In Ho Chi Minh City, ice is delivered daily to restaurants from a factory which has to meet certain standards of hygiene (the water is at least chlorinated). In rural areas the ice could be made from river (sewer?) water. Another problem is that even clean ice often makes its way to its destination in a filthy sack. Completely avoiding ice would be a good idea, but that's not easy advice to follow in a hot, tropical country.

Water Purification The simplest way of purifying water is to boil it thoroughly. Consider purchasing a water filter for longer trips into the countryside. Chlorine tablets (Puritabs, Steritabs or other brand names) will kill many pathogens, but not some parasites like giardia and amoebic cysts. Iodine is more effective in purifying water and is available in tablet form (such as Potable Aqua). Follow the directions carefully and remember that too much iodine can be harmful.

Medical Problems & Treatment

Self-diagnosis and treatment can be risky, so you should always seek medical help. Although we do give drug dosages in this section, they are for emergency use only. Correct diagnosis is vital.

An embassy, consulate or five-star hotel can usually recommend a local doctor or clinic. The facilities in Ho Chi Minh City (see Medical Services later) are generally good but it's a sensible idea to ensure you're in reasonable health before departing. Antibiotics should ideally be administered only under medical supervision. Take only the recommended dose at the prescribed intervals and use the whole course, even if the illness seems to be cured. Stop immediately if there are any serious reactions and don't use the antibiotic if you are unsure that you have the correct one. Some people are allergic to commonly prescribed antibiotics such as penicillin or sulpha drugs; carry this information (eg, on a bracelet) when travelling.

Environmental Hazards

Heat Exhaustion Dehydration and salt deficiency can cause heat exhaustion. Take time to acclimatise to high temperatures, drink sufficient liquids and do not do anything too physically demanding. Sweating makes you lose a lot of salt, and this can lead to fatigue and muscle cramps. Putting extra salt in your food (a teaspoon a day is probably too much) will solve this, but increase your water intake if you do. Using soy sauce is another method of increasing salt intake.

Heatstroke This serious and occasionally fatal condition can occur if the body's heat-regulating mechanism breaks down and the body temperature rises to dangerous levels. Long, continuous periods of exposure to high temperatures with insufficient fluids can leave you vulnerable to heatstroke.

Infectious Diseases

Diarrhoea Simple things like a change of water, food or climate can all cause a mild bout of diarrhoea, but a few rushed toilet trips with no other symptoms is not indicative of a major problem.

Dehydration is the main danger with any diarrhoea, particularly in children or the elderly as it can occur quite quickly. Under all circumstances *fluid replacement* (at least equal to the volume being lost) is the most important thing to remember. Weak black tea with a little sugar, soda water or soft drinks allowed to go flat and diluted 50% with clean water are all good. With severe diarrhoea, a rehydrating solution is preferable to replace minerals and salts lost. Commercially available oral rehydration salts (ORS) are very useful; add them to boiled or bottled water. In an emergency you can make up a solution of six teaspoons of sugar and half a teaspoon of salt to a litre of boiled or bottled water. You need to drink at least the same volume of fluid that you are losing in bowel movements and vomiting. Urine is the best guide to the adequacy of replacement – if you have small amounts of concentrated urine, you need to drink more. Keep drinking small amounts often. Stick to a bland diet as you recover.

Gut-paralysing drugs such as Lomotil or Imodium can be used to bring relief from the symptoms, though they do not actually cure the problem. Only use these drugs if you do not have access to toilets, eg, if you *must* travel. For children under 12 years Lomotil and Imodium are not recommended. Do not use these drugs if the person has a high fever or is severely dehydrated.

In certain situations antibiotics may be required: diarrhoea with blood or mucus (dysentery), any diarrhoea with fever, profuse watery diarrhoea, persistent diarrhoea not improving after 48 hours and severe diarrhoea. These suggest a more serious cause of diarrhoea and in these situations gut-paralysing drugs should be avoided. A stool test may be necessary to diagnose what bug is causing your diarrhoea.

Hepatitis Hepatitis is a general term for inflammation of the liver. It is a common disease worldwide. There are several different viruses that cause hepatitis, and they differ in the way that they are transmitted. The symptoms are similar in all forms of the illness, and include fever, chills, headache, fatigue, feelings of weakness and aches and pains, followed by loss of appetite, nausea, vomiting, abdominal pain, dark urine, light-coloured faeces, jaundiced (yellow) skin and yellowing of the whites of the eyes. People who have had hepatitis should avoid alcohol for some time after the illness, as the liver needs time to recover.

Hepatitis A is transmitted by contaminated food and drinking water. You should seek medical advice, but there is not much you can do apart from resting, drinking lots of fluids, eating lightly and avoiding fatty foods. Hepatitis E is transmitted in the same way as hepatitis A; it can be particularly serious in pregnant women.

There are almost 300 million chronic carriers of hepatitis B in the world. It is spread through contact with infected blood, blood products or body fluids, eg, through sexual contact, unsterilised needles and blood transfusions, or contact with blood via small breaks in the skin. Other risky situations include having a shave, tattoo or body piercing with contaminated equipment. The symptoms of hepatitis B may be more severe than type A and the disease can lead to long-term problems such as chronic liver damage, liver cancer or a long-term carrier state. Hepatitis C and hepatitis D are spread in the same way as hepatitis B and can also lead to long term complications.

There are vaccines against hepatitis A and B, but there are currently no vaccines against the other types of hepatitis. Following the basic rules about food and water (hepatitis A and E) and avoiding risky situations (hepatitis B, C and D) are important preventative measures.

HIV & AIDS Infection with the Human Immunodeficiency Virus (HIV) may lead to Acquired Immune Deficiency Syndrome (AIDS), which is a fatal disease. Any exposure to blood, blood products or body fluids may put an individual at risk. The disease is often transmitted through sexual contact or dirty needles – vaccinations, acupuncture, tattooing and body piercing can be potentially as dangerous as intravenous drug use. HIV/AIDS can also be spread through infected blood transfusions.

If you do need an injection, ask to see the syringe unwrapped in front of you, or take a needle and syringe pack with you. However, fear of HIV infection should never preclude treatment for serious medical conditions.

Official figures on the number of people with HIV/AIDS in Vietnam are vague. Despite the fact that health education messages relating to HIV/AIDS can be found nationwide, the official line is that infection is largely limited to sex workers and drug users. Condoms are widely available in Ho Chi Minh City.

Sexually Transmitted Diseases Gonorrhoea, herpes and syphilis are among these diseases; sores, blisters or rashes around the genitals and discharges or pain when urinating are common symptoms. In some STDs, such as wart virus or chlamydia, symptoms may be less marked or not observed at all, especially in women. Syphilis symptoms eventually disappear completely but the disease continues and can cause severe problems in later years. While abstinence from sexual contact is the only 100% effective prevention, using condoms is also effective. There is no cure for herpes or AIDS.

Typhoid Typhoid fever is a dangerous gut infection caused by contaminated water and food. It is imperative that medical help be sought immediately.

In its early stages sufferers may feel they have a bad cold or flu on the way, as early symptoms are a headache, body aches and a fever which rises a little each day until it is around 40°C (104°F) or more. The victim's pulse is often slow relative to the degree of fever present – unlike a normal fever where the pulse increases. There may also be vomiting, abdominal pain, diarrhoea or constipation.

In the second week the high fever and slow pulse continue and a few pink spots may appear on the body; trembling, delirium, weakness, weight loss and dehydration may occur. Complications such as pneumonia, perforated bowel or meningitis may occur.

Typhoid is not a serious health risk in Ho Chi Minh City.

Malaria This serious and potentially fatal disease is spread by mosquito bites. When travelling in areas where malaria is extremely important to avoid exposure to mosquito bites to prevent this disease. Symptoms range from fever, chills and sweating, headache, diarrhoea and abdominal pains, to a vague feeling of ill-health. Seek medical help immediately if malaria is suspected. Without treatment malaria can rapidly deteriorate into something more serious and can even be fatal.

If medical care is not available, malaria tablets can be used for treatment. You need to use a malaria tablet which is different from the one you were taking when you contracted malaria. Your doctor should be able to advise you on this before you leave your home country.

Travellers are advised to prevent mosquito bites at all times. The main messages are as follows:

- Wear light-coloured clothing.
- Wear long trousers and long-sleeved shirts.
- Use mosquito repellents containing the compound DEET on exposed areas (prolonged overuse of DEET may be harmful, especially to children, but its use is considered preferable to being bitten by disease-transmitting mosquitoes).
- Avoid perfumes or aftershave.
- Use a mosquito net impregnated with mosquito repellent (permethrin) – it may be worth taking your own.
- Impregnating clothes with permethrin effectively deters mosquitoes and other insects.

Dengue Fever This viral disease is transmitted by mosquitoes and occurs mainly in tropical and subtropical areas of the world. Generally, there is only a small risk to travellers except during epidemics, which are usually seasonal (during and just after the rainy season).

The *Aedes aegypti* mosquito, which transmits the dengue virus, is most active during the day, unlike the malaria mosquito, and is found mainly in urban areas, in and around human dwellings.

Signs and symptoms of dengue fever include a sudden onset of high fever, headache, joint and muscle pains (hence its old name, breakbone fever), and nausea and vomiting. A rash of small red spots appears three to four days after the onset of fever. Dengue is commonly mistaken for other infectious diseases, including influenza.

You should seek medical attention if you think you may be infected. Infection can be diagnosed by a blood test. There is no specific treatment for dengue. Avoid asparin, as it increases the risk of haemorrhaging.

There is no vaccine against dengue fever. The best prevention is to avoid mosquito bites at all times – see the Malaria section earlier for more details.

Cuts, Bites & Stings

Bedbugs & Lice Bedbugs live in various places, but particularly in dirty mattresses and bedding, evidenced by spots of blood on bedclothes or on the wall. Bedbugs leave itchy bites in neat rows. Calamine lotion or Stingose spray may help.

All lice cause itching and discomfort. They make themselves at home in your hair (head lice), your clothing (body lice) or in your pubic hair (crabs). You catch lice through direct contact with infected people or by sharing combs, clothing and the like. Powder or shampoo treatment will kill the lice and infected clothing should then be washed in very hot, soapy water and left in the sun to dry.

Bites & Stings Bee and wasp stings are usually painful rather than dangerous. However, in people who are allergic to them severe breathing difficulties may occur and require urgent medical care. Calamine lotion or Stingose spray will give relief and ice packs will reduce the pain and swelling. There are some spiders with dangerous bites but antivenins are usually available. Scorpion stings are notoriously painful and some can be fatal.

Cuts & Scratches Wash well and treat any cut with an antiseptic such as povidone-iodine. Where possible avoid bandages and Band-Aids, which can keep wounds wet. Coral cuts are notoriously slow to heal and if they are not adequately cleaned small pieces of coral can become embedded in the wound.

Cuts and scratches can easily get infected in the tropical climate. Wash cuts out with boiled or bottled water, use an antiseptic, keep them dry and keep an eye on them; nasty cases require use of an antibiotic cream. Cuts on your feet and ankles are particularly troublesome – a new pair of sandals can quickly give you an abrasion which can be difficult to heal. Try not to scratch mosquito bites for the same reason.

Women's Health

Gynaecological Problems Excessive sweating, and the use of antibiotics, synthetic underwear or contraceptive pills can lead to fungal vaginal infections, especially when travelling in hot climates. STDs are a major cause of vaginal problems.

Pregnancy It is not advisable to travel to some places while pregnant as some vaccinations normally used to prevent serious diseases are not advisable during pregnancy (eg, yellow fever). In addition, some diseases, like malaria, may be much more serious for pregnant women than they would be otherwise (and may increase the risk of a stillborn child).

Medical Services

Hospitals and clinics suited to visitors are:

The Emergency Centre (☎ 829 2071, 829 6485) 125 ĐL Le Loi, District 1. Operates 24 hours. Doctors speak English and French.

The Optical Treatment Centre (☎ 829 8732) 280 Đ Dien Bien Phu, District 3

The Pasteur Institute (☎ 823 0352) 167 Đ Pasteur, District 3. Has the best facilities in Vietnam for medical tests. However, you need to be referred here by a doctor.

Cho Ray Hospital (Benh Vien Cho Ray; ☎ 855 4137/8, fax 855 7267) 201B ĐL Nguyen Chi Thanh, District 5. With 1000 beds, it's one of the largest medical facilities in Vietnam. There is a section for foreigners on the 10th floor. About one-third of the 200 doctors speak English and there are 24-hour emergency facilities. The hospital was built in the 1970s, before reunification, and some of the equipment still dates from that period.

Binh Dan Hospital is said to have belonged to President Thieu during the days when he ruled South Vietnam. This hospital is still one of the best in Vietnam, and treats Communist Party and government officials, but it's too far from the centre to be of much use to visitors. It's approximately 13km north-west of the city centre, in the Tan Binh District.

There are several foreign doctors resident in Ho Chi Minh City.

You can contact Dr F Boudey at the Heart Institute (☎ 865 1586, ext 221), at 520 Đ Nguyen Tri Phuong, District 10.

The OSCAT/Asia Emergency Assistance International Clinic, or AEA (☎ 829 8520, fax 829 8551), in the Hannam Office Building, 65 Đ Nguyen Du, District 1, has a medical services program for resident expats and dental treatments. An annual fee buys you regular treatment, emergency medical care and evacuation 24 hours a day. You can also contact International SOS Assistance (☎ 829 4386, fax 824 2862), at 151 Đ Bis Vo Thi Sau, District 3, for information about its health plan and evacuation services.

Dental care in Vietnam is cheap enough (US$20 for a root canal!). The dentists may not have state-of-the-art technology, but most are knowledgeable.

You can try Dr Tran Ngoc Dinh (☎ 832 4598, 839 9463), at 355 Đ Nguyen Trai, District 1, who speaks English; ditto for Dr Do Dinh Hung (☎ 864 0587, 890 4605), at 281A Đ Cach Mang Thang Tam, Ward 7, Tan Binh District. There is also the Orthodontology Centre (☎ 835 7595) at 263 ĐL Tran Hung Dao, District 1. You'll have to decide yourself what you think of the service at the Ho Chi Minh City Dentistry Academy, at 201A ĐL Nguyen Chi Thanh, District 5, near Cho Ray Hospital.

Pharmacies are everywhere – some good, but many not. One good pharmacy is at 678 Đ Nguyen Dinh Chieu, District 3. The owner speaks excellent English and French and can get rarer medicines not normally kept in stock within a couple of hours. There are also a couple of good pharmacies on Đ De Tham in the Pham Ngu Lao area.

WOMEN TRAVELLERS

Like Thailand and other predominantly Buddhist countries, Vietnam is, in general, free of serious hassles for female Western travellers. At least, that applies to women who are easily recognised as foreigners.

Attitudes Towards Women

As in most parts of Asia, Vietnamese women are given plenty of hard work to do but have little authority at the decision-making level. Vietnamese women proved to be highly successful as guerrillas and brought plenty of grief to US soldiers during the Vietnam War. After the war, their contribution received plenty of lip service, but all the important government posts were given to men. In the countryside, you'll see women doing such jobs as farm labour, crushing rocks at construction sites and carrying baskets weighing up to 60kg. It's doubtful that most Western men are capable of such strenuous activity.

Vietnam's two-children-per-family policy appears to be benefiting women, and more women are delaying marriage to get an education. About 50% of students are female, but their skills don't seem to be put to much use after graduation.

Prostitute Vigilantes Western women can travel around Vietnam with few hassles, but it's a different story for some Asian women who choose to travel in Vietnam, particularly those who are young and accompanied by a Western male. Strangely, Asian women travelling in Vietnam with a Western male companion may automatically be labelled a 'Vietnamese whore'. The fact that the couple could be married (or just friends) doesn't seem to occur to anyone, nor does it seem to register that the woman might not be Vietnamese at all.

Women in this situation are occasionally subjected to verbal abuse, though it will be spoken entirely in Vietnamese which means she may not realise that insults are being hurled at her. Most of this abuse will come from Vietnamese men (including teenagers).

The problem is basically that Vietnamese men believe Western men are out to steal their women. For racially mixed couples in Vietnam, no easy solution exists. There's no need to be overly paranoid, and we've already received several recent letters from mixed race couples who reported having no such experiences in Vietnam. Still, others have reported such abuse, so it may help to at least be aware, and take a few precautions:

- If you do face a confrontation, don't blow your top; maintain cool and walk away.
- Dress 'like a foreigner' – sewing patches on your clothing with Japanese or Chinese characters can work wonders. One traveller got good results by sewing a Korean flag onto her backpack.
- The Western male might be strongly tempted to physically assault a Vietnamese man who is insulting his Asian wife or girlfriend, but this could lead to a brawl with serious consequences. Before you act, remember that some of the spectators could be the man's brothers and they may retaliate violently.

GAY & LESBIAN TRAVELLERS

On the whole, Vietnam is a relatively hassle-free place for homosexuals. There are no laws on same-sex relationships in Vietnam, nor much in the way of official harassment.

Common local attitudes suggest a general social prohibition, though the lack of any laws make things fairly safe (even if the authorities do break up a party on occasion). Major headlines were made in 1997 with Vietnam's first gay male marriage, and again in 1998 at the country's first lesbian wedding, in the Mekong Delta.

With the vast number of same-sex travel partners, gay or not, it is fair to say there is little scrutiny over how travelling foreigners are related. However it would be prudent not to flaunt your sexuality. Likewise with heterosexual couples, passionate public displays of affection are considered a basic no-no.

Perhaps the best way to tap into what's what is on the Net. Check out Utopia at www.utopia-asia.com. The site is full of information and contacts, including detailed sections on the legality of homosexuality in Vietnam and some local gay terminology.

Douglas Thompson's *The Men of Vietnam* is a comprehensive gay travel guide to Vietnam. The book can be ordered at the Website mentioned earlier.

DISABLED TRAVELLERS

Remember that Vietnam is still a developing country, and such concerns as handicapped rights just aren't hot political issues. Physically challenged travellers will have to deal with such things as multistorey hotels lacking lifts, pavements blocked by street vendors, high kerbs and motorcycle riders who slow down only when they hit something.

Ho Chi Minh City is not a good city for the disabled, despite the fact that many Vietnamese are disabled with war injuries. Tactical problems include a lack of pedestrian footpaths and the ubiquitous squat toilets.

SENIOR TRAVELLERS

There is a deep and definite sense of respect for the elderly in Vietnam, though seniors are likely to encounter problems similar to those that affect disabled people. Ho Chi Minh City poses no special problems for the elderly beyond the chaotic traffic and (possibly) pickpockets who may view older people as soft targets. And, as in other Asian countries, it is not uncommon to be elbowed out of line at a post office by a one metre tall, 97-year-old woman.

There are no discounts as such for pensioners, nor international cards that are officially recognised, but it may be worth flashing your card to see what you can get.

Senior travellers should be extra careful about keeping all vaccinations up to date. Any special medications required should also be brought along.

HO CHI MINH CITY FOR CHILDREN

Ho Chi Minh City is a relatively good city for kids, with a number of appealing attractions, though keeping children happy and entertained can prove challenging at times. In general, foreign children have a good time in Vietnam, mainly because of the overwhelming amount of attention they attract. The Vietnamese absolutely adore children, and if you bring the kids you can expect that everyone will want to fuss over and play with them!

At both the War Remnants Museum and History Museum, there are water puppet performances daily (see the Things to See & Do chapter for details). The city zoo is another big draw-card for kids, and adult kids as well. Playgrounds are scarce, though some city parks feature amusement park attractions. Of course a cyclo ride in itself should keep most kids enthralled for a while, not to mention some of the best ice cream in South-East Asia! Those travelling with kids can score serious points by taking them out to the Saigon Water Park.

The main risk to children comes from Ho Chi Minh City's horrendous traffic. It's bad enough for adults to deal with the reckless driving, but for children this is an especially serious hazard.

Daycare centres are notable for their absence, though it will not be difficult to hire a babysitter if you need one. Finding a babysitter who can speak English will be more difficult, but certainly not impossible.

Babies and unborn children can present their own peculiar problems when travelling. Lonely Planet's *Travel with Children* by Maureen Wheeler gives a rundown on health precautions to be taken with kids and advice on travel during pregnancy.

USEFUL ORGANISATIONS

Commercial Organisations

Vietcochamber is supposed to initiate and facilitate contacts between foreign business and Vietnamese companies. Vietcochamber publishes a listing of government companies and their contact details.

The following are some government and trade organisations that offer various services to investors and businesspeople. They may be worth contacting for any business dealings in the city:

Vietcochamber (Chamber of Commerce & Industry of Vietnam; Chi Nhanh Phong Thuong Mai Va Cong Nghiep Viet Nam) (☎ 823 0331, 823 0339, fax 829 4472) 171 Đ Vo Thi Sau, District 3
Foreign External Affairs Office (☎ 822 3032, 822 4311) 6 Đ Thai Van Lung, District 1
Foreign Economic Relations Service (☎ 829 2991) 45–47 Đ Ben Chuong Duong, District 1
Foreign Trade & Investment Development Center (☎ 829 2391, fax 822 2983) 92–96 ĐL Nguyen Hue, District 1
People's Committee of Ho Chi Minh City (☎ 829 1056) 86 Đ Le Thanh Ton, District 1
State Committee for Cooperation & Investment (☎ 829 4674, fax 822 3905) 178 Đ Nguyen Dinh Chieu, District 3
Vietnam Trade Information Centre (☎ 829 8734) 35–37 Đ Ben Chuong Duong, District 1

Aid Organisations

As a developing country, Vietnam needs all the help it can get, and there are a number of international aid organisations filling that role. Unfortunately, most of the following relief organisations do not accept donations or volunteers.

FAO (United Nations Food & Agriculture Organization; TC Luong Thuc Va Nong Nghiep) (☎ 829 0781) 2 Đ Phung Khac Khoan, District 1
ICRC (International Committee of the Red Cross; UB Chu Thap Do Quoc Te) (☎ 822 2965) 70 Đ Ba Huyen Thanh Quan, District 3
UNDP (United Nations Development Program; Chuong Trinh Cua LHQ Ve Phat Trien) (☎ 829 5821, fax 829 5865) 2 Đ Phung Khac Khoan, District 1
UNHCR (United Nations High Commission for Refugees; Cao Uy LHQ Ve Nguoi Ti Nan) (☎ 844 5895, fax 844 5896) 257 Đ Hoang Van Thu, Tan Binh District
UNICEF (United Nations International Children's Emergency Fund; Quy Nhi Dong LHQ) (☎ 291006) 2 Đ Phung Khac Khoan, District 1

LIBRARIES

The Municipal Library is at 34 Đ Ly Tu Trong, District 1. Nearby, at 69 Đ Ly Tu Trong is the General Sciences Library with a total of 500 seats in its reading rooms.

SCHOOLS

Expat schools around the city include:

ABC Kindergarten (☎ 822 8807) 5 Đ Nguyen Thi Dieu, District 3
École Française Colette (☎ 829 1992, fax 829 1992) 124 Đ Cach Mang Thang Tam, District 3
International Grammar School (☎ 822 3337, fax 823 0000) 236 Đ Nam Ky Khoi Nghia, District 3
International School (☎ 887 4022) 649A Đ Vo Truong Toan, An Dien Ward, Thu Duc District
Saigon Kids (☎ 829 1324, fax 822 8439) 72/7C Đ Tran Quoc Toan, District 3
Saigon Southern School (☎ 873 0226) South Saigon Highway, Tan Phu Ward, District 7

DANGERS & ANNOYANCES

Theft

The Vietnamese are convinced that their cities are very dangerous and full of criminals. Although the locals generally exaggerate the danger, crime rates have risen significantly in the past couple of years. *Do not* underestimate the skills of the thieves of Ho Chi Minh City, especially around Đ Dong Khoi and ĐL Nguyen Hue. One traveller recently had this to say:

> Muggings are a regular problem now in Ho Chi Minh as I found out in three hours there – my wallet containing my passport, money etc was torn from around my neck by the passenger on a Honda Om. We were by no means the only victims. Extreme vigilance is called for.

Especially watch out for drive-by thieves on motorcycles – they specialise in snatching handbags and cameras from tourists riding in cyclos. Many are also proficient at grabbing valuables from the open window of a car and speeding away with the loot. Foreigners have occasionally reported having their glasses and hats snatched too.

Pickpocketing often involves the most unlikely kinds of people. Even cute little kids, women with babies and newspaper vendors seem to be practitioners of the art. It is currently a serious problem, especially in tourist areas of Ho Chi Minh City. The children often wander right into cafes and restaurants where foreigners are eating, ostensibly to sell newspapers or postcards. In the process – and often with the help of another child accomplice – they can relieve you of your camera, or any other item, if you've set it down on an adjacent seat. If you must set things down while you're eating, at least take the precaution of fastening these items to your seat with a strap or chain. Remember, any luggage that you leave unattended for even a moment will grow legs and vanish. Not all of the kids, however, are thieves, but it is always a good idea to keep a close eye on your belongings.

Despite all this, you should not be overly paranoid. Don't assume that everyone's a thief – most Vietnamese are very poor but reasonably honest.

To avoid theft, probably the most sensible advice one can follow is to not bring anything valuable that you don't need. Expensive watches, jewellery and electronic gadgets invite theft, but do you really need these things while travelling?

If robbed, it is likely the most help the local police will be is in writing a report for the insurance company.

Violence

Unlike in some Western cities, recreational homicide is not a popular sport in Ho Chi Minh City. In general, violence against foreigners is extremely rare, and strict laws are in place to deter physical threats to non-Vietnamese. Vietnamese thieves prefer to pick your pocket or grab your bag and then run away – knives, guns, sticks and other weapons are almost never used. However, Vietnamese newspapers have started reporting a recent upsurge in violent robberies. So far, the victims have been overwhelmingly Vietnamese – perhaps the thieves are reluctant to get involved with foreigners.

Con Artists

Compared with some other countries (the Philippines and Thailand come to mind), Vietnam is relatively free of con artists who try to draw travellers into 'practice' card games, 'sure-fire investments' and great bargains on 'rare gems' that can always be 'resold at a profit'. But the Vietnamese are starting to learn some of the tricks that can be played on naive tourists in order to separate them from their money. You can never anticipate every scam you might encounter, so perhaps the best advice is to maintain a healthy scepticism and be prepared to walk away when unreasonable demands are made for your money.

There have been persistent reports in the tourist zones (especially around Đ Dong Khoi and ĐL Nguyen Hue) of single male travellers being approached in the evening by women who appear to be prostitutes. Those foreigners foolish enough to even talk to these women for a couple of minutes may suddenly be approached by a very angry, screaming man claiming that the foreigner is trying to rape his wife. He makes a big scene, a crowd gathers and he demands US$100 or so in compensation.

Beggar Fatigue

Just as you're about to dig into the scrumptious Vietnamese meal you've ordered, you feel someone gently tugging on your shirtsleeve. You turn around to deal with this latest 'annoyance' only to find it's someone who looks like they haven't eaten for a week.

You are looking into the face of poverty. How do you deal with these situations? If you're like most people, not very well.

So what can you do to help these street people, many of whom are malnourished, illiterate and have no future? Good question – please send us suggestions. On occasion, we've given food to beggars; at least this is one way to feed the hungry without having to give money never knowing how it will actually be spent.

Noise

One thing that can be insidiously draining on your energy during a visit to Ho Chi Minh City is the noise from the streets. At night, there is often a competing cacophony from motorcycles, dance halls, cafes, video parlours, karaoke lounges, restaurants and so on. Taxis might as well have a permanent siren attached.

Most Vietnamese seem to be immune to noise. Fortunately, the racket subsides around 10 or 11 pm, as few clubs stay open later than midnight. On the other side of the coin, though, the Vietnamese are very early risers; most people are up and about from around 5 am onwards. This means that traffic and street noise starts early. It's worth trying to get a hotel room at the back so that the effect of noise is diminished. Other than that, perhaps you could consider bringing a set of earplugs.

LEGAL MATTERS

Civil Law

The French gave the Vietnamese the Napoleonic Code, much of which has still to be repealed, even though these laws may conflict with later statutes. Since reunification, Soviet-style laws have been applied to the whole country with devastating consequences for private property owners. The recent economic reforms have seen a flood of new property legislation, much of it the result of advice from the United Nations (UN), the International Monetary Fund and other international organisations. The rapid speed at which legislation is being enacted is a challenge for those who must interpret and enforce the law.

At the time of writing, the biggest trial since reunification was under way at the stunning French-built city courthouse on Đ Ly Tu Trong. The case, involving alleged wrongdoing on the part of 74 customs officials at Saigon Harbour, revolved around smuggled electronics. Authorities even had to erect a temporary prison near the courthouse to accommodate all the accused.

Still, most legal disputes are settled out of court. In general, you can accomplish more with a carton of cigarettes and a bottle of good cognac than you can with a lawyer.

For information regarding the development of Vietnam's legal code, contact the Vietnam Law & Legal Forum at 21C Đ Ton Duc Thang, District 1.

Drugs

You may well be approached with offers to buy marijuana and occasionally opium. Giving in to this temptation is risky at best. There are many plain-clothes police in Vietnam – just because you don't see them doesn't mean they aren't there. If arrested, you could be subjected to a long prison term and/or a large fine.

The illegal drug export market has also been doing well and Vietnam's reputation is such that customs officials at your next destination might be inclined to search your luggage thoroughly. In short, drug use in Vietnam is a very perilous activity and taking some home with you is just plain stupid.

Police

The problem of police corruption has been acknowledged in official newspapers. The same problems that plague many developing countries' police forces – very low pay and low levels of training – certainly exist in Ho Chi Minh City. The government has attempted to crack down on abuses and has warned that any police caught shaking down foreign tourists will be arrested and drummed out of the service.

The crackdown has dented the enthusiasm of the police to confront foreigners directly with demands for bribes. However, it has not eliminated the problem altogether.

BUSINESS HOURS

The Vietnamese rise early (and consider sleeping in to be a sure indication of illness). Offices, museums and many shops open between 7 and 8 am and close between 4 and 5 pm. Lunch time is taken very seriously, and virtually everything shuts down for 1½ hours between noon and 1.30 pm. Government workers tend to take longer breaks, so figure on getting nothing done from 11.30 am to 2 pm.

Most government offices are open until noon Saturday. Sunday is a holiday. Many museums are closed Monday. Temples on the tourist circuit are usually open all day every day. Many small privately owned shops, restaurants and street stalls stay open seven days a week, often until late at night. Consulates are notorious for keeping absurdly short business hours and for closing on every holiday, from Shakespeare's birthday to National Girl Guide Week.

Vietnamese tend to eat their meals by the clock, and disrupting someone's meal schedule is considered rude. This means that you generally shouldn't pay visits to people during lunch (unless invited).

PUBLIC HOLIDAYS & SPECIAL EVENTS

Politics affects everything, including public holidays. As an indication of Vietnam's new openness, Christmas, New Year's Day, Tet (Lunar New Year) and Buddha's Birthday were re-established as holidays after a 15-year lapse.

The following is a list of Vietnam's public holidays:

New Year's Day (Tet Duong Lich) 1 January

Anniversary of the Founding of the Vietnamese Communist Party (Thanh Lap Dang CSVN) 3 February – the Vietnamese Communist Party was founded on this date in 1930.

Liberation Day (Saigon Giai Phong) 30 April – the date on which Saigon surrendered is commemorated nationwide as Liberation Day. Many cities and provinces also commemorate the anniversary of the date, in March or April 1975, on which they were 'liberated' by the North Vietnamese Army.

International Workers' Day (Quoc Te Lao Dong) 1 May – also known as May Day, this falls back-to-back with Liberation Day, giving everyone a two-day holiday.

Ho Chi Minh's Birthday (Sinh Nhat Bac Ho) 19 May

Buddha's Birthday (Phat Dan) Eighth day of the fourth moon (usually June)

National Day (Quoc Khanh) 2 September – commemorates the proclamation of the Declaration of Independence of the Democratic Republic of Vietnam by Ho Chi Minh in 1945.

Christmas (Giang Sinh) 25 December

Special prayers are held at Vietnamese and Chinese pagodas when the moon is full or just the thinnest sliver. Many Buddhists eat only vegetarian food on these days, which, according to the Chinese lunar calendar, fall on the 14th and 15th days of the month and from the last (29th or 30th) day of the month to the first day of the next month.

Festivals

The following major religious festivals include the lunar date (check against any Vietnamese calendar for the Gregorian dates):

Tet (Tet Nguyen Dan) First to seventh days of the first moon – the Vietnamese Lunar New Year is the most important festival of the year and falls in late January or early February. This public holiday is officially three days, but many people take an entire week off work and few businesses are open.

Holiday of the Dead (Thanh Minh) Fifth day of the third moon – people pay solemn visits to graves of deceased relatives, specially tidied up a few days before, and make offerings of food, flowers, joss sticks and votive papers.

Buddha's Birth, Enlightenment and Death Eighth day of the fourth moon – this day is celebrated at pagodas and temples which, like many private homes, are festooned with lanterns. Processions are held in the evening. This festival has been redesignated a public holiday.

Summer Solstice Day (Tiet Doan Ngo) Fifth day of the fifth moon – offerings are made to spirits, ghosts and the God of Death to ward off epidemics. Human effigies are burned to satisfy the requirements of the God of Death for souls to staff his army.

Wandering Souls Day (Trung Nguyen) Fifteenth day of the seventh moon – this is the second-largest Vietnamese festival of the year. Offerings of food and gifts are made in homes and pagodas for the wandering souls of the forgotten dead.

Mid-Autumn Festival (Trung Thu) Fifteenth day of the eighth moon – this festival is celebrated with moon cakes of sticky rice filled with lotus seeds, watermelon seeds, peanuts, the yolks of duck eggs, raisins, sugar and other such things. This festival is like Christmas Day for children, who carry colourful lanterns in the form of boats, unicorns, dragons, lobsters, carp, hares, toads etc in an evening procession accompanied by the banging of drums and cymbals.

Confucius' Birthday Twenty-eighth day of the ninth moon.

DOING BUSINESS

The recent liberalisation of rules has had a dramatic effect on foreign joint-venture operations. Some of the most successful joint ventures to date have involved hotels, though some of these investments are clear cases of real estate speculation (foreigners cannot buy land directly, but businesses with a Vietnamese partner can). The leading foreign investors are the Koreans, Singaporeans and Taiwanese. There has also been a large amount of Overseas Vietnamese money invested.

Ho Chi Minh City's foreign investment environment, however, has grown shaky as of late. The crippling economic crisis that gripped Asia in recent years has had a substantial effect on Vietnam. Countless promising joint business ventures, in particular those depending on Asian funding, have collapsed.

Stories abound of foreigners being burned in business deals in Vietnam..Expats have come to call this phenomena getting kicked out. While multinational companies and huge hotel chains can afford to dump a few million dollars into a risky venture, a lot of smaller start-up companies and individuals have literally lost their shirts. In such a shaky environment, the quality of hospitality services (especially restaurants) is in a constant state of flux, as ownership, management and staff frequently turn around. Frustratingly, many places which were once running a shipshape business just aren't what they used to be, and the challenge is often discovering places that have managed to maintain the high recommendation they once received. This caveat in mind, it is not to say opportunities do not exist, but tread lightly, and be aware that there is often more than meets the eye.

On paper, it all looks good. In practice, the rule of law barely exists in Vietnam these days. Local officials interpret the law any way it suits them, often against the wishes of . This poses serious problems for joint ventures – foreigners who have gone to court in Vietnam to settle civil disputes have generally fared pretty badly. It's particularly difficult to sue a state-run company, even if that company committed obvious fraud. The government has gained a reputation for suddenly cancelling permits, revoking licences and basically tearing up written contracts. There is no independent judiciary.

One successful foreign entrepreneur drew this analogy: 'Vietnamese do business like they drive – that is to say, recklessly...'

Foreigners who stay in Vietnam long term and attempt to do business can expect periodic visits from the police collecting taxes and donations. Often they will direct their requests towards the Vietnamese employees rather than confront a foreign manager directly. It's just one of those things that makes doing business in Vietnam so exciting. Good luck..

The mammoth Vietnamese bureaucracy, official incompetence, corruption and the ever-changing rules and regulations continue to irritate foreign investors. On paper, intellectual property rights are protected, but enforcement is lax.

Vietnam's legal system is complex, but fortunately today there are several Vietnamese and foreign law firms available in Ho Chi Minh City to help.

For foreign language interpretation and translation services, consider contacting BEST Services (☎ 830 0363), at 81A Đ Nguyen Son Ha, or the Hoang Hue Office Service Centre (☎/fax 821 3616) at 44 Đ Ngo Duc Ke, District 1.

Personal and corporate bank accounts can be set up at Vietcombank, or at one of several foreign banks in Ho Chi Minh City (see the Banks listing earlier in this chapter).

WORK

From 1975 to about 1990, Vietnam's foreign workers were basically technical specialists and military advisers from Eastern Europe and the former Soviet Union. The declining fortunes of the former Eastern Bloc have caused most of these advisers to be withdrawn.

Vietnam's opening to capitalist countries has suddenly created more work opportunities for Westerners, though less so today in the corporate sector than a few years ago. Today some of the best-paid Westerners living in Vietnam are those working for the diplomatic corps or official foreign aid organisations such as the UN, or those hired by private foreign companies attempting to set up joint-venture operations. People with certain high-technology skills may also find themselves much in demand and able to secure high pay and cushy benefits.

Foreigners who look like Rambo have occasionally been approached by talent scouts wanting to recruit them to work as extras in war movies. Watch for ads in the *Vietnam News* for leads. But for most travellers, the main work opportunities will be teaching a foreign language.

English is by far the most popular foreign language with Vietnamese students. Some foreign language students in Vietnam also want to learn French and Japanese. There is also a limited demand for teachers of German, Spanish, Chinese and Korean.

Government-run universities in Vietnam hire some foreign teachers. Pay is generally around US$2 per hour, but benefits such as free housing and unlimited visa renewals are usually thrown in. Teaching at a university requires some commitment (eg, you may have to sign a one-year contract).

There is also a budding free market in private language centres and home tutoring – this is where most newly arrived foreigners seek work. Pay in the private sector is slightly better than in the government sector – figure on perhaps US$4 per hour to start – however it is likely that these private schools won't be able to offer the same benefits as a government-run school.

Some English schools to consider contacting are:

BEST Language Centre (☎ 843 5979, fax 846 5589) 391 Đ Nam Ky Khoi Nghia, District 3
International English School (☎ 835 3390) 101 ĐL Nguyen Van Cu, District 5
Outerspace Language School (☎ 822 0515) 54 Đ Dinh Tien Hoang, District 1
TESCAN (☎ 824 5619) 35 Đ Le Thanh Ton, District 1

To be legally employed a business visa is required. One possible way around the visa hurdle is to sign up for Vietnamese language lessons at a university, but be aware that you may actually be expected to attend class and study.

Private tutoring pays even better – up to US$15 per hour. In this case, you are in business for yourself. The authorities may or may not turn a blind eye to such activities.

Some Western journalists and photographers manage to make a living in Ho Chi Minh City by selling their stories and pictures to Western news organisations and domestic English-language media outlets. Most journalists, however, are forced to work freelance and pay can vary from decent to dismal.

Volunteer Work

There are various nongovernment organisations (NGOs), including religious, environmental and humanitarian aid groups with offices in Ho Chi Minh City.

If you're looking to volunteer in Vietnam, you may wish to contact the NGO Resource Centre in Hanoi (☎ 832 8570, fax 832 8611, ngocentr@netnam.org.vn), at the La Thanh Hotel at 218 Pho Doi Can. This organisation has links with most international NGOs in Vietnam and can sell you a copy of their *Vietnam NGO Directory* (US$10), containing detailed listings and contacts.

Getting There & Away

AIR

The majority of flights into and out of Vietnam are through Ho Chi Minh City. As such, many flights to and from Hanoi connect through Ho Chi Minh City and other Asian cities.

Departure Tax

Vietnam's departure tax is US$10 for international flights and US$1.60 for domestic flights. It can be paid in Vietnamese dong or US dollars. Children under age two years of age are exempt.

Other Parts of Vietnam

There are direct flights between Ho Chi Minh City and most major cities in Vietnam. Pacific Airlines is the only company besides Vietnam Airlines to offer domestic flights. Both companies charge the same fares on domestic flights, but Pacific Airlines' rates are cheaper on their scant international routes.

Australia

Vietnam Airlines offers direct flights between Ho Chi Minh City and both Sydney and Melbourne.

The weekend travel sections of papers like the *Age* (Melbourne) or the *Sydney Morning Herald* are good sources of discount travel information. Also check out *Escape*, a magazine published by STA Travel, the Australian-based travel organisation which has offices worldwide.

Also well worth trying is Flight Centre. It has numerous branches in Australia, including Melbourne (☎ 03-9670 0477), Sydney (☎ 02-9233 2296) and Brisbane (☎ 07-3229 9958).

Cambodia

There are daily flights between Phnom Penh and Ho Chi Minh City on either Royal Air Cambodge or Vietnam Airlines.

There is a US$5 airport tax to fly out of Cambodia. One-month visas for Cambodia are available upon arrival at Phnom Penh Airport for US$20.

Canada

There are currently no direct flights between Canada and Vietnam. Most Canadian travellers transit in Hong Kong.

Getting discount tickets in Canada is much the same as in the USA – go to the travel agents and shop around until you find a good deal.

Travel CUTS (☎ 888-838 2887) is Canada's national student bureau and has offices in a number of Canadian cities including Vancouver, Edmonton, Toronto and Ottawa – you don't necessarily have to be a student to use them.

China

China Southern Airlines and Vietnam Airlines fly several routes between Ho Chi Minh City and major cities in China.

Hong Kong

Hong Kong is the second most popular point for departures to Vietnam, after Bangkok. Hong Kong's flag carrier, Cathay Pacific Airways, and Vietnam Airlines offer a daily joint service between Hong Kong and Ho Chi Minh City which takes about 2½ hours. The most popular ticket is an open jaw, which allows you to fly from Hong Kong to Ho Chi Minh City and return from Hanoi to Hong Kong (or vice versa).

A travel agent in Hong Kong specialising in discount air tickets and customised tours to Vietnam is Phoenix Services (☎ 2722 7378, fax 2369 8884), at Room B, 6th floor, Milton Mansion, 96 Nathan Rd, Tsimshatsui, Kowloon.

Continental Europe

Vietnam Airlines operates flights between Paris and Ho Chi Minh City via Bangkok. Some tickets have a 60-day limit.

Cheaper Paris–Ho Chi Minh City flights are operated by Aeroflot (via Moscow),

Lauda Air (via Vienna) and Malaysia Airlines (via Kuala Lumpur).

One French travel agent specialising in tickets/tours to Asia is Nouvelles Frontières (☎ 08-03 33 33 33).

Japan

Vietnam Airlines shares a direct routes between Tokyo or Osaka and Ho Chi Minh City with Japan Airlines. Cheaper flights are available on Korean Air via Seoul.

Korea

Korean Air, Asiana Airlines and Vietnam Airlines all fly the Seoul–Ho Chi Minh City route at least three times weekly.

A good travel agency for discount tickets is Joy Travel Service (☎ 776 9871, fax 756 5342) at 10th floor, 24–2 Mukyo-dong, Chung-gu, Seoul.

Laos

Lao Aviation and Vietnam Airlines offer daily joint services between Vientiane and Ho Chi Minh City.

Malaysia

Malaysia Airlines and Vietnam Airlines have a joint service from Kuala Lumpur to Ho Chi Minh City, taking about three hours.

Singapore

Singapore Airlines and Vietnam Airlines offer a daily joint service on the Ho Chi Minh City–Singapore route. Most flights from Singapore continue to Hanoi.

Taiwan

Taiwan's China Airlines offers a joint service with Vietnam Airlines between Ho Chi Minh City and Taipei. The flight time is around three hours.

There are no diplomatic relations between Taiwan and Vietnam, so visa processing goes via Bangkok and takes 10 working days.

A long-running discount travel agent with a good reputation is Jenny Su Travel (☎ 02-2594 7733, 2596 2263, fax 2592 0068) at 10th floor, 27 Chungshan N Rd, Section 3, Taipei.

Thailand

Bangkok, only 80 minutes flying time from Ho Chi Minh City, has emerged as the main port of embarkation for air travel to Vietnam.

Thai Airways International (THAI), Air France and Vietnam Airlines offer daily Bangkok–Ho Chi Minh City services. Many choose an open jaw ticket, which flies people into either Ho Chi Minh City or Hanoi, from where they set out overland before flying back to Bangkok from the other city.

Khao San Rd in Bangkok is the budget travellers' headquarters and the place to look for bargain ticket deals.

UK

There are no direct flights between the UK and Vietnam, but relatively cheap tickets are available on the London–Hong Kong run. From Hong Kong, Asia's hub city, it's easy enough to make onward arrangements to Vietnam.

To find out what's going, there are a number of magazines in Britain that have good information about flights and agents. These include *Trailfinder*, free from the Trailfinders Travel Centre in Earl's Court, and *Time Out*, a weekly entertainment guide widely available in the UK.

Discount tickets are available almost exclusively in London. To begin with, try calling STA Travel (☎ 020-7937 1221), Trailfinders (☎ 020-7938 3366) or Campus Travel (☎ 020-7730 8111).

USA

At the time of writing, no US air carriers were flying into Vietnam.

China Airlines and EVA Air (both Taiwanese) typically offer the cheapest fares on US-Vietnam flights, all of which transit in Taipei.

Other cariers flying US-Vietnam are Cathay Pacific (via Hong Kong), Singapore Airlines (via Singapore), THAI (via Bangkok) and Asiana (via Seoul).

Airline Offices

Vietnam Airlines also acts as the sales agent for Lao Aviation (Hang Khong Lao).

Air Travel Glossary

Cancellation Penalties If you have to cancel or change a discounted ticket, there are often heavy penalties involved; insurance can sometimes be taken out against these penalties. Some airlines impose penalties on regular tickets as well, particularly against 'no-show' passengers.

Courier Fares Businesses often need to send urgent documents or freight securely and quickly. Courier companies hire people to accompany the package through customs and, in return, offer a discount ticket which is sometimes a phenomenal bargain. However, you may have to surrender all your baggage allowance and take only carry-on luggage.

Full Fares Airlines traditionally offer 1st class (coded F), business class (coded J) and economy class (coded Y) tickets. These days there are so many promotional and discounted fares available that few passengers pay full economy fare.

Lost Tickets If you lose your airline ticket an airline will usually treat it like a travellers cheque and, after inquiries, issue you with another one. Legally, however, an airline is entitled to treat it like cash and if you lose it then it's gone forever. Take good care of your tickets.

Onward Tickets An entry requirement for many countries is that you have a ticket out of the country. If you're unsure of your next move, the easiest solution is to buy the cheapest onward ticket to a neighbouring country or a ticket from a reliable airline which can later be refunded if you do not use it.

Open-Jaw Tickets These are return tickets where you fly out to one place but return from another. If available, this can save you backtracking to your arrival point.

Overbooking Since every flight has some passengers who fail to show up, airlines often book more passengers than they have seats. Usually excess passengers make up for the no-shows, but occasionally somebody gets 'bumped' onto the next available flight. Guess who it is most likely to be? The passengers who check in late.

Promotional Fares These are officially discounted fares, available from travel agencies or direct from the airline.

Reconfirmation If you don't reconfirm your flight at least 72 hours prior to departure, the airline may delete your name from the passenger list. Ring to find out if your airline requires reconfirmation.

Restrictions Discounted tickets often have various restrictions on them – such as needing to be paid for in advance and incurring a penalty to be altered. Others are restrictions on the minimum and maximum period you must be away.

Round-the-World Tickets RTW tickets give you a limited period (usually a year) in which to circumnavigate the globe. You can go anywhere the carrying airlines go, as long as you don't backtrack. The number of stopovers or total number of separate flights is decided before you set off and they usually cost a bit more than a basic return flight.

Transferred Tickets Airline tickets cannot be transferred from one person to another. Travellers sometimes try to sell the return half of their ticket, but officials can ask you to prove that you are the person named on the ticket. On an international flight tickets are compared with passports.

Travel Periods Ticket prices vary with the time of year. There is a low (off-peak) season and a high (peak) season, and often a low-shoulder season and a high-shoulder season as well. Usually the fare depends on your outward flight – if you depart in the high season and return in the low season, you pay the high-season fare.

The complete list of Ho Chi Minh City airline offices is as follows:

Aeroflot (☎ 829 3489, fax 829 0076) 4H ĐL Le Loi, District 1
Air France (☎ 829 0891, fax 823 0190) 130 Đ Dong Khoi, District 1
Asiana Airlines (☎ 822 2663, fax 822 2710) 141–3 ĐL Ham Nghi, District 1
British Airways (☎ 829 1288, fax 823 0030) 58 Đ Dong Khoi, District 1
Cathay Pacific Airways (☎ 822 3203, fax 825 8276) 58 Đ Dong Khoi, District 1
China Airlines (☎ 825 1388, fax 825 1390) 132–4 Đ Dong Khoi, District 1
China Southern Airlines (☎ 829 1172, fax 829 6800) 52B Đ Pham Hong Thai, District 1
Emirates Airlines (☎ 822 8000, fax 822 8080) The Landmark, 5B Đ Ton Duc Thang, District 1
EVA Air (☎ 822 4488, fax 822 3567) 32 Đ Ngo Duc Ke, District 1
Garuda Indonesia (☎ 829 3644, fax 829 3688) 132–4 Đ Dong Khoi, District 1
Japan Airlines (☎ 821 9098, fax 842 2189) 115 ĐL Nguyen Hue, District 1
KLM-Royal Dutch Airlines (☎ 823 1990, fax 823 1989) 2A–4A Đ Ton Duc Thang, District 1
Korean Air (☎ 824 2878, fax 824 2877) 65 ĐL Le Loi, District 1
Lauda Air (☎ 829 7117, fax 829 5832) 9 Đ Dong Khoi, District 1
Lufthansa Airlines (☎ 829 8529, fax 829 8537) 132–4 Đ Dong Khoi, District 1
Malaysia Airlines (☎ 829 2529, fax 824 2884) 132–4 Đ Dong Khoi, District 1
Pacific Airlines (☎ 820 0978, fax 820 0980) 177 Đ Vo Thi Sau, District 3
Royal Air Cambodge (☎ 844 0126, fax 842 1578) 343 Đ Le Van Sy, Tan Binh District
Singapore Airlines (☎ 823 1583, fax 823 1554) Suite 101, Saigon Tower, 29 ĐL Le Duan, District 1
Swissair (☎ 824 4000, fax 823 6550) Saigon Center, 65 ĐL Le Loi, District 1
Thai Airways International (THAI) (☎ 829 2810, fax 822 3465) 65 Đ Nguyen Du, District 1
United Airlines (☎ 823 4755, fax 823 0030) 58 Đ Dong Khoi, District 1
Vasco (☎ 842 2790, fax 844 5224) 114 Đ Bach Dang, Tan Son Nhat Airport, Tan Binh District
Vietnam Airlines (☎ 829 2118, fax 823 0273) 116 ĐL Nguyen Hue, District 1

You must reconfirm all reservations for flights out of the country.

BORDER CROSSINGS

There are currently six places at which foreigners may cross overland into Vietnam. In addition to the Moc Bai land border crossing into Cambodia, there are also two legal ways into Laos, and three into China. These journeys are beyond the scope of this city guide. Refer to Lonely Planet's guidebook *Vietnam* for further details.

There are no legal moneychanging facilities on the Vietnamese side of any of these crossings, so be sure to have some US dollars cash (preferably small denominations) handy. Try to find a bank or legal moneychanger – black marketeers have a well-deserved reputation for short-changing and outright theft.

Vietnamese police at the land border crossings are notoriously problematic. Most travellers find that it's much easier to exit Vietnam overland than it is to enter that way. Countless foreigners making the land crossings have reported attempts by Vietnamese customs agents to solicit bribes. Travellers at the border crossings (especially into Laos and China) are routinely asked for an immigration fee and/or a customs fee. Of course they know this is illegal, but the Vietnamese border guards are well practised at collecting your money.

BUS

Other Parts of Vietnam

Vietnam has an extensive network of dirt-cheap buses and other passenger vehicles which covers virtually every corner of the country. However, few travellers use them, for reasons that will become obvious in the following paragraphs.

Road safety is not one of Vietnam's strong points. The Vietnamese intercity road network of two-lane highways is becoming more and more dangerous due to the rapid increase in the number of motor vehicles. Vietnam does not have an emergency rescue system or even a proper ambulance network – if something happens to you out on the road, you could be hours from even rudimentary medical treatment.

If possible, try to travel during daylight hours only. Indeed, many drivers refuse to drive after dark in rural areas because the unlit highways often have huge potholes, occasional collapsed bridges and lots of bicycles and pedestrians (including dogs and chickens) who seem oblivious to traffic. However, if you like living dangerously, there are some overnight buses.

Public buses generally come in four flavours: Korean-made (a few years old), Russian-made (circa 1970), American-made (circa 1965) and increasingly rare French-made (antique). Package tour groups tend to travel on modern, Japanese-made buses with air-conditioning and cushy seats.

It's fair to say that riding the public buses will give you ample opportunity to have 'personal contact' with the Vietnamese people. If you're looking to meet locals, what better way than to have a few sitting on your lap! As one reader says:

> I enjoyed the bus riding scene, the scenery and the conversations (gesturing) with people. Although I'd rate the conditions as terrible, the riding community suffered, slept and ate together.

Figuring out the bus system is anything but easy. Ho Chi Minh City has several bus stations, and responsibilities are divided according to the location of the destination (whether it is north or south of the city) and the type of service being offered (local or long-distance, express or non-express.

Most long-distance buses depart in the early morning. Often, half a dozen vehicles for the same destination will leave at the same time, usually around 5.30 am. For details on routes and long-distance bus depots, see the Getting Around chapter.

Classes The appellation express *(toc hanh)* is applied rather loosely in Vietnam. Genuine express buses are considerably faster than local buses, which drop off and pick up locals and their produce at each cluster of houses along the highway. But many express buses are the same decrepit vehicles used on local runs, except that they stop less frequently.

Reservations Buses normally leave early in the morning, so if you don't plan to bargain with the bus driver, you might conside showing up at the bus station the day befor departure and purchasing a ticket.

Costs Costs are negligible, even though foreigners sometimes pay five times the going rate. Depending on the type of ticket, i works out to around US$0.02 per kilometre

Open Date Ticket In backpacker haunts throughout Vietnam, you'll see lots of signs advertising the Open Date Ticket or just Open Ticket. Basically, this is a bus service catering to foreign budget travellers. The buses run between Ho Chi Minh City and Hanoi and you may enter and exit the bus at any major city along the route. You are not obliged to follow a fixed schedule.

Essentially, there are two tickets available: Ho Chi Minh City–Hué for as little as US$27, Hué–Hanoi for as low as US$16. Shorter individual legs of the trip can be purchased for less. Buying minibus tickets all along the way costs a bit more, but you achieve maximum flexibility.

Although it really isolates you from the locals, the Open Tickets are a temptation and many people go for them. Look for them at cafes in the Pham Ngu Lao Area.

Cambodia

The only frontier crossing between Cambodia and Vietnam that is open to Westerners is at Moc Bai. Most travellers to and from the Cambodian borders prefer to travel by taxi (see the Car & Motorcycle section later), though there are public buses between Phnom Penh and Ho Chi Minh City.

Although land travel through Cambodia is not especially recommended, the situation is considered relatively safe on the main highway between Ho Chi Minh City and Phnom Penh. However, it would still be wise to make inquiries before proceeding, and to realise that flying is safest of all.

Buses run every day between Ho Chi Minh City (via Moc Bai) and Phnom Penh. The cost is US$5 or US$12, depending on whether you take the air-con coach or an old De Soto rattletrap. In Ho Chi Minh City, you purchase tickets from the Phnom Penh

Bus Garage, at 155 ĐL Nguyen Hue, District 1, adjacent to the Rex Hotel, but the bus departs at 5 am from 145 Đ Nguyen Du. The biggest disadvantage of this bus is that you must wait for everybody to clear customs at the border, a procedure that can take hours.

There is a faster and cheaper way, although it's a bit more complicated. You can board one of the many bus tours heading for the Caodai Great Temple at Tay Ninh (for as little as US$4). But instead of going to Tay Ninh, you get off sooner at Go Dau, where the highway forks. There will be motorcycle taxis waiting here, and for as little as US$0.50 you can get a ride to the border crossing at Moc Bai. At the border, you must walk across, and you'll find air-con share taxis waiting on the Cambodian side to take you to Phnom Penh for US$5 per person.

MINIBUS

Tourist-style minibuses can be booked through most hotels and cafes. Popular destinations include the Mekong Delta and Cu Chi tunnels. Privately owned minibuses are more comfortable than the huge public buses. However, the level of comfort varies – only with a charter can you be assured that the driver won't pack the passengers in like sardines.

There are two categories of minibus – public and chartered.

Public Minibuses The public minibuses (actually privately owned) cater to the domestic market. They depart when full and will pick up as many passengers as possible along the route. They may also drive around town before departure, hunting for additional customers before actually heading out to the highway. Such minibuses will usually become ridiculously crowded as the journey progresses and are not comfortable by any means. The frequent stops to pick up and discharge passengers (and arrange their luggage and chickens) can make for a slow journey. In other words, public minibuses are really a small-scale version of the large public buses. Public minibuses congregate in the general vicinities of the bus stations.

Just next to the Saigon Hotel and the mosque on Đ Dong Du, District 1, is where you catch minibuses to Vung Tau. This is an unofficial bus stop and there is always the possibility that the location will be suddenly moved. In other words, inquire first.

Chartered Minibuses A large majority of independent travellers in Vietnam choose this form of transport above all others. Chartered minibuses are just what the name implies. Some cater exclusively to foreigners, but well-heeled Vietnamese also travel this way.

This is the deluxe class – air-conditioning is standard and you can be certain of having enough space to sit comfortably. Such luxury, of course, is something you must pay for – prices will be a lot higher than what you'd pay on public buses. Nevertheless, it's still very cheap by Western standards. Budget hotels and cafes are the best places to inquire about these vehicles.

If a chartered minibus isn't full, the driver may still pick up some passengers en route. However, any reputable company puts a limit on the number of passengers – the driver should pick up no more people than there are empty seats and should not pick up anybody with excessive luggage.

TRAIN

Trains from Saigon train station, or Ga Sai Gon (☎ 844 3952, 844 0218, 823 0105), at 1 Đ Nguyen Thong, District 3, serve cities along the coast north of Ho Chi Minh City.

The main thing to remember about Vietnamese trains is that odd-numbered ones travel southward and even-numbered ones travel northward. The one running between Ho Chi Minh City and Hanoi is known as the *Reunification Express*.

Other Parts of Vietnam

The 2600km Vietnamese railway system (Duong Sat Viet Nam) runs along the coast between Hanoi and Ho Chi Minh City, and links the capital with Haiphong and other northern towns. While sometimes even slower than buses, the trains offer a more relaxing way to get around. Large-bodied

PHIL WEYMOUTH

The *Reunification Express* runs the length of Vietnam, from Hanoi to Ho Chi Minh City.

Westerners will find that the trains offer more leg and body room than the jam-packed buses. Dilapidated as the tracks, rolling stock and engines may appear, the trains are much safer than the country's kamikaze bus fleet. Furthermore, the railway authorities have been rapidly upgrading the facilities to accommodate foreign tourists – even air-conditioned sleeping berths are now obtainable on the express trains.

One key factor to take into account when deciding whether to go by train or bus is the hour at which the train gets to where you want to go – trying to find a place to stay at 3 am is likely to be very frustrating.

Even the express trains in Vietnam are slow by Western standards, but conditions are improving as the tracks and equipment are being upgraded. The quickest train journey between Hanoi and Ho Chi Minh City takes 34 hours at an average speed of 50km/h. The slowest express train on this route takes 41 hours, averaging 40km/h for the 1726km trip. Slow local trains go from Ho Chi Minh City to such places as Nha Trang and Qui Nhon.

Petty crime is a problem on Vietnamese trains, especially if you travel in budget class. Thieves have become proficient at grabbing packs through the windows as trains pull out of stations. To protect your belongings, always keep your backpack or suitcase near you and lock or tie it to something, especially at night. If you book a soft sleeper, try to get the bottom berth; there is a storage chamber underneath the board where you can stash your bag and sleep at ease knowing the only way in is to roll you off.

Another hazard is that children frequently throw rocks at the train. Many conductors will insist that you keep down the metal window shields to prevent injury to passengers. Unfortunately, these shields obstruct the view.

There is supposedly a 20kg limit for luggage carried on Vietnamese trains. Enforcement isn't strict, but if you have too much stuff you might have to send it in the freight car and pay a small surcharge. This is a hassle that you'll probably want to avoid. Bicycles can also be sent in the freight car. Just make sure that the train you are on *has* a freight car (most have) or your luggage will arrive later than you do.

Eating is no problem – there are vendors in every train station who board the train and practically stuff food, drinks, cigarettes and lottery tickets into your pockets. However, the food that is supplied by the railway company (free, as part of the cost of the ticket for some long journeys) could be better. It's a good idea to stock up on your favourite munchies and beverages before taking a long trip.

Schedules As stated before: odd-numbered trains travel southward; even-numbered trains travel northward. The fastest service is provided by the *Reunification Express*, which runs between Hanoi and Ho Chi Minh City, making only a few quick stops en route. If you want to stop at some obscure point between the major towns, you'll have to use one of the slower local trains. Aside from the main Hanoi–Ho Chi Minh City run, there are small spur lines that link Hanoi with Haiphong and the Chinese border.

Seven *Reunification Express* trains depart Saigon station every day between 10.35 am and 10.30 pm. The same number of daily trains depart Hanoi between 5.30 am and 5.25 pm.

In addition, there are local trains. The train schedule changes so frequently (about every six months) that there's little point in reproducing the whole thing here. The timetables for all trains are posted at major stations and you can copy these down or pick one up. It's important to realise that the train schedule is bare bones during Tet. Even the *Reunification Express* is suspended for nine days, starting four days before Tet and continuing four days after.

It's *very* important that you hang on to your ticket until you've exited the train station at your final destination. Some travellers have discarded their tickets while leaving the train only to find that the gatekeepers won't allow them to exit the station without a ticket. In this situation, you could be forced to purchase another ticket at the full price. The purpose of this system is to catch people who have sneaked aboard without paying.

Classes There are six classes of train travel: half seat, hard seat, soft seat, hard berth, soft berth and super berth. Since it's all that the vast majority of Vietnamese can afford, half seat and hard seat are usually packed and are very uncomfortable. Hard seat is tolerable for day travel, but overnight it can be even less comfortable than the bus, where at least you are hemmed in and thus propped upright.

Soft seat carriages have vinyl-covered seats rather than the uncomfortable benches of hard seat.

Hard sleeper has three tiers of beds (six beds per compartment). Because it necessitates clambering up a ladder, the upper berth is cheapest, followed by the middle berth and finally the lower berth. The best bunk to claim is the one in the middle, because the bottom berth is usually invaded by seatless travellers during the day. There is no door to separate the compartment from the corridor.

Soft sleeper has two tiers (four beds per compartment) and all bunks are priced the same. These compartments have a door. The best trains have two categories of soft sleeper, one with air-con and one without. At the present time, air-con is only available on the very fastest express train.

Reservations The supply of train seats is often insufficient to meet demand. Reservations for all trips should be made at least one day in advance. For sleeping berths, you may have to book passage three or more days before the date of travel. Bring your passport and visa when buying train tickets. Though such documents are never checked at bus stations, train personnel may ask to have a look at them.

You need not necessarily go to the train station to get your ticket. Many travel agencies, hotels and cafes are in the business of purchasing train tickets for a small commission. The Saigon train station ticket office is open from 7.15 to 11 am and from 1 to 3 pm daily. In the Pham Ngu Lao backpackers' area, commission-free train tickets can also be purchased from the convenient Saigon Railways Tourist Company (☎ 836 7640, fax 836 9031) at 275C Đ Pham Ngu Lao, District 1. It's open from 7.30 to 11.30 am and from 1 to 4.30 pm.

If you arrive early (eg, 7.30 am) at a train station in central Vietnam, you may be told that all tickets to Hanoi are sold out. However, this may simply mean that there are no tickets *at the moment*, but more may become available after 8 pm when Hanoi phones through the details of unsold tickets. Again, buying through a travel agency could eliminate this hassle. Of course, not much can be done if all the seats really are sold out.

In any city, reservations can be made only for travel originating in that city. For this reason – and because train stations are often far from the main part of town – it is a good idea to make reservations for onward travel as soon as you arrive in a city.

Costs One disadvantage of train travel is that foreigners are supposed to pay a surcharge of around 400% over and above what Vietnamese pay. It works out at about US$100 for a Ho Chi Minh City–Hanoi ticket in a hard-sleeper compartment. This is compared to US$150 to fly the same route.

The actual price you pay for a ticket depends on which train you take – the fastest trains are the most expensive.

China

It is possible to enter/exit Vietnam by train at the Chinese border crossings at the Friendship Pass and the Lao Cai–Hekou border. These journeys are beyond the scope of this city guide. Refer to Lonely Planet's guidebook *Vietnam* for further details.

CAR & MOTORCYCLE

Other Parts of Vietnam

Inquire at almost any tourist cafe or hotel to arrange car rental (with driver). Renting from a licensed agency is safer, albeit more expensive, but you needn't go to the most expensive places like Saigon Tourist. The agencies in the Pham Ngu Lao area generally offer the lowest prices.

The same agencies can also advise you on where to rent self-drive motorbikes. The danger factor of Vietnamese roads and traffic aside, motorbiking is a popular way to travel for many, especially in the Mekong Delta region.

Other Countries

There are share taxis direct from Ho Chi Minh City to the Moc Bai border crossing, some costing as little as US$5 per person. In Ho Chi Minh City, Kim Cafe, (☎ 836 9859), at 270 Đ De Tham, District 1, is one place to book these, but most other travel agencies can make similar arrangements.

BICYCLE

Vietnam is an appealing, if dangerous, place for long-distance cycling. Most of the terrain in and around Ho Chi Minh City is flat (or only moderately hilly) and most major roads are of a serviceable standard.

Bicycles can be transported around the country on the top of buses or in train luggage compartments.

HITCHING

Hitching is never entirely safe in any country in the world, and we don't recommend it. Travellers who decide to hitch should understand that they are taking a small but potentially serious risk. People who do choose to hitch will be safer if they travel in pairs and let someone know where they are planning to go.

BOAT

Other Parts of Vietnam

Passenger and goods ferries to the Mekong Delta depart from a dock (☎ 829 7892) at the river end of ĐL Ham Nghi. There is a daily service to the provinces of An Giang and Vinh Long and to the towns of Ben Tre (eight hours), Camau (30 hours; once every four days), Mytho (six hours; departs at 11 am) and Tan Chau. Buy your ticket on the boat. Simple food may be available on board. Be aware that these ancient vessels lack even the most elementary safety gear, such as life jackets.

There is also a hydrofoil service to Vung Tau for US$10 each way. The hydrofoil leaves Ho Chi Minh City at 6.45, 8 and 10.30 am and 2.45 pm. Return departures are at 8.30 am and 1, 4 and 4.30 pm. Contact the booking office (☎ 829 7892) at 6A Đ Nguyen Tat Thanh, District 2.

Neighbouring Countries

Vietnam has 3451km of intriguing coastline, so it's a shame that there's so little chance of arriving on these scenic shores by boat. If you have connections in the shipping industry, you might get on a freighter. A number of luxury cruise liners offer stopovers in Ho Chi Minh City.

ORGANISED TOURS

From Ho Chi Minh City

Even if you're not the sort of person inclined to take organised tours, there are good reasons to consider doing so in Ho Chi Minh City. First of all, there's Vietnam's decrepit transport system to contend with. Slugging it out on crowded, frequently stopping buses is bad enough, but many of the places worth seeing are not even accessible by bus. Then there is the issue of cost – labour is cheap, so by choosing your tour operator carefully you need not spend a pile of money. There is also the benefit of having a guide and interpreter who can add value to your trip, as well as making good travelling companions.

And you can usually avoid the image of big tour buses and hordes of camera-clicking tourists – it's easy to arrange tours for small groups (three to 10 persons is typical). Even if you've come to Vietnam by yourself, you should have no difficulty finding other travellers to accompany you and split the cost – indeed, the travel agencies in Ho Chi Minh City specialise in arranging this for you.

For a listing of travel agents and tour operators in Ho Chi Minh City, see the Organised Tours section in the Getting Around chapter.

From Abroad

Package tours of Ho Chi Minh City are sold by agencies worldwide. Nearly all these tours follow one of a dozen or so set itineraries. You really could fly to Ho Chi Minh City and make all the arrangements after arrival, so the only thing you gain by booking ahead is that you might save a little time. However, if your time is more precious than money, a pre-booked package tour could be right for you.

Nearly all package tours to Vietnam include a stop in Ho Chi Minh City. Tours booked outside Vietnam are not a total rip-off, given what you get (visa, air tickets, tourist-class accommodation, food, transport, a guide etc), but then again, they're not cheap.

Almost any travel agency can book you onto a standard mad-dash minibus tour around Vietnam. More noteworthy are the adventure tours arranged for people with a particular passion. These can include speciality tours for cyclists, trekkers, birdwatchers, war veterans, 4WD enthusiasts and Vietnamese cuisine buffs. If you have a particular interest and want to organise a group tour, you might like to surf, or advertise on, the Internet.

Consider contacting the following speciality travel outfits:

Australia

Griswalds Vietnamese Vacations (☎ 02-9564 5040, fax 02-9564 1373, ✉ binh@magna.com.au) PO Box 501, Leichhardt, NSW 2040. Their slogan: 'Your dong is safe in our hands!'
Web site: www.magna.com.au/~binh.html

Orbitours (☎ 02-9954 1399, fax 9954 1655) PO Box 834, 3rd floor, 73 Walker St, North Sydney, NSW 2059

Peregrine
Sydney: (☎ 02-9290 2770) 5/38 York St, Sydney, NSW 2000
Melbourne: (☎ 03-9662 2800; fax 9663 8618) 258 Lonsdale St, Melbourne, Victoria 3000

Canada

Club Adventure (☎ 514-699 7764, fax 699 8756) 200 Rene-Levesque, Lery, Quebec J6N 3N6
Web site: www.clubadventure.com

Global Adventures (☎ 800-781 2269, ☎ 604-940 2220, fax 940 2233) Runs 12-day sea kayaking trips in scenic Halong Bay.
Web site: www.portal.ca/~global

France

Nouveau Monde Voyages (☎ 10 43 29 40 40, fax 10 46 34 19 67) 8 rue Mabillon, Paris 75006

Germany

Geoplan Touristik (☎ 307-954021, fax 954025) Steglitzer Damm 96B, D-12 169, Berlin

Netherlands

Baobab Reizen (☎ 20-627 51 29, fax 624 54 01, ✉ baobob@dds.nl) Haarlemmerstraat 24–26, Amsterdam 1013 ER

Tradewind Holidays (☎ 20-661 01 01, fax 642 01 37) PO Box 70449, Amsterdam 1007 KK

New Zealand

Adventure World (☎ 649-524 5118, fax 520 6629) 101 Great South Rd, Auckland

Go Orient Holidays (☎ 649-379 5520, fax 377 0111) 151 Victoria St West, Auckland

UK

Asian Journeys (☎ 1604-234855, fax 234866) 32 Semilong Rd, Northampton NN2 6BT

USA

Asia Transpacific Journeys (☎ 800-642 2742) PO Box 1279, Boulder, CO 80306. Offers

unique and adventure-laden trekking tours and cycling trips to suit all budgets.
Web site: www.SoutheastAsia.com

Asian Pacific Adventures (☎ 800-825 1680, 323-935 3156) 826 South Sierra Bonita Ave, Los Angeles, CA 90036. Arranges cycling trips.

China Span (☎ 425-882 8686, fax 882 8880) 18419 NE 27th Way, Redmond, WA 98052. Runs photographic speciality tours to Vietnam.
Web site: www.chinaspan.com

The Global Spectrum (☎ 800-419 4446, @ gspectrum@gspectrum.com) Suite 204, 1901 Pennsylvania Ave NW, Washington, DC 20006

Latitudes-Expeditions East (☎ 800-580 4883, 415-398 0458, fax 680 1522) 870 Market St, Suite 482, San Francisco, CA 94102. South-East Asian specialist running small group expeditions to Vietnam.
Web site: www.weblatitudes.com

Sea Canoe International Adventures (☎ 800-444 1043, fax 888-824 5621). Offers kayaking trips on rivers and lakes near the Chinese border, and in Halong Bay.
Web site: www.seacanoe.com

Vietnam Tours (☎ 206-824 9946, fax 824 9982)
Web site: www.bmi.net/vntours/index.html

Wild Card Adventures (☎ 800-590 3776, fax 360-387 9816, @ info@awildcard.com) 751 Maple Grove Rd, Camano Island, WA 98292 (close to Seattle). Customised Vietnam travel itineraries and unusual destinations.
Web site: www.awildcard.com

Warning

The information in this chapter is particularly vulnerable to change: Prices for international travel are volatile, routes are introduced and cancelled, schedules change, special deals come and go, and rules and visa requirements are amended. Airlines and governments seem to take a perverse pleasure in making price structures and regulations as complicated as possible. You should check directly with the airline or a travel agent to make sure you understand how a fare is supposed to work.

The upshot of this is that you should get opinions, quotes and advice from as many airlines and travel agents as possible before you part with your hard-earned cash. The details given in this chapter should be regarded as pointers and are not a substitute for your own careful, up-to-date research.

Vietnam

Vidotour (☎ 829 1438, fax 829 1435, @ vidotour@bdvn.vnmail.vnd.net) 41 Đ Dinh Tien Hoang, District 1, Ho Chi Minh City. Offers a spectrum of upmarket tours to points north and south in Vietnam. Also do a range of Indochina tours.

GETTING THERE & AWAY

Getting Around

THE AIRPORT

Tan Son Nhat Airport was one of the three busiest airports in the world in the 1960s, thanks to Uncle Sam. The runways are still lined with lichen-covered, mortar-proof aircraft-retaining walls and other military structures from those halcyon days.

Today, the airport is still Vietnam's busiest air hub.

TO/FROM THE AIRPORT

Tan Son Nhat Airport is 7km from central Saigon. In general, metered taxis are your best bet and cost around US$5 between the airport and the city centre. There are also unmetered taxis, but these are no cheaper.

The metered fare is calculated in Vietnamese dong, and should usually cost under 60,000d (about US$5) You'll need to add one zero to the fare showing on the meter – for example 5500 would be 55,000d. Be sure the driver switches on the meter *after* you get into the taxi – a common way to pull in a few extra dong is to turn on the meter while waiting for customers, so it has already been going a few minutes before you're even inside the car.

By all means, if your driver complies with using the meter and does not give you a rigmarole about it not working, a tip of about US$1 should be in order. You can expect the driver to recommend a hotel where he can collect a commission for delivering you. In many cases they're good, so if you don't know where you're staying, it might not hurt to have a look. If you don't care to deal with this, you can ask to be dropped at a place in this book or, if you're a budget traveller, in the Pham Ngu Lao area, the backpackers' area in District 1 (still known as Saigon) – they all know where it is.

There is also Skybus, which runs from 7 am to 11 pm between the airport and the Vietnam Airlines office on ĐL Nguyen Hue. The cost is only US$2, but it hasn't proved tremendously popular, largely because Vietnam Airlines is in a pricey neighbourhood where few budget travellers want to go. If they got their act together and stopped on Đ Pham Ngu Lao, the service could be a big hit.

To get to the airport, you can call a taxi (see the Taxi section later). Some of the cafes in the Pham Ngu Lao area also do runs to the airport – these places even have sign-up sheets where you can book share taxis for US$2 per person. This, no doubt, will prove considerably cheaper than the limousine service available at the front desk of the Rex Hotel.

If you are travelling light enough to take a motorcycle taxi to Tan Son Nhat Airport, you may have to walk the short distance from the airport gate to the terminal. Still, it's doubtful you'll save much money this way, and the last thing you need on your way home is to be in a crash.

BUS

Local City Bus Few foreigners make use of the city buses, though they are safer than cyclos, if less aesthetic. Now that Ho Chi Minh City's People's Committee has resolved to phase out cyclos, some money is finally being put into the badly neglected public transport system.

At present, there are only three bus routes, though undoubtedly more will be added. No decent bus map is available and bus stops are mostly unmarked, so it's worth summarising the three bus lines, which are as follows:

Saigon–Cholon Buses depart from central Saigon at Me Linh Square (by the Saigon River) and continue along ĐL Tran Hung Dao to Binh Tay Market in Cholon, then return along the same route. The bus company running this route is an Australian joint venture – buses have air-conditioning and video movies and the driver is well dressed! All this for US$0.20. Buy your ticket on board from the female attendant (sharply dressed in a blouse and skirt).

Mien Dong–Mien Tay Buses depart from Mien Dong bus station (north-east Saigon), pass through Cholon and terminate at Mien Tay bus station on the western edge of town. The fare is US$0.40.

Van Thanh–Mien Tay Buses depart from Van Thanh bus station (east Ho Chi Minh City), pass through Cholon and terminate at Mien Tay bus station. The fare is US$0.40.

Long-Distance Bus Inter-city buses depart from and arrive at a variety of stations around Ho Chi Minh City. In general, you will find that these buses are extremely crowded, as well as being unreliable and unsafe – but at least they are dirt cheap.

Cholon bus station is the most convenient place to get buses to Mytho and other Mekong Delta towns. The Cholon bus station is at the very western end of ĐL Tran Hung Dao B, in District 5, close to the Binh Tay Market.

Less conveniently located than Cholon station, Mien Tay bus station (Ben Xe Mien Tay; ☎ 825 5955) has even more buses to points south of Ho Chi Minh City (basically the Mekong Delta). This enormous station is about 10km south-west of Saigon in An Lac, a part of Binh Chanh District. There are buses from central Saigon to Mien Tay bus station which depart from the Ben Thanh bus station (near Ben Thanh Market). Express buses (which receive priority treatment at ferry crossings) and minibuses from Mien Tay bus station serve Bac Lieu, Camau, Cantho, Chau Doc, Long Xuyen and Rach Gia.

Buses to places north of Ho Chi Minh City leave from Mien Dong bus station (Ben Xe Mien Dong; ☎ 829 4056), which is in Binh Thanh District – about 5km from central Saigon on National Highway 13 (Quoc Lo 13, the continuation of Đ Xo Viet Nghe Tinh). The station is just under 2km north of the intersection of Đ Xo Viet Nghe Tinh and Đ Dien Bien Phu. To get there, you can take a bus from Ben Thanh bus station, near Ben Thanh Market. There are express services from Mien Dong bus station to Buon Ma Thuot, Danang, Haiphong, Hanoi, Hué, Nam Dinh, Nha Trang, Pleiku, Quang Ngai, Qui Nhon, Tuy Hoa and Vinh. All express buses leave between 5 and 5.30 am daily.

Vehicles departing from Van Thanh bus station (Ben Xe Van Thanh; ☎ 829 4839) serve destinations within a few hours of Ho Chi Minh City, mostly in Song Be and Dong Nai provinces. For travellers, most important are probably the buses to Dalat and Vung Tau. Van Thanh bus station, at 72 Đ Dien Bien Phu, Binh Thanh District, is about 1.5km east of the intersection of Đ Dien Bien Phu and Đ Xo Viet Nghe Tinh. As you head out of Saigon, go past where the numbers on Đ Dien Bien Phu climb up into the 600s.

Buses to Tay Ninh, Cu Chi and points north-east of Saigon depart from the Tay Ninh bus station (Ben Xe Tay Ninh; ☎ 849 5935), in Tan Binh District, west of the centre. To get there, head all the way out on Đ Cach Mang Thang Tam. The station is about 1km past where Đ Cach Mang Thang Tam merges with Đ Le Dai Hanh.

An assortment of decrepit US vans, Daihatsu Hijets and Citroën Traction 15s leave Van Thanh bus station for Baria, Cho Lau, Ham Tan, Long Dien, Long Hai, Phu Cuong, Phu Giao, parts of Song Be Province, Vung Tau and Xuan Loc. Three-wheelers (*xe lams*, see later in this chapter) go to Tay Ninh bus station in Tan Binh District. Vehicles leave when full (and we mean *full*). Van Thanh bus station is open from 6 am to about 6 pm.

Just next to the Saigon Hotel and the mosque on Đ Dong Du is where you catch buses to Vung Tau. This is a bus stop, not an official bus station and so there is always the possibility that it will be suddenly moved. In other words, inquire first.

METRO

Ho Chi Minh City does not yet have a metro (subway), nor is one under construction.

However, a team of foreign consultants has been called in and a feasibility study is under way. It's not likely that the metro will be completed within the life span of this book. Nevertheless, it's nice to be optimistic. And when the ribbon-cutting ceremony for the Ho Chi Minh City metro finally occurs, just remember that you read it here first.

CAR & MOTORCYCLE

Car Self-drive cars for hire are not yet available, but – considering the traffic – it's hard to imagine why anybody would want to drive if they didn't have to. On the other hand, it's easy enough to hire a car with driver included. Labour is cheap at around US$5 per day, so hiring a local to confront the chaos is only a small part of the rental fee for the vehicle.

Travel agencies, hotels and cafes are all into the car rental business. Most of the vehicles are relatively recent Japanese and Korean machines – everything from subcompacts to minibuses. However, it's still possible to enjoy a ride in a vintage vehicle from the 1950s or '60s.

Not long ago, boat-like classic American cars (complete with tail fins and impressive chrome fenders) were popular as 'wedding taxis'. These added considerable charm to Vietnamese weddings, but have fallen out of fashion – prestige these days means a white Toyota. Nevertheless, some of the old vehicles can be hired for excursions in and around Ho Chi Minh City. Aside from these road hogs you'll see the occasional French-built Renaults and Citroëns. The former Soviet Union chips in with vehicles made by Lada, Moskvich and Volga.

A cheap Russian-built rental car can be had for about US$4 per hour, US$25 per day (under eight hours and under 100km) or US$0.15 to US$0.25 per kilometre. Small Japanese cars can be rented for US$5 per hour, US$35 per day or US$0.35 per kilometre. A minivan can carry up to 12 people and be rented for US$6 per hour, US$40 per day or US$0.40 per kilometre.

Government regulations require that all cars carrying foreigners need a special permit (which simply means that the vehicle owner pays a special tax) and a licensed guide in the car at all times. While this might sound like a noble effort to protect foreigners, the result will certainly be an increase in prices. Bureaucracy is something you pay for.

Motorcycle If you're brave, you can rent a motorcycle and really earn your 'I Survived Saigon' T-shirt. Many say that this is the fastest and easiest way to get around Ho Chi Minh City and that's probably true, as long as you don't crash into anything.

Be very careful, and if you plan to ride a motorcycle, it's strongly recommended that you spend some time riding on the back of one to acclimatise to the insanity of Ho Chi Minh City traffic patterns (or lack thereof). People drive like maniacs, and side-view mirrors, if they exist at all, are almost always turned inward (which act as a great way to check yourself out, but does little to improve safety).

You can hire a local person to be your guide, translator and motorcycle driver – this is generally worth the additional expense (about US$5 per day). Nevertheless, many travellers like the stimulation of the self-drive experience. Motorcycle rentals are ubiquitous in places where tourists congregate; the Pham Ngu Lao area is as good as any to satisfy this need. Ask at the cafes and hotels for ideas on where to find rentals.

A 50cc motorcycle, officially designated a moped (see below), can be rented for US$5 to US$10 per day. Before renting one, make sure it's rideable. The rental company will probably want security – your passport, visa or a cash deposit. It's better to use your own lock rather than the one supplied (renters have been known to have an accomplice with an extra key steal the bike, thus forcing the renter to buy a new one).

The legal definition of a moped is any motor-driven two-wheeled vehicle less than 100cc, even if it doesn't have bicycle pedals. Motorcycles are defined as two-wheeled vehicles with engines 100cc and larger. In Vietnam, no driving licence is needed to drive a moped, while to drive a motorcycle you will need an international driving licence endorsed for motorcycle operation. But expats remaining in the country over six months are expected to obtain a Vietnamese driving licence. The Vietnamese licence will be valid only for the length of your visa!

Most places have parking lots *(giu xe)* for bicycles and motorcycles – usually just a roped-off section of sidewalk – where they'll charge US$0.20 to guard your vehicle (bike theft is a major problem).

Locals are required to have liability insurance on their motorcycles, but foreigners are not covered and there is currently no way to arrange this locally.

The government has been talking about making the use of safety helmets a legal requirement. However, most Vietnamese disdain wearing them, in part because of the expense and also because of the tropical heat. You can purchase high-quality safety helmets in Vietnam for about US$40, or buy a low-quality eggshell helmet for US$15. As a last resort, you might consider purchasing a slightly battered US Army helmet from Dan Sinh (or the 'War Surplus') Market (see War Souvenirs in the Shopping chapter) – the bullet holes might provide ventilation.

Purchase Foreigners lacking a resident's visa are not strictly supposed to own a motorcycle in Vietnam. However, some people have found that it is possible to buy a bike but register it in the name of a Vietnamese friend or, in some cases, the name of the shop. The big question is what to do with the bike when you are finished with it. You might be able to sell it back (at a discount) to the shop where you bought it.

Japanese-made motorcycles are the best available, but are very expensive. Unless you can get an exceptionally good deal on a used Honda, the best alternative is to buy a Russian-made Minsk 125cc which sells brand new for around US$500. It's a petrol pig, but a powerful bike and it's very easy to find spare parts and people who can do repairs (though repair shops frequently overcharge). The two-stroke engine burns oil like mad and the spark plugs frequently become oil-fouled, so always carry a spare spark plug and spark plug wrench.

TAXI

Air-conditioned metered taxis cruise the streets, but it's often easier to phone for one. There are currently 15(!) companies in Ho Chi Minh City offering metered taxis and they charge almost exactly the same rates. Flagfall is around US$0.50 and US$0.50 for each kilometre thereafter.

The competitors are: Airport Taxi (☎ 844 6666), Ben Thanh Taxi (☎ 842 2422), Cholon Taxi (☎ 822 6666), Davi Taxi (☎ 829 0290), Festival Taxi (☎ 845 4545), Gia Linh Taxi (☎ 822 6699), Mai Linh Taxi (☎ 822 6666), Nguyen Tran Taxi (☎ 835 0350), Red Taxi (☎ 844 6677), S Taxi (☎ 821 2121), Saigon Taxi (☎ 842 4242), Saigon Tourist Taxi (☎ 822 2206), Tanaco Taxi (☎ 822 0350), Taxico (☎ 820 2020) and Vina Taxi (☎ 842 2888).

CYCLO

The cyclo or pedicab *(xich lo,* short for the French *cyclo-pousse)* is the best invention since sliced bread. Cyclos offer a cheap, attractive (but slow) way to get around sprawling Ho Chi Minh City. Riding in one of these clever contraptions will also give you the moral superiority that comes with knowing you are being kind to the environment – certainly kinder than all those speed-crazed drivers on their whining, wheezing, smoke-spewing motorcycles.

Cyclos can be hailed along major thoroughfares almost any time of the day or night, though for safety reasons we do not recommend taking them after dark.

In Ho Chi Minh City, many of the drivers are former South Vietnamese army soldiers and quite a few know at least basic English, while others are quite fluent. Each has a story of war, re-education, persecution and poverty to tell.

In an effort to control Ho Chi Minh City's rapidly growing traffic problems, there are presently 51 streets on which cyclos are prohibited to ride. As a result, your driver must often take a circuitous route to avoid these trouble spots since the police will not hesitate to fine him. For the same reason, the driver may not be able to drop you off at the exact address you want though he will bring you to the nearest side street. Many travellers have gotten angry at their cyclo drivers for this. Try to have some sympathy, since it is not their fault. Perhaps the authorities would have served the city better by allowing the quiet and atmospheric cyclos carte blanche and forcing the cars to take an alternative route.

Short hops around the city centre should cost about US$0.80; central Saigon to central Cholon costs about US$1.60. Overcharging is the norm, so negotiate a price beforehand and have the exact change ready. Renting a cyclo for US$1 per hour is a fine idea if you will be doing much touring. Be sure, though, to have your money counted out and ready before getting on a cyclo. It also pays to have the exact money – drivers will sometimes claim they cannot make change for a 10,000d note.

Enjoy cyclos while you can – the municipal government intends to phase them out. It no longer registers new cyclos, has closed down cyclo factories and forbids their manufacture. However, enterprising locals have started manufacturing fake licence plates in an effort to thwart the ban on new cyclos. One effect of these pirate cyclos *(xe bo trong)* is that if your driver gives you a bad time and you copy down his licence number to report him to the police, the number may turn out to be a dud.

JOHN BANAGAN

As a result of a campaign to modernise the city, cyclos may soon be a thing of the past.

XE LAM

The xe lam (sometimes called Lambretta) connects the various bus stations. There is a useful xe lam stop on the north-west corner of Đ Pham Ngu Lao and Đ Nguyen Thai Hoc, where you can catch a ride to the Mien Tay bus station for the Mekong Delta.

HONDA OM

A quick (if precarious) way around town is to ride on the back of a motocycle taxi *(Honda om)*. You can either try to flag someone down (most drivers can use whatever extra cash they can get) or ask a Vietnamese to find a Honda om for you. The accepted rate is comparable to what cyclos charge.

BICYCLE

A bicycle is a good, slow and relatively safe way to get around the city and see things. Bikes can be rented from a number of places – many hotels, cafes and travel agencies can accommodate you.

A good place to buy a decent (ie, imported) bicycle is Federal Bike Shop (☎ 833 2899), which has three locations, all in District 1: 139H Đ Nguyen Trai, 158B Đ Vo Thi Sau and 156 Đ Pham Hong Thai. Cheaper deals may be found at some of the shops around 288 Đ Le Thanh Ton, District 1 (on the corner of Đ Cach Mang Thang Tam). You can also buy bike components: Czech and French frames, Chinese derailleurs, headlamps etc. A decent bicycle with foreign components costs about US$100. In Cholon, try the bicycle shops on ĐL Ngo Gia Tu, just south-west of ĐL Ly Thai To (near An Quang Pagoda). In District 4 there are bicycle parts shops along Đ Nguyen Tat Thanh, just south of the Ho Chi Minh Museum.

For cheap and poorly assembled domestic bicycles and parts, try the ground floor of Cua Hang Bach Hoa, the department store on the corner of ĐL Nguyen Hue and ĐL Le Loi. Vikotrade Company, at 35 ĐL Le Loi, District 1, across the street from the Rex Hotel, also has locally made components.

For on-the-spot bicycle repairs, look for an upturned army helmet and a hand pump sitting next to the curb. There is a cluster of bicycle repair shops around 23 Đ Phan Dang Luu, Phu Nhuan District.

Bicycle parking lots are usually just roped-off sections of a pavement. For US$0.20 you can leave your bicycle knowing that it will be there when you get back (bicycle theft is a big problem). When you pull up, your bicycle will have a number written on the seat in chalk or stapled to the handlebars. You will be given a reclaim chit (don't lose it!). If you come back and your bicycle is gone, the parking lot is supposedly required to replace it.

BOAT

You can easily hire a motorised 5m boat to see the city from the Saigon River. Be warned – there have been countless unpleasant incidents with bag snatching and pickpocketing at the Bach Dang Pier at the base of ĐL Ham Nghi. It's better to go to the area nearby where you see the ships offering dinner cruises. There will always be someone hanging around looking to charter a boat – ask them to bring the boat to you, rather than you go to the boat (they can easily do this).

The price should be US$5 per hour for a small boat or US$10 to US$15 for a larger and faster craft. Interesting destinations for short trips include Cholon (along Ben Nghe Channel) and the zoo (along Thi Nghe Channel). Note that both channels are fascinating, but filthy – raw sewage is discharged into the water. Foreigners regard the channels as a major tourist attraction, but the government considers them an eyesore and has already launched a program to move local residents out. The channels will eventually be filled in and the water diverted into underground sewer pipes. At that point, the only possible channel cruises will be by submarine.

For longer trips up the Saigon River, it would be worth chartering a fast speedboat from Saigon Tourist. Although these cost US$20 per hour, you'll save money when you consider that a cheap boat takes at least five times longer for the same journey. Splitting the cost between a small group of travellers makes a lot of economic sense and it can be more fun boating with others.

Although cruising the Saigon River can be interesting, it pales in comparison with the splendour of the canals in the Mekong Delta region. One traveller wrote:

> We hired a small boat with driver and female guide for US$5 for an hour for two people and were able to go up the Cholon Channel and see life on the waterfront. The bridges are too low for regular tourist craft. It was extremely interesting to see how these stilt-house dwellers live. We were told that already when the water level is low 'pirate boys' board the boats demanding money, but we had no problems. We were able to take many interesting photographs.

But another traveller had a different attitude:

> Boat trips through the Ben Nghe Channel to Cholon are a bit of a rip-off. The pieces of plastic and the water-plants in the very dirty water make the motor stop every two or three minutes. This forces the boat owner to stop and do a cleaning job which takes much time. We spent 35 minutes drifting on 5km of stinking water without any protection from the rain. There are better places in Vietnam to do boat journeys, such as Cantho, Nha Trang, Hoi An and Hué, to name a few.
>
> **Gorrit Goslinga**

Since you hire boats by the hour, some will go particularly slowly because they know the meter is running. You might want to set a time limit from the outset – three hours should be plenty.

Ferries across the Saigon River leave from Ben Pha Thu Thien, a dock near Me Linh Square. They run every half-hour or so from 4.30 am to 10.30 pm, and the fare is US$0.08. To get on these vessels, you have to run the gauntlet of greedy boat owners and pickpockets.

WALKING

Exploring the city on foot is an excellent idea, but there is one drawback – the traffic. Foreigners frequently make the mistake of thinking that the best way to cross a busy Vietnamese street is to run quickly across it. Sometimes this works and sometimes it gets you creamed. Locals cross the street slowly – very slowly – giving the motorcycle drivers sufficient time to judge their position

Whitewashing Nature

Visitors to Ho Chi Minh City have often wondered why the lower half of all the trees are painted white. Theories posited by tourists have included: (1) the paint protects the trees from termites; (2) the paint protects the trees from Agent Orange; (3) it is some government official's idea of Art Nouveau; and (4) it is an ancient Vietnamese tradition. It turns out that the mystery of the white trees has a much simpler explanation – the trees are painted white so people don't bump into them at night.

so they can pass to either side of you. Motorcycles will *not* stop or even slow down, but they *will* try to avoid hitting you. Remember, make no sudden moves.

For an interesting self-guided walking tour of District 1, see the Things to See & Do chapter.

ORGANISED TOURS

There are surprisingly few day tours available of Ho Chi Minh City itself, though no doubt Saigon Tourist can come up with something in exchange for a hefty fee. Travellers' cafes and travel agents can arrange a car with a guide to tour the sights. Cyclos are also a popular way to see the city.

There are heaps of tours to the outlying areas of Cu Chi, Tay Ninh and the Mekong Delta. Some of the tours are day trips and other are overnighters. The cheapest tours are available from cafes and agencies in the Pham Ngu Lao area (see following Travel Agencies section). These places also arrange trips north to Dalat, Nha Trang, Hoi An, Hué, and so forth.

Travel Agencies

Saigon Tourist (Cong Ty Du Lich Thanh Pho Ho Chi Minh) is Ho Chi Minh City's official government-run travel agency. Saigon Tourist owns, or is a joint-venture partner in, over 70 hotels and numerous restaurants around town, plus a car-rental agency, the Vietnam Golf and Country Club and tourist traps like Binh Quoi Tourist Village.

The way Saigon Tourist became so big is simple: the hotels and restaurants were liberated from their former capitalist (mostly ethnic Chinese) owners after 1975, most of whom subsequently fled the country. The entire upper-level management of this state company is former Viet Cong (no kidding) and attitudes towards foreigners are still decidedly cool. To be fair, Saigon Tourist has in the past few years been wisely investing much of the profits back into new hotels and restaurants. The company keeps growing – if Vietnam ever establishes a stock market, Saigon Tourist shares will be blue chip.

Vietnam Tourism is the national government's tourist agency and is open from 7.30 to 11.30 am and from 1 to 4.30 pm Monday to Saturday. Vietnam Tourism seems to have a slightly better attitude than Saigon Tourist, but both agencies do their best to overcharge for their mediocre service.

There are plenty of other travel agencies in Ho Chi Minh City, virtually all of them joint ventures between government agencies and private companies. These places can provide cars, book air tickets and extend your visa. Some of these places charge the same as Saigon Tourist and Vietnam Tourism, while others are much cheaper. Competition between the private agencies is keen, and you can often undercut Saigon Tourist's tariffs by 50% if you shop around.

Perhaps the best way to approach choosing who to go with is to visit several tour operators and see what's being offered (and for how much). You'll find, in fact, that they're all rather similar in standard and price. Most of the guides are excellent, though this can be hit or miss. The best thing is to speak with other travellers who have just arrived back from a tour and find out the latest.

If one operator stands out from the pack, it's Sinhbalo Adventures (see the Mid-Range & Top End agencies listing, below). This unique outfit specialises in customised adventure tours, such as trekking in national parks and motorbiking the Ho Chi Minh Trail. It's headed up by Mr Le Van Sinh, owner of Sinh Cafe and Vietnam's best-travelled tour guide.

A line-up of some local travel agencies catering to the backpacker market follows, but should only be used as a starting point:

Travel Agencies – Budget

Ben Thanh Tourist (☎ 886 0365, fax 836 1953) 45 Đ Bui Vien, District 1
Fiditourist (☎ 835 3018) 195 Đ Pham Ngu Lao, District 1
Kim Cafe (☎ 836 9859) 270 Đ De Tham, District 1
Linh Cafe (☎ 836 7016, 836 0643) 291 Đ Pham Ngu Lao, District 1
Nam Duong Travel Agency (☎ 836 9630, fax 836 9632) 213 Đ Pham Ngu Lao, District 1. Specialises in domestic and international air-ticketing.
Sinh Cafe (☎ 836 7338, fax 836 9322) 248 Đ De Tham, District 1

Travel Agencies – Mid-Range & Top End

Ann Tours (☎ 833 2564, fax 832 3866, ⓔ anntours@yahoo.com) 58 Đ Ton That Tung, District 1
Atlas Tours (☎ 822 4122, fax 829 8604) 164 Đ Nguyen Van Thu, District 1
Ben Thanh Tourist (☎ 829 8597, fax 829 6269) 121 ĐL Nguyen Hue, District 1
Cholon Tourist (☎ 835 9090, fax 835 5375) 192–194 Đ Su Van Hanh, District 5
Fiditourist (☎ 829 6264) 71–73 Đ Dong Khoi, District 1
Global Holidays (☎ 822 8453, fax 822 8454) 106 ĐL Nguyen Hue, District 1
Hung Vi/Superb Travel (☎ 822 5111, fax 824 2405) 110A ĐL Nguyen Hue, District 1
Mai Linh Co (☎ 825 8888, fax 822 4496) 64 ĐL Hai Ba Trung, District 1
Saigon Tourist (☎ 829 8129, fax 822 4987) 49 Đ Le Thanh Ton, District 1
Sinbalo Adventures (☎ 836 7682, fax 836 7682, ⓔ sinhle@hcm.vnn.vn, www.sinhbalo.com) 34 Đ Bui Ven, District 1
Star Tours (☎ 824 4673, fax 824 4675) 166 Đ Nam Ky Khoi Nghia, District 3
Vietnam Tourism (☎ 829 1276, fax 829 0775) 69–71 Đ Nam Ky Khoi Nghia, District 3
Vinatour (☎ 829 7026, fax 829 9868) 28 Đ Le Thi Hong Gam, District 1
Vita Tours (☎ 823 0767, fax 824 3524) 52 ĐL Hai Ba Trung, District 1
Youth Tourist (☎ 829 4580) 292 Đ Dien Bien Phu, District 3

Things to See & Do

HIGHLIGHTS

The Vietnam (American) War is a topic that still fascinates foreigners, and many of Ho Chi Minh City's tourist attractions focus on this interest. In central Saigon, the most intriguing sites for war buffs include the War Remnants Museum and Reunification Palace. A day trip to the Cu Chi tunnels (see the later Excursions chapter) is also most rewarding.

If you'd rather pursue the topic of religion, be sure to check out the Giac Lam Pagoda, Jade Emperor Pagoda and Vinh Nghiem Pagoda. A day-long excursion to Tay Ninh is required to visit the incredible Caodai Great Temple. Another worthwhile excursion is to the One Pillar Pagoda.

Buying and selling is the heart and soul of Ho Chi Minh City. The best place to get a look at the city's lively commercial side is to visit Ben Thanh Market, Binh Tay Market or Andong Market. These bustling indoor markets are tourist attractions in themselves even if you don't wish to buy anything (see the later Shopping chapter).

Boat trips on the Saigon River are always a great way to take refuge from the urban pandemonium. Further afield, beach buffs are sure to appreciate either the glitter of commercialised Vung Tau or the tranquillity of barely developed Long Hai.

WALKING TOUR (MAPS 3 & 4)

Ho Chi Minh City's immense sprawl makes it somewhat impractical to see all of it on foot, but a one-day walking tour through the city centre, District 1, is certainly possible.

The **Pham Ngu Lao area**, a likely place to start, is the hotel and restaurant centre for budget travellers. It has nothing of interest for Western tourists beyond satisfying basic needs such as eating, drinking, socialising and sleeping. But it's a different story for some Saigonese; Pham Ngu Lao is where they go to look at the hippies. Yes it's true – Western backpackers (locally dubbed *tay balo*, which means foreigner with backpack) have become something of a tourist attraction, much like the hill tribes of the Central Highlands.

After a short walk north up Đ Nguyen Thai Hoc to the New World Hotel (a major landmark), turn right along Đ Le Lai to the huge indoor **Ben Thanh Market**. The market is at its bustling best in the morning. You may want to do your actual souvenir buying later in the day, at a time when you can haul the goods straight back to your hotel.

From the market, cross the large roundabout (very carefully!) where you'll see a statue of Tran Ngyuen Han. One short block south of here, on Đ Pho Duc Chinh, is the praiseworthy **Fine Arts Museum**. After touring the exhibits, zigzag west to ĐL Ham Nghi and turn north again on Đ Ton That Dam and stroll through the colourful **outdoor street market**. At the northern terminus, turn west at the 'T' on Đ Huyen Thuc Khang to Đ Pasteur and out to ĐL Le Loi, the large boulevard leading to the grand, recently restored **Municipal Theatre**.

From the theatre, head back up ĐL Le Loi, and turn north at the Rex Hotel up ĐL Nguyen Hue. At the northern end is the old **Hôtel de Ville**. You'll have to admire it from the outside because it's now home to the local People's Committee – requests to visit the interior are normally abruptly rejected. However, a one-block walk along Đ Le Thanh Ton will bring you to the **Museum of Ho Chi Minh City**, where visitors are warmly received.

The popular **War Remnants Museum** is just a few blocks to the north (technically in District 3) along Đ Nam Ky Khoi Nghia then left on Đ Vo Van Tan. You'll have to pay attention to your watch because the museum is closed for lunch from 11.45 am to 1.30 pm.

Nearby is **Reunification Palace**, which most likely you'll have to visit after lunch. It's only open from 7.30 to 11 am and from 1 to 4 pm.

Later in the afternoon you can stroll the length of ĐL Le Duan, stopping to look at

Notre Dame Cathedral and the grand **Central Post Office.** At the end of the boulevard are the shaded grounds of the **zoo & botanical gardens**, in the grounds of which is the excellent **History Museum**. Just across from the main gate you'll find the quiet **Ho Chi Minh Military Museum.**

A few blocks to the north along Đ Nguyen Binh Khiem will bring you to the **Jade Emperor Pagoda**, a colourful way to end your tour. By this time you will most likely be tired enough to head for your hotel, take a shower, get a cold drink and prepare yourself for tackling the nightlife of Ho Chi Minh City.

CITY CENTRE

A large number of the city's major sights are within the city centre in, and on the periphery of, District 1 (stretching east from the Pham Ngu Lao area to the zoo & botanical gardens). The self-guided walking tour described earlier will take you to most of the must-sees in this part of the city; the museums listed below are en route.

Museums

Fine Arts Museum (Map 3) This classic yellow and white building, with a few modest Chinese influences, at 97A Đ Pho Duc Chinh, District 1 (☎ 829 4441), houses one of the more interesting collections in Vietnam. Even if you are not interested in the collection, just enter the huge hall and admire its Art Nouveau windows and floors. The 1st floor seems to have housed revolutionary art in former times. Those pieces are either in storage, thrown out, or you find them in some back rooms close to the toilet. On the 1st floor now you find changing exhibitions of officially accepted contemporary art. Much of it kitsch or desperate attempts to master abstract art, but occasionally something brilliant is displayed here. Some of the recent art is for sale at private galleries in the rear courtyard, and prices are generally fair.

MASON FLORENCE

The stunning French-colonial facade of the Fine Arts Museum is arguably its main attraction.

The 2nd floor displays the old politically correct art. Some of this stuff is pretty crude – pictures of heroic figures waving red flags, children with rifles, a wounded soldier joining the Communist Party, innumerable tanks and weaponry, grotesque Americans and heroic depictions of Ho Chi Minh. Nevertheless, it's worth seeing because Vietnamese artists managed to be less dull and conformist than their counterparts in Eastern Europe. Once you've passed several paintings and sculptures of Uncle Ho, you will see that those artists who studied before 1975 managed to somehow transfer their own aesthetics into the world of prescribed subjects. Surprisingly, the Vietnamese Communists seem to have only prescribed the subjects, but not the style. Most impressive are some drawings of prison riots in 1973. On the floor are some remarkable abstract paintings. Maybe the most striking thing about these politically correct paintings is that all Vietnamese military heroes look a bit more European than Asian.

The 3rd floor displays a good collection of older art, mainly Funan Oc-Eo sculptures. These Oc-Eo pieces strongly resemble the styles from ancient Greece and Egypt. You will also find the best Cham pieces outside Danang. Also interesting are the many pieces of Indian art, often of an elephant's head. Other pieces clearly originated in Angkor culture.

A cafe is in the garden in front of the museum and is a preferred spot for elderly gentlemen to exchange stamp collections and sip iced tea.

The Fine Arts Museum, or Bao Tang My Thuat, charges admission US$0.40. It's open from 7.45 to 11.15 am and from 1.30 to 4.15 pm Monday to Saturday

JOHN BANAGAN

Reproductions in oil are a local speciality.

MASON FLORENCE

Incense offerings at a Buddhist temple, Cholon

JOHN BANAGAN

Forget long and short grain, here's real variety.

MARK KIRBY

'Army surplus': a US army helicopter ends its days at the War Remnants Museum.

PHIL WEYMOUTH

A red flag is dwarfed by capitalist monumentalism.

JOHN BORTHWICK

Fireworks on sale for Tet

JOHN BANAGAN

French facade, local flourish

MICHELLE BENNETT

Detail, Buddhist temple

PHIL WEYMOUTH

Ho Chi Minh City was largely built in colonial times.

Museum of Ho Chi Minh City (Map 3) Housed in a neoclassical structure built in 1886 and once known as Gia Long Palace, the Museum of Ho Chi Minh City (☎ 829 974165), on Đ Ly Tu Trong, District 1, on the corner of Đ Nam Ky Khoi Nghia, is a singularly beautiful building. The museum displays artefacts from the various periods of the Communist struggle for power in Vietnam. The photographs of anti-colonial activists executed by the French appear out of place in the gilded 19th century ballrooms, but then again, the contrast helps you get a feel for the immense power and self-confident complacency of colonial France. There are also photos of Vietnamese peace demonstrators in Saigon demanding that US troops get out and the historic photo of the martyrdom of Thich Quang Duc, the monk who set himself on fire to protest the policies of President Ngo Dinh Diem.

Some of the information plaques are in Vietnamese only, but other exhibits include documents in French or English and many others are self-explanatory if you know some basic Vietnamese history. Some of the guides speak English, and will often latch on to you in various rooms or on each floor and provide excellent if unrequested guided tours. There are donation boxes next to the visitors' books in various parts of the museum where you can leave a tip for the guides (US$1 is appropriate). Most of the guides do fine work and get paid nothing for it.

The exhibition begins in the first room on the left (as you enter the building), which covers the period from 1859 to 1940. There are interesting displays relating to traditional handicrafts and small industry – fishing and farming tools, looms, lacquerware, ceramics, wood carving and an old fire cart adorned with Chinese characters. Other exhibits focus on the physical geography and flora and fauna of Ho Chi Minh City (including a curious-looking school of stuffed fish dangling on threads in an empty fish tank).

On the 2nd floor are exhibits that show how the 'Saigon puppet regime fell', including a world map detailing the countries that supported North Vietnam during the war with the US. Nearby there is a collection of miniature models of the humble dwellings of revolutionary leaders. One of the most interesting items on display is a *xe keo*, the predecessor to the cyclo, a man-pulled wooden hand cart. Also notable is the *ghe* (a long, narrow rowboat), with a false bottom in which arms were smuggled. The weight of the contraband caused the boat to sit as low in the water as it would have if it had had no false bottom. Nearby is a small diorama of the Cu Chi tunnels. An adjoining room has examples of infantry weapons used by the Viet Cong (VC) and various captured South Vietnamese and US medals, hats and plaques. A map shows Communist advances during the dramatic collapse of South Vietnam in early 1975. There are also photographs of the liberation of Saigon.

Deep underneath the building is a network of reinforced concrete bunkers and fortified corridors. The system, branches of which stretch all the way to Reunification Palace, included living areas, a kitchen and a large meeting hall. In 1963, President Diem and his brother hid here immediately before fleeing to a Cholon church where they were captured (and shortly thereafter killed).

It is worth a stroll around the grounds outside the museum, where there is some interesting military hardware. On the east side of the building (along Đ Pasteur), you'll find a Soviet tank, a US Huey UH-1 helicopter and an anti-aircraft gun. In the garden fronting Đ Nam Ky Khoi Nghia is the US-built F-5E jet used by a renegade South Vietnamese Air Force pilot to bomb the Presidential Palace (now Reunification Palace) on 8 April 1975. The museum grounds, incidentally, are one of the most popular places for Saigonese to have wedding portraits shot – rather than feature the war relics, however, most prefer the grand building as a backdrop. The stunning staircase inside the museum also lends itself as a set piece.

Admission is US$0.80. It's open from 8 to 11.30 am and from 2 to 4.30 pm Tuesday to Sunday.

War Remnants Museum (Map 3) Once known as the Museum of Chinese and American War Crimes, this museum's name has been changed to avoid offending the sensibilities of Chinese and American tourists. However, the pamphlet handed out at reception pulls no punches: it's entitled *Some Pictures of US Imperialists' Aggressive War Crimes in Vietnam.*

Whatever the current name, the War Remnants Museum (☎ 829 0325), at 28 D Vo Van Tan, District 3, at the intersection with D Le Qui Don, has become perhaps the most popular museum in Ho Chi Minh City with Western tourists. Many of the atrocities documented were well publicised in the West, but it is one thing for US anti-war activists to protest against Pentagon policies and quite another for the victims of these military actions to tell their own story. No matter which side of the political fence you stand on, the museum is well worth a visit – if for no other reason than to act as a sobering reminder that war is anything but glorious. Ironically, the War Remnants Museum is in the former US Information Service building.

In the yard of the museum, US armoured vehicles, artillery pieces, bombs and infantry weapons are on display. There is also a guillotine that the French used to deal with Viet Minh 'troublemakers'. Many of the photographs illustrating US atrocities are from US sources, including photos of the infamous My Lai Massacre. There is a model of the 'tiger cages' used by the South Vietnamese military to house VC prisoners on Con Son Island and pictures of genetically deformed babies, their birth defects attributed to the widespread spraying of chemical herbicides by the US. An adjacent room has exhibits displaying counter-revolutionary war crimes committed by saboteurs within Vietnam after 1975. Counter-revolutionaries are portrayed as being allied with both the US and Chinese imperialists.

The main objection to the museum comes, not surprisingly, from American tourists, many of whom complain that it is one-sided. There are some unnecessarily crude comments placed under the photos, such as one of a US soldier picking up a horribly mangled body to show the photographer, and a caption that reads 'this soldier seems satisfied'. And, of course, there is official amnesia when it comes to the topic of the many thousands of people tortured and murdered by the VC.

Politically neutral war historians will perhaps be more disturbed by the lack of context and the incompleteness of some of the photos and exhibits. For example, it's surprising, that there are no photos of Thich Quang Duc, the monk who burned himself to death to protest the war (see the boxed text Human Sacrifice in this chapter). Or photos of the Kent State students in the USA who were shot while protesting US policies. Hopefully, beyond the recently added installation entitled *War & Peace: Vietnam after 35 Years*, the museum will be further expanded to include an even larger slice of the war's history.

Despite these criticisms, there are few museums in the world which drive home the point so well that modern warfare is horribly brutal and that many of the victims are civilians. Even those who adamantly supported the war will have a difficult time not being horrified by photos of innocent children mangled by US bombing, napalming and artillery shelling. There are also scenes of torture – it takes a strong stomach to look at these. You'll also have a rare chance to see some of the experimental weapons used in the 'American War' which were at one time military secrets, an example being the flechette (an artillery shell filled with thousands of tiny darts).

Entry costs US$0.80 (children under 15 free). Explanations are writt n in Vietnamese, English and Chinese. It's open from 7.30 to 11.45 am and from 1.30 to 4.45 pm daily.

Excellent **water puppet performances** can be also seen here in the small theatre near the museum ticket office. There is no fixed schedule: once a minimum of five customers show up, the 30 minute show goes on. Entry costs US$2.

Reunification Palace (Map 3) It was to this building – then known, variously, as Independence Palace or the Presidential Palace – that the first Communist tanks to enter Saigon rushed, on the morning of 30 April 1975. After crashing through the wrought-iron gates in a dramatic scene recorded by photo-journalist Neil Davis and shown around the world, a soldier ran into the building and up the stairs to unfurl a Viet Cong flag from the 4th floor balcony. In an ornate 2nd floor reception chamber, General Minh, who had become head of state only 43 hours before, waited with his improvised cabinet. 'I have been waiting since early this morning to transfer power to you', Minh said to the VC officer who entered the room. 'There is no question of your transferring power', replied the officer, 'you cannot give up what you do not have'.

Reunification Palace, or Hoi Truong Thong Nhat (☎ 829 0629), at 106 Đ Nguyen Du, District 1, is one of the most fascinating sights in Ho Chi Minh City, both because of its striking modern architecture and because of the eerie feeling you get as you walk through the deserted halls. The building, once the symbol of the South Vietnamese government, is preserved almost as it was on that day in April 1975 when the Republic of Vietnam, which hundreds of thousands of Vietnamese and 58,183 Americans had died trying to save, ceased to exist. Some recent additions include a statue of Ho Chi Minh and a video viewing room where you can watch the latest version of Vietnamese history in a variety of languages. The national anthem is played at the end of the tape and you are expected to stand up – it would be considered rude not to do so.

In 1868, the residence for the French Governor-General of Cochinchina was built on this site. The residence gradually expanded and became known as Norodom Palace. When the French departed, the palace became home for South Vietnamese President Ngo Dinh Diem. So hated was Diem that his own air force bombed the palace in 1962 in an unsuccessful attempt to kill him. Recognising that he had an image problem, the president ordered a new residence to be built on the same site but this time with a sizeable bomb shelter in the basement. The new mansion was designed by Paris-trained Vietnamese architect Ngo Viet Thu – work began in 1962 and was completed in 1966. Diem did not get to see his dream house because he was slain by his own troops in 1963. The new building was named Independence Palace and was home for South Vietnamese President Nguyen Van Thieu, until his hasty departure in 1975. The Communists renamed it Reunification Palace (Hoi Truong Thong Nhat).

The building, both inside and out, is an outstanding example of 1960s architecture: it is much more interesting up close than you would expect if viewed from the street. Reunification Palace has an airy and open atmosphere and its spacious chambers are tastefully decorated with the finest modern Vietnamese art and crafts. In its grandeur, the building feels worthy of a head of state.

The ground floor room with the boat-shaped table was often used for conferences. Upstairs, in the Presidential Receiving Room (the one with the red chairs in it, called Phu Dau Rong, or the Dragon's Head Room), the president of South Vietnam received foreign delegations. The president sat behind the desk; the chairs with dragons carved into the arms were used by his assistants. The chair facing the desk was reserved for foreign ambassadors. Next door is a meeting room. The room with gold-coloured chairs and curtains was used by the vice president. In an exquisite example of how far the wheel has turned, today, for US$1, you can sit in the former president's chair and have your photo taken.

In the back of the structure is the area in which the president lived. Check out the model boats, horse tails and severed elephant feet. On the 3rd floor there is a card playing room with a bar and a movie screening chamber. The 3rd floor also boasts a terrace with a heliport – there is still a moribund helicopter parked here, but it costs US$1 admission if you want to walk around the helipad to take advantage of the photo opportunities. The 4th floor has a dance hall.

Perhaps most interesting of all is the basement with its network of tunnels, telecommunications centre and war room (with one of the best maps of Vietnam you'll ever see pasted to the wall). One tunnel stretches all the way to Gia Long Palace, which is now the Museum of Ho Chi Minh City.

The museum is open from 7.30 to 11 am and from 1 to 4 pm daily, except when official receptions or meetings are taking place. English- and French-speaking guides are on duty during these hours. Each guide is assigned to a particular part of the palace, so you will have numerous guides as you move from room to room. The entrance fee is US$3 for foreigners (free for Vietnamese).

History Museum (Map 3) One of Ho Chi Minh City's best museums, the History Museum, or Vien Bao Tang Lich Su (☎ 829 8146), is a welcome relief for those overwhelmed by the amount of war-related displays in other city museums.

Built in 1929 by the Société des Études Indochinoises and once the National Museum of the Republic of Vietnam, the gorgeous Chinese-style building is just inside the main entrance to the zoo, on Đ Nguyen Binh Khiem. You can enter through the main entrance here, but you'll need to pay the entrance fee to the zoo as well if you do (US$0.50). Otherwise, there is a second entrance for the museum only about 20m north of the gate on Đ Nguyen Binh Khiem. Inside the main door you're immediately confronted by a big statue of guess who?

The museum has an excellent collection of artefacts illustrating the evolution of the cultures of Vietnam, from the Bronze Age Dong Son civilisation (13th century BC to 1st century AD) and the Oc-Eo (Funan) civilisation (1st to 6th centuries AD), to the Chams, Khmers and Vietnamese. There are many valuable relics taken from Cambodia's Angkor Wat. The museum is open from 8 to 11.30 am and 1.30 to 4.30 pm daily and from 8.30 am to 4.30 pm Sunday.

At the back of the building on the 3rd floor is a research library (☎ 829 0268) with numerous books on Indochina from the French period. It's open Monday to Saturday.

The museum stages 20-minute **water puppet performances,** similar to the show at the War Remnants Museum; shows begin when a minimum of five patrons have arrived with the US$1 admission fee.

Ho Chi Minh Military Museum (Map 3) Opened in 1996, this museum, Bao Tang Chien Dich Ho Chi Minh, at 2 Đ Le Duan, District 3, is a branch of the No 7 Army Museum – which was closed to the public at the time of writing. Displays centre on Ho Chi Minh and the military campaign leading up to the dramatic capture of Saigon in 1975.

In the central room a giant floor map outlines how the Communists advanced into South Vietnam. On request, staff will air a short video documentary (in English, French or Vietnamese) on the screen above the display which treats the events building up to the day Saigon fell.

Adjoining rooms on the first storey feature period tools and transport, as well as a large collection of vintage film cameras. Though of less interest, more items are displayed on the second level, as well as giant stained glass windows portraying patriotic war scenes.

Outside, US, Chinese and Soviet war materiel is on display, including a Cessna A-37 of the South Vietnamese Air Force and a US-built F-5E Tiger with the 20mm nose gun still loaded. The tank on display is one of the tanks that broke into the grounds of what is now Reunification Palace on 30 April 1975.

The museum is just across from the main gate of the zoo on Đ Nguyen Binh Khiem. Displays are labelled in English, and a short English pamphlet complete with historical photos is also provided. Entry costs US$0.40. It's open from 8 to 11 am and from 1.30 to 4.30 pm Tuesday to Saturday.

Ho Chi Minh Museum Formerly known as Uncle Ho's Museum for Mementos, Bao Tang Ho Chi Minh (☎ 940 1094), at 1 Đ Nguyen Tat Thanh, District 4, is in the old customs house, just across Ben Nghe Channel on the quayside end of DL Ham Nghi.

This building was (and still is) nicknamed the Dragon House, or Nha Rong, and was built in 1863. The tie between Ho Chi Minh (1890–1969) and the museum building is tenuous: 21-year-old Ho, having signed on as a stoker and galley-boy on a French freighter, left Vietnam from here in 1911, beginning 30 years of exile in France, the Soviet Union, China and elsewhere.

The museum houses many of Ho's personal effects, including some of his clothing (he was a man of informal dress), sandals, his beloved US-made Zenith radio and other memorabilia. Most of the explanatory signs in the museum are in Vietnamese, but if you know a little about Uncle Ho (Bac Ho), you should be able to follow most of the photographs and exhibits.

In the evening until midnight the photogenic facade of the building is illuminated, making for a good photo opportunity (but bring a tripod). The museum is open from 7.30 to 11.30 am and from 1.30 to 9 pm daily.

Ton Duc Thang Museum (Map 3) This small, rarely visited museum, Bao Tang Ton Duc Thang (☎ 822 4887), on Đ Ton Duc Thang, District 3, is dedicated to Ton Duc Thang, Ho Chi Minh's successor as president of Vietnam, who was born in Long Xuyen, An Giang Province, in 1888. He died in office in 1980, and the museum (housed in a classic Soviet-style concrete shell), was built in 1988, on the 100th anniversary of his birth.

On display here are many of Ton Duc Thanh's personal belongings, including clothing and books, and his modest bedroom set. A large collection of photos illustrate his role in the Vietnamese Revolution, including the time in 1933 he spent imprisoned on Con Dao Island. The highlight of the museum is a chillingly realistic recreation of prisoners slaving away in the rice mill cellar of the 19th century French-built prison. Very well done, the display includes its own built-in light show!

The museum, thoughtfully restored in early 1999, is worth a look when you're in the area. It's located along the waterfront, half a block north of the Tran Hung Dao statue in Me Linh Square. Entry is free and an English pamphlet is sold for US$0.80. It's open from 8 to 11 am and from 2 to 6 pm Tuesday to Sunday.

MASON FLORENCE

Relegated to distant second in Vietnam's gallery of heroes, Uncle Ho's successor Ton Duc Thang.

Places of Worship

Notre Dame Cathedral (Map 3) Notre Dame Cathedral, built between 1877 and 1883, is set in the heart of Ho Chi Minh City's government quarter. The cathedral is on Đ Han Thuyen, facing down Đ Dong Khoi. It has a neo-Romanesque form and two 40m-high square towers, tipped with iron spires, that dominate the city's skyline. In front of the cathedral (in the centre of the square bounded by the main post office) is a statue of the Virgin Mary. If the front gates are locked, try the door on the side of the building that faces Reunification Palace.

Unusually, this cathedral has no stained-glass windows. The glass was a casualty of fighting during WWII. A number of foreign travellers worship here and the priests are allowed to add a short sermon in French or English to their longer presentations in Vietnamese. The 9.30 am Sunday mass might be the best one for foreigners to attend.

Jade Emperor Pagoda (Map 2) The Jade Emperor Pagoda (known in Vietnamese as Phuoc Hai Tu and Chua Ngoc Hoang), built in 1909 by the Cantonese

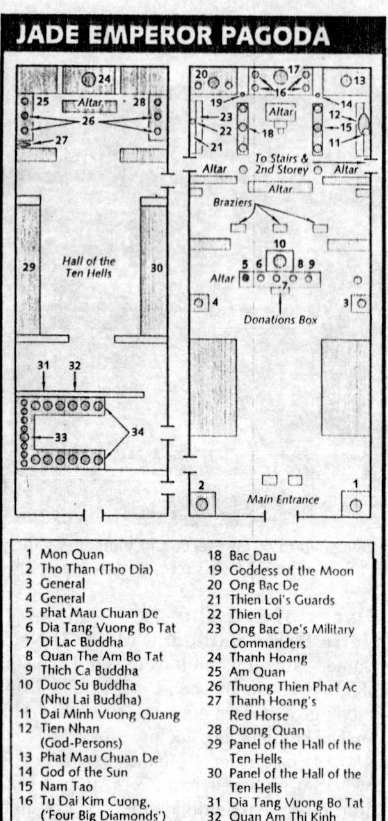

(Quang Dong) congregation, is truly a gem of a Chinese temple. It is one of the most spectacularly colourful pagodas in Ho Chi Minh City, filled with statues of phantasmal divinities and grotesque heroes. The pungent smoke of burning joss sticks fills the air, obscuring the exquisite woodcarvings decorated with gilded Chinese characters. The roof is covered with elaborate tile work. The statues, which represent characters from both the Buddhist and Taoist traditions, are made of reinforced papier-mâché.

As you enter the main doors of the building, Mon Quan, the God of the Gate, stands to the right in an elaborately carved wooden case. Opposite him, in a similar case, is Tho Than (Tho Dia), the God of the Land. Straight on is an altar on which are placed, from left to right, figures of: Phat Mau Chuan De, mother of the Five Buddhas of the Cardinal Directions; Dia Tang Vuong Bo Tat (Ksitigartha), the King of Hell; the Di Lac Buddha (Maitreya), the Buddha of the Future; Quan The Am Bo Tat (Avalokiteçvara, Guanyin in Mandarin Chinese), the Goddess of Mercy; and a bas-relief portrait of the Thich Ca Buddha. Behind the altar, in a glass case, is the Duoc Su Buddha, also known as the Nhu Lai Buddha. The figure is said to be made of sandalwood.

To either side of the altar, against the walls, are two especially fierce and menacing figures. On the right (as you face the altar) is a 4m-high statue of the general who defeated the Green Dragon. He is stepping on the vanquished dragon. On the left is the general who defeated the White Tiger, which is also being stepped on.

The Taoist Jade Emperor, Ngoc Hoang, presides over the main sanctuary, draped in luxurious robes. He is flanked by the Tu Dai Kim Cuong (Four Big Diamonds), his four guardians, so named because they are said to be as hard as diamonds. In front of the Jade Emperor stand six figures, three to each side. On the left is Bac Dau, the Taoist God of the Northern Polar Star and God of Longevity, flanked by his two guardians; and on the right is Nam Tao, the Taoist God of the Southern Polar Star and God of Happiness, also flanked by two guardians.

In the case to the right of the Jade Emperor is 18-armed Phat Mau Chuan De, one form of the Goddess of Mercy. Two faces, affixed to her head behind each ear, look to either side. On the wall to her right, at a height of about 4m, is Dai Minh Vuong Quang, who was reincarnated as Sakyamuni, riding on the back of a phoenix. Below are the Tien Nhan (literally, the 'god-persons').

In the case to the left of the Jade Emperor sits Ong Bac De, a reincarnation of the Jade Emperor, holding a sword. One of his feet is resting on a turtle while the other rests on a snake. On the wall to the left of Ong Bac De, about 4m off the ground, is Thien Loi, the God of Lightning, who slays evil people. Below Thien Loi are the military commanders of Ong Bac De (on the lower step) and Thien Loi's guardians (on the upper step). At the top of the two carved pillars that separate the three alcoves are the Goddess of the Moon (on the left) and the God of the Sun (on the right).

Out the door on the left-hand side of the Jade Emperor's chamber is another room. The semi-enclosed area to the right (as you enter) is presided over by Thanh Hoang, the Chief of Hell; to the left is his red horse. Of the six figures lining the walls, the two closest to Thanh Hoang are Am Quan, the God of Yin (on the left), and Duong Quan, the God of Yang (on the right). The other four figures, the Thương Thien Phat Ac, are gods who dispense punishments for evil acts and rewards for good deeds. Thanh Hoang faces in the direction of the famous Hall of the 10 Hells. The carved wooden panels lining the walls graphically depict the varied torments awaiting evil people in each of the 10 Regions of Hell. At the top of each panel is one of the Judges of the 10 Regions of Hell examining a book in which the deeds of the deceased are inscribed.

On the wall opposite Thanh Hoang is a bas-relief wood panel depicting Quan Am Thi Kinh standing on a lotus blossom – a symbol of purity. On the panel, Quan Am Thi Kinh is shown holding her son. To her left is Long Nu, a very young Buddha who is her protector. To her right is Thien Tai, her guardian spirit, who knew the real story all along. Above her left shoulder is a bird bearing prayer beads.

To the right of the panel of Quan Am Thi Kinh is a panel depicting Dia Tang Vuong Bo Tat, the King of Hell.

On the other side of the wall is a fascinating little room in which the ceramic figures of 12 women, overrun with children and wearing colourful clothes, sit in two rows of six. Each of the women exemplifies a human characteristic, either good or bad (as in the case of the woman drinking alcohol from a jug). Each figure represents one year in the 12 year Chinese calendar. Presiding over the room is Kim Hoa Thanh Mau, the Chief of All Women.

Off to the right of the main chamber, stairs lead up to a 2nd floor sanctuary and balcony.

The Jade Emperor Pagoda, at 73 Đ Mai Thi Luu, District 3, is in a part of the city known as Da Kao (or Da Cao). To get there, go to 20 Đ Dien Bien Phu and walk half a block north-westward (to the left as you head out of Ho Chi Minh City towards Thi Nghe Channel).

Tran Hung Dao Temple (Map 2) This small temple is dedicated to Tran Hung Dao, a national hero, who in 1287 vanquished an invasion force, said to have numbered 300,000 men, that had been dispatched by the Mongol emperor Kublai Khan. The temple, at 36 Đ Vo Thi Sau, District 3, is a block north-east of the telecommunications dishes that are between Đ Dien Bien Phu and Đ Vo Thi Sau. It's open from 6 to 11 am and from 2 to 6 pm Monday to Friday.

Lẹ Van Tam Park, between the antenna dishes and ĐL Hai Ba Trung, was built in 1983 on the site of the Massiges Cemetery, burial place of French soldiers and settlers. The remains of French military personnel were exhumed and repatriated to France. Another site no longer in existence is the tomb of the 18th century French missionary and diplomat Pigneau de Béhaine, Bishop of Adran, which was completely destroyed after reunification.

Tan Dinh Church (Map 2) Notable for its ornate masonry, this is one of Ho Chi Minh City's most architecturally splendid cathedrals, and well worth a look if you're in the area. Mass is held at 5.15 am and 5 pm daily, with services at 5, 6.15, 7.30 and 9 am and at 4, 5.30 and 7 pm Sunday. Confession is held between 2 and 6 pm Saturday.

Tan Dinh Church is in District 3, near the Tan Dinh Market, a short walk north of the intersection of ĐL Hai Ba Trung and ĐL Vo Thi Sau.

Xa Loi Pagoda (Map 2) Xá Loi Vietnamese Buddhist Pagoda, at 89 Đ Ba Huyen Thanh Quan, District 3, near Đ Dien Bien

Human Sacrifice

Thich Quang Duc was a monk from Hué who travelled to Saigon and publicly burned himself to death in June 1963 to protest the policies of President Ngo Dinh Diem. A photograph (which has since become internationally famous) of his act was printed on the front pages of newspapers around the world. His death soon inspired a number of other self-immolations.

Many Westerners were shocked less by the suicides than by the reaction of Tran Le Xuan (Madame Nhu, the president's notorious sister-in-law), who happily proclaimed the self-immolations a 'barbecue party' and said, 'Let them burn and we shall clap our hands.' Her statements greatly added to the already substantial public disgust with Diem's regime: the US press labelled Madame Nhu the Iron Butterfly and Dragon Lady. In November 1963, both President Diem and his brother Ngo Dinh Nhu (Madame Nhu's husband) were killed by Diem's own soldiers. Madame Nhu was outside the country at the time (fortunately for her) and was last reported to be living in Rome.

The Thich Quang Duc Memorial (Dai Ky Niem Thuong Toa Thich Quang Duc) is at the intersection of Đ Nguyen Dinh Chieu and Đ Cach Mang Thang Tam, District 3 (Map 2), just around the corner from the Xa Loi Pagoda.

Phu, was built in 1956 and is famed as the repository of a sacred relic of the Buddha. In August 1963, truckloads of armed men under the command of President Ngo Dinh Diem's brother, Ngo Dinh Nhu, attacked Xa Loi Pagoda, which had become a centre of opposition to the Diem government. The pagoda was ransacked and 400 monks and nuns, including the country's 80-year-old Buddhist patriarch, were arrested. This raid, and others elsewhere, helped solidify opposition among Buddhists to the Diem regime, a crucial factor in the US decision to support the coup against Diem. This pagoda was also the site of several self-immolations by monks protesting against the Diem regime and the Vietnam War.

Women enter the main hall of Xa Loi Pagoda by the staircase on the right as you come in the gate; men use the stairs on the left. The walls of the sanctuary are adorned with paintings depicting the Buddha's life.

A monk preaches at the temple from 8 to 10 am Sunday. On days of the full moon and new moon, special prayers are held from 7 to 9 am and 7 to 8 pm. The temple is open from 7 to 11 am and from 2 to 5 pm daily.

Mariamman Hindu Temple (Map 3) Mariamman Hindu Temple, the only Hindu temple still in use in Ho Chi Minh City, is a little piece of southern India in the centre of Ho Chi Minh City. Though there are only 50 to 60 Hindus in Ho Chi Minh City – all of them Tamils – this temple, known in Vietnamese as Chua Ba Mariamman, is also considered sacred by many ethnic Vietnamese and ethnic Chinese. Indeed, it is reputed to have miraculous powers. The temple was built at the end of the 19th century and dedicated to the Hindu goddess Mariamman.

The lion to the left of the entrance used to be carried around Ho Chi Minh City in a street procession every autumn. In the shrine in the middle of the temple is Mariamman, flanked by her guardians – Maduraiveeran (to her left) and Pechiamman (to her right). In front of the figure of Mariamman are two *lingas* (phallic symbols). Favourite offerings placed nearby often include joss sticks, jasmine, lilies and gladioli. The wooden stairs, on the left as you enter the building, lead to the roof, where you'll find two colourful towers covered with innumerable figures of lions, goddesses and guardians. Take off your shoes before stepping onto the slightly raised platform.

After reunification, the government took over the temple and turned part of it into a factory for joss sticks. Another section was occupied by a company producing seafood for export – the seafood was dried in the sun on the roof. The whole temple is to be returned to the local Hindu community.

Mariamman Temple, at 45 Đ Truong Dinh, District 1, is only three blocks west of Ben Thanh Market. It's open from 7 am to 7 pm daily.

Saigon Central Mosque (Map 3) Built by south Indian Muslims in 1935 on the site of an earlier mosque, the Saigon Central Mosque, at 66 Đ Dong Du, District 1, is an immaculately clean and well-kept island of calm in the middle of bustling central Saigon. In front of the sparkling white and blue structure, with its four nonfunctional minarets, is a pool for ritual ablutions – required by Islamic law before prayer. As with any mosque, take off your shoes before entering the sanctuary.

The simplicity of Saigon Central Mosque is in marked contrast to the exuberance of Chinese temple decorations, and the rows of figures and statuettes and elaborate ritual objects in Buddhist pagodas. Islamic law strictly forbids using human or animal figures for decoration.

Only a handful of ethnic Indian Muslims remain in Ho Chi Minh City: most of the community fled in 1975. As a result, prayers – held five times a day – are sparsely attended except on Friday, when several dozen worshippers (mainly non-Indian Muslims) are present. The mass emigration also deprived the local Muslim community of much of its spiritual leadership: very few Muslims knowledgeable in traditional rites and practices and Arabic – the language of the Koran – remain.

There are 12 other mosques serving the 5000 or so ethnic Vietnamese Muslims in Ho Chi Minh City.

Phung Son Tu Pagoda (Map 5) Phung Son Tu Pagoda, at 338 Đ Yersin, District 1, only 1km from central Saigon, was built by the Fujian congregation in the mid-1940s and is more typical of Ho Chi Minh City's Chinese pagodas. The interior is often hung with huge incense spirals that burn for hours. Worshippers include both ethnic Chinese and ethnic Vietnamese. Phung Son Tu Pagoda is dedicated to Ong Bon, Guardian Spirit of Happiness and Virtue, whose statue is behind the main altar in the sanctuary. On the right-hand side of the main hall is the multi-armed Goddess of Mercy.

ANDERS BLOMQVIST

Phung Son Tu Pagoda: dedicated to Ong Bon, Guardian Spirit of Happiness and Virtue

Parks

Zoo & Botanical Gardens (Map 3) The zoo and botanical gardens (Thao Cam Vien) are pleasant places for a relaxing stroll, which you can do in the shade of giant tropical trees that thrive amidst the lakes, lawns and flower beds. The zoo facilities are still a bit run-down, but in recent years they seem to be improving.

The botanical gardens, founded in 1864, were one of the first projects undertaken by the French after they established Cochinchina as a colony. They were once one of the finest such gardens in Asia, but this is certainly no longer true. The emphasis now is on the fun fair, with kiddie rides, fun house, miniature train and house of mirrors.

Just inside the main gate, across from the History Museum, is the **Temple of King Hung Vuong**. The Hung kings are said to have been the first rulers of the Vietnamese nation, having established their rule in the Red River region before being invaded by the Chinese. On the north side of the temple is a large cast iron Elephant sculpture, which was a gift from the King of Siam (now Thailand) during his first visit to Indochina, in 1930.

The main gate of the zoo is on Đ Nguyen Binh Khiem at the intersection of ĐL Le Duan, District 3. There is another entrance on Đ Nguyen Thi Minh Khai, near the bridge over Thi Nghe Channel.

The limited food sold here is generally expensive and not too good. Just outside the main gate (along Nguyen Binh Khiem St) there are numerous food stalls selling excellent rice dishes, soup and drinks at reasonable prices.

Cong Vien Van Hoa Park (Map 3) Next to the old Cercle Sportif, an elite sporting club during the French period, the bench-lined walks of Cong Vien Van Hoa Park are shaded with avenues flanked by enormous tropical trees.

This place still has an active sports club, although now you don't have to be French to visit. There are 11 tennis courts, a swimming pool and a club house, which all have a grand colonial feel about them. It's worth a look for the pool alone. There are Roman-style baths

MASON FLORENCE

Apart from *Homo sapiens*, not many of the species in this picture are native to Ho Chi Minh City.

with a coffee shop overlooking the colonnaded pool.

The tennis courts are available for hire at a reasonable fee. Hourly tickets are on sale for use of the pool and you can buy a bathing costume on the grounds if you don't have one. The antique dressing rooms are quaint but note that there are no lockers! Other facilities include a gymnasium, table tennis tables, weight-lifting apparatus, wrestling mats and ballroom dancing classes.

In the morning, you can often see people here practising the art of *thai cuc quyen* (t'ai chi), or slow-motion shadow boxing.

Within the park is a small-scale model of the Cham towers in Nha Trang.

Cong Vien Van Hoa Park is adjacent to Reunification Palace. There are entrances across from 115 Đ Nguyen Du and on Đ Nguyen Thi Minh Khai.

Other Attractions

Hôtel de Ville (Map 3) Ho Chi Minh City's gingerbread Hôtel de Ville is not a place to stay, despite the name. One of the city's most prominent landmarks, it was built between 1901 and 1908, after years of the sort of architectural controversy peculiar to the French. Situated at the northwestern end of ĐL Nguyen Hue and facing the river, the white-on-pastel-yellow Hôtel de Ville, with its ornate facade and elegant interior lit with crystal chandeliers, is now the somewhat incongruous home of the Ho Chi Minh City People's Committee.

The building is officially called the People's Committee Building, though few outside the government care to call it that. Whatever it's called, you'll have to content yourself with admiring the exterior only. The building, perhaps the most photographed in Vietnam, is not open to the public and requests by tourists to visit the interior are rudely rebuffed.

For gecko fans: at night, the exterior of the building is usually covered with thousands of the creatures feasting on insects.

Binh Soup Shop (Map 2) It might seem strange to introduce a restaurant in the sightseeing section of this book rather than the Places to Eat section, but there is more to this shop than just the soup. The Binh Soup Shop was the secret headquarters of the VC in Saigon. It was from here that the VC planned the attack on the US embassy and other places in Saigon during the Tet offensive of 1968. One has to wonder how many American soldiers must have eaten here, unaware that the waiters, waitresses and cooks were VC infiltrators.

The historic Binh Soup Shop (☎ 844 3775), at 7 Đ Ly Chinh Thang, District 3, starts serving *pho* (Vietnam's breakfast of champions) to hungry customers at 6 am. By the way, the soup isn't bad.

NORTH OF CITY CENTRE

Places of Worship

Dai Giac Pagoda (Map 2) This Vietnamese Buddhist pagoda, at 112 Đ Nguyen Van Troi, Phu Nhuan District, is built in a style characteristic of pagodas constructed during the 1960s. In the courtyard, under the unfinished, 10 level, reddish-pink tower inlaid with porcelain shards, is an artificial cave made of volcanic rocks, in which there is a gilded statue of the Goddess of Mercy. In the main sanctuary, the 2.5m gilt Buddha has a green neon halo, while below, a smaller white reclining Buddha (in a glass case) has a blue neon halo.

Vinh Nghiem Pagoda (Map 2) Vinh Nghiem Pagoda, inaugurated in 1971, is noteworthy for its vast sanctuary and eight-storey tower, each level of which contains a statue of the Buddha. It was built with help from the Japan-Vietnam Friendship Association, which explains the presence of Japanese elements in its architecture. At the base of the tower (which is open only on holidays) is a shop selling Buddhist ritual objects. Behind the sanctuary is a three-storey tower that serves as a repository for carefully labelled ceramic urns containing the ashes of people who have been cremated. Beware: the sheer number of incense vendors (and beggars) can overwhelm you as you enter the grounds. The pagoda is just off Đ Nguyen Van Troi, in District 3, and is open from 7.30 to 11.30 am and from 2 to 6 pm daily.

Le Van Duyet Temple (Map 2) This temple is dedicated to Marshal Le Van Duyet (pronounced zyet; 1763–1831), who is buried here with his wife. The marshal was a South Vietnam general and viceroy who helped put down the Tay Son Rebellion and reunify Vietnam. When the Nguyen Dynasty came to power in 1802, he was elevated by Emperor Gia Long to the rank of marshal. Le Van Duyet fell into disfavour with Gia Long's successor, Minh Mang, who tried him posthumously and desecrated his grave. Emperor Thieu Tri, who succeeded Minh Mang, restored the tomb, fulfilling a prophesy of its destruction and restoration. Le Van Duyet was considered a great national hero in the South before 1975, but is disliked by the Communists because of his involvement in the expansion of French influence.

The temple itself was renovated in 1937 and has a distinctly modern feel to it. Since 1975, the government has done little to keep it from becoming dilapidated. Among the items on display are a portrait of Le Van Duyet, some of his personal effects (including European-style crystal goblets) and other antiques. There are two wonderful life-size horses on either side of the entrance to the third and last chamber, which is kept locked.

During celebrations of Tet and the 30th day of the seventh lunar month (the anniversary of Le Van Duyet's death), the tomb is thronged with pilgrims. Vietnamese used to come here to take oaths of good faith if they could not afford the services of a court of justice. The tropical fish are on sale to visitors. The caged birds are bought by pilgrims and freed to earn merit. The birds are often recaptured (and liberated again).

Le Van Duyet Temple, at 131 Đ Dinh Tien Hoang, Binh Thanh District, is 3km from the centre of Saigon, near where ĐL Phan Dang Luu becomes ĐL Bach Dang.

CHOLON

Places of Worship

An Quang Pagoda (Map 5) An Quang Pagoda, on Đ Su Van Hanh, District 10, near the intersection with Đ Ba Hat, gained some notoriety during the Vietnam War as the home of Thich Tri Quang, a powerful monk who led protests against the South Vietnamese government in 1963 and 1966. When the war ended, you would have expected the Communists to be grateful. Instead, he was placed under house arrest and later thrown into solitary confinement for 16 months. Thich Tri Quang was eventually released and is said to still be living at An Quang Pagoda.

Tam Son Hoi Quan Pagoda (Map 5) Known to the Vietnamese as Chua Ba Chua, at 118 Đ Trieu Quang Phuc, District 5, near the corner of ĐL Tran Hung Dao, this pagoda was built by the Fujian congregation in the 19th century and retains most of its original rich ornamentation. The pagoda is dedicated to Me Sanh, the Goddess of Fertility. Both men and women – but more of the latter – come here to pray for progeny.

To the right of the covered courtyard is the deified general Quan Cong, with a long, black beard. He is flanked by two guardians, the mandarin general Chau Xuong on the left (holding a weapon) and the administrative mandarin Quan Binh on the right. Next to Chau Xuong is Quan Cong's sacred red horse.

Behind the main altar (directly across the courtyard from the entrance) is Thien Hau, the Goddess of the Sea, who protects fisherfolk and sailors. To the right is an ornate case in which Me Sanh, in white, sits surrounded by her daughters. In the case to the left of Thien Hau is Ong Bon. In front of Thien Hau is Quan The Am Bo Tat, enclosed in glass.

Across the courtyard from Quan Cong is a small room containing ossuary jars and memorials in which the dead are represented by their photographs. Next to this chamber is a small room containing the papier-mâché head of a dragon of the type used by the Fujian congregation for dragon dancing. There is a photograph of a dragon dance on the wall between Quan Cong's red horse and Me Sanh.

Thien Hau Pagoda (Map 5) Thien Hau Pagoda, also known as Ba Mieu, Pho Mieu and Chua Ba, is at 710 Đ Nguyen Trai, District 5. It was built by the Cantonese congregation in the early 19th century. Of late it has become something of a showcase for tours operated by Saigon Tourist and Vietnam Tourism, which may explain the recent extensive renovations. This pagoda is one of the most active in Cholon.

The pagoda is dedicated to Thien Hau (also known as Tuc Goi La Ba), Goddess of the Sea. It is said that Thien Hau can travel over the oceans on a mat and ride the clouds to wherever she pleases. Her mobility allows her to save people in trouble on the high seas.

Thien Hau is very popular in Hong Kong (where she's called Tin Hau) and in Taiwan (where her name is Matsu). This might explain why Thien Hau Pagoda is included on so many tour-group agendas (tourists from both those places have reputations for free spending).

Though there are guardians to either side of the entrance, it is said that the real protectors of the pagoda are the two land turtles who live here.

Above the roof-line of the interior courtyard there are intricate ceramic friezes. Near the pagoda's huge braziers are two miniature wooden structures in which a small figure of Thien Hau is paraded around on the 23rd day of the third lunar month. On the main dais are three figures of Thien Hau, one behind the other, all flanked by two servants or guardians. To the left of the dais is a bed for Thien Hau. To the right is a scale-model boat, and on the far right is the goddess Long Mau, Protector of Mothers and Newborns. It's open from 6 am to 5.30 pm.

Nghia An Hoi Quan Pagoda (Map 5) Nghia An Hoi Quan Pagoda, at 678 Đ Nguyen Trai, District 5, not far from Thien Hau Pagoda, was built by the Chaozhou congregation and is noteworthy for its gilded woodwork. There is a carved wooden boat over the entrance and inside, to the left of the doorway, is an enormous representation of Quan Cong's red horse with its groom. To the right of the entrance is an elaborate altar in which a bearded Ong Bon stands holding a stick. Behind the main altar are three glass cases. In the centre is Quan Cong and to either side are his assistants, Chau Xuong on the left and Quan Binh on the right. To the right of Quan Binh is an especially elaborate case for Thien Hau. It's open from 4 am to 6 pm.

Cholon Mosque (Map 5) The clean lines and lack of ornamentation of the Cholon Mosque are in stark contrast to nearby Chinese and Vietnamese pagodas. In the courtyard is a pool for ritual ablutions. Note the tile *mihrab* (the niche in the wall indicating the direction of prayer, which is towards Mecca). The mosque was built by ethnic Tamil Muslims in 1932. Since 1975, it has served the ethnic Malaysian and Indonesian Muslim communities. It's at 641 Đ Nguyen Trai, District 5, and is open all day Friday and at prayer times on other days.

Quan Am Pagoda (Map 5) Quan Am Pagoda, at 12 Đ Lao Tu, District 5, one block off Đ Chau Van Liem, was founded in 1816 by the Fujian congregation. The temple is named for Quan The Am Bo Tat, Goddess of Mercy.

This is the most active pagoda in Cholon and the Chinese influence is obvious. The roof is decorated with fantastic scenes, rendered in ceramic, from traditional Chinese plays and stories. The tableaux include ships, houses, people and several ferocious dragons. The front doors are decorated with very old gold and lacquer panels. On the walls of the porch are murals in slight relief, picturing scenes of China from the time of Quan Cong. There are elaborate woodcarvings on roof supports above the porch.

Behind the main altar is A Pho, the Holy Mother Celestial Empress, gilded and in rich raiment. In front of her, in a glass case, are three painted statues of Thich Ca Buddha, a standing gold Quan The Am Bo Tat, a seated laughing Ameda and, to the far left, a gold figure of Dia Tang Vuong Bo Tat, King of Hell.

In the courtyard behind the main sanctuary, in the pink-tile altar, is another figure of A Pho. Quan The Am Bo Tat, dressed in white embroidered robes, stands nearby. To the left of the altar is her richly ornamented bed. To the right of the altar is Quan Cong, flanked by his guardians. To the far right, in front of another pink altar, is the black-faced judge Bao Cong.

Phuoc An Hoi Quan Pagoda (Map 5) Phuoc An Hoi Quan Pagoda, at 184 Đ Hung Vuong, District 5, near the intersection with Đ Thuan Kieu, was built in 1902 by the Fujian congregation and is one of the most beautifully ornamented pagodas in Ho Chi Minh City. Of special interest are the many small porcelain figures, the elaborate brass ritual objects and the fine woodcarvings on the altars, walls, columns and hanging lanterns. From outside the building you can see the ceramic scenes, each containing innumerable small figurines, which decorate the roof.

To the left of the entrance is a life-size figure of the sacred horse of Quan Cong. Before leaving on a journey, people make offerings to the horse. They then stroke the horse's mane before ringing the bell around its neck. Behind the main altar, with its stone and brass incense braziers, is Quan Cong, to whom the pagoda is dedicated. Behind the altar to the left is Ong Bon and two servants. The altar to the right is occupied by representations of Buddhist (rather than Taoist) personages. In the glass case are a plaster Thich Ca Buddha and two figures of the Goddess of Mercy, one made of porcelain and the other cast in brass.

Ong Bon Pagoda (Map 5) Ong Bon Pagoda, also known as Chua Ong Bon and Nhi Phu Hoi Quan, at 264 ĐL Hai Thuong Lan Ong, District 5, was built by the Fujian congregation and is dedicated to Ong Bon, Guardian Spirit of Happiness and Virtue. The wooden altar is intricately carved and gilded.

As you enter the pagoda, there is a room to the right of the open-air courtyard. In it, behind the table, is a figure of Quan The Am Bo Tat in a glass case. Above the case is the head of a Thich Ca Buddha.

Directly across the courtyard from the pagoda entrance, against the wall, is Ong Bon, to whom people come to pray for general happiness and relief from financial difficulties. He faces a fine, carved wooden altar. On the walls of this chamber are rather indistinct murals of five tigers (to the left) and two dragons (to the right).

In the area on the other side of the wall with the mural of the dragons is a furnace for burning paper representations of the wealth people wish to bestow upon deceased family members. Diagonally opposite is Quan Cong flanked by his guardians Chau Xuong (to his right) and Quan Binh (to his left). It's open from 5 am to 5 pm.

Ha Chuong Hoi Quan Pagoda (Map 5) The Ha Chuong Hoi Quan Pagoda, at 802 Đ Nguyen Trai, District 5, is a typical Fujian pagoda. It is dedicated to Thien Hau Thanh Mau, Goddess of the Sea, who was born in Fujian.

The four carved stone pillars, wrapped in painted dragons, were made in China and brought to Vietnam by boat. There are interesting murals to either side of the main altar. Note the ceramic relief scenes on the roof.

Ha Chuong Hoi Quan Pagoda becomes extremely active during the Lantern Festival, a Chinese holiday held on the 15th day of the first lunar month (the first full moon of the new lunar year).

Cha Tam Church (Map 5) It is in Cha Tam Church, at 25 Đ Hoc Lac, District 5, at the western end of ĐL Tran Hung Dao, that President Ngo Dinh Diem and his brother Ngo Dinh Nhu took refuge on 2 November 1963, after fleeing the Presidential Palace during a coup (see History in the Facts about Ho Chi Minh City chapter). When their efforts to contact loyal military officers (of whom there were almost none) failed, Diem and Nhu agreed to surrender unconditionally and revealed where they were hiding.

The coup leaders sent an M-113 armoured personnel carrier to the church and the two were taken into custody. But before the vehicle reached central Saigon, the soldiers had killed Diem and Nhu by shooting them at point-blank range and then repeatedly stabbing their bodies.

When news of the deaths was broadcast on radio, Saigon erupted in celebration.

Portraits of the two were torn up and political prisoners, many of whom had been tortured, were set free. The city's nightclubs, closed because of the Ngos' conservative Catholic beliefs, reopened. Three weeks later, US president John F. Kennedy was assassinated. As Kennedy's administration had supported the coup against Diem, some conspiracy theorists have speculated that he was killed by Diem's family in retaliation. Then again, there are theories that Kennedy was murdered by the Soviets, the Cubans, left-wing radicals, right-wing radicals, the CIA and the Mafia.

Cha Tam Church, built around the turn of the century, is an attractive white and pastel-yellow structure. The statue in the tower is of François Xavier Tam Assou (1855–1934), a Chinese-born vicar apostolic (delegate of the pope) of Saigon. Today, the church has a very active congregation of 3000 ethnic Vietnamese and 2000 ethnic Chinese.

Vietnamese-language masses are held from 5.30 to 6 am Monday to Saturday and from 5.30 to 6.30 am, 8.30 to 9.30 am and 3.45 to 4.45 pm Sunday. Chinese-language masses are held from 5.30 to 6 pm Monday to Saturday and from 7 to 8 am and 5 to 6 pm Sunday.

Cho Quan Church (Map 5) Cho Quan Church, at 133 Đ Tran Binh Trong, District 5, between Đ Tran Hung Dao and Đ Nguyen Trai, was built by the French about 100 years ago and is one of the largest churches in Ho Chi Minh City. This is the only church we've seen in the city where the figure of Jesus on the altar has a neon halo. The view from the belfry is worth the steep climb. The church is open from 4 to 7 am and 3 to 6 pm Monday to Saturday, and from 4 to 9 am and 1.30 to 6 pm Sunday. Sunday masses are held at 5, 6.30 and 8.30 am, and 4.30 and 6 pm.

Khanh Van Nam Vien Pagoda (Map 5) Built between 1939 and 1942 by the Cantonese congregation, Khanh Van Nam Vien Pagoda, at 46/5 Đ Lo Sieu, District 11, is said to be the only Taoist pagoda in all of Vietnam. The number of true Taoists in Ho Chi Minh City is said to number only 4000. However, since most Chinese practice a mixture of Taoism and Buddhism, true Taoists can be true Buddhists without there being any contradiction.

A few metres from the door is a statue of Hoang Linh Quan, chief guardian of the pagoda. There is a Yin and Yang symbol on the platform on which the incense braziers sit. Behind the main altar are four figures: Quan Cong (on the right) and Lu Tung Pan (on the left) represent Taoism; between them is Van Xuong representing Confucianism; and behind Van Xuong is Quan The Am Bo Tat, Goddess of Mercy.

In front of these figures is a glass case containing seven gods and one goddess, all of which are made of porcelain. In the altars to either side of the four figures are Hoa De (on the left), a famous doctor during the Han Dynasty, and Huynh Dai Tien (on the right), a disciple of Laotse (Thai Thuong Lao Quan in Vietnamese).

Upstairs is a 150cm-high statue of Laotse. Behind his head is a halo consisting of a round mirror with fluorescent lighting around the edge.

Off to the left of Laotse are two stone plaques with instructions for inhalation and exhalation exercises. A schematic drawing represents the human organs as a scene from rural China. The diaphragm, agent of inhalation, is at the bottom. The stomach is represented by a peasant ploughing with a water buffalo. The kidney is marked by four Yin and Yang symbols, the liver is shown as a grove of trees and the heart is represented by a circle with a peasant standing in it, above which is a constellation. The tall pagoda represents the throat and the broken rainbow is the mouth. At the top are mountains and a seated figure representing the brain and the imagination, respectively. The 80-year-old chief monk says that he has practised these exercises for the past 17 years and hasn't been sick one day.

The pagoda operates a home at 46/14 Đ Lo Sieu for 30 elderly people who have no families. Each of the old folk, most of whom are women, have their own wood stove made of brick and can cook for themselves. Next door, also run by the pagoda, is a free medical clinic which offers Chinese herbal medicines and acupuncture treatments to the community. Before reunification, the pagoda ran (also free of charge) the school across the street.

Prayers are held from 8 to 9 am. To reach Khanh Van Nam Vien Pagoda, turn off Đ Nguyen Thi Nho (which runs perpendicular to Đ Hung Vuong) between numbers 269B and 271B. The pagoda is open daily from 6.30 am to 5.30 pm.

Phung Son Pagoda (Map 5) Phung Son Pagoda, at 1408 ĐL 3 Thang 2, District 11, near the intersection with Đ Hung Vuong, is also known as Phung Son Tu and Chua Go and is extremely rich in statuary made of hammered copper and bronze, wood and ceramic. Some statues are gilded while others, beautifully carved, are painted. This Vietnamese Buddhist pagoda was built between 1802 and 1820 on the site of structures from the Oc-Eo (Funan) period, which was a contemporary of the early centuries of Christianity. In 1988, a Soviet archaeological team carried out a preliminary excavation and found the foundations of Funanese buildings, but work was stopped pending authorisation for a full-scale dig.

Once upon a time, it was decided that Phung Son Pagoda should be moved to a different site. The pagoda's ritual objects – bells, drums, statues – were loaded onto the back of a white elephant for transport to the new location, but the elephant slipped because of the great weight and all the precious objects fell into a nearby pond. This event was interpreted as an omen that the pagoda should remain at its original location. All the articles were retrieved, except for the bell, which locals say was heard ringing whenever there was a full or new moon until about a century ago.

The main dais, with its many levels, is dominated by a gilded A Di Da Buddha seated under a canopy flanked by long mobiles resembling human forms without heads. A Di Da is flanked by Quan The Am Bo Tat (on the left), and Dai The Chi Bo Tat (on the right). To the left of the main dais is

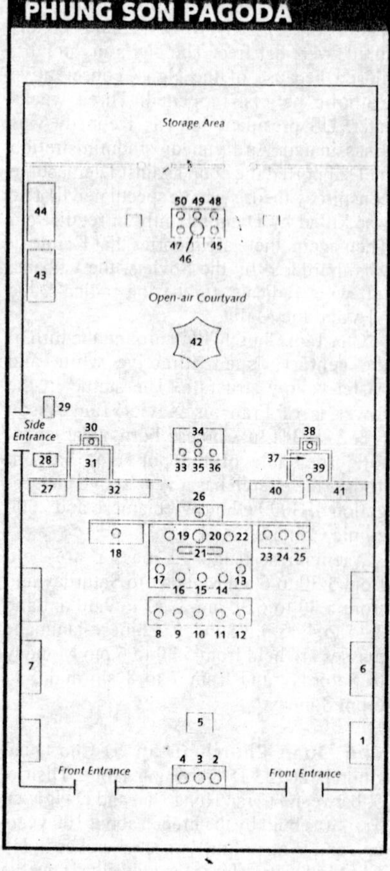

an altar with a statue of Bodhidharma, who brought Buddhism from India to China. The statue, which is made of Chinese ceramic, has a face with Indian features.

As you walk from the main sanctuary to the room with the open-air courtyard in the middle, you come to an altar with four statues on it, including a standing bronze Thich Ca Buddha of Thai origin. To the right is an altar with a glass case containing a statue made of sandalwood. The statue is claimed to be Long Vuong, the Dragon King, who brings rain. Around the pagoda building are a number of interesting monks' tombs.

PHUNG SON PAGODA

1 Dia Tang Vuong Bo Tat
2 Guardian
3 Guardian of the Pagoda
4 Tieu Dien, a Guardian
5 Donations Box
6 Judges of the Ten Regions of Hell
7 Judges of the Ten Regions of Hell
8 Van Thu Bo Tat
9 Quan The Am Bo Tat
10 A Di Da Buddha
11 Dai The Chi Bo Tat
12 Pho Hien Bo Tat
13 Guardian
14 Dai The Chi Bo Tat
15 A Di Da Buddha
16 Quan The Am Bo Tat
17 Guardians
18 Bodhidharma
19 Quan The Am Bo Tat
20 A Di Da Buddha
21 Statuettes of Quan the Am Bo Tat, Her Guardians & Thich Ca Buddha as a Child
22 Dai The Chi Bo Tat
23 Lang Nu
24 Quan The Am Bo Tat
25 Thien Tai
26 Memorial Tablets, Portraits of Ancestor Monks
27 Memorial Tablets, Portraits of Ancestor Monks
28 Desk with Old Photos of Monks Under Glass
29 Desk with Old Paper Money Under Glass
30 Statue of Hue Minh, Founder of the Pagoda
31 Rosewood Platform
32 Memorial Tablets, Portraits of Ancestor Monks
33 Thich Ca Buddha
34 Ameda
35 Bronze Thich Ca Buddha
37 Rosewood Platform
38 Statue of Head Monk Hue Thanh, Successor to Hue Minh
39 Sandalwood Statue of Long Vuong
40 Memorial Tablets, Portraits of Ancestor Monks
40 Memorial Tablets, Portraits of Ancestor Monks
42 Miniature Mountain made of Volcanic Rocks
43 Rosewood Platforms
44 Rosewood Platforms
45 Guardian
46 18-armed Chuan De
47 Guardian
48 Dai The Chi Bo Tat
49 A Di Da Buddha
50 Quan The Am Bo Tat

Prayers are held three times a day from 4 to 5 am, 4 to 5 pm and 6 to 7 pm. The main entrances are locked most of the time because of problems with theft, but the side entrance (to the left as you approach the building) is open from 5 am to 7 pm.

NORTH OF CHOLON

Places of Worship

Giac Lam Pagoda (Map 6) Giac Lam Pagoda, at 118 Đ Lac Long Quan, Tan Binh District, about 3km from Cholon, dates from 1744 and is believed to be the oldest pagoda in greater Ho Chi Minh City. Because the last reconstruction here was in 1900, the architecture, layout and ornamentation remain almost unaltered by the modernist renovations that have transformed so many other religious structures in Vietnam. Ten monks live at this Vietnamese Buddhist pagoda, which also incorporates aspects of Taoism and Confucianism. It is well worth the trip out here from central Saigon.

To the right of the gate to the pagoda compound are the ornate tombs of venerated monks. The *bo de* (bodhi, or pipal) tree in the front garden was the gift of a monk from Sri Lanka. Next to the tree is a regular feature seen in Vietnamese Buddhist temples, a gleaming white statue of Quan The Am Bo Tat standing on a lotus blossom (a symbol of purity).

The roof-line of the main building is decorated, inside and outside, with unusual blue-and-white porcelain plates. Through the main entrance there is a reception hall lined with funeral tablets and photos of the deceased. Roughly in the centre of the hall, near an old French chandelier, is a figure of 18-armed Chuan De. Note the carved hardwood columns which bear gilded Vietnamese inscriptions written in *nom* characters (Vietnamese script). The wall to the left is covered with portraits of great monks from previous generations. Their names and other biographical information are recorded on the vertical red tablets in gold nom characters. A box for donations sits nearby. Shoes should be removed when passing from the rough red floor tiles to the smaller, white-black-and-grey tiles.

On the other side of the wall from the monks' funeral tablets is the main sanctuary, which is filled with countless gilded figures. On the dais in the centre of the back row sits A Di Da (pronounced **ah**-zee-dah), the Buddha of the Past (Amitabha). To his right is Kasyape and to his left Anand; both are disciples of the Thich Ca Buddha (the historical Buddha Sakyamuni, whose real name was Siddhartha Gautama). Directly in front of A Di Da is a statue of the Thich Ca Buddha, flanked by two guardians. In front of Thich Ca is a tiny figure of the Thich Ca Buddha as a child. As always, he is clothed in a yellow robe.

The fat laughing fellow, seated with five children climbing all over him, is Ameda. To his left is Ngoc Hoang, the Taoist Jade Emperor, who presides over a world of innumerable supernatural beings. In the front row is a statue of the Thich Ca Buddha with two Bodhisattvas on each side. On the altars along the side walls of the sanctuary are various Bodhisattvas and the Judges of the 10 Regions of Hell. Each of the judges is holding a scroll resembling the handle of a fork.

The red and gold Christmas-tree-shaped object is a wooden altar bearing 49 lamps and 49 miniature statues of Bodhisattvas. People pray for sick relatives or ask for happiness by contributing kerosene for use in the lamps. Petitioners' names and those of ill family members are written on slips of paper that are attached to the branches of the tree.

The frame of the large bronze bell in the corner looks like a university bulletin board because petitioners have attached to it lists of names: the names of people seeking happiness and the names of the sick and the dead, placed there by relatives. It is believed that when the bell is rung, the sound will resonate to the heavens above and the heavens below, carrying with it the attached supplications.

Prayers here consist of chanting to the accompaniment of drums, bells and gongs and they follow a traditional rite seldom performed these days. Prayers are held from 4 to 5 am, 11 am to noon, 4 to 5 pm and 7 to 9 pm daily.

The best way to get to Giac Lam Pagoda from Cholon is to take ĐL Nguyen Chi Thanh or ĐL 3 Thang 2 to Đ Le Dai Hanh. Go north-westward on Đ Le Dai Hanh and turn right onto Đ Lac Long Quan. (Beware: the numbering on Đ Lac Long Quan is extremely confusing, starting over from 1 several times and at one point jumping to four digits. In many places, odd and even numbers are on the same side of the street.) Walk 100m and the pagoda gate will be on your left. It is open to visitors from 6 am to 9 pm.

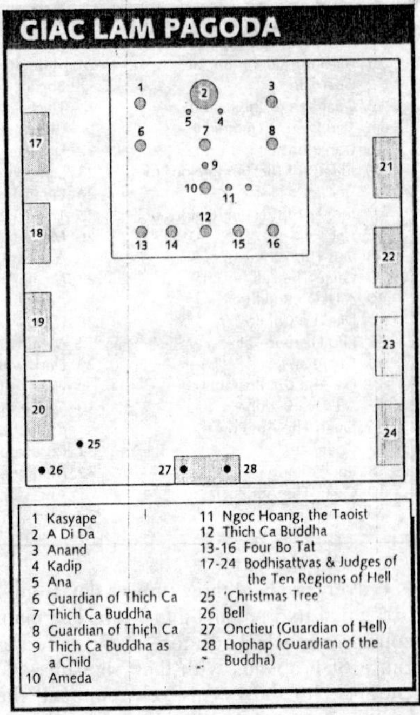

Giac Vien Pagoda (Map 7) Giac Vien Pagoda is architecturally similar to Giac Lam. Both share an atmosphere of scholarly serenity, though Giac Vien, which is right next to Dam Sen Lake in District 11, is in a more rural setting. Giac Vien Pagoda was founded by Hai Tinh Giac Vien about 200 years ago. It is said that Emperor Gia Long, who died in 1819, used to worship at Giac Vien. Today, about 10 monks live at the pagoda.

The pagoda is in a relatively poor part of the city. Because of the impossibly confusing numbering on Đ Lac Long Quan, the best way to get to Giac Vien Pagoda from Cholon is to take ĐL Nguyen Chi Thanh or ĐL 3 Thang 2 to Đ Le Dai Hanh. Turn left (south-west) off Đ Le Dai Han onto Đ Binh

SANCTUARY OF GIAC VIEN PAGODA

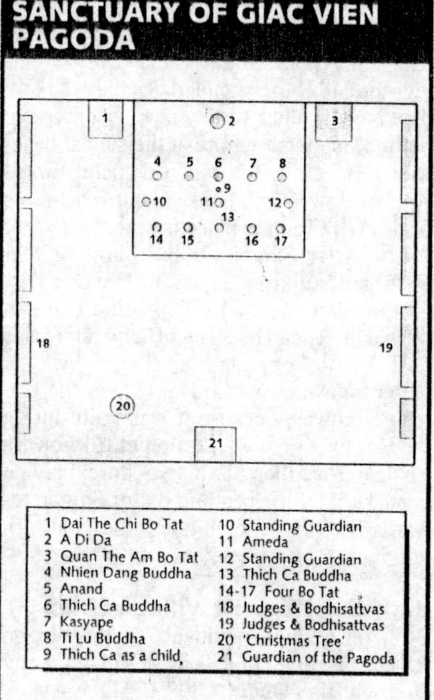

Thoi and turn right (north) at Đ Lac Long Quan. The gate leading to the pagoda is at 247 Đ Lac Long Quan.

Pass through the gate and go several hundred metres down a potholed, dirt road, turning left at the T-intersection and right at the fork. You will pass several impressive tombs of monks on the right before arriving at the pagoda itself.

The first chamber as you enter the pagoda is lined with funeral tablets. At the back of the second chamber is a statue of Hai Tinh Giac Vien, holding a horse-tail switch. Nearby portraits are of his disciples and successors as head monk. A donation box sits to the left of the statue. Opposite Hai Tinh Giac Vien is a representation of Chuan De, who is flanked by two guardians.

The main sanctuary is on the other side of the wall behind the Hai Tinh Giac Vien statue. A Di Da is at the back of the dais. Directly in front of him is the Thich Ca Buddha, flanked by his disciples Anand (on the left) and Kasyape (on the right). To the right of Kasyape is the Ti Lu Buddha; to the left of Anand is the Nhien Dang Buddha. At the foot of the Thich Ca Buddha is a small figure of Thich Ca as a child. Fat, laughing Ameda is seated with children climbing all over him; on either side of him stand guardians. In the front row of the dais is Thich Ca with two Bodhisattvas on each side.

In front of the dais is a fantastic brass incense basin with fierce dragon heads emerging from each side. On the altar to the left of the dais is Dai The Chi Bo Tat, on the altar to the right is Quan The Am Bo Tat. The Guardian of the Pagoda is against the wall opposite the dais. Nearby is a 'Christmas tree' similar to the one in Giac Lam Pagoda. Lining the side walls are the Judges of the 10 Regions of Hell (holding scrolls) and 18 Bodhisattvas.

Giac Vien Pagoda is open to the public from 7 am to 7 pm daily. Prayers are held from 4 to 5 am, 8 to 10 am, 2 to 3 pm, 4 to 5 pm and 7 to 9 pm daily.

Parks

Dam Sen Park (Map 5) Dam Sen Park, at 3 Đ Hoa Binh, District 11, near the Giac Vien Pagoda, boasts the fanciest facilities of all Ho Chi Minh City's parks and is a highly popular place with Saigonese families and lovers. The park, centred around enormous Dan Sen Lake, features several gardens done in different themes, a Chinese-style tea house, water rides, and it even has a monorail running though it. Other attractions include the Sea Biology Museum, Underwater-World Cave and pools decorated with giant white swans and galloping horses.

Entry costs US$1.60.

Ho Ky Hoa Park (Map 2) Ho Ky Hoa Park (whose name means Lake and Gardens), is a children's amusement park in District 10, just off ĐL 3 Thang 2. It is near the Hoa Binh Theatre and behind Vietnam Quoc Tu Pagoda. There are paddleboats, rowboats and sailboats for hire. Fishing is allowed in the lakes and a small swimming pool is open to the public for part of the year. The cafes are open year-round and there are also two arcades of Japanese video games. Within the park boundaries is the rather expensive Ky Hoa Hotel. Ho Ky Hoa Park is open from 7 am to 9.30 pm daily. It is always crowded on Sundays.

SUBURBAN ATTRACTIONS

Orchid Farm

There are a number of orchid farms *(vuon cay kieng)* in suburban Ho Chi Minh City, but most are concentrated in the Thu Duc District. These places raise more than orchids. The Artex Saigon Orchid Farm, east of Ho Chi Minh City, is the largest of all, with 50,000 plants representing 1000 varieties. It is primarily a commercial concern, but visitors are welcome to stop by to relax in the luxurious garden.

The farm, founded in 1970, uses revenues from the sale of orchid flowers for its operating budget, but makes its real profit selling orchid plants, which take six years to mature and are thus very expensive. In addition to varieties imported from overseas, the farm has a collection of orchids native to Vietnam. Ask to see the orange-yellow Cattleya orchid variety called Richard Nixon; they have another variety named for Joseph Stalin. The nurseries are at their most beautiful just before Tet, when demand for all sorts of flowers and house plants reaches its peak. After Tet, the place is bare.

The Artex Saigon Orchid Farm (☎ 896 6686) is 15km from Saigon in Thu Duc District, a rural part of Ho Chi Minh City, on the way to Bien Hoa. The official address is 5/81 Xa Lo Vong Dai, but this highway is better known as Xa Lo Dai Han or the Korean Highway, because it was built during the war by Koreans. At kilometre 14 on Xa Lo Dai Han there is a two-storey police post. Turn left (if heading out of Saigon towards Bien Hoa), continue 300m and turn left again.

PABLO GARCIA GASTAR

Orchids are a thriving local export industry.

Binh Quoi Tourist Village (Map 2)

Built on a small peninsula in the Saigon River, the Binh Quoi Tourist Village, Lang Du Lich Binh Quoi (☎ 899 1831), is a slick tourist trap operated by Saigon Tourist. Backpackers are few on the ground, but upmarket tourists get brought out here by the busload and some city-weary locals also seem to like it.

The village is essentially a park featuring boat rides, water puppet shows, a restaurant, a swimming pool, tennis courts, a camping ground, a guesthouse, bungalows and amusements for the kids. The park puts in a plug for Vietnam's ethnic minorities by staging traditional-style minority weddings accompanied by music. There are some alligators kept in an enclosure for viewing, but so far no alligator-wrestling shows. River cruises can be fun – the smaller cruise boats have 16 seats and the larger ones have 100 seats.

Next door to the water puppet theatre, you can make bookings for the local nightlife. A sign in English advertises all sorts of fun activities:

> Saigon Tourist Brings You: *Magical Evenings.* Sunset cruise, traditional show, dinner under the stars. Daily: cruise and dinner show US$20 (5.30 to 9 pm); cultural show alone US$5 (7 to 8 pm).

Binh Quoi Bungalows (☎ 899 1831 or 899 4103, 1147 Đ Xo Viet Nghe Tinh, Binh Quoi) is perhaps one of the better value places to stay here. Built on stilts above the water, the bungalows give you a little taste of traditional river life in the Mekong Delta, but with air-conditioning and tennis courts. The standard price range here is US$10 to US$18. Room No 44 goes for US$22 and has the best views of the river.

Binh Quoi Tourist Village is 8km north of central Saigon in the Binh Thanh district. You can get there by cyclo, motorcycle or taxi. A much slower alternative is to charter a boat from the Me Linh Square area on the Saigon River.

Saigon Water Park

The recently completed Saigon Water Park (☎ 897 0456) is a giant oasis in the suburbs of Ho Chi Minh City. This refreshing complex on the banks of the Saigon River is chock-full of pools and water rides: loop-the-loop slides, a children's wading pool and even a wave pool.

The setting of this Australian-built leisure land is the complete antithesis to most of Asia's kitsch theme parks and is the perfect antidote for anyone who needs to cool down from an overdose of pagodas and museums.

Though perhaps not a top priority for those with only a day or two to soak up the sights of the city, anyone with kids and a half-day to spare will quickly come to appreciate this wet and wonderful playground on a sweltering Ho Chi Minh City day. There is also a restaurant with fine views over the river.

The park is open from 11 am to 7 pm Monday to Saturday 8 am to 8 pm Sunday and public holidays. The best time to avoid the crowds is between 11 am and 2 pm on weekdays (most Vietnamese stay out of the midday sun).

The all-you-can-splash entry fee is US$4.30. People under 1.1m in height (ie, some children and low-stature adults) pay US$2.50.

Saigon Water Park is on Đ Kha Van Can, in the Thu Duc District (near Go Dua Bridge). It's too far for cyclos, but you can take a metered taxi for about US$4.

The park also runs an air-con minibus shuttle costing US$0.40 one-way. The bus departs to/from the Ben Thanh Market every hour on the half-hour. The opening hours are 9 am to 5 pm Monday to Friday, from 9 am to 8 pm Saturday and from 8 am to 8 pm Sunday and public holidays.

WHAT'S FREE

Some of Ho Chi Minh City's greatest attractions require little or no outlay of dong.

Days could be spent just wandering the streets of the city, discovering architectural masterpieces and exploring the city's parks, lakes, temples and pagodas.

Ho Chi Minh City's bustling markets (see the Shopping chapter later) provide a colourful close-up look at how local Vietnamese merchants vend their wares. The city's myriad art galleries provide even more places to explore.

ACTIVITIES

Swimming

Ho Chi Minh City's tropical climate makes swimming the ideal way to stay cool and get exercise. If you don't make it to excellent Saigon Water Park (see Suburban Attractions earlier in this chapter), there are several fine swimming pools at plush tourist hotels. You needn't stay at these hotels to use the facilities, but you must pay an admission fee of US$5 to US$10 per day. Hotels offering access to their pools include the Embassy (not so good), Omni, Equatorial, Metropole, Palace and Rex. About the only major hotel which does not offer public access to its pool is the New World.

There are a number of public pools where local Vietnamese go and some of the newer ones are in very good condition. These pools charge by the hour and it works out to be very cheap if you're staying only a short time. One such place is the Olympic-sized Lam Son Pool (☎ 358 028) at 342 D Tran Binh Trong, District 5. The weekday charge is around US$0.50 per hour and rises to US$1 on weekends. For US$1.50 per hour you can visit the pool at the Workers' Club at 55B Đ Nguyen Thi Minh Khai, District 3.

The International Club (Map 2; ☎ 865 7695), at 285B Đ Cach Mang Thang Tam, District 10, also has a good outdoor swimming pool, as well as sauna and steam rooms, an exercise gym and beauty salon. The bizarre interior of the place resembles an old hotel, but it is very popular with expats and attracts a good number of Asian businessmen looking to wind down from the stresses of corporate Vietnam. Entry to the pool costs US$1.50 Monday to Friday and US$2.25 on weekends. There is also a massage service, and a US$9 ticket entitles you to a 45 minute rub-down and all-day use of the club's facilities. The management here is serious about keeping its massage legitimate: the rules and regulations posted in the massage rooms state clearly that 'all club employees, male and female, are required to wear underwear at all times'!

Water-skiing

Perhaps sewage-skiing would be a more apt term. The Saigon River is pretty murky and there is no telling what sort of contagious diseases you might contract by frolicking in the bubbling broth. Nevertheless, some brave – or foolish – foreigners have on occasion rented a speedboat from Saigon Tourist (or elsewhere) and headed upstream to Bien Hoa (30km east of Saigon) where the water is merely brown rather than black. Probably you'd be better off heading down to the Mekong River for this activity, though that will require at least an overnight trip.

Massage

Perhaps the best rub-down in Ho Chi Minh City is at the Vietnamese Traditional Medicine Institute (☎ 839 6697) at 185 Đ Cong Quye, District 1. Here you can enjoy a no-nonsense massage performed by well-trained blind masseuses (a team of three men and five women). The cost is just US$2 per hour in a fan room (air-con comfort will set you back an extra dollar). There is also a sauna room available here for US$1.50 per hour, though the institute does not offer fluffy new age music or aromatherapy remedies. Walk-in service is from 9 am to 8 pm daily.

Most upmarket hotels offer some kind of massage service (some more legitimate than others). Another interesting option is the International Club (see the Swimming entry earlier in this chapter).

Golf

The Vietnam Golf and Country Club is another cash cow brought to you by Saigon Tourist. It's actually a joint venture with a Taiwan-based company (it's rumoured the Taiwanese were more interested in the appreciating value of the real estate than the 36 hole golf course). The course was the first in Vietnam to provide night golfing under floodlights.

The club, Cau Lac Bo Golf Quoc Te Viet Nam (☎ 832 2084, fax 832 2083), at 40–42 Đ Nguyen Trai, Thu Duc District, is in Lam Vien Park, about 15km east of central Saigon. Membership ranges from US$5000 to US$60,000, but paying visitors are welcome. It may be worth coming here to use the driving range, which costs US$10, or you can play a full round for US$50. Other facilities include tennis courts and a swimming pool.

Song Be Golf Resort (☎ 855 800, fax 855 516), in Song Be Province, is a slick Singaporean-Vietnamese joint venture 20km north of Saigon. Unfortunately, this resort is for members and their guests only; membership costs from US$7000 up to US$75,000. The villas cannot be purchased, but they can be leased for 50 years.

The Rach Chiec Driving Range (☎ 896 0756) is a good place to practice your swing. A one month membership costs US$70 and gets progressively cheaper the longer you join for. Clubs (US$4 to US$6) and shoes (US$6) are available to rent, and a local instructor can be hired for US$12 per hour. The range is open from 6 am to 10 pm daily. It's in An Phu Village, a 20 minute drive north along Highway 1 from central Saigon.

In the pipeline is a golf course at Gia Dinh Park (Cong Vien Gia Dinh). This is in the northern part of the Phu Nhuan District, close to the airport. When completed, it will certainly be the closest golf course to central Saigon.

Bowling

The Saigon Superbowl (☎ 885 0188, fa: 845 8119) is near the airport at A43 Đ Truong Son, Tan Binh District. There are 32 lanes here, though at peak times there can be a two hour wait for a lane. You can entertain yourself in the meantime at the adjacent video game arcade. Bowling costs US$3 (US$4 after 5 pm). Shoe rental is US$0.50.

The Bowling Centre (☎ 864 3784) is in the International Club at 285B Đ Cach Mang Thang Tam, District 10. There are 12 lanes here and 65 video game machines. It's open from 10 am until midnight daily.

Fitness Clubs

Most major hotels in Ho Chi Minh City will allow you to use their facilities (gymnasium, pool, sauna, tennis courts etc) for the payment of a reasonable daily fee. You do not need to be a guest at the hotel, though the hotel has the right to refuse you (which they might do if the facilities become overcrowded). The fees vary, so you'll need to make inquiries locally.

Hash House Harriers

This loosely strung organisation meets once a week for a jogging session followed by a drinking session. The times and meeting places change, as do the people organising it, but at the time of writing it was 2.30 pm on Sunday at the Oscar Hotel. Look for the latest announcements on the notice board at the Norfolk Hotel (117 Đ Le Thanh Ton, District 1). Announcements may also appear in expat pubs around town or in local magazines.

Roller Skating

There is a roller skating rink in Cong Vien Van Hoa Park, adjacent to Reunification Palace, and another rink across from the Saigon Star Hotel at 204 Đ Nguyen Thi Minh Khai, District 3.

Nha Van Hoa is a small park in Cholon on the south side of ĐL Tran Hung Dao between Đ Ngo Quyen and ĐL Nguyen Tri Phuong. Unusually, it's a park with nightlife. Features include an outdoor stage with live music (awful wailing, but they try), an indoor roller skating rink and video game arcade. There is also a disco of sorts, including a karaoke hall with dance lessons.

LANGUAGE COURSES

Universities require that you study 10 hours per week. Lessons usually last for two hours, for which you pay tuition of around US$5. The vast majority of foreign language students enrol at the General University of Ho Chi Minh City, Truong Dai Hoc Tong Hop (Map 2) at 12 Đ Binh Hoang, District 5. It's near the south-west corner of ĐL Nguyen Van Cu and ĐL Tran Phu.

An alternative to government-run language courses, the privately-run BEST Language Centre (☎ 830 0366, fax 830 0364) is at 81A Đ Nguyen Son Ha, District 3.

Places to Stay

The tourist boom of the early 90s initially created a shortage of hotel space, but overbuilding, the recent economic crisis in Asia and a decline in tourist arrivals has now produced a glut. At the time of writing there were well over 100 new mini-hotels vying for customers, and a handful of joint-venture high-rise hotels stalled flat in the middle of construction – some say they'll never be completed. This means that travellers are now in a good negotiating position, whether you're at a grungy guesthouse or a top-end hotel. Today, rooms can be found in four-star hotels (many operating with as low as 20% occupancy) for as little as US$88!

Even at the fanciest hotels, it's possible to get discounts if you're staying long term (which often means three days or more). Booking through some foreign or domestic travel agencies can also net you a discount. For practical purposes, the rates quoted in this book are the short-term, walk-in rates.

Another factor to take into account is tax. There is a Value Added Tax (VAT) of 10% imposed by the Vietnamese government (in cheaper places this is generally figured into the room price) and top end hotels often tack on a 5% service fee.

HOTELS

Most of the large hotels *(khach san)* and guesthouses *(nha khach* or *nha nghi)* are government-owned or foreign-Vietnamese joint ventures. As well as large hotels, there is also a rapidly increasing number of private and joint-venture mini-hotels. Sadly, with the number of fantastic old French-colonial buildings in Ho Chi Minh City, a scant few have been renovated for tourist lodging, and those that have remain out of the budget for many travellers. The city's potential for charming bed and breakfast-type inns is completely untapped.

It's always a good idea to take a look at a room to make sure that you're getting what you wanted and that you are not paying for something you don't need.

Official policy is to insist that capitalist tourists pay double what Vietnamese pay but, even so, the prices are still reasonable. Some hotels give a big discount to Overseas Vietnamese, a policy that most foreigners regard as overtly racist.

Many hotels will insist that you leave your passport or visa with reception so that they can register you with the police. While police registration was indeed required in the past, this is no longer true in Ho Chi Minh City (but *is* true in many less-developed provinces). What the hotels are doing is simply holding your documents because they want to be sure you don't run off with the towels or TV – police registration has nothing to do with it. While there's nothing wrong with the staff checking your documents, there's really no need for them to take your valuable papers away from you, assuming that you paid for your room in advance. If you resent this, then say so.

Security

Hotel security can be a problem – especially in the cheapest places. Some hotels have a latch where you can fix a padlock to the outside of your room's door – if so, use your own lock. Aside from locking the door to your room, keep your bags in the cabinets or closets that are often provided for this purpose and lock these with a padlock, or cable and padlock combination. This way you won't have to worry about hotel employees with room keys. If there is a safe in your room or at reception, you should make use of it.

Reservations

Even during the busiest season, there is seldom much need for reservations in Ho Chi Minh City – you can always find a place to stay. Moreover, a reservation usually nullifies any chance of negotiating the room tariff.

However, if you do book ahead by fax or email, most hotels (including budget guesthouses) can arrange airport pickup.

DORMITORIES

While there are dormitories *(nha tro)* in Ho Chi Minh City, most of these are officially off-limits to foreigners. In this case, the government's motives are not simply to charge you more money for accommodation – there is a significant chance of getting robbed while sleeping in a Vietnamese dormitory. Also, by Western standards, many of these places are substandard.

Luckily, the concept of a relatively upmarket, foreigner-only dormitory has caught on. Many of these dormitories are actually regular hotel rooms with just two or four beds; you can find these in some backpacker hotels in the Pham Ngu Lao area.

COSTS

For the purposes of this book, budget accommodation is defined as costing less than US$25. From US$25 to US$60 would be mid-range and anything over that is top end. It's important to realise that many Vietnamese hotels offer a wide range of prices in the same building. For example, on budget hotel listed here has room prices running from US$12 to US$70. Cheap rooms are almost always on the top floor because few hotels have lifts and most guests paying US$70 are not keen to walk up seven storeys or more.

WHERE TO STAY

Different categories of travellers have staked out their own turf in Ho Chi Minh City. Budget travellers tend to congregate around the Pham Ngu Lao area, at the western end of District 1. Travellers with a little more cash to spare tend to prefer the more upmarket hotels concentrated around Đ Dong Khoi, on the eastern side of District 1. French travellers seems to have an affinity for District 3. Cholon attracts plenty of people from Hong Kong and Taiwan – but Western backpackers are rare. Despite the availability of cheap accommodation, it seems that the herd instinct is too powerful a force to resist.

If you don't really know where you want to stay, but you're limited by your budget, it's best to take a taxi to the Pham Ngu Lao area and proceed on foot. Touts from the hotels hang around the airport looking for business, and taxi drivers will often shove hotel name cards into your hands. Remember, if the hotels weren't paying commissions the touts wouldn't bother. If you don't want to lug your bags around (which also makes you a prime target for cyclo drivers and kids who will persist in taking to you a 'great' hotel) you might consider dropping your gear at one of the travellers' cafes. Most won't mind keeping an eye on it for you and they'll happily show you the programs they're offering. It shouldn't take too long to find something.

PLACES TO STAY – BUDGET

The vast majority of popular budget accommodation is found in the Pham Ngu Lao area, Ho Chi Minh City's very own backpackers' ghetto. Closer to the city centre there are a number of cheap places scattered around the Dong Khoi area and in Cholon.

Pham Ngu Lao Area (Map 4)

Đ Pham Ngu Lao, Đ De Tham and Đ Bui Vien form the few blocks that are the heart of the budget-traveller haven. These streets and the adjoining alleys, collectively known as Pham Ngu Lao, contain a treasure-trove of cheap accommodation and cafes catering to the budget end of the market. At last count there were close to 100 places to stay in the area.

Be warned: a major construction project is under way to redevelop the northern side of Đ Pham Ngu Lao into the enormous Saigon Commercial Center. It is estimated the project will take to around late 2002 and will generate a considerable amount of dust and noise.

Near the bottom of the barrel is the ***Liberty 3 Hotel*** *(☎ 836 9522, fax 836 4557, 187 Đ Pham Ngu Lao)*, a state-run monstrosity near the corner of Đ De Tham. It's cheap but rundown and in dire need of a facelift (or a ball and chain). Fan singles/doubles cost US$5/6.50 and air-con doubles are US$12 to US$16.

The first place in this neighbourhood to offer dormitory accommodation was the

Tan Thanh Thanh Hotel *(☎ 886 1751, fax 836 7027,* **@** *ththanhhotel@tlnet.com.vn, 205 Đ Pham Ngu Lao)*. Dorm beds start at US$3 and private rooms cost from US$5 to US$10.

Another old favourite with travellers is the pleasant and friendly ***Hotel 211*** *(☎ 836 7353, fax 836 1883, 211 Đ Pham Ngu Lao)*. It has dorm beds for US$3, while singles/doubles cost US$7/8 with fan or US$10/12 with air-con. All rooms have a private bath with hot water.

Another clean and friendly place is the new ***Mai Phai Hotel*** *(☎ 836 5868, fax 837 1575, 209 Đ Pham Ngu Lao)*. Rooms feature minibar, satellite TV, and IDD phone. Rates here are very reasonable at US$12 to US$20, which includes breakfast at the in-house restaurant.

The ***Ocean Hotel*** *(☎ 836 8231, 217 Đ Pham Ngu Lao)* has fan rooms for US$8. Air-con rates are US$12/15. Up the street a little, similar rates and slightly better standards prevail at the popular ***Hotel 269*** *(☎ 836 7345, fax 836 8171, 269 Đ Pham Ngu Lao)*.

Some travellers have had good things to say about the ***Quyen Thanh Hotel*** *(☎ 836 8570, fax 836 9946, 212 Đ De Tham)*. Air-con rates begin at US$15 and larger rooms cost US$20. There is an excellent souvenir shop on the ground floor.

The new, 32-room ***Southern Hotel*** *(☎ 837 0922, fax 837 0923,* **@** *southernhotel @hcm.vnn.vn, 216 Đ De Tham)* is at the top end of the budget hotels in the area. Rooms are spacious and squeaky clean, and all feature minibar and satellite TV. Rooms range from US$12/15 to US$30/50.

Another recommended place on this street is the ***Hotel 265*** *(☎ 836 1883, 265 Đ De Tham)*, with dorm beds for US$3 and air-con rooms from US$10/12. Practically next door is the equally good ***Le Le 2*** *(☎ 836 8585, fax 836 8787)* – also known as the Vinh Guesthouse – with air-con comfort for US$8 to US$15. Ditto for the ***Peace Hotel*** *(☎ 836 8824, 272 Đ De Tham)* across the street.

The ***Lan Anh Hotel*** *(☎ 836 5197, fax 836 5196, 252 Đ De Tham)* is another spiffy place which charges from US$7 to US$18.

The friendly owner at the ***Anh Dao Guesthouse*** *(☎ 836 7351, 235 Đ De Tham)* has basic fan singles for US$4 and US$5, doubles for US$6 and US$8; add a couple of dollars for air-con. There are similar rates at the ***Thanh Ngi Guesthouse*** *(☎ 836 7917, 207 Đ De Tham)*, the ***Thanh Thanh*** *Guesthouse (☎ 836 8813, 191–193 Đ De Tham)* and the ***Hoang Anh Mini-Hotel*** *(☎ 836 7815, 266 Đ De Tham)*.

The ***Ngoc Dang Mini-Hotel*** *(☎ 836 9419, 254 Đ De Tham)* charges US$7 to US$10 for fan rooms and US$12 to US$18 for air-con.

Near the corner of Đ De Tham, the ***A Hotel*** *(☎ 836 8566, fax 836 0442, 34 ĐL Tran Hung Dao)* would be a nicer place to stay if it weren't right on the noisy main boulevard. Still, it's friendly enough and cheap – dorm beds cost US$3 and fan rooms are US$7/8.

Friendly ***Bao Chau Hotel*** *(☎ 836 7579, 355 Đ Pham Ngu Lao)* is a decent value at US$6/8 for fan singles/doubles, or US$12 for an air-con room. Also in the neighbourhood is the ***Hai Son Hotel*** *(☎ 836 9024, fax 836 0221, 357 Đ Pham Ngu Lao)*, which has Chinese-speaking staff and charges US$18/20 for air-con singles/doubles with satellite TV. It's a similar operation at the nearby, neon-lit ***Tan Kim Long Hotel*** *(☎ 836 8136, fax 836 8230, 365 Đ Pham Ngu Lao)*.

The ***My Man Mini-Hotel*** *(☎ 836 7544, 373/20 Đ Pham Ngu Lao)* is down a tiny alley behind the Thai Binh Market and, yes, the name is both English and Vietnamese. Rooms with air-con cost US$10 to US$15. In the same alley you'll find the ***Coco Loco Guesthouse*** *(☎ 837 2647, 373/2 Đ Pham Ngu Lao)*, which charges US$5/7 for fan rooms and US$8 to $12 for air-con rooms. One more place tucked away in this alley is the ***Nhat Thai Hotel*** *(☎ 836 0184, 373/10 Đ Pham Ngu Lao)*, whose literature promises to 'serve you devotedly and perfectly'. Air-con rooms rent for US$10 and US$12.

In the same vicinity is warm-hearted Madam Cuc's ***Hotel 127*** *(☎ 836 8761, fax*

836 0658, 127 Đ Cong Quynh). This place is raved about for its welcoming reception. Rooms cost US$7 to US$20. Nearly opposite, at No 168, is the ***Tuan Anh Hotel*** *(☎ 835 6989)*, where rooms cost US$23.

Just one block north-west of Thai Binh Market is ***Hoang Yen Mini-Hotel*** *(Map 2; ☎ 839 1348, fax 829 8540, 83A Đ Bui Thi Xuan)*. The owner speaks French, but not much English. Singles/twins are US$14/18 and the tariff includes breakfast.

About 100m south of, and parallel to, Đ Pham Ngu Lao is Đ Bui Vien, which is rapidly being transformed into a solid string of guesthouses and mini-hotels in the US$6 to US$12 range. By the demographics you can tell this street has been written up well in Japanese guidebooks.

We've personally found ***Hotel 64*** *(☎ 836 5073, fax 836 0658, 64 Đ Bui Vien)* to be a good one. Others on Bui Vien named for their address include the ***41 Guesthouse*** *(☎ 836 5228)*, ***96 Guesthouse*** *(☎ 836 0764)* and ***Guesthouse 97*** *(☎ 836 8801, fax 836 4899)*.

Larger places on Đ Bui Vien include the ***Hai Duong Hotel*** *(☎ 836 9080, fax 836 9022)* at No 82, the ***Hong Kong Mini-Hotel*** *(☎ 836 4904)* at No 22 and ***Hong Quyen Hotel*** *(☎/fax 836 8829)* at No 31.

Mid-size spots to consider include ***Hotel Hong Loi*** *(☎ 836 8076, 47 Đ Bui Vien)*, the ***Van Trang Hotel*** *(☎ 836 8969, fax 836 4230, 80 Đ Bui Vien)*, ***Tuan Anh Guesthouse*** *(☎ 836 0166, fax 836 0427, Đ 103 Bui Vien)* and ***Vu Chau Hotel*** *(☎ 836 8464, 37 Đ Bui Vien)*.

Đ Bui Vien's smaller guesthouses include the ***Hop Thanh Guesthouse*** *(☎ 836 7108, 112 Đ Bui Vien)*, ***Linh Thu Guesthouse*** *(☎ 836 8421, 72 Đ Bui Vien)*, ***Minh Phuc Guesthouse*** *(☎ 836 0537, 58 Đ Bui Vien)*, ***Phuong Lan Guesthouse*** *(☎ 836 9569, 70 Đ Bui Vien)*, ***Thanh Guesthouse*** *(☎ 836 9222, 53 Đ Bui Vien)* and ***Vuong Hoa Guesthouse*** *(☎ 836 9491, 36 Đ Bui Vien)*.

Hai Ha Mini-Hotel *(☎ 836 5565, fax 836 7256)* at No 78, ***Phuong Hoang Mini-Hotel*** *(☎/fax 836 8631)* at No 25 and ***Huy Doc Hotel*** (☎ 837 0538, fax 836 9591) at No 74. All have satellite TV. ***Minh Chau Guesthouse*** *(☎/fax 836 7588, @ minhchauhotel@hcm.vnn.vn, 75 Đ Bui Vien)* offers email services.

Mini-Hotel Alley (Map 4) Perhaps the closest concentration of lodgings in Ho Chi Minh City is in the alley one street south of Đ De Tham. The alley is flanked by (and addressed as an extension of) Đ Bui Vien and Đ Pham Ngu Lao. These places are all recent constructions, and are virtually identical. Most are family-run and the price range hovers between US$6 and US$10 for fan rooms, while bigger air-con rooms (some with balconies) generally cost between US$12 and US$18. Due to space contraints, we have not marked the hotels of this alley on the Pham Ngu Lao map (Map 4), however they can all be found in the strip we have designated Mini-Hotel Alley.

Right in the middle of the alley, we can recommend ***Mini-Hotel Cam*** *(☎ 836 7622, @ kevinkien@hcm.fpt.vn, 40/31 Đ Bui Vien)* for cleanliness and safety.

There have been a stream of good reports on both ***Bi Saigon*** and ***Bee Saigon*** *(☎ 836 0678, fax 836 7947)*. Both these mini-hotels are at 185/26 Đ Pham Ngu Lao.

Other travellers have praised ***Hung Mini-Hotel*** *(☎ 836 7[illegible]8, 40/14 Đ Bui Vien)* and ***40/18 Guesthouse*** *(☎/fax 836 7495)* at 40/18.

Both the ***Giang Mini-Hotel*** *(☎ 836 7495, 40/26 Đ Bui Vien)* and ***Hoang Hoa Guesthouse*** *(☎ 836 1915, @ honghoa@bdvn.vnd.net, 182/28 Đ Pham Ngu Lao)* offer email services, the latter with satellite TV.

Others squeezed into the Đ Pham Ngu Lao-half of the alley include the ***Chau Long Mini-Hotel*** *(☎ 836 9667, fax 837 0116)* at 185/8, ***Dung Hotel*** *(☎ 836 7049)* at 185/6, ***Hotel Thao Nhi*** *(☎ 836 0020)* at 185/26 and ***Mini-Hotel Xinh*** *(☎ 836 7339)* at 185/14.

On the Đ Bui Vien half are ***Hotel Thanh*** *(☎ 836 1924)* at 40/6, ***Linh Mini-Hotel*** *(☎/fax 836 9641)* – 40/10, ***Mi Mi Guesthouse*** *(☎ 836 9645)* at 40/5 and ***Mini-Hotel Hau*** *(☎ 836 9536)* at 40/9. You might want to try the ***Titi Mini-Hotel*** *(☎ 836 0156)* at 40/12, ***Quang Guesthouse*** *(☎ 836 9079)* at 40/7, ***Mini-Hotel Huong*** *(☎ 836 9158)* at 40/19 or the *Ngu Lan Guesthouse* (☎ *836 0566*) at 40/11. Two of the newest additions here are *Ly Ly* (☎ *837 1717*) at 40/2 and ***Phong*** (☎ *836 5221*) at 40/14.

In the next alley up from here, between the popular Zen and Bodhi Tree vegetarian restaurants, is the friendly ***Linh Linh Hotel*** (☎ *836 1851, 175/14 Đ Pham Ngu Lao*).

Miss Loi's Neighbourhood (Map 4) A quiet alternative about 10 minutes' walk from Đ Pham Ngu Lao is a string of guesthouses along a narrow alley connecting Đ Co Giang and Đ Co Bac. This area is close to the hoopla, but far enough away for you not to have to deal with touts every time you step outside. To reach the guesthouses walk south-east on Đ Co Bac and turn left after you pass the *nuoc mam* (fish sauce) shops.

The first hotel to appear here was ***Miss Loi's Guesthouse*** (☎ *836 7973, 178/20 Đ Co Giang*). Fan rooms cost US$8 to US$10 and air-con rooms are US$12. Zany Miss Loi throws in breakfast free and even has her own beauty salon! Many of her neighbours are jumping into this business and the area seems destined to develop into another budget-travellers' haven.

Directly across from Miss Loi's is the six-room ***Xuan Thu Guesthouse*** (☎ *836 9335 178/17 Đ Co Giang*). Dorm beds cost US$3, US$5/6 for a fan single or US$8 for a fan double and US$10 for an air-con double. Breakfast is included in the tariff. Similar rates prevail next door at the new ***Bich Hong*** (☎ *836 0841, 171/16–32 Đ Co Bac*).

Other alternatives in the area include the slightly weathered ***Guesthouse Thanh*** (*71/1E Đ Co Bac*), across from Bich Hong, and the quiet ***Ngoc Hue Guesthouse*** (☎ *836 0089, fax 835 5350,* ⓔ *nghue@kst.cinetvn.com, 171/22 Đ Co Bac*), set back from the alleyway; fan rooms go for US$6, or US$10/12 for air-con singles/doubles.

Two more places to consider are ***Kim Loan Guesthouse*** (☎ *836 8351, fax 836 7687,* ⓔ *ntkimloan@hcm.vnn.vn, 171/1 Đ Co Bac*), which has large rooms from US$6 to US$10, and neighbouring ***Minh Guesthouse*** (☎ *836 4153, 171/3 Đ Co Bac*), which charges the same.

Other Neighbourhoods (Map 4) There are several more options on the streets splintering off from the roundabout with the mounted-horseman statue near the New World Hotel. Consider checking out the ***Oriole Hotel*** (☎ *832 3494, fax 839 5919, 74 Đ Le Thi Rieng*). It's a friendly mini-hotel with comfortable and clean air-con rooms from US$15 to US$24.

There are several choices near the Ben Thanh Market, north of the Pham Ngu Lao area. The ***Galaxy Hotel*** (☎ *822 3283, fax 829 2799, 190 Đ Le Thanh Ton*) has gone a bit downhill recently, but then again so have the rates. Fan rooms rent for US$10, and air-con rooms cost US$18 and US$20.

Dong Khoi Area (Map 3)

Nga Quan (☎ *824 2471, fax 829 2235, 10/1 Đ Ho Huan Nghiep*) is a friendly choice, tucked down a narrow alley in the heart of downtown Saigon. Quiet air-con rooms with satellite TV, minibar and bathtub rent for US$20 – decidedly good value.

New Hotel (☎ *824 1812, 14 Đ Ho Huan Nghiep*) is close to the foregoing and offers air-con singles from US$14 to US$23 and doubles from US$19 to US$29. Single/double suites cost US$49/54.

One of the better deals in the city centre is the ***Khach San Dien Luc*** (☎ *822 9058, fax 822 9385, 5/11 Đ Nguyen Sieu*). This place is owned and run by the local electricity company and has the sterility and look of a new hospital. Rooms cost from US$15 to US$25 and feature IDD phones and satellite TV.

In the shadow of the plush Embassy Hotel is the large and somewhat neglected ***Tao Dan Hotel*** (☎ *823 0299, 35A Đ Nguyen Trung Truc*). Most of the guests could be described as budget business travellers. Prices are US$20 to US$25 with air-con.

The ***Hotel 69*** (☎ *829 1513, fax 829 6604, 69 ĐL Hai Ba Trung*) is a friendly and conveniently-located mini-hotel. Rooms are fairly basic, but decent value; singles/twins start at US$16/22.

The ***Rose Hotel*** (*Map 3;* ☎ *829 5947, fax 829 5913, 28–34 Đ Pasteur*) is an oldie but a goodie. Air-con singles/doubles with satellite TV and IDD phones cost US$20/25 and include breakfast. The hotel features a small rooftop swimming pool and garden terrace.

Cholon (District 5) (Map 5)

The ***Phuong Hoang Hotel*** *(☎ 855 1888, fax 855 2228, 411 DL Tran Hung Dao)* is in an eight-storey building. Also known as the Phoenix Hotel, this place is in central Cholon. Rooms with fan/air-conditioning cost US$12/22.

The ***Song Kim Hotel*** *(☎ 855 9773, 84–86 Đ Chau Van Liem)* is a grungy and somewhat disreputable establishment with twin rooms for US$8 with fan or US$11 with air-con. You can do better for marginally more money.

Just up the street is the ***Truong Thanh Hotel*** *(☎ 855 6044, 111–117 Đ Chau Van Liem)*. It's definitely a budget place. Rooms with fan are US$8 to US$10, while air-con costs US$15.

Half a block away is the ***Thu Do Hotel*** *(☎ 855 9102, 125 Đ Chau Van Liem)*. It looks very much like a dump, a distinction it shares with the Truong Thanh. Rooms cost a modest US$8 to US$11.

The very basic ***Tan Da Hotel*** *(☎ 855 5711, 17–19 Đ Tan Da)* is close to the upmarket Arc En Ciel Hotel. Rooms with fan/air-con cost US$11/18.

The ***Bat Dat Hotel II*** *(☎ 855 5902, 41 Đ Ngo Quyen)* is the cheap cousin of the pricey Bat Dat Hotel. At the Bat Dat II, twins are US$12 to US$20.

The ***Hoa Binh Hotel*** *(☎ 835 5113, fax 835 3941, 1115 ĐL Tran Hung Dao)* is a seven-storey building which has seen better days. Still, it's cheap. Doubles with fan/air-con cost just US$7/14.

PLACES TO STAY – MID-RANGE

Pham Ngu Lao Area (Map 4)

The Pham Ngu Lao area boasts a number of slightly upmarket places that cater both to backpackers who don't mind shelling out a bit more for a nice room, and moneybags who prefer to be where the action is without sacrificing comfort.

Room rates at the attractive ***Hanh Hoa Hotel*** *(☎ 836 0245, fax 836 1482, @ hanhhoahotel@hcm.vnn.vn, 237 Đ Pham Ngu Lao)*, with satellite TV, range from US$17 to US$25 and are decent value.

Another hotel which has managed to inch its way into backpacker central is the sleek ***Le Le Hotel*** *(☎ 836 8686, fax 836 8787, 171 Đ Pham Ngu Lao)*. This place has an elevator and satellite TV. Rooms cost US$15 to US$50.

The ***Giant Dragon Hotel*** *(☎ 836 4759, fax 836 7279, 173 Đ Pham Ngu Lao)* has plush rooms with satellite TV. Costs range from US$25 to US$65.

North of Đ Pham Ngu Lao, the ***Rang Dong Hotel*** *(☎ 832 2106, fax 839 3318, 81–83 Đ Cach Mang Thang Tam)* is a sizeable and spiffy choice and reasonably priced. Rates range from US$26 to US$65. Nearby, the ***Saigon Royal Hotel*** *(☎ 829 4846, fax 822 5346, 12D Đ Cach Mang Thang Tam)* is also nice enough and has even cheaper rates – US$15 to US$40.

The ***Liberty 4 Hotel*** *(☎ 836 5822, fax 836 4556, 265 Đ Pham Ngu Lao)* offers excellent views from its 9th floor restaurant. The rooms are quite nice, but it's questionable whether it's worth the price – US$40 to US$130.

The three star ***Vien Dong Hotel*** *(☎ 836 8941, fax 836 8812, 275A Đ Pham Ngu Lao)* has budget rooms costing US$30 and deluxe suites for US$70, inclusive of breakfast, VAT and service charges. The hotel features full amenities including a fine rooftop restaurant, an Asian and halal food restaurant and the popular Cheers nightclub.

Virtually next door to the giant New World Hotel is the ***Palace Saigon Hotel*** *(☎ 833 1353 or 835 9421, 82 Đ Le Lai)*. It has doubles for US$25 to US$35.

Dong Khoi Area (Map 3)

The ***Spring Hotel*** *(☎ 829 7362, fax 822 1383, 44–46 Đ Le Thanh Ton)* is an attractive place with a somewhat Japanese feel to it. Doubles range from US$25 to US$59 and include breakfast at the in-house restaurant.

The ***Saigon Hotel*** *(☎ 829 9734, fax 829 1466, 47 Đ Dong Du)* is across the street from the Saigon Central Mosque. Doubles

PLACES TO STAY

cost US$47 to US$95. Deluxe rooms and suites come equipped with satellite TV.

Aptly named, the ***Grand Hotel*** *(☎ 823 0163, fax 823 5871, 12 Đ Ngo Duc Ke)* – formerly known as the Dong Khoi – is a charming choice. This recently renovated landmark is notable for its spacious suites with 4.5m-high ceilings and French windows. It's on the corner of Đ Dong Khoi and rates range from US$40 to US$140.

The contemporary ***Asian Hotel*** *(☎ 829 6979, fax 829 7433, 146–150 Đ Dong Khoi)* is a fine place to stay and is notable for its restaurant. Single/double rooms start from US$50/65.

The ***Bong Sen Hotel*** *(☎ 829 1516, fax 829 8076, 117–123 Đ Dong Khoi)* is affectionately called 'the BS' by travellers. It offers air-con twins for US$28 to US$160. Formerly called the Miramar Hotel, the Bong Sen is also signposted as the Lotus Hotel, which is a translation of its Vietnamese name.

The new ***Bong Sen Annexe*** *(☎ 823 5818, fax 823 5816, 61–63 ĐL Hai Ba Trung)* is an attractive choice and popular with small group tours. Economy rooms cost US$45/60, city-view rooms are US$55/70, and junior suites are US$80/95. Eating at the Ca Noi Restaurant on the 8th floor is recommended.

Nearby, the ***Fimex Hotel*** *(☎ 822 0082, fax 822 0085, 40–42 ĐL Hai Ba Trung)* is a nice new mini-hotel with rates from US$25 to US$40, including VAT, service and breakfast. A similar place worth consideration is the ***Chuson Hotel*** *(☎ 823 1390, fax 822 1647, 22 ĐL Hai Ba Trung)*, just down the street. Standard rooms go for US$26 to US$35, deluxe rooms for US$45 and suites for US$55. All rates include breakfast and a fruit bucket.

The ***Nam Phuong Hotel*** *(☎ 822 4446, fax 829 7459, 46 ĐL Hai Ba Trung)* has clean rooms, and weary people will be thankful for the lift (a rarity in such tall, thin mini-hotels). Rooms cost US$35 to US$45.

The ***Huong Sen Hotel*** *(☎ 829 1415, fax 829 0916, 66–70 Đ Dong Khoi)* has a decent in-house restaurant on the 6th floor and a Baskin Robbins ice cream shop on the street level. Rooms charges are US$40 to US$100 for twins.

The ***Embassy Hotel*** *(☎ 823 1981, fax 823 1978, 35 Đ Nguyen Trung Truc)* is a medium-size place not far from Reunification Palace. It has a restaurant, karaoke bar, live music in the evening and superb air-conditioning. Twins are US$35 to US$50.

The ***Orchid Hotel*** *(☎ 823 1809, fax 829 2245, 29A Đ Don Dat)* is a decent place on the corner with Đ Thai Van Lung with an array of amenities, including karaoke and 24-hour room service. Singles/doubles range from US$35/45 to US$60/70.

District 3 (Map 3)

This district attracts a large number of French travellers, possibly because of the local French-style architecture. If you speak French, you may have a chance to use it here.

On the north side of Cong Vien Van Hoa Park is the ***Bao Yen Hotel*** *(☎ 829 9848, 9 Đ Truong Dinh)*. Prices are a very reasonable US$12 to US$15 and all rooms come with air-con.

One place that gets the thumbs up from French travellers is the ***Guesthouse Loan*** *(☎ 844 5313)*. This place is also known as the No 3 Ly Chinh Thang Hotel, which is also its address. Prices are US$18 to US$24 and all rooms have air-con and hot water.

The ***Que Huong Hotel*** *(☎ 829 4227, fax 829 0919, 167 ĐL Hai Ba Trung)* – also known as the Liberty Hotel – is two blocks from the French consulate. Singles/doubles cost from US$40/50 to US$60/75. Suites cost US$85. The lunch buffet in the ground floor restaurant is good value at US$2.

The ***Victory Hotel*** *(☎ 823 1755, fax 829 9604, 14 Đ Vo Van Tan)* is just one block north-west of Reunification Palace and is in far better shape than the palace itself. Rates are US$25 to US$55.

The ***Saigon Star Hotel*** *(☎ 823 0260, fax 823 0255, 204 Đ Nguyen Thi Minh Khai)* is modern and luxurious. It features satellite TV, two restaurants and a coffee shop, the Moonlight Karaoke Club and a business centre with email services. Rates are currently discounted, ranging from US$45 to US$68. The same rates apply at the nearby all-suite

Chancery Saigon Hotel *(☎ 829 0152, fax 825 1464, @ chancery@hcm.vnn.vn, 196 L Nguyen Thi Minh Khai)*, which includes all service charges, VAT, continental breakfast and airport transfers.

Tan Binh & Phu Nhuan Districts (Map 2)

These are the areas out towards the airport in the northern part of the city.

The ***Tan Son Nhat Hotel*** *(☎ 844 0517, fax 844 1324, 200 ĐL Hoang Van Thu)* was built as a guesthouse for top South Vietnamese government officials. In 1975, the North Vietnamese Army (NVA) inherited it. A ground floor room used by South Vietnamese prime minister Tran Thien Khiem has been preserved exactly as it was in 1975, plastic fruit and all. There is a small swimming pool out the back. Rates are moderate at US$28 to US$45.

Almost within walking distance of the airport is the ***Mekong Travel Hotel*** *(☎ 844 1024, fax 844 4809, 243A ĐL Hoang Van Thu)*. Single/twin rooms in this opulent place cost US$24/30, while suites will set you back US$50. It's certainly one of the better deals near the airport.

Just next door to the Mekong is the pleasant ***Garden Plaza Hotel*** *(☎ 842 1111, fax 842 4370, 309B Đ Nguyen Van Troi)*. This Singapore joint venture is Vietnam's first atrium-style hotel. Rates are US$55 to US$75.

The ***Chains First Hotel*** *(☎ 844 1199, fax 844 4282, 18 Đ Hoang Viet)* boasts a coffee shop, gift shop, tennis courts, sauna, massage services, three restaurants, swimming pool, business centre and a free airport shuttle service. Single/twin rooms start at US$35/55. Management throws in breakfast and a basket of fruit.

Cholon (District 5) (Map 5)

The ***Chau Hotel & Restaurant*** *(☎ 835 0517, fax 836 2248, 1127 ĐL Tran Hung Dao)* is a new place with 26 spotlessly clean singles/doubles/triples for US$22/25/35, including breakfast. The in-house Chinese restaurant is recommended.

The five-storey ***Dong Khanh Hotel*** *(☎ 835 2410, 2 ĐL Tran Hung Dao)* is the pride and joy of Ho Chi Minh City Tourist and a popular place for wedding parties. Single/doubles start from US$30/60. The restaurant here is also worthy of a plug.

The 20-room ***Tokyo Hotel*** *(☎ 835 7558, fax 835 2505, 106–108 Đ Tran Tuan Khai)* has all the modern conveniences at nice prices, plus friendly staff. Doubles cost US$28 to US$50.

The ***Arc En Ciel (Rainbow) Hotel*** *(☎ 855 4435, fax 855 0332, 52–56 Đ Tan Da)* is a prime venue for tour groups from Hong Kong and Taiwan. It includes the Rainbow Disco Karaoke. Rooms cost from US$30/40. The hotel is on the corner with ĐL Tran Hung Dao.

A near neighbour to the Arc En Ciel is the ***Van Hoa Hotel*** *(☎ 855 4182, fax 856 3118, 36 Đ Tan Da)*. It seems a good place and rooms cost US$25 to US$40.

The ***Bat Dat Hotel*** *(☎ 855 5817 or 855 5843, 238–244 ĐL Tran Hung Dao)* is across from the Arc En Ciel. This formerly cheap place is now plush and offers twins from US$35 to US$60.

The ***Hanh Long Hotel*** *(☎ 835 1087, fax 835 0742, 1027 ĐL Tran Hung Dao)* is a newer place. The name means Happy Dragon, but some might say otherwise.

The ***Cholon Hotel*** *(☎ 835 7058, fax 835 5375, 170–174 Đ Su Van Hanh)* is good value. The desk clerks speak English and Chinese. Squeaky clean singles/twins cost US$15/20.

Right next door is the privately owned ***Cholon Tourist Mini-Hotel*** *(☎ 835 7100, fax 835 5375, 192–194 Đ Su Van Hanh)*. It's also of a high standard and caters to the Taiwanese market. Rooms cost US$22/28.

Next to Cholon Tourist, ***Anh Quoc Hotel*** *(☎ 835 9447, fax 839 6872, 196 Đ Su Van Hanh)* has respectable air-con rooms for US$20.

The ***Andong Hotel*** *(☎ 835 2001, 9 ĐL An Duong Vuong)*, right at the intersection with ĐL Tran Phu, is a clean place. All rooms have hot water, telephone, air-conditioning and refrigerator. Twin rooms cost US$20 to US$25.

Right inside Andong Market is the ***Caesar Hotel*** *(☎ 835 0677, fax 835 0106, 34–36*

ĐL An Duong Vuong), a slick Taiwanese joint venture. It is probably easiest to ask taxis or cyclos to take you to the market. Room prices have come down recently to US$28 to US$40, including breakfast.

District 11

About 1km north of central Cholon is the ***Phu Tho Hotel*** *(☎ 855 1309, fax 855 1255, 527 Đ 3 Thang 2)*. The price range is US$40 to US$50, with breakfast and airport transfers included. There is a huge restaurant on the lowest three floors with built-in karaoke facilities.

The ***Goldstar Hotel*** *(☎ 855 1646, fax 855 1644, 174–176 Đ Le Dai Hanh)* has clean singles/doubles for US$32/45. All rooms have private bath, refrigerator and air-con. The upper floors give a good view of the race track.

PLACES TO STAY – TOP END

District 1 (Map 3)

One of the most historic old hotels in the city is the venerable ***Continental Hotel*** *(☎ 829 9201, fax 824 1772, 132–134 Đ Dong Khoi)*, the setting for much of the action in Graham Greene's novel *The Quiet American*. During the war, journalists used to sit on the terrace – known as the Continental Shelf – and sip beers. The terrace, though, is now closed. Just across the street from the Municipal Theatre, the hotel dates from the turn of the century and received its last renovation in 1989 - unfortunately at the hands of its current owner, Saigon Tourist. They could have done better. The Continental charges US$89 to US$199 for rooms (including breakfast and fruit). The building also houses the offices of China Airlines, Garuda Indonesia, Malaysia Airlines and Lufthansa Airlines.

Another classic hotel is the enormous ***Rex Hotel*** *(☎ 829 6043, fax 829 6536, 141 ĐL Nguyen Hue)*. Its ambience of mellowed kitsch dates from the time it served as a hotel for US military officers. Twins and suites cost US$79 to US$760. Amenities here include a large gift shop, tailor, unisex beauty parlour, photocopy machines, massage service, acupuncturist, a swimming pool on the 6th floor, an excellent restaurant on the 5th floor, a coffee shop on the ground floor and a beautiful view from the large 5th-floor rooftop veranda, which features caged birds and potted bonsai bushes shaped like animals.

The posh ***Caravelle Hotel*** *(☎ 823 4999, fax 824 3999, 19 Lam Son Square)*, once owned by the Catholic Diocese of Saigon, is now one of the city's finest accommodations. Standard rooms start from US$89, while suites cost from US$200 to US$900. The *real* ***Hard Rock Cafe*** is on the 10th floor and is open from 4 pm to midnight; upstairs on the rooftop is the popular ***Saigon Saigon*** bar.

The 291-room ***Hotel Sofitel Plaza Saigon*** *(☎ 824 1555, fax 824 1666, 17 ĐL Le Duan)* is the newest of the city's fancy hotels. There are two fine in-house restaurants, as well as the L'Elysee Bar, which has a delightful terrace, and a rooftop swimming pool. Rates start at a modest US$209 and climb to US$1450 for the Presidential Suite.

The ***Majestic Hotel*** *(☎ 829 5514, fax 829 5510, 1 Đ Dong Khoi)* is on the Saigon River. Following an extensive renovation it can reclaim its title as one of the city's most majestic hotels. Prices here are US$120 to US$550, though at the time of writing 40% discounts were being offered.

The ***Palace Hotel*** *(☎ 829 2840, fax 824 4230, 56–66 ĐL Nguyen Hue)* offers superb views from the 14th floor restaurant. Rates range from US$40 to US$165, with breakfast included. The Palace has an imported-food shop, a dance hall, the Sky View Bar on the 15th-floor terrace and a small swimming pool on the 16th floor.

In the same neighbourhood is the ***Saigon Prince Hotel*** *(☎ 822 2999, fax 824 1888, 63 ĐL Nguyen Hue)*. Glittering, luxury twins cost US$145 to US$300, but a 20% discount is standard. Expats say it has the best massage service in town.

The ***Kim Do Hotel*** *(☎ 822 5914, fax 822 5915, 133 ĐL Nguyen Hue)* is a fancy pleasuredome brought to you by Saigon Tourist. Rates are US$70 to US$250. It's fair to say you get what you pay for at this place.

The enormous ***New World Hotel*** (Map 4; *☎ 822 8888, fax 823 0710, 76 Đ Le Lai)* is a

JOHN BORTHWICK

The Continental Hotel by day, Dong Khoi area

MASON FLORENCE

The Rex Hotel at night, Dong Khoi area

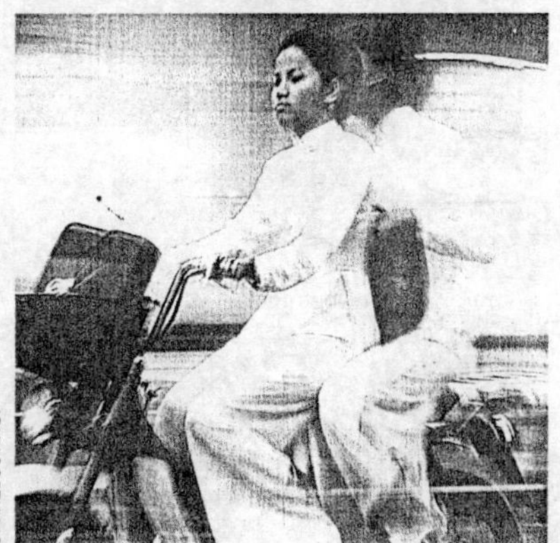

JOHN BANAGAN

Ho Chi Minh City's chief form of fast transport

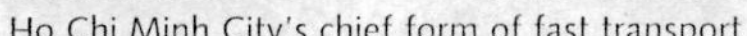

JOHN BORTHWICK

The architecture is from France, but the streetscape (Cholon) is wholly Ho Chi Minh City.

GARRETT CULHANE
One of innumerable streetside eateries.

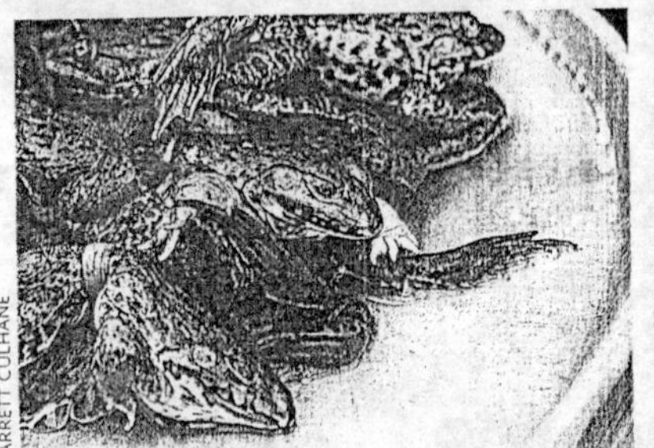
GARRETT CULHANE
Frogs on a tray, before...

PHILIP GAME
Frogs on a tray, after. Bon appétit.

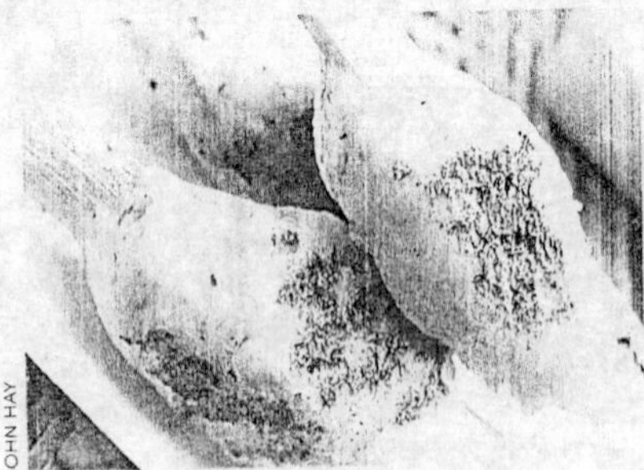
JOHN HAY
Grilled prawn mousse on sugar cane

RICHARD I'ANSON
Raw ingredients

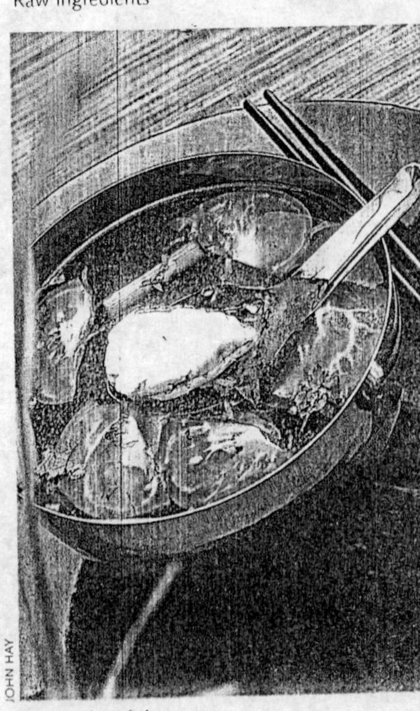
JOHN HAY
Fresh, clear fish soup

slick luxury tower and one of the most upmarket hotels in Ho Chi Minh City. The clientele tends toward Chinese-speaking tour groups from Hong Kong and Taiwan, but anyone with hard currency is welcome. Singles/twins start at US$105/185, while a presidential suite goes for a cool US$850. Credit cards, thankfully, are accepted.

On the road to the airport is the ***Saigon Lodge Hotel*** *(☎ 823 0112, fax 825 1070, 215 Đ Nam Ky Khoi Nghia)*. This place boasts the usual top-end hotel amenities, plus satellite TV and halal food. Twins are US$60 to US$115 or you can rent the penthouse for US$280.

The ***International Hotel*** *(☎ 829 0009, fax 829 0066, 19 Đ Vo Van Tan)* maintains plush standards; rooms are US$75 to US$150.

The ***EPCO Hotel*** *(☎ 825 1125, fax 822 3556, 120 Đ Cach Mang Thang Tam)* is one of the plushest hotels in the city. The price range for twins is US$55 to US$175.

The ***Sol Chancery Hotel*** *(☎ 829 9152, fax 825 1464, 196 Đ Nguyen Thi Minh Khai)* is a popular business hotel. Rooms cost US$60 to US$80.

The large ***Mercure Hotel*** *(☎ 824 2525, fax 824 2533, 79 ĐL Tran Hung Dao)* is a nice upmarket option between backpackers' central and the Ben Thanh Market. Single/twin rooms cost US$90/110. Suites are US$165 to US$200.

Another short walk south from the cheap guesthouses and budget cafes is the debonair ***Windsor Saigon Hotel*** *(☎ 836 7848, fax 836 7889, 193 ĐL Tran Hung Dao)*. It has all the amenities, including a white stretch Cadillac limo! The fancy Four Seasons Restaurant here gets good reviews as does the excellent bakery/deli, offering pastries, fine wine, cheese and *real* sausages. Room rates range from US$65 for studios to US$100 for apartments.

The ***Norfolk Hotel*** *(☎ 829 5368, fax 829 3415, 117 Đ Le Thanh Ton)* is an Australian joint venture and all rooms boast satellite TV and a minibar. Twins cost US$65 to US$145, including breakfast.

Not far away is the ***Tan Loc Hotel*** *(☎ 823 0028, fax 829 8360, 177 Đ Le Thanh Ton)*. It has twins for US$45 to US$100.

The ***Oscar Saigon Hotel*** *(☎ 823 1818, fax 829 2758, 68A ĐL Nguyen Hue)* is a Hong Kong joint venture formerly known as the Century Saigon Hotel. Rooms are US$50 to US$105.

The ***Riverside Hotel*** *(☎ 822 4038, fax 825 1417, 18 Đ Ton Duc Thang)* is very close to the Saigon River. This grand old colonial building has been renovated and now features a good restaurant and bar. Doubles cost US$70 to US$200, but at the time of writing discounts of 30% were available.

The ***Empress Hotel*** *(☎ 832 2888, fax 835 8215, 136 Đ Bui Thi Xuan)* is a snazzy place where twins cost US$50 to US$200.

The ***Metropole Hotel*** *(☎ 832 2021, fax 832 2019, 148 Đ Tran Hung Dao)* has been the subject of reports of overcharging and even theft of cameras and luggage from rooms. If you want to stay, official rates are US$86 to US$149.

Phu Nhuan District (Map 2)

The ***Omni Hotel*** *(☎ 844 9222, fax 844 9200, 251 Đ Nguyen Van Troi)* is the poshest accommodation on the way the airport. This place has everything from room safes and a florist, to a pool and health club. The price for all this comfort is US$189 to US$920 per night.

Cholon (District 5)

The ***Equatorial Hotel*** *(Map 2; ☎ 839 0000, fax 839 0011, 242 Đ Tran Binh Trong)* is one of Cholon's newest and plushest accommodation options. The price range at this place is US$90 to US$280.

LONG-TERM RENTALS

Finding a Flat

Despite the fact that there are some 15,000 expats living in Ho Chi Minh City, there does not appear to be a shortage of good-quality rental accommodation. Unfortunately, living cheaply is not easy if you don't happen to be Vietnamese. Unless you get married to a Vietnamese national and move in with the family, there isn't much chance of renting a worker's flat (which cost only US$50 per month). The police will not permit it.

The budget market is served chiefly by the mini-hotels scattered all around town. Discounts can be negotiated for long-term rentals at almost any hotel. If you've got a big budget, but don't need a large space, even the big five-star luxury hotels offer steep discounts to long-termers. The name of the game is negotiation. It's wise, however, to first stay in the hotel for at least one night before agreeing to anything.

Aside from the backpacker guesthouses or mini-hotels, it is possible to find private houses and apartments to rent for around US$200 to US$500 per month. It's also possible to arrange to stay in the homes of local people, but they must register you with the police. The police can – and often do – arbitrarily deny such registration requests and will force you to stay in a hotel or guesthouse licensed to accept foreigners.

Real estate agents who cater to the expat market advertise in the *Vietnam Economic Times*, *Vietnam Investment Review* and the *Vietnam News* daily newspaper; you do not generally deal directly with landlords. Shop around for the best deal, and don't be afraid to negotiate.

Serviced Apartments

Well-heeled expats with a liberal budget have two basic options – villas or specially built luxury flats. Villas seem more popular and Ho Chi Minh City has a large supply. Villas that can be rented by foreigners typically cost from US$2000 to US$5000 a month. The luxury apartments are a new phenomena – some well known places in this category include the ***Landmark*** *(☎ 822 2098)*, ***Parkland*** *(☎ 898 9000)*, ***Riverside*** *(☎ 899 7405)*, ***Cityview Apartments*** *(☎ 822 1111)*, ***Apartments 27AB*** *(☎ 822 4109)*, ***Stamford Court*** *(☎ 899 7405)*, ***Saigon Village*** *(☎ 865 0287)*, ***Sedona Suites*** *(☎ 822 9666)* and ***Regency Chancellor Court*** *(☎ 822 5807)*.

Places to Eat

One of the delights of Ho Chi Minh City is the amazing cuisine. You'll never have to look very far for food – restaurants *(nha hang)* of one sort or another seem to be in every nook and cranny. If you are willing to sacrifice plush surroundings, you can eat a complete meal for under US$1. On the other hand, if you have some cash just burning a hole in your pocket, the upmarket restaurants of Ho Chi Minh City will accommodate you. Keep an eye out for affordable lunch specials – the competition is high and prices (even at top-notch hotels) criminally low!

Both Vietnamese and Western food are widely available and English-language menus are becoming increasingly common. Central Saigon is the place to look for fine Western and Vietnamese food. Cholon's speciality is, naturally, Chinese food. Many hotel restaurants offer Vietnamese and Western food at prices varying from reasonable to ridiculous. Check the price list first to avoid indigestion later.

Most local Vietnamese restaurants do not have prices on the menu. You must definitely ask the total price when you place your order because overcharging is common. Vietnamese diners know this and will always ask, so don't be shy about speaking up. If you don't, be prepared for a surprise when the bill finally comes.

FOOD

Wherever you go in Ho Chi Minh City you'll find *pho*. This is noodle soup, and it's delicious. As opposed to northerners, who dump tablespoons of MSG into their pho, Saigonese prefer to add sugar.

The other staple is, of course, rice *(cơm)*, likewise sold at street stalls all over the city. Be certain that at some point you sample Vietnamese spring rolls *(cha gio)*, an inexpensive Vietnamese speciality found everywhere.

Nuoc mam (pronounced something like nuke mom) is a type of fermented fish sauce – instantly identifiable by its distinctive smell – without ... plete. Most ... it, but a few ... made by ferm... large ceramic va...

If nuoc mam is... you, try *mam tom*, a p... ...p sauce which US soldiers ... ...s called Viet Cong tear gas.

Salt with chilli and lemon juice is often served as a condiment and most Westerners seem to like it. Soy sauce is also readily available and makes a good, less smelly substitute for nuoc mam.

For breakfast, rice porridge *(chao trang)* or some kind of meat sandwich is popular. Hué-style (ie, from central Vietnam) beef noodle soup is another favourite.

Vietnamese vegetarian cooking *(an chay)* is an integral part of Vietnamese cuisine. However, the majority of Vietnamese do indeed eat meat most of the time. An important exception occurs on the first and 15th days of the lunar month – festival days in which devout Buddhists normally avoid eating meat.

DRINKS

Aside from the wide variety of delicious and exotic foods, the Vietnamese also produce many excellent drinks. Vietnamese coffee is prime stuff, but there is one qualifier – you'll need to dilute it with hot water. The Vietnamese like their coffee so strong and sweet that it will turn your teeth inside out. Ditto for Ovaltine and Milo, which are regarded as desserts rather than drinks.

Unfortunately, tea is not very good in the southern part of Vietnam. The best Vietnamese tea is from the northern part of the country, or is imported. The Vietnamese never put milk and sugar into their tea and are amazed when they see foreigners do so.

Bottled mineral water *(nuoc suoi)* is found everywhere and is safe to drink. A Vietnamese speciality is carbonated water with freshly squeezed lemon, sugar and ice

...nut milk *(nuoc dua)* ... a chilled coconut is su... refreshing. Many so-called im... soft drinks and beers are not ...ported at all, but made locally by foreign joint ventures.

Memorise the words *bia hoi*, which means draft beer. There are signs advertising it everywhere, and most cafes have it on the menu. Quality varies, but is generally OK. The best thing is the price, averaging US$0.40 per litre! Places that serve bia hoi usually also have good, cheap food. Vietnamese wine, usually made from rice, is good only for cooking, though if you're desperate for a cheap drink you could do worse. Ho Chi Minh City also has a wide selection of imported and locally brewed bottled beer.

PLACES TO EAT – DISTRICTS 1 & 3 (MAPS 3 &4)

Food Stalls

Noodle soup is available all day long at street stalls and hole-in-the-wall shops everywhere. A large bowl of delicious beef noodles costs around US$0.50. Just look for the signs that say Pho. One famous Ho Chi Minh City ***pho shop*** is between the two *ao dai* tailors at 258–260 and 264/1 Đ Pasteur, but there are countless places to seek out:

> The best noodle soup that I had was in the Ben Thanh Market itself. The food stalls inside the market were clean, the food fresh and the soup very tasty. It's also a fun place to eat because you quickly become the centre of attention.
>
> **John Lumley-Holmes**

Sandwiches with a French look and a very Vietnamese taste are sold by street vendors. Fresh French baguettes are stuffed with something resembling pâté (don't ask) and cucumbers seasoned with soy sauce. A sandwich costs between US$0.50 and US$1, depending on what it's filled with and whether you are overcharged. Sandwiches filled with imported French soft cheese cost a little more. Baguettes a la carte cost about US$0.16.

Markets always have a wide selection of food items, often on the ground floor or in the basement. Clusters of food stalls can be found in Thai Binh, Ben Thanh and Andong markets.

Backpackers' Cafes & Restaurants (Map 4)

Đ Pham Ngu Lao and Đ De Tham form the axis of Ho Chi Minh City's budget eatery haven. Western backpackers easily outnumber the Vietnamese here, and indeed the locals have trouble figuring out the menus (banana muesli does not translate well into Vietnamese).

A long-running hang-out for budget travellers is ***Kim Cafe*** *(☎ 835 9859, 272 Đ De Tham)*. This is a very good place to meet people, arrange trips and get travel information at the tour office next door. An nearly identical set-up exists at the nearby ***Sinh Cafe*** *(☎ 836 7338, 248 Đ De Tham)*.

The ***Saigon Cafe***, at195 Đ Pham Ngu Lao, on the corner of Đ De Tham, is worthy of a plug and, along with ***Cafe 333*** (also on Đ De Tham), is where the largest numbers of expats congregate. ***Bin Cafe***, at 274 Đ De Tham, is also popular and proudly advertises 'no MSG or animal fat' cooking. Other contenders on the block include the ***Sasa Cafe***, at 240 Đ De Tham, and ***Lucky Cafe***, at 224 Đ De Tham.

Around the corner, on Đ Pham Ngu Lao, are several more backpacker hang-outs serving up decent Vietnamese and Western food at low prices. The ***Lotus Cafe***, at 197 Đ Pham Ngu Lao, ***Cafe 215***, at 215 Đ Pham Ngu Lao, and ***Linh Cafe***, at 291 Đ Pham Ngu Lao, are all good, and all are run by friendly people.

The best place for authentic Vietnamese food in backpackers' central is ***Thuong Chi*** *(☎ 836 7225, 40/29 Đ Bui Vien)*, mid-way down Mini-Hotel Alley (one street south of Đ De Tham). This place is spotlessly clean, friendly and serves superb food (try the Hué-style spring rolls for US$1.60).

If you're feeling spring-rolled out, head for ***Cafe Van*** *(☎ 836 0636, 169B Đ De Tham)*, on the corner of ĐL Tran Hung Dao. Also known as the Sandwich Box, this is a fine eatery run by a British and Vietnamese couple (Peter is also a tour leader) who serve up excellent sandwiches, baked potatoes with all the fixings and Ho Chi Minh City's best chilli. They also offer takeaway and free delivery.

For some reason or another, Indian food goes with the backpacker territory and there are a handful of places to feast on real curries and *nan*. For North Indian/Pakistani food, try ***Trang Indian Restaurant*** *(☎ 836 9186, 239 Đ Pham Ngu Lao)*. ***An Do***, at 222 Đ De Tham, and ***Sunshine Indian Restaurant***, at 236 Đ De Tham, are two more places you might check out.

There is respectable Italian grub at ***Good Morning Vietnam*** *(☎ 837 1894, 197 Đ De Tham)*. Other places serving pizza and pasta include ***Cappuccino***, at 222 Đ De Tham, near Sinh Cafe, as well as at ***Ngoc Phuong***, at 203 Đ Pham Ngu Lao. ***Margherita***, at 175/1 Pham Ngu Lao, takes the cake for being the cheapest.

For local point-and-eat rice-for-the-people fare *(con ban dan)*, try the ground floor of ***Kim's Guesthouse***, at 91 Đ Bui Vien, not to be confused with Kim's Cafe & Bar (or Kim Cafe). There is also good beef noodle soup across the street at ***Pho Bo***, next to the 96 Guesthouse, as well as at ***Pho Thanh Canh***, at 55 Đ Nguyen Cu Trinh, about 300m from Guesthouse 127.

Finally, perhaps the area's most unexpected eatery, ***Penny Lane,*** which specialises in Russian BBQ!

Vegetarian (Map 4)

On the first and 15th days of the lunar month, food stalls around the city – especially in the markets – serve vegetarian versions of meaty Vietnamese dishes. While these stalls are quick in serving customers, a little patience is required – good home cooking takes time, but it's worth the wait.

In the Pham Ngu Lao area, ***Zen*** *(☎ 839 1545, 175/6 Đ Pham Ngu Lao)* is in a narrow alley two streets east of Đ De Tham. Its food is excellent and very cheap. Equally recommended are the nearby ***Bodhi Tree I & II*** (Cay Be De in Vietnamese).

The owners of the ***Tin Nghia*** *(☎ 821 2538, 9 ĐL Tran Hung Dao)* are strict Buddhists. This simple establishment is about 200m from Ben Thanh Market, a short walk from the Pham Ngu Lao area. It serves an assortment of cheap and delicious traditional Vietnamese food prepared without meat, chicken, fish or egg. Instead, tofu, mushrooms and vegetables are used. It is open from 8 am to 2 pm and from 4 pm to 9 pm daily.

In the Đ Dong Khoi area, you might try the excellent vegetarian fare at ***Com Chay 39*** *(Map 3; ☎ 824 4556, 39 Đ Dong Du)*, across from the mosque.

Vietnamese (Map 3)

Ancient Town *(☎ 829 9625, 211 Đ Dien Bien Phu)*, also know as Pho Xua, serves dishes from the three regions of Vietnam in a beautifully restored colonial villa. The charming owner, Isabelle Nhu Loan, was a well-known Vietnamese actress in California before she returned to open the restaurant. An excellent jazz band plays in the courtyard some nights.

Cool Restaurant *(☎ 829 1364, 30 Đ Dong Khoi)*, also known as Kinh Bac, is situated in

SIMON BORG

Saigon's cuisine, like its culture, is a melange of different cultural and regional influences.

a narrow, rambling building of several rooms with tasteful, tropical decor influenced by traditional northern Vietnamese pagoda design. Cool also serves tasty specialties from the north, centre and south of the country. Set meals cost from around US$6.

Not far from Cool, ***Tan Nam*** *(☎ 829 8634, 60–62 Đ Dong Du)* is yet another place offering traditional decor and fine food.

Bo Tung Xeo Restaurant *(☎ 825 1330, 31 Đ Ly Tu Trong)*, also known as Quan Luong Son, is a true Ho Chi Minh City institution and highly popular with Saigonese and expats alike. This *very* local eatery serves amazingly cheap and tasty Vietnamese food. The house specialty is tender marinated beef *bo tung xeo* (about US$2 a portion, including a salad) which you grill over charcoal at the table. Bo tung xeo (literally 'to cut piece by piece') refers to an ancient form of torture (you might ask after you've finished eating). There are also excellent seafood dishes on the menu. The staff speak English.

The popular ***Mandarine Restaurant*** *(☎ 822 9783, 11A Đ Ngo Van Nam)* is perhaps Ho Chi Minh City's best Vietnamese restaurant. The selection here of fine, traditional food is superb, and the pleasant decor makes it an all-round good bet. One of the house specialities worth trying is the Hanoi-style fish cakes *(cha ca)*. Just up the road from Mandarine, ***Hoi An*** *(☎ 823 1049, 11 Đ Le Thanh Ton)* is a recent arrival on Ho Chi Minh City's upmarket Vietnamese food scene. The cooking is Hué-style (hence the name Hoi An) and the woodsy decor is tastefully traditional.

The ***Lemon Grass Restaurant*** *(☎ 822 0496, 4 Đ Nguyen Thiep)* is another personal favourite. You'd be hard-pressed to find anything bad on the menu, so if you can't decide what to order just pick something at random. Two women in traditional clothing play musical instruments while you eat. Aspiring interior designers should come here and check out the bamboo decor.

Vietnam House *(☎ 829 1623, 93–95 Đ Dong Khoi)* is on the corner with Đ Mac Thi Buoi. The cuisine is Vietnamese-style, as is the decor. In the 2nd-floor dining room, a traditional, four piece ensemble plays from 7.30 pm. The best part is the bar and lounge on the 1st floor where a pianist plays from 5.30 pm until late at night. The restaurant is open from 10 am until midnight.

The atmospheric ***Han Han*** *(☎ 822 6705, 178A Đ Nguyen Van Thu)* is one of the newest places in town for fine Vietnamese fare. They serve an eclectic mix of southern, Hué-style and northern dishes and prices are very reasonable. Han Han is just north of the city centre, near Le Van Tam Park.

Another place serving Hué-style dishes is the ***Tib Cafe***, at 187 ĐL Hai Ba Trung, District 3. It makes a good choice for dinner – and their jackfruit salad is superb.

Along Đ Ngo Duc Ke in District 1 are a strip of excellent restaurants serving good, cheap Vietnamese food. At No 19, ***Restaurant 19*** *(☎ 829 8882)* serves a very tasty variation on Hanoi's cha ca and good Thai dishes as well. Nearby, ***Restaurant 13*** is highly popular with locals and expats alike.

Asian (Map 3)

The best Indian food in District 1 is at ***Urvashi*** *(27 Đ Hai Trieu)*, just off ĐL Nguyen Hue by the Harbour View Tower office building. Wonderful Southern Indian dishes are the house speciality.

Chao Thai *(☎ 824 1457, 16 Đ Thai Van Lung)* is the best of Ho Chi Minh City's Thai restaurants, both for food and atmosphere. Their US$6.50 lunch set is good value.

The International Hotel *(☎ 829 0009, 19 Đ Vo Van Tan, District 3)* is the venue for the ***Fook Yuen Cantonese Restaurant***. This place dishes up dim sum from 7 am to 3 pm, then reopens for set meals from 5.30 to 10 pm.

For Japanese food, ***Ohan*** *(☎ 824 4896, 71–73 Đ Pasteur)* may be slightly pricier than other Japanese places but the food and service are top-notch.

Sagano *(☎ 822 2182, 17/A9 Đ Le Thanh Ton)* has decent fare, a pleasant atmosphere and is centrally located. Across the street, ***A-Un*** *(☎ 829 3635, 42 Đ Le Thanh Ton)* offers a mix of inexpensive Japanese and Chinese dishes.

Akatonbo *(☎ 824 4928, 39 ĐL Hai Ba Trung)* is clean, cheap and tasty. Just across the street, ***Heiwa En*** serves good Chinese-style Japanese dishes like dumplings *(gyoza)*.

Nishimura *(Map 2; ☎ 844 9222, 251 ĐL Nguyen Van Troi, Phu Nhuan District)*, in the Omni Saigon Hotel, is a very upmarket choice. ***Kampachi*** *(Map 2; ☎ 839 0000, 242 Đ Tran Binh Trong, District 1)*, in the Equatorial Hotel, is another snazzy place with a sushi bar.

The best Indian food in District 1 is at ***Indian Heritage*** *(☎ 823 4687, 12 Đ Thai Van Lung)*, in the Xuan Huong Hotel. It serves an excellent US$5 lunch buffet. Nearly across the street, ***Ashoka*** *(☎ 823 1372, 17A/10 Đ Le Thanh Ton)* is another good Indian place and likewise moderately priced.

Also recommendable is ***Tandoor*** *(☎ 824 4839, 103 Đ Vo Van Tan)*. For really cheap Indian food, you have to go the atmospheric, cult-like ***canteen*** *(66 Đ Dong Du)* behind the mosque and opposite the Saigon Hotel.

Sari Indo *(☎ 829 5011, 48 Đ Dong Du)* specialises in Indonesian cuisine.

Excellent Korean BBQ and fresh seafood are served in the solid string of restaurants along Đ Thi Sach (running south from the T-intersection at Đ Le Thanh Ton). Beware the touts!

French (Map 3)

Restaurant Bibi *(☎ 829 5783, 8A/8D2 Đ Thai Van Lung)* is another great place for casual French bistro fare. Run by a Frenchman named, you guessed it, Bibi, the bright Mediterranean decor creates a pleasant atmosphere in which to dine.

Just next door to the famed Lemon Grass Restaurant (see entry in the Vietnamese listings in this chapter) in the Đ Dong Khoi area is ***Augustin*** *(829 2941, 10 Đ Nguyen Thiep)*, a popular spot serving bistro-style food. Many consider it Ho Chi Minh City's best cheap French restaurant.

La Fourchette *(☎ 836 9816, 9 Đ Ngo Duc Ke)* is another excellent choice in District 1 for authentic yet inexpensive French food.

Moving upmarket is ***Camargue*** *(☎ 824 3148, 16 Đ Cao Ba Quat)*, housed in a charming restored villa with a tropical open-air terrace. Favoured by well-off expatriate businesspeople, it's an attractive, atmospheric spot with excellent food. The menu includes a variety of dishes complimented by a well-appointed wine list. It's at the expensive end of the spectrum and you could easily spend $20 on food alone. Camargue, also home to trendy Vasco's Bar, is a short walk from the Municipal Theatre.

If you insist on an expensive French restaurant dining experience, ***Le Caprice*** *(☎ 822 8337, 5B Đ Ton Duc Thang)* can accommodate you. It is on the top floor of the Landmark building. It's a very high-class place; the views are stunning, and unfortunately so are the prices.

The food is also fine at ***La Cigale*** *(☎ 844 3930, 158 Đ Nguyen Dinh Chin, Phu Nhuan District)*, where you can dine in little private cubicles. It's on the way to the airport and just opposite the Omni Hotel.

Though a bit out of the way (Map 2; Binh Thanh District) ***Le Bordeaux*** *(☎ 822 2342, F7–8, Đ D2, Commune 25)* is considered by many to be Ho Chi Minh City's best French restaurant. Don't let the address put you off – the food is more creative.

L'Etoile *(☎ 829 7939, 180 ĐL Hai Ba Trung)* serves terrific French food but doe not get the crowds it used to.

The ***Brodard Cafe*** *(☎ 822 3966, 131 Đ Dong Khoi)* is an oldie but a goodie. Despite ongoing renovations, the decor is still vintage 1960s. This place is known for decent French food and its prices are OK. It's on the corner of Đ Nguyen Thiep.

International (Map 3)

Madame Dai's Bibliotheque *(☎ 823 1438, 84A Đ Nguyen Du)* is another true Saigon institution. Here guests dine on a mix of French and Vietnamese dishes in the cosy home of Madame Dai, a charming retired lawyer and former member of the pre-1975 National Assembly of South Vietnam. The restaurant walls are lined with Madame Dai's extensive collection of old books (hence the name bibliotheque, library in French), and on some nights classical music is performed upstairs. Call ahead for reservations.

Panorama 33 *(☎ 910 0492, 37 Đ Ton Duc Thang)* is a restaurant and lounge bar located on the 32nd and 33rd storeys of the

Saigon Trade Center – the city's tallest building. As one would expect, given the location, there are amazing views, especially from the outdoor seating area. The food is not bad either. Panorama 33 is open from 10 am to 11 pm daily.

The Liberty Restaurant *(☎ 829 9820, 80 Đ Dong Khoi)* is a joint venture with the state-run Ben Thanh Tourist. Despite its government connections, it's known for cheap, good Vietnamese food. It also serves (more expensive) Chinese and Western food. This place was popular in the days before 1975, when it was known as the Tu Do Restaurant.

The ***Givral Restaurant*** *(☎ 829 2747, 169 Đ Dong Khoi)*, across the street from the Continental Hotel, has excellent selections of cakes, homemade ice cream and yoghurt. Aside from the junk food, there's French, Chinese, Vietnamese and Russian cuisine on the menu.

A stone's throw from the Rex Hotel, the ***Rex Garden Restaurant*** *(☎ 824 2799, 86 Đ Le Thanh Ton)* is in an attractive setting and serves good Vietnamese and French food. You can dine in air-con comfort, or dine outside surrounded by views of the past and present – on one side the rear courtyard of the Museum of Ho Chi Minh City, and on the other a row of tennis courts where Ho Chi Minh City's nouveaux riches swat at little yellow balls in the heat.

The ***Liberty Restaurant*** *(☎ 829 9820, 80 Đ Dong Khoi)* is a joint venture with the state-run Ben Thanh Tourist. Despite its government connections, it's known for cheap, good Vietnamese food, plus (more expensive) Chinese and Western food. There is live music upstairs in the evening performed by a Vietnamese band. The Liberty's popularity goes back to before 1975, when it was known as the Tu Do Restaurant.

Maxim's Dinner Theatre *(☎ 829 6676, 15 Đ Dong Khoi)*, next to the Majestic Hotel, is very much what the name implies – a restaurant with live musical performances. The menu includes Chinese and French food. The sea slug and duck web has disappointed a few travellers but the creme caramel and vanilla souffle should not be missed. There is a very dark nightclub upstairs (free entry) with a live band playing 1960s tunes. Maxim's is open from 11 am to 11 pm, but is usually empty until dinner. Reservations are recommended on weekends.

The popular Swiss-Vietnamese run ***Sapa Restaurant & Bar*** *(☎ 829 5754, 26 Đ Thai Van Lung)* is a fine place to sample bona fide Swiss cuisine or relax over a drink. The menu features schnitzel and cheese fondue.

Next door to Sapa at No 24, the French-run ***Why Not?*** *(☎ 822 6138)* is worth checking out for good European food or a game of darts.

Annie's Pizza *(Map 4; ☎ 839 2577, 21 Đ Bui Thi Xuan)* does the best pepperoni and mozzarella in town. If you don't feel like trekking over there, just ring them up for a home delivery.

The best authentic Italian food in town is found in District 3 at ***Ristorante Pendolasco*** *(☎ 820 3552, 142 Đ Vo Thi Sau)*. Highly atmospheric and somewhat less pricey is ***Santa Lucia*** *(☎ 822 6562, 14 ĐL Nguyen Hue)* in District 1.

For good German fare, check out ***Gartenstadt*** *(☎ 822 3623, 34 Đ Dong Khoi)*, a popular expat business lunch spot. ***Bavaria*** *(Map 4; ☎ 822 2673, 20 Đ Le Anh Xuan)* is another worthy German restaurant and Bavarian-style pub.

Mogambo's Cafe *(☎ 825 1311, 20 Đ Bis Thi Sach)* is noted for its stunning Polynesian decor and juicy steaks. This place is a restaurant, pub and hotel.

One of the trendiest bar/restaurants in town is the popular, Latinesque ***Globo Cafe*** *(☎ 822 8855, 6 Đ Nguyen Thiep)* in District 1.

Cafe Latin *(☎ 822 6363, 25 Đ Dong Du)* is Vietnam's first tapas bar. There is a superb wine collection and fresh bread baked daily. The attached ***Billabong Restaurant*** is notable for Aussie food and other international cuisine.

The ***Tex-Mex Cantina*** *(☎ 829 5950, 24 Đ Le Thanh Ton)* features Mexican food with a Texan twist. It is distinguished by being the only Mexican restaurant in Ho Chi Minh City. There's everything you'd expect, including a relaxed atmosphere, a band, a pool table and chilli con carne.

Just across from the Tex-Mex Cantina, the ***Marine Club*** *(☎ 829 2249, 17A4 Đ Le Thanh Ton)* is a popular piano bar-restaurant serving French standards and wood-fired, brick-oven-cooked pizzas (call for free delivery).

The ***Paloma Cafe*** *(☎ 829 5813, 26 Đ Dong Khoi)* is a stylish place with wooden tables, white tablecloths, polished silverware, aggressive air-conditioning and waiters who need to be tipped. Judging from the crowd that packs in every night, they must be doing something right – it's very popular with young, fashion-conscious Vietnamese.

Also popular with young Vietnamese is Ho Chi Minh City's only Czech restaurant, ***Hoa Vien*** *(☎ 825 8605, 30 Đ Mac Dinh Chi)*. The big drawcard is the draught Pilsner Urquell beer.

For a good late-night bowl of noodles, try the trendy ***ABC Restaurant*** *(☎ 823 0388, 172H Đ Nguyen Dinh Chieu)*. It's open until about 3 am.

You can get your fill of snake, turtle, deer antler and other exotic dishes at ***Tri Ky Restaurant*** *(☎ 844 2299, 478 Đ Nguyen Kiem)* in District 3.

Cafes (Map 3)

The stylish ***Dong Du Cafe*** *(☎ 823 2414, 31 Đ Dong Du)* dishes up great homemade ice cream, coffee and, if you're still hungry, a bit of Italian food.

Some of the best coffee in town is found at ***Java*** *(☎ 821 4742, 65 ĐL Le Loi)*, on the ground floor of the Saigon Trade Center. ***Monaco Cafe & Restaurant*** *(☎ 825 6387, 59 Đ Pasteur)* is just behind the Rex Hotel. It serves light food and drinks, but coffee is the house speciality.

For old-world atmosphere, ***Bo Gia Cafe*** in the Đ Dong Khoi area is hard to top. It's in the Tiem Sach Bookshop at 20 Đ Ho Huan Nghiep – look for the outdoor tables on the sidewalk. The ***Montana Cafe*** *(☎ 829 5067, 40E Đ Ngo Duc Ke)* is a trendy cafe and bar, open all day. The sandwiches are good – and save room for its ice cream.

Mogambo Cafe *(☎ 825 1373, 20 Đ Thi Sach)*, on the corner of ĐL Hai Ba Trung, is noted for its Polynesian decor. This place is a pub, cafe and guesthouse.

There are good salads, sandwiches and freshly baked pastries at ***Paris Deli*** *(☎ 821 6127, 65 ĐL Le Loi)* on the ground floor of the Saigon Trade Center. This place was retro-modelled on a Parisian bistro, and their breakfast and lunch sets (US$2 and US$3.50, respectively) are worth checking out. Paris Deli has a second branch in the neighbourhood *(☎ 829 7533, 31 Đ Dong Khoi)*.

A cheaper alternative for fresh bread and other sweet things is the ***Saigon Bakery*** *(☎ 820 2083, 281C ĐL Hai Ba Trung)*.

A good source of Italian cakes, tarts, ice cream and the like is ***Ciao Cafe*** *(☎ 825 1203, 72 ĐL Nguyen Hue)*. Its other Western food is also OK, as is its Vietnamese. It's open for breakfast, lunch and dinner. A second branch of ***Ciao Cafe*** *(☎ 822 9796, 21–23 Đ Nguyen Thi Minh Khai)* does coffee, spaghetti, sandwiches, cakes, pastries – and great pizza.

Luna Cafe is another nearby place, across the street from Khai Silk on Đ Mac Thi Buoi.

Spago Cafe & Restaurant *(☎ 822 3907, 158 Đ Dong Khoi)* is a stylish spot which bills itself as the fashion corner cafe (it's on the corner of Đ Ly Tu Trong, a short walk down Đ Dong Khoi from Notre Dame Cathedral). Just south of here, set behind the small park, the Chi Linh Coffee Shop (see Coffee Shops in the Entertainment chapter) is a pleasant place to sip a coffee and people-watch.

Goody *(☎ 824 2110, 133 ĐL Hai Bai Trung)* is a trendy place that serves respectable Italian-style ice cream and light food. It's in District 1, a short walk from the French consulate.

Ice Cream Shops (Map 3)

Some of the best Vietnamese ice cream *(kem)* in Ho Chi Minh City is served at the three shops called ***Kem Bach Dang*** *(☎ 829 2707)*. Two of them are on ĐL Le Loi, on opposite corners of Đ Pasteur (Kem Bach Dang 1 is at 26 ĐL Le Loi and the other is at No 28). The third branch is at 67 ĐL Hai Ba Trung, on the corner with ĐL Le Loi. All three serve ice cream, hot and cold drinks and cakes at very reasonable prices. A US$1.50 speciality is ice cream served in a baby coconut with candied fruit on top *(kem trai dua)*.

America's response is ***Baskin-Robbins*** *(☎ 829 5775, 128A Đ Pasteur)*. It will cost you a fair bit to try all 31 flavours, as prices here are not low. There is another branch of '31' in the Huong Sen Hotel, at 66–70 Đ Dong Khoi, and a third yet at the Saigon Superbowl in the Tan Binh District.

Self-Catering (Maps 2 & 3)

Simple meals can easily be assembled from fruits, vegetables, French bread, croissants, cheese and other delectables sold in the city's markets and at street stalls. But avoid the unrefrigerated chocolate bars – they taste like they were left behind by the Americans in 1975. Apparently, the chocolate is repeatedly melted by the midday sun and rehardened at night, and quickly becomes a ball of rancid mush.

Finding yourself daydreaming about Kellogg's Frosties, Pringle's potato chips, Twining's tea or Campbell's soup? A good place to satisfy these urges is ***Minimart***, at 101 Đ Nam Ky Khoi Nghia, on the 2nd floor of the Saigon Intershop (just off of ĐL Le Loi). Minimart is open from 9 am to 6 pm daily.

Co-op Mart Cong Quyen (shopping mall) *(☎ 839 4973, 189C Đ Cong Quyen)* is highly popular place with local Saigonese. It offers reasonable prices on food items (eat in and take away) and consumer goods. The mall is near the Pham Ngu Lao area, at the western terminus of Đ Bui Thi Xuan.

About 100m toward the Thai Binh Market from here is ***Hanoi Mart***, at 51 Đ Cong Quyen, another large new supermarket.

The ***Dong Khanh Department Store***, at 850 ĐL Tran Hung Dao, also has a good supermarket with a range of imported goodies.

The ***Saigon Superbowl***, at A43 Truong Son, Tan Binh District, near the airport, offers Western-style mall culture. There is a supermarket here, not to mention a Kentucky Fried Chicken, Donut Magic and Jollibee Fast Food. There is even a place to cash travellers cheques to pay for it all.

In the Saigon Food Center, just opposite the local fire brigade, ***Citimart*** *(☎ 836 4588, 393B ĐL Tran Hung Dao)* is one of the larger supermarkets in town.

The ***Gourmet Shop*** *(☎ 844 9222, 251 Đ Nguyen Van Troi, Phu Nhuan District)*, at the Omni Hotel, is a treasure trove of rare items like cranberry sauce, French cheese, Sri Lankan tea and frozen cherry cheesecake. ***Megamart*** *(☎ 822 2578, 71 Đ Pasteur)* is a competitor in the imported food business.

Le Tonneau *(☎ 822 4522 75 Đ Mac Thi Buoi)*, just near the corner of Đ Dong Khoi, sells a wide selection of imported wines and spirits.

Cora *(☎ 061-833 180)* is a giant supermarket and shopping mall beamed right out of middle America to the northern suburbs of Ho Chi Minh City. The broad aisles feature food, kitchenware, electronics and clothing. The attached shopping mall has trendy shops and boutiques, a bakery and a Kentucky Fried Chicken. Cora is right on Highway 1 (about 30km from the city centre, past the Dong Nai River, near the town of Bien Hoa). It's way too far for a cyclo ride but taxi and buses (leaving from the Ben Thanh Market; US$0.40) can get you there.

PLACES TO EAT – CHOLON (MAP 5)

Cholon boasts many fine restaurants, though the classier ones are more expensive than in central Saigon. A far bigger problem than price, though, is the lack of comfortable chairs. Even many of the upmarket places leave you no choice but to sit on stools with no back support. This is hard to reconcile – do Cholonese have stronger-than-normal backbones or is it a plot by the local acupuncturists to drum up business? After all, even the budget cafes in the Pham Ngu Lao area have plastic chairs with backs on them. Nevertheless, if you search diligently you should find some place to eat that won't leave you in traction the next day.

If you want to pig out on pastries, Cholon is certainly the best place in Vietnam to do it. One fine bakery after another can be found along ĐL Tran Hung Dao. Two of the best we found are side by side near the intersection of ĐL Tran Hung Dao and Đ Trieu Quang Phuc: ***Do Thanh***, at 106–108 Đ Trieu Quang Phuc; and ***Hue Hue***, at 368 ĐL Tran Hung Dao.

If you haven't ruined your appetite with pastries, check out some of the local Chinese restaurants. Two highly popular indoor/outdoor restaurants are ***Nam Son***, at 520 Đ Nguyen Trai, and nearby ***My Huong***, at 131 Đ Nguyen Tri Phuong. Both serve all kinds of good food, including superb noodle soup with duck.

There is good chicken noodle soup at ***Pho Ga Chu Sang***, at 204 Đ Hai Thuong Lan Ong. Just next door, ***Hòng Phat***, at 206 Đ Hai Thuong Lan Ong, serves recommendable noodle soup with pork.

The ***Arc En Ciel Hotel***, at 52–56 Đ Tan Da, on corner of ĐL Tran Hung Dao B, has a good restaurant on the top floor (also with comfortable seats).

My Phuc Nguyen, at 3 ĐL Tran Hung Dao, sells tasty Singapore-style BBQ beef and pork jerky for about US$1. It's across the street from the Dong Khanh Hotel (on the corner of Đ An Binh, where ĐL Tran Hung Dao B begins). There are no seats at all – take-away service only.

Tiem Com Chay Giac Ngo 1, at 124 Đ Nguyen Tri Phuong, dishes up excellent vegetarian food and has an English menu. There is a second branch, ***Giac Ngo 2***, at 16 Đ Hau Giang, just on the edge of Districts 5 and 6, near the Binh Tay Market.

About 20m east of Giac Ngo 2, on the corner of Đ Hau Giang and Đ Pham Dinh Ho, ***Tiem An Nam Long*** is noteworthy for tasty wok-fried dishes and pavement seating. There is an English menu with no prices, but everything is cheap – most dishes cost under US$2.

Tiem Com Chay Phat Huu Duyen *(527 Đ Nguyen Trai)* is a small but popular Chinese vegetarian restaurant near the southern terminus of Đ Phuoc Hung. It's open from 7.30 am to 10 pm. A few doors down from here, the atmospheric ***Chinese Restaurant***, at 545 Đ Nguyen Trai, specialises in Taiwanese-style fried chicken; you can watch it being prepared in an old-style wooden cart in front of the restaurant.

Food Stalls (Map 3)

There are clusters of ***food stalls*** in the Andong and Binh Tay markets, where you can score cheap noodle and rice dishes. Everything is fresh and excellent.

PLACES TO EAT – BINH THANH DISTRICT (MAP 2)

There is a ***waterfront restaurant*** at the Binh Quoi Tourist Village, 8km from central Saigon in the Binh Thanh District. You can have dinner a la carte for under US$10 or buy a package deal tha includes dinner, a water puppet show and a river cruise. It costs US$20 for the whole evening. Quoi Island is chock-a-block with ***waterfront cafes***. They're popular with both expats and locals and costs are reasonable.

DINNER CRUISES (MAP 3)

Wining and dining while floating on the Saigon River is not the worst way to spend an evening. The ***floating restaurants*** are all government-owned and are docked just opposite the Riverside Hotel, in District 1. Most start boarding at 6 pm, depart the pier at 8 pm and return at 10 pm. Prices vary from US$5 to US$10 for dinner a la carte, though you could spend significantly more if you go heavy on the booze. Tickets for the cruise can be bought at the pier and you can call for information (☎ 822 5401). Most of the cruise boats offer live music and dancing.

Entertainment

Saigon, as it was known during the Vietnam (American) War, was notorious for its riotous nightlife. Pubs staffed with legions of prostitutes were major centres of R & R (rest and recreation) for US soldiers. In Saigon, a DJ noted, 'You can boogie till you puke'.

Reunification, in 1975, put a real damper on evening activities. After reunification, the pubs were shut down and the prostitutes were encouraged to find other employment, like stoop labour in the rice paddies. The rest of the population was introduced to enlightened socialist forms of entertainment.

Today, however, the pubs and discos have definitely staged a comeback, though what little prostitution there is must keep a low profile to protect Ho Chi Minh City's family image. Periodic crack down and clean-up campaigns – publicly aimed at controlling drugs, prostitution and excessive noise – continue to keep Ho Chi Minh City's nightlife decidedly on the quiet side.

Though the city's pubs still tend to be male-oriented businesses, more and more places are sufficiently toned-down for a single woman to feel comfortable. Amenities in the better places include air-conditioning, decent pub grub and taped background music.

Central Saigon is the place to be on Sunday and holiday nights (and lately Saturday nights as well). The streets are jam-packed with young Saigonese going cruising *(di troi)* on bicycles and motorcycles. Everyone is dressed in their fashionable best (often with the price tag still attached). The mass of slowly moving humanity is so thick on Đ Dong Khoi that you may have to wait until dawn to get across the street! It is utter chaos at intersections, where eight, 10 or more lanes of two-wheeled vehicles intersect without the benefit of traffic lights, safety helmets or sanity.

Near the Municipal Theatre, fashionably dressed young people take a break from cruising to watch the endless procession, lining up along the street next to their cycles. The air is electric with the glances of lovers and animated conversations among friends. Everyone is out to see and be seen – it's a sight you shouldn't miss.

BARS

Pham Ngu Lao Area (Map 4)

When it comes to nightlife, budget backpacker land has a few hot spots. The latest place is the popular ***Allez Boo Bar*** *(☎ 836 9522, 187 Đ Pham Ngu Lao)*, which is done up in dimly-lit tropical bamboo decor. The bar is easy to spot, right on the corner with Đ De Tham.

Bar Rolling Stones, *(☎ 836 0395, 287 Đ Pham Ngu Lao)*, and the ***Long Phi Bar*** *(☎ 836 9319, 163 Đ Pham Ngu Lao)* are both known for their late hours, loud music and party atmosphere. Near the corner of Đ Pham Ngu Lao and Đ De Tham is the slightly mellower ***Guns and Roses Bar*** *(☎ 836 0845, 207 Đ Pham Ngu Lao)*.

The budget-minded should try the unnamed draught beer *(bia hoi)* at the place at 161 Đ Pham Ngu Lao, a Vietnamese watering hole where you can sample the local brew for US$0.40 per litre.

Of course, there are always the travellers' cafes (see the earlier Places to Eat chapter), many which stay open late serving cheap food and drinks.

Dong Khoi Area (Map 3)

For wider nightlife choices, head down to the central area around Đ Dong Khoi.

Vasco's Bar, at 16 Đ Cao Ba Quat, shares the lovely villa housing the exquisite French restaurant Camargue. It's a trendy place (popular with expats) and features a pleasant outdoor terrace.

Apocalypse Now *(☎ 824 1463, 2C Đ Thi Sach)* has long led the pack. The music is loud and the patrons are from all walks of life – and apocalyptically rowdy.

For a more civilised atmosphere, try the excellent ***No 5 Ly Tu Trong*** *(☎ 825 6300)*. Named for its address, it is run by long-term

Swiss resident, Heinz. The decor of this restored French-colonial villa is stylish and sleek. Expats congregate here, swapping yarns. Good music, tasty food and beer, billiards and friendly staff all contribute to the pleasant atmosphere.

The legendary imitation ***Hard Rock Cafe*** *(☎ 822 1023, 22–24 Mac Thi Buoi)* has mellower music than the name suggests. It certainly is a popular spot.

On the 11th floor rooftop of the Caravelle Hotel you will find ***Saigon Saigon*** *(☎ 823 4999)*. It offers top-notch views and real atmosphere. However prices are also top-notch.

Another excellent place to take in the view of the rising Ho Chi Minh City skyline is ***Panorama 33*** *(☎ 910 0492, 37 Đ Ton Duc Thang)*, which occupies the 32nd and 33rd floors of the Saigon Trade Center, the city's tallest building. You can enjoy a coffee or cocktails in air-con comfort, but the place to be is really outside on the terrace. Panorama is open from 10 am to 11 pm daily.

The ***Montana Cafe*** *(☎ 829 5067, 40E Đ Ngo Duc Ke)* is centrally located between ĐL Nguyen Hue and Đ Dong Khoi, and has a diverse menu, billiards and satellite TV. The atmosphere is relaxed but chic. (See the Places to Eat chapter, earlier.)

Sheridan's Irish House *(☎ 823 0973, 19 Đ Le Thanh Ton, District 1)* is an Irish pub beamed straight from the backstreets of old Dublin. Curiously, in the same building, upstairs from the pub, there is a small Chinese restaurant beamed straight from the back alleys of Shanghai!

The ***Tex-Mex Cantina*** *(☎ 829 5950, 24 Đ Le Thanh Ton)* serves the best margarita on the rocks this side of Hong Kong and is also notable for its billiards tables. (See the Places to Eat chapter, earlier.)

Wannabe ranch hands should check out ***Wild West*** *(☎ 829 5127, 33 ĐL Hai Ba Trung)*. The live music here is loud and the billiards tables are busy.

Not far from Wild West is ***Hien & Bob's Place*** *(☎ 823 0661, 43 ĐL Hai Ba Trung)*, a long-running expat hangout which advertises the coldest beer in town and American-style sandwiches.

Yet another theme bar is the ***Cafe 58*** *(☎ 829 0206, 56–60 ĐL Hai Ba Trung)*. They have a good billiards table and the bar sees a good mix of foreign and local clientele. If you're tired of hearing this week's pop hit played *over and over*, Cafe 58 has one of the best CD collections in Vietnam. The Vietnamese name is Cafe Ai Cap – look for the neon sign.

DISCOS & CLUBS

Two of the hottest new nightclubs in town are Hazzard (Map 3; ☎ 822 5478, 104 Đ Hai Ba Trung, District 1) and Monaco (Map5; ☎ 835 1723, 651 Đ Tran Hung Dao, District 5).

Tropical Rainforest *(Map 3; ☎ 825 7783, 5–15 Đ Ho Huan Nghiep)* – called Mua Rung in Vietnamese – is done up in Amazonian rainforest-theme decor. It is one of Ho Chi Minh City's hottest dance spots and, surprisingly, is brought to you by Saigon Tourist (it's not just lounge music anymore!). The US$4 door charge entitles you one free drink. Their cocktail list features such perennials as Envy, Seduction and – our personal favourite – Orgasm.

Planet Europe *(☎ 885 0184)*, located in the Saigon Superbowl (Map 2; Tan Binh District), is a flashy place that serves food and has a happy hour that lasts from 6.30 to 9 pm. If dancing isn't your thing, they can accommodate you with karaoke.

Cheers *(☎ 839 205.*¯ is the disco inside the Vien Dong Hotel (Map 4; 275A Đ Pham Ngu Lao, District 1). This popular place charges a US$7 admission and features live rhythms from a Filipino house band.

Junction 5 *(☎ 839 0000)* is inside the plush Equatorial Hotel (Map 2; 242 Đ Tran Binh Trong, District 5). This place has a house band dishing up live music.

The New World Hotel (Map 4; 76 Đ Le Lai, District 1) chips in with ***Catwalk*** *(☎ 824 3760)*. The disco and ***Garden Pub*** is particularly big with Hong Kongers, who also appreciate that there are in-house karaoke booths a few steps away.

There is dancing with a live band at the ***Rex Hotel*** *(Map 3; ☎ 829 6043, fax 829 6536, 141 ĐL Nguyen Hue, District 1)*, from 7.30 to 11 pm nightly.

BALLROOM DANCING

Vietnam is one of the few places left where a major component of the nightlife is ballroom dancing. Interestingly, these *soirées dansantes* have become more and more like mutated discos in recent years – and the guests are likely to be affluent young people dressed in jeans and the latest designer bootlegs – but the principle is the same.

One place to find ballroom disco is at ***Nha Van Hoa Lao Dong*** which is in Cong Vien Van Hoa Park (Map 3), enter from Đ Nguyen Thi Minh Khai – it's on the north side, just west of Đ Huyen Tran Cong Chua. Admission costs US$1 and it's open from 8 to 10 pm Thursday, Saturday and Sunday. It's a similar scene at ***Cau Lac Bo,*** on the waterfront side of Đ Ben Chuong (Map 4), just south of ĐL Ham Nghi, on the Saigon River.

COFFEE SHOPS

Coffee shops can be found everywhere and anywhere in Ho Chi Minh City. These should not be confused with cafes, which serve complete meals (see Cafes in the Places to Eat chapter). Coffee shops don't do meals, but most usually have snacks. Key features of Vietnamese coffee shops are superbly comfortable lawn chairs (which always face towards the street) and plenty of *loud* music. The chairs are wonderful, but the music usually consists of Vietnamese pop songs, which seldom appeal to non-Vietnamese. Worse still, more and more coffee shops are being set up with karaoke sound systems, which allow you to create your own noise. Nevertheless, you might find these coffee shops quite enjoyable if you're deaf or if you visit during an electrical outage. They are also a good place to take refuge from a sudden downpour.

Chi Linh Coffee Shop *(☎ 824 2936)* deserves special mention. This outdoor drinking establishment is in a park-like garden on Đ Dong Khoi between Đ Ly Tu Trong and Đ Le Thanh Ton (Map 3). You can sit in the park, listen to music, drink a beer or coffee and relax away an afternoon or evening. No food is served.

In the Pham Ngu Lao area, you might try the string of indoor-outdoor places on Đ De Tham, between Đ Bui Vien and ĐL Tran Hung Dao.

POP & ROCK

To really taste Ho Chi Minh City's youth culture, you have to catch one of its pop music shows. It matters little where you go, since it's very much the same from one venue to the next. The music is almost entirely Western bubble gum pop hits from the '60s and '70s. An essential difference from Western-style performances is that each vocalist (accompanied by a house band) gets to perform one or two songs. The singers seem to have a uniform of sorts – a sequins and satin outfit with a permapress hairdo. The best band always plays at the end of the concert, forcing you to sit through the rest. If you're lucky, you might get to see a very rare performance by a foreign band (a while back, a Russian heavy metal band called Vomit was threatening to make a tour!).

There's an ***outdoor venue*** on Đ Ly Tu Trong between Đ Nam Ky Khoi Nghia and Đ Pasteur, District 1 (Map 3). There is no admission fee – you just pay for your drinks. Shows are at 8 pm nightly. Two nights a week they play traditional Vietnamese music with folk instruments – which are largely drowned out by the waves of mushy synthesised sound. The other five nights feature modern and pop music – which sounds very similar to the traditional music.

An outdoor amphitheatre called ***Trong Dong*** is in the south-west part of Cong Vien Van Hoa Park (Map 4), on the corner of Đ Cach Mang Thang Tam and Đ Nguyen Du, District 1. Admission costs around US$1. The official address is 8 Đ Cach Mang Thang Tam. There is an ***unnamed place*** with similar music up the road, at 126 Đ Cach Mang Thang Tam.

JAZZ (MAP 3)

The beats of the mighty Hoa Soty (literally, 'Fire Mountain'), led by 70-something pianist and local hero La Thanh, can be heard Monday, Friday and Saturday at ***L'Elysee*** *(☎ 824 1555)* in the posh Sofitel Plaza Saigon Hotel at 141 ĐL Nguyen Hue. The bar's name is French for Elysian Fields.

It is a stylish place. If you're hungry, there is a good light-bite menu to choose from.

The ***Saxophone Lounge*** *(☎ 822 8305)* in the New World Hotel, at 76 Đ Le Lai, has live jazz every night, starting at 9 pm.

THEATRE

Various forms of Vietnamese theatre are performed around the country by dozens of state-funded troupes and companies. Ho Chi Minh City has several places where you can catch traditional or classical music, opera, ballet and a variety of theatrical performances (see the Theatre & Puppetry section in the Facts about Ho Chi Minh City chapter). Performance-types and starting times vary greatly, so check the local papers before heading out.

Municipal Theatre (Map 3)

The ***Municipal Theatre*** *(☎ 829 1249, 829 1584)*, or Nha Hat Thanh Pho, is on Đ Dong Khoi smack between the upmarket Continental and Caravelle hotels. It faces up ĐL Le Loi. It was built in 1899 for use as a theatre, but later served as the heavily fortified home of the South Vietnamese National Assembly. To coincide with Saigon's 300-year anniversary, the theatre underwent a painstakingly thorough restoration.

Each week, the Municipal Theatre offers a different program, which could be Eastern European-style gymnastics, nightclub music or traditional Vietnamese theatre. Most performances start at 8 pm nightly. Refreshments are sold during intermission and public toilets are in the basement.

Hoa Binh Theatre (Map 2)

The huge ***Hoa Binh Theatre complex*** *(☎ 865 5199, 14 ĐL 3 Thang 2, District 10)* – also known as Nha Hat Hoa Binh, or Peace Theatre – often has several performances taking place simultaneously in its various halls, the largest of which seats 2300 people. The complex is next to the Vietnam Quoc Tu Pagoda. The ticket office is open from 7.30 am until the end of the evening show.

Evening performances, which begin at 7.30 pm, are usually held once or twice a week. Shows range from traditional and modern Vietnamese plays to Western pop music and circus acts. In the 2300-seat hall, well-known Vietnamese pop singers begin performances at 8.30 pm and run through to about 11.30.

Films are screened all day, every day, beginning at 8.30 am. Some of the films – from France, Hong Kong and the USA (Disney productions are a favourite) – are still live-dubbed (someone reads a translation of the script over the PA system), leaving the original soundtrack at least partly audible. A weekly schedule of screenings is posted outside the building next to the ticket counter.

The disco on the ground floor is open from 8 to 11 pm Tuesday to Sunday. Admission is US$2.

Conservatory of Music (Map 4)

Performances of both traditional Vietnamese and Western classical music are given at the ***Conservatory of Music*** *(☎ 824 3774, 112 Đ Nguyen Du)*, which is near Reunification Palace. Concerts are held at 7.30 pm Monday and Friday evening during the two annual concert seasons, from March to May and from October to December.

Students aged seven to 16 attend the conservatory, which performs all the functions of a public school in addition to providing instruction in music. The music teachers here have been trained in France, Britain and the USA, as well as the former Eastern Bloc. The school is free, but most of the students come from well-off families because only the well-to-do can afford the prerequisite musical instruments.

The theatre's Vietnamese name is Nhac Vien Thanh Pho Ho Chi Minh.

Ben Thanh Theatre (Map 3)

The ***Ben Thanh Theatre*** *(☎ 823 1652, 6 Mac Dinh Chi)* hosts a variety of entertainment: music, ballet, fashion shows, and cross-cultural events.

Mang Non Theatre (Map 3)

The ***Mang Non Theatre*** *(☎ 822 2051, 193 Đ Dong Khoi, District 1)*, has performances of water puppets *(mua roi ngoc)* and 'dry' puppetry *(mua roi can)*. Two dry shows take place at 8 am and 11.15, Sundays. There are no 'wet' shows. Tickets cost US$1.10, or US$0.80 for children. The English translation of the venue is Bamboo Shoot Theatre.

Nha Hat Cai Luong Theatre (Map 4)

Nha Hat Cai Luong Theatre, or Tran Huu Trang, at 136 ĐL Tran Hung Dao, is very convenient to the Pham Ngu Lao area and a good place to see contemporary theatre *(cai luong)* performances. Schedules are irregular, so to find out what's playing and head over the theatre ticket office, or try calling this cellular phone number (in Vietnam only): ☎ 090728957. Tickets cost around US$2 to US$3.

Maxim's Dinner Theatre (Map 3)

Maxim's Dinner Theatre *(☎ 829 6676, 15 Đ Dong Khoi)*, a Ho Chi Minh City institution, is a restaurant with live musical performances. Cultural shows run nightly from 6.45 to 9 pm, and a *phong tra* (literally, 'tea room')show runs from 9.30 to 11.30 pm (see the Places to Eat chapter, earlier).

WATER PUPPETRY (MAP 3)

This art really comes from the north (see Theatre & Puppetry in the Facts about Ho Chi Minh City chapter), and is best seen in Hanoi. In recent years, though, it has been introduced to the south, as it has been a big hit with tourists. There are two places where you can see water puppet shows in Ho Chi Minh City. The best venue in Ho Chi Minh City is the ***War Remnants Museum***, at 28 Đ Vo Van Tan; a similar set up is at the ***History Museum***, on the grounds of the zoo (see the Things to See & Do chapter for more information on these places). Shows do not run on a fixed schedule but commence when there are at least five customers.

CULTURE CLUBS

These are really geared towards the domestic audience, but you might have some interest in seeing what sort of culture the government produces for the masses. Some venues for Vietnamese cultural entertainment include the ***Youth House of Culture*** *(4 Đ Pham Ngoc Thach, District 1)*, the ***Children's House of Culture*** *(4 Đ Tu Xuong, District 3)* and the ***Workers' Club*** *(55B Đ Xo Viet Nghe Tinh, District 1)*.

CINEMAS

Most maps of Ho Chi Minh City have cinemas *(rap)* marked with a special symbol. Western movies, either subtitled or dubbed, vie with trashy Vietnamese kung fu flicks and cheesy love stories. It is best to phone ahead to find out what is showing (and, if possible, what is subtitled, as opposed to overdubbed).

Vietnamese censors take a dim view of nudity and sex – murder and mayhem are OK. Traditionally, the government has favoured movies about victorious wars and the life and times of Ho Chi Minh. Gripping stuff.

The ***Archive Film Club*** *(Map 2; ☎ 822 2324, 212 Đ Ly Chinh Thang, District 3)* is perhaps the most popular venue to catch subtitled foreign films. The seats here are hard as rock, so you might consider bringing a cushion.

Out by the airport is the ***Tan Son Nhat Cinema*** *(Map 2; ☎ 823 1128, 186 Đ Nguyen Van Troi, Phu Nhuan District)*, a multiscreen complex with more comfortable seating than the Archive – but the theatres are a bit claustrophobic.

There are several cinemas in the city centre, though foreign language screenings are rare. They include the ***Rap Mang Non***, on Đ Dong Khoi 100m from the Municipal Theatre. There is also ***Rap Dong Khoi*** (Map 3), at 163 Đ Dong Khoi, District 1 and, in the Pham Ngu Lao area, the ***Cong Nhan Cinema*** *(Map 4; ☎ 836 9556, 30 ĐL Tran Hung Dao, District 1)*.

Video Parlours

An adjunct to Ho Chi Minh City's cinemas are its unauthorised video parlours. Vietnam's opening to the outside world is creating massive headaches for the country's censors. Despite their best efforts, customs agents haven't been able to hold back the tide of video tapes being smuggled into Vietnam. The pirating of video tapes has become bi

One of the joys of Asian travel: bountiful fruit

RICHARD I'ANSON

Fresh produce is everywhere.

GARRETT CULHANE

A baker sells French bread on the street.

KRAIG LIEB

If it walks or crawls, you can cage it and sell it.

PHIL WEYMOUTH

Stall holders, Cholon Market

PHIL WEYMOUTH

What better way to wash down a meal?

GARRETT CULHANE

GARRETT CULHANE

Some like it hot

GREG ELMS

That was then...this is Apocalypse Now.

PHIL WEYMOUTH

The Municipal Theatre, Dong Khoi area

MASON FLORENCE

Saigon Water Park, Thu Duc, has proved a hit with tourists and locals.

business and the tapes are sold or rented all over the country. Kung fu movies from Hong Kong and pornography from the West and Japan are much in demand. Ditto for the latest MTV tapes. Such spiritual pollution is bad enough, but a thornier problem for the culture police are videos about the Vietnam War. Illegal but popular war movies include *Rambo, Apocalypse Now, Full Metal Jacket, Platoon, The Deer Hunter, Good Morning Vietnam, Born on the 4th of July, Air America* and *Heaven and Earth.*

Since many Vietnamese cannot afford video equipment, budding entrepreneurs have set up instant mini-theatres consisting of a VCR, a few chairs and curtains to keep out nonpaying onlookers. The admission price is very low, in the order of US$0.25. Some of these video parlours provide food and beverage services.

SPECTATOR SPORTS

Venues

Phu Tho Racetrack When South Vietnam fell in 1975, one of the first things Hanoi did was to ban debauched, capitalistic pastimes such as gambling. Horse-racing tracks – mostly found in the Saigon area – were shut down. This only forced Vietnam's gambling fraternity to go underground. Later, however, the government's need for hard cash caused a rethink of official policy towards gambling.

The ***Phu Tho Racetrack*** – Cau Lac Bo TDTT; Truong Dua Phu Tho – *(☎ 864 9322, 2 Đ Le Dai Hanh, District 11)*, which dates from around 1900, reopened in 1989. Much of the credit for the reopening goes to Philip Chow, a Chinese-Vietnamese businessman who fled to Hong Kong as a youth but returned to Vietnam in 1987. After getting the track up and running, Chow was rewarded for his efforts by being sacked. Government officials, sensing the opportunity to line their own pockets, saw no reason to keep an entrepreneur on the payroll.

Ever the optimist, Chow approached the government with a proposal to reopen the Duc Hoa Thung Racetrack, 45km from central Saigon. Realising that this could draw business away from its own monopoly, they flatly refused.

Like the state lottery, the racetrack is extremely lucrative. But this has not prevented grumbling about just where the money is going, and widespread allegations about the drugging of horses. And though the minimum legal age for jockeys is 14 years, most look like they are about 10.

The overwhelming majority of gamblers are Vietnamese, though there is no rule prohibiting foreigners from joining in. The minimum bet is 2000d; the maximum 20,000d, but you can buy as many stubs as you want. Races are held Saturday and Sunday afternoons, starting at 12.30 pm; entrance is free. Plans to introduce off-track betting have so far not materialised. However, illegal bookmaking (bets can be placed in gold!) offers one form of competition to the government-owned monopoly.

The Phu Tho Racetrack is also the venue for periodic motorcycle races, though it's a little uncertain if you'll be able to see this. Illegal street racing is a recent fad, often with fatal results. To get the racers off the street, the municipal government has permitted occasional legal races at Phu Tho Racetrack. To keep the fatality rate down, motorcycle size has been limited to 50cc and 100cc. There is some corporate sponsorship of the races, with winners often receiving a new Yamaha or Honda.

Unlike the horse races, motorcycle races do not run to regular schedules. Furthermore, motorcycle racing is controversial – some consider the sport decadent and want it banned. Make local inquiries to find out what the current situation is.

City Stadium The Ho Chi Minh City stadium, San Van Dong Hoa Lu, is on the corner of Đ Dinh Tien Hoang and Đ Nguyen Thi Minh Khai, District 1 (one block west of the zoo). This is the place where Ho Chi Minh City's major sporting events are held.

Street Sports

The Vietnamese are incredibly skilled at badminton (shuttlecock). Other favourites include volleyball and table tennis. It can be amazing to watch badminton, even if you don't play. Competitions take place regularly in front of a church called Nha Thoi, in District 6.

Though not a pleasant experience for animals and animal lovers, the back alleys near the river in Cholon are the venues for illegal cock fights.

TV Sports

Football (soccer) is the No 1 sport with spectators. The FIFA World Cup is not shown on Vietnamese free-to-air TV, but it is broadcast on satellite TV (and copied onto pirated video tapes and distributed the very same day).

Tennis has considerable snob appeal with Vietnam's nouveaux riches – trendy Vietnamese like nothing better than to catch the games on TV. But though the upper crust likes to play, there is a shortage of public tennis courts.

Shopping

In recent years, Ho Chi Minh City has blossomed into a shoppers' paradise, catering to both tourists and the local market. With Vietnam's recent economic reforms, today's Saigonese, in particular the youth, have fully embraced the craze for material goods (demonstrated by the myriad of fashionable boutiques and shopping malls springing up around the city).

Whether or not you wish to buy anything, your first commercial encounter will likely be with the 'you buy something from me' women and children who pedal postcards, books (mostly bootlegged photocopies) and maps. A reasonable amount of bargaining is called.

In general, items sold with no visible price tags must be bargained for – expect the vendor to start the bidding at two to five times the real price. Tagged items may be negotiable, but more often than not the prices are fixed.

To the Western mind, one of the odd things about shopping in Ho Chi Minh City is the tendency for vendors of the same product to congregate all in one spot. For example, it's not uncommon for 50 or more shops and stalls selling TVs to all cram together on one street, while there is a dearth of such shops elsewhere. This situation is found in other parts of Asia: there are streets devoted, in turn, to CDs, watches, jewellery, glasses, stationery, cloth, clothing, cameras etc. The shops offer little to choose between them – prices, quality and selection are nearly identical in all adjacent businesses. At least in theory, cut-throat competition like this should create a buyers' market. In practice, Vietnamese shopkeepers wouldn't be in business if they were not making a profit.

As a general principle, try to find a shop that: 1) does not cater particularly to tourists, and 2) puts price tags on all its items. In touristy areas, items sold with no visible price tags must be bargained for – expect the vendor to start the bidding at two to five times the real price. Though the touristy areas are where the best selection of souvenir goods are sold, you may find a better deal if you are willing to hunt around the back alleys and markets of Ho Chi Minh City, where the rents are lower.

WHAT TO BUY

Hot items on the tourist market include lacquerware, items with mother-of-pearl inlay, wood carvings and ceramics (from fine celadon to enormous elephants), embroidered items (hangings, tablecloths, pillow cases, pyjamas and robes), blinds made of hanging bamboo beads (many travellers like the replica of the *Mona Lisa*), reed mats, Chinese-style carpets, jewellery, leatherwork, bird cages and aromatic cinnamon wood boxes and toothpick holders.

RICHARD I'ANSON

Chinese-style porcelain and ceramics are popular with souvenir hunters.

Other items which make attractive souvenirs include the colourful clothing and crafts produced by Vietnam's prolific hill tribes. Despite its distance from the mountainous Central Highlands and northern Vietnam, where these people live, an increasing selection of ethnic minority products are finding their way to shops in Ho Chi Minh City.

Assuming you are an automobile collector and have sufficient funds to support such an expensive habit, Ho Chi Minh City is a worthwhile place to check out for old cars. During the Vietnam (American) War, Saigon had a large population of resident US technical advisors, businesspeople, journalists, diplomats and CIA agents, many of whom bought imported US and European cars for personal use. When South Vietnam suddenly collapsed in 1975, the Americans had to flee abruptly, abandoning their vehicles in the process. There are also a dwindling number of classic old French cars, left behind from the colonial era.

WHERE TO SHOP

Dong Khoi Area (Map 3)

Central Saigon is *the* place to shop. However something to remember is that this area is also by far the worst in the city for street crime. Đ Dong Khoi and Đ Nguyen Hue are thick with shops geared towards the tourist traffic, but are also where the largest number of scams and rip-offs and take place. When shopping (or just strolling, for that matter) in this area, be *very* careful of your belongings: skilled pairs of motorcycle cowboys perform like world-class acrobats and can swipe your bag and be hundreds of metres away by the time it registers that you've been robbed!

Arts & Handicrafts Đ Dong Khoi has a reputation as the centre for handicrafts, though many shop owners can be rapacious and will drive a hard bargain. Not surprisingly, you can expect high prices and, of course, bargaining is *de rigueur*. By way of compensation, there is a fairly wide selection of goods here. Remember that the 'antiques' are almost certainly fakes, which is OK, as long as you don't pay 'antique' prices.

Heritage (☎ 823 5438), at 53 Đ Dong Khoi, is an attractive shop selling reproduction Vietnamese arts and crafts: ceramics, carved statues, folk paintings and textiles. Heritage can also tailor *ao dai* (the national dress of Vietnam). It's open from 8.30 am to 10 pm daily.

Nearby, Precious Qui (☎ 825 6817), at 27 Đ Dong Khoi, specialises in lacquerware and accessories (interesting forks and spoons) fashioned from buffalo horn. They also stock a limited selection of celadon ceramic ware.

Authentique Interiors (☎ 822 1333), at 38 Đ Dong Khoi, is another trendy place that sells a tasteful selection of furniture, lacquerware and accessories. There is a gallery on the second storey with a rotating roster of exhibitions. The shop and gallery are open from 9 am to 9 pm daily.

Made in Vietnam (☎ 822 0841), at 26B Đ Le Thanh Ton, sells a wide selection of local crafts and home decorations, including ceramics, lighting and rattan furniture.

The Home Zone (☎ 822 8022), at 41 Đ Dinh Tien Hoang, near the corner of ĐL Le Duan, is another interesting place to look for locally made home furnishings.

Celadon Green (☎ 823 6816), at 29 Đ Dong Du, specialises in celadon tableware and also carries a few interesting bits of lacquerware. Another place to find high quality celadon wares is Celadon Legend (☎ 823 6853), at 71A Đ Le Thanh Ton, which is attached to the Rex Hotel.

Opposite the Omni Hotel (on the way to the airport) is Lamson Art Gallery (Map 2; ☎ 844 1361), at 106 Đ Nguyen Van Troi, Phu Nhuan District. This place sells exquisite, but relatively expensive, lacquerware, rattan, ceramics, woodcarvings – and more. It's worth stopping by to have a look at the artisans at work.

'Ethnic Minority' Goods East Meets West (☎ 823 1553), at 24 ĐL Le Loi, which is attached to the Rex Hotel, specialises in colourful hill tribe clothing and paraphernalia.

Nam Kha Silk Collection (☎ 822 5115), at 29B Đ Dong Khoi, sells a very nice collection of ethnic minority clothing.

Fine Art From simple greeting cards with silk paintings on the front (US$0.50) to wood-block prints, oil paintings, lacquer paintings and watercolours, Ho Chi Minh City is an excellent city for art hunters. Even much of the mass-produced stuff, most of which is very affordable, looks great at home.

The cheaper stuff (US$10 to US$50) is sent to touristy galleries and hotel gift shops. It's important to know that there are quite a few forgeries around – just because you spot a painting by a famous Vietnamese artist does not mean that it's an original, though it may still be an attractive work of art. Higher-standard works are generally put on display in one of the city's more exclusive galleries.

Published out of Hong Kong, *Asian Art News* magazine (e asianart@netvigator.com) is an excellent source on what's happening in the Vietnamese art market. Several of Vietnam's top galleries advertise here. You might also take a look at the online Gallery Cyclo at www.destinationvietnam.com.

A wide variety of oil paintings, watercolours, lacquer paintings and paintings on silk can be bought from Ho Chi Minh City's expanding array of art galleries. Typical prices for paintings are in the US$30 to US$50 range, but the artists may ask 10 times that. The following galleries should provide a good starting point for art hunters.

Duc Minh Art Gallery (☎ 823 2449) 23 Đ Ly Tu Trong
Saigon Gallery (☎ 829 7102) 5 Đ Ton Duc Thang
Saigon Tourist Art Gallery (☎ 829 7473) 55 Đ Dong Khoi
Tu Do Gallery (☎ 823 1785) 142 Đ Dong Khoi
Vinh Loi Gallery (☎ 822 2006) 41 Đ Ba Huyen Thanh Quan
Xuan Gallery (☎ 829 1277) 32 Đ Vo Thi Sau

The Ho Chi Minh City Association of Fine Arts (☎ 823 0026), at 218A Đ Pasteur, is another place where aspiring young artists display their latest works. There are also several upmarket galleries on the first level of the Fine Arts Museum. These include the Blue Space, Nhat Le and Lac Hong galleries.

If you've bought a masterpiece in need of proper framing, Saigon Art Frame (☎ 823 2753), at 74 E2 ĐL Hai Ba Trung, is a reputable place with reasonable prices and good quality materials.

Antiques There are quite a number of stores in Ho Chi Minh City offering real and fake antique Vietnamese handicrafts. A Vietnamese speciality is the instant antique, with a price tag of a few dollars for a teapot, ceramic dinner plate or wood carving. Of course, it's OK to buy fake antiques, as long as you aren't paying genuine antique prices.

There are also some shops in the city that deal in real antiques and high quality reproductions.

If you're looking to export, most of the colonial era stuff is not difficult to get out of the country, but for the older Vietnamese and Chinese items you'll want to be sure you have the proper paperwork. A problem occurs if you've bought an antique (or something which looks antique) and didn't get an official export certificate:

> When I was in the airport a customs officer eyed out two porcelain vases I had bought and told me that I should go to the Department of Culture to have them assessed or pay a fine of US$20. Of course, there was no representative of the Department of Culture at the airport to make such an evaluation, so getting them assessed would require me to miss my flight.
>
> Anna Crawford Pinnerup

Just what happens to confiscated antiques is a good question. Some say that the authorities sell them back to the souvenir shops. You might call it recycling.

Reputable shops can advise you on the formalities of certification.

Indochine House (☎ 822 7318), at 27 Đ Dong Du, is a charming shop specialising in early 20th century rescued relics (mostly produced during the period when much of Saigon was built by French colonists). It sells fine art and memorabilia, furniture, old photos and prints, plus some older Asian ceramics. It's open from 9.30 am to 6.30 pm daily.

Nguyen Freres (☎ 822 9654), at 2A ĐL Le Duan, is another contender, dealing with a similar selection. About half of their stock is real antiques and the rest is reproduction furniture and household knick-knacks. It's open from 10 am to 7 pm daily – to 6 pm Sunday.

Clothing Ho Chi Minh City has a wide selection of silk clothes and accessories, most which are cheap. The most popular item with women is the elegant ao dai. Ready-made ao dai start at about US$20, while the custom-tailored sets are considerably more. There are also male ao dai available – these are a looser-fit and come with a silk-covered head wrap to match the top of the outfit. Prices vary by store and by the fabric chosen.

If you want to buy custom-made clothing for your friends, you'll need their measurements. As a general rule, you get best results when you're personally measured by the tailor or seamstress.

Ho Chi Minh City is an excellent place to pick up hand-embroidered clothing and accessories. T-shirts are ever-popular items with travellers. A printed T-shirt costs around US$2, while an embroidered design will cost maybe US$3.50. However, don't believe the sizes on the labels – large in Asia is often equivalent to medium in the West, and a tumble through a clothes dryer will instantly make it a small.

Sandals are a practical item in the tropical heat. At around US$4, they certainly are worth the money. Finding large sizes to fit Western feet can be a problem though. Make sure they are very comfortable before you purchase them – some tend to be poorly made and will give you blisters.

The best place to find ready-made silk garments, as well as embroidery and drawings on silk, is along Đ Dong Khoi. Two well-known places are Khai Silk (☎ 823 4634), at 98 Đ Mac Thi Buoi, and Vietsilk (☎ 823 4860), at 21 Đ Dong Khoi, though a stroll along Đ Dong Khoi will turn up plenty of other choices.

For ready-made women's fashions try Coco (☎ 822 8219), at 2A ĐL Le Duan, a stylish boutique just next door to Homezone. Other places that are worth checking out are Thai Fashion, at 92H Đ Le Thanh Ton, and Down Under Fashions at 229 Đ Le Thanh Ton.

For Western-style fashions and men's suits, there are numerous tailor shops in central Saigon and in Cholon. Several upmarket hotels have in-house tailors. Custom-made suits for men can also be tailored at several shops along Đ Dong Khoi.

T-shirts and conical straw hats are available from vendors along Đ Dong Khoi and ĐL Nguyen Hue.

Ao Dai Ao dai (pronounced ow-yai), the flowing silk blouse slit up the sides and worn over pantaloons, are tailored at many shops in and around the city centre.

Si Hoang (☎ 829 9156) has two locations: 36–38 Đ Ly Tu Trong, District 1 and 258–260 Đ Pasteur, District 3. A couple of doors down from the latter branch, at 264/1 Đ Pasteur, is another ao dai maker called Nha (☎ 823 0745); these places are nearly opposite the Pasteur Institute.

You might also try Ao Dai Thanh Chau (☎ 823 1032) at 244 Đ Dinh Tien Hoang. This is a very famous place with local Saigonese, though it's a bit far from the city centre. Vietnam Silk (☎ 829 2607, fax 843 9279), at 183 Đ Dong Khoi, opposite the Continental Hotel, is one of many places along the tourist shopping strip in the city centre which can tailor ao dai. You might also check out the stalls in the Ben Thanh Market or the Saigon Intershop area on ĐL Le Loi (Map 3).

Embroidery In addition to the shops along Đ Dong Khoi, Kieu Giang (☎ 824 1343), at 71C Đ Le Thanh Ton and Kim Phuong (☎ 829 0844), at 77 Đ Le Thanh Ton, are both excellent places to find high quality embroidery. They are both attached to the Rex Hotel, on the same side of Đ Le Thanh Ton (opposite the Hôtel de Ville).

Hats Women all over the country wear conical hats to keep the sun off their faces (they also function like umbrellas in the rain). If you hold a well-made conical hat up to the light, you'll be able to see that between the layers of straw material are paper cut-outs with artistic designs. Conical hats generally sell for about US$1 in the tourist areas, but can be bought for about a quarter of that price at the markets.

Coffee & Wine Very close to the Rex Hotel, the Monaco Cafe & Restaurant (☎ 825 6387), at 59 Đ Pasteur, is more a place to sit and sip java than a coffee wholesaler, but it's as good a place as any to pick up high quality beans.

Just off of Đ Dong Khoi, PL Chateau (☎ 825 6288), at 63 Đ Mac Thi Buoi, sells top-grade caffeine and also hands out cards that entitle you to a free espresso. At a few doors down, Le Tonneau (☎ 822 4522), at 75 Đ Mac Thi Buoi, stocks an excellent collection of imported wines and spirits.

Gems & Jewellery Vietnam produces some good gems and jewellery, but there are plenty of fakes and flawed gems around. This doesn't mean that you can't buy something if you think it's beautiful, but don't think that you'll find a cut diamond or polished ruby for a fraction of what you'd pay at home. Some travellers have actually thought that they could buy gems in Vietnam and sell these at home for a profit. Such business requires considerable expertise and good connections in the mining industry.

Books In the early days of Vietnamese tourism, in the late 1980s and early 1990s, Ho Chi Minh City's bookshops tended to primarily stock material of the technical and instructional variety, printed by the government for the edification of the people. While there are still strict controls on the import of foreign books and periodicals, an increasing number of English and French books and magazines (those that have passed the screening for social correctness by the Ministry of Culture) are now available.

Strangely, even as the Vietnamese government desperately strives to bring more tourists into the country, it *still* does not permit the import of most travel guides produced outside of Vietnam. In the meantime, while the authorities turn a blind eye, around-the-clock photocopiers spin off bootlegs of Lonely Planet books.

If you're tempted to buy black-market books, remember that though copied books generally cost one-third to half of the price of the genuine article, they also fall apart twice as fast.

Viet My Bookstore (☎ 822 9650), at 41 Đ Dinh Tien Hoang, has a number of imported books and magazines published in English, French and Chinese. Directly across from the upmarket Sofitel Plaza Saigon Hotel, the shop's English-language name is Stern's Books. It's open from 7.45 am to 9.30 pm daily.

Hieu Sach Xuan Thu (☎ 822 4670), at 185 Đ Dong Khoi, and Fahasa (☎ 822 5446), at 40 ĐL Nguyen Hue, are two of the better government-run bookshops. You should at least manage to find a good dictionary or some maps here, and a few books in English and French.

Also worth checking out is newsstand/bookshop Bookazine(☎ 829 7455), at 28 Đ Dong Khoi. Opening hours are 8 am to 10 pm daily.

The atmospherically old-world Tiem Sach Bookshop (☎ 824 4388), at 20 Đ Ho Huan Nghiep, has a massive library of mostly used English and French titles. It also operates a cosy cafe and ice cream parlour. It's open from 8.30 am to 10 pm daily.

Xunhasaba (☎ 823 0724, fax 824 1321), at 25B Đ Nguyen Binh Khiem, is the Vietnamese acronym for State Enterprise for Export & Import of Books & Periodicals.

The best area to look for maps, books and stationery is along the north side of ĐL Le Loi, between the Rex Hotel and Đ Nam Ky Khoi Nghia. There are many small privately run shops, and also the large government-run Saigon Bookstore (☎ 829 6438), at 60–62 ĐL Le Loi.

Stamps & Coins Postage stamps set in collector's books are readily available at post offices, at some hotel gift shops, souvenir shops and bookshops and, of course, from the ubiquitous street vendors. Many of the same places sell old coins and currency.

As you enter the Central Post Office (☎ 829 6555), at 2 Đ Cong Xa Paris, immediately to your right is a counter selling stationery and pens. It also has some decent stamp collections. Also, as you face the entrance from the outside, to your right are a few stalls which have stamp collections and other goods, such as foreign coins and banknotes. You can even find old stuff from the South Vietnamese regime. Prices are variable; about US$2 will get you a decent set of late model stamps already mounted in a book, but the older and rarer collections cost more.

Perhaps the best place to look is Cotevina, at 18 Đ Dinh Tien Hoang, the government corporation which issues Vietnamese stamps. The range dates from the 1960s to the present.

Many bookshops and antique shops along Đ Dong Khoi sell overpriced French-Indochinese coins, old banknotes and packets of Vietnamese stamps.

Eyeglasses In Ho Chi Minh City you'll find plenty of opticians willing to sell eyeglasses for as little as US$10. Although the price is hard to beat, cheap glasses are just that. Ultra-cheap eyeglass frames made in Vietnam or imported from China are mostly rubbish: the frames rust and soon break. These same shops usually sell European-made frames for a much higher price, but beware of primitive equipment used for grinding the lenses.

A lot of opticians in Ho Chi Minh City make cheap eyeglasses with easily breakable frames and misaligned lenses. One place which offers quality (albeit at a higher price) is Saigon Optic, at 46 Đ Pham Ngoc Thach. Good things have also been said about Kinh Italy (☎ 823 0483) at 10 Đ Cach Mang Thang Tam.

Pham Ngu Lao Area (Map 4)

The Pham Ngu Lao budget zone offers good pickings and has steadily acquired a string of downmarket shops geared towards backpackers. Prices are reasonable, rapacious bargaining is rare, staff speak English and there is a wide selection of interesting items. While the crime rate is less severe than the Dong Khoi area, Pham Ngu Lao has its fair share of thieves, so beware.

Check out the shops along Đ Pham Ngu Lao, Đ De Tham and Đ Bui Vien. It's also productive to look at some of the stalls at Ben Thanh Market.

'Ethnic Minority' Goods Check out Sapa 2 (☎ 837 2307), at 235 Đ Pham Ngu Lao, and their other branch, Sapa 3, located nearby at 223 Đ De Tham.

Clothing At the budget end of the scale, T-shirts and conical straw hats are available from vendors along Đ De Tham.

If you're in the market for a tailored suit, expats have good things to say about Huy Hoang (☎ 839 5904), at 36 Đ Ton That Tung, which is near the Huyen Si Cathedral (a short walk from the Pham Ngu Lao area).

Music & Electronics Ho Chi Minh City has an astounding collection of CDs and audio tapes for sale, most of which are pirated. The official word is that this illegal practice will be cleaned up by the authorities, but don't hold your breath waiting.

In addition to traditional and contemporary Vietnamese hits, you'll also find the latest pop songs from Hong Kong, Taiwan and Japan and, latterly, music for a growing and devoted core of avant-garde types who prefer rock 'n' roll from the West.

Electronic goods sold in Vietnam are actually not such a great bargain. You'd be better off purchasing these items in duty-free ports such as Hong Kong and Singapore. Still, the prices charged in Vietnam are not all that bad, mainly due to smuggling, which results in de facto duty-free goods. Bear in mind, though, only those items imported legally by an authorised agent will include a warranty card valid in Vietnam.

The street market that runs along Đ Huynh Thuc Khang and Đ Ton That Dam, in the Dong Khoi area, sells everything. The area was known as the Electronics Black Market until early 1989, when it was legalised. It's now generally called the Huynh Thuc Khang Street Market or else the Electronics Street Market, though it doesn't have an official name.

Coffee & Wine Vietnamese coffee is prime stuff and is amazingly cheap if you know where to buy it. The best grades come from Buon Ma Thuot in the Central Highlands. The beans are roasted in butter. Obviously, price varies according to quality and also with the seasons. You can buy whole beans or have them ground into powder at no extra charge.

One popular souvenir item is the Vietnamese one-cup coffee dripper. These are compact and lightweight, and typically cost about US$0.25, though tourist shops usually mark the price up to about US$1.

The city's major markets have the best prices and widest selection of coffee. We scored some top-grade caffeine from Van Ly Huong at Stall No 905, Zone 3, in Ben Thanh Market. This market is also the best place to find the peculiar coffee drippers used by the Vietnamese. Get a stainless-steel one rather than aluminium – the latter is cheaper, but more hassle to use. And if you're buying whole beans, you'll also be able to pick up a coffee grinder.

Duc Thanh (☎ 836 8884), at 129 Đ Bui Vien, sells a variety of fresh local coffees and teas, and doubles as a small cafe.

Rubber Stamps & Carved Seals (Maps 4 &5) No bureaucracy, Communist or otherwise, can exist without the official stamps and seals that provide the *raison d'être* for legions of clerks. Some travellers find these make a interesting keepsake.

Most Vietnamese own carved seals (called name chops) bearing their name, an old tradition borrowed from China. You can have one made too, but ask a local to help translate your name into Vietnamese.

The need for stamps and seals is catered to by the numerous shops strung out along the street just north of the New World Hotel (Map 4), on the opposite side of the street to the hotel. If you want your own seal, you might want to get it carved in Cholon (Map 5), using Chinese characters, since these are certainly more artistic – though less practical – than the romanised script (*quoc ngu*, see the Language chapter) used by most Vietnamese today.

Books On Đ De Tham there are a handful of shops dealing in used paperbacks and bootleg CDs, where you can also swap books (usually two of yours for one of theirs).

War Souvenirs In places frequented by tourists, it's easy to buy what looks like equipment left over from the Vietnam War. However, almost all of these items are reproductions and your chances of finding anything original are slim. Enterprising back-alley tailors turn out US military uniforms, while metalcraft shops have learned how to make helmets, bayonets, dog tags and Zippo lighters engraved with soldier poetry. The lighters seem to be the hottest-selling item. You can pay extra to get one that's been beat up to look like a war relic, or just buy a new shiny one for less money.

Two things you should seriously think twice about purchasing are weapons and ammunition, *even if fake.* You may have several opportunities to buy old bullets and dud mortar shells. Most of these items are either reproductions or deactivated, but metal scavengers from the countryside occasionally turn up in the markets with real bullets that are still useable (with the gunpowder still inside). Real or not, it's illegal to carry ammunition and weapons on airlines and many countries will arrest you if any such goods are found in your luggage. Customs agents in Singapore are particularly strict and thorough, and travellers carrying souvenir ammunition and weapons have been arrested there.

If you're after a chic pair of combat boots or rusty dog tags, Dan Sinh (or the 'War Surplus') Market is the place to shop. It's also the best market for electronics and other types of imported machinery – you could easily renovate a whole villa from the goods on sale here.

The market is at 104 Đ Yersin, (Map 4; near the intersection of Đ Nguyen Cong Tru). The front of the market is lined with stalls selling automobiles and motorcycles, but directly behind the pagoda building you can find reproductions of what appears to be second-hand military gear.

Stall after stall sells everything from gas masks and field stretchers to rain gear and mosquito nets. You can also find Zippo lighters, canteens, duffel bags, ponchos and boots. If you're in the market for one, this is the place to pick up a second-hand flak jacket (demand has slumped since the Vietnam War ended and the prices are now very competitive). Be warned, though, as exorbitant overcharging of foreigners looking for a poignant souvenir is common.

Eyeglasses Try the Cua Hang Mat Kinh Optical Shop (☎ 836 8028) at 195 Đ De Tham.

Department Stores

Tax Department Store (Map 3) The Tax Department Store, or Cua Hang Bach Hoa, is the biggest department store in Ho Chi Minh City and is on the corner of ĐL Le Loi and ĐL Nguyen Hue. Built as the Grands Magasins Charner about seven decades ago, this three-storey emporium, which for years was run by the government and had a pathetic selection of goods, has been privatised, and floor space is now rented to individual businesses. Items for sale include consumer electronics, blank and pirated cassette tapes, locally produced bicycles and parts, domestic alcoholic beverages, stationery, little globes of the world labelled in Vietnamese, sports equipment, cheap jewellery and synthetic clothing.

Just across ĐL Nguyen Hue is Saigon Tourist's duty-free shop

Outdoor Markets

Huynh Thuc Khang Street Market (Map 4) The street market that runs along Đ Huynh Thuc Khang and Đ Ton That Dam, in the Dong Khoi area, sells *everything*. The area used to be known as the Electronics Black Market until early 1989, when it was legalised. It's now generally called the Huynh Thuc Khang Street Market, although it doesn't have an official name.

You can still buy electronic goods of all sorts – from electric mosquito zappers to VCRs – but the market has expanded enormously to include food, clothing, washing detergent, lacquerware, condoms, pirated

GARRETT CULHANE

Is it legal? Don't ask. *Whatever* you want, the Huynh Thuc Khang Street Market will have it.

cassettes, posters of celebrities such as Ho Chi Minh, Mariah Carey and Mickey Mouse, smuggled bottles of Johnny Walker, Chinese-made Swiss army knives and just about anything else to satisfy your material desires. About half the items have marked prices, otherwise the tariff is subject to negotiation.

Thai Binh Market (Map 4) This small outdoor market in the Pham Ngu Lao area deals primarily in food items: meat, vegetables and fruit. There is nothing (yet) by way of souvenirs, but it is a colourful scene to check out if you're staying in backpacker land.

Xa Tay Market (Map 5) A few steps away from the Cholon Mosque, this is another busy little street market well worth strolling through if you're pagoda-hopping in District 5. The market occupies the southern end of Đ Phu Dong Thien Vuong.

Indoor Markets

Ho Chi Minh City has a number of incredibly huge indoor markets selling all manner of goods. They are some of the best places to pick up the conical hats and ao dai for which Vietnam is famous.

Old Market (Map 4) Despite the name, this is not a place to find antiques. Rather, the Old Market is where you can most easily buy imported (black-market?) foods, wines, shaving cream, shampoo etc. However, this is not the place to look for electronics or machinery, for that go to the Tan Dinh.

When asking or giving directions, there is a problem using the Vietnamese name for this market (Cho Cu) because written or pronounced without the correct tones it means penis. Your cyclo driver will no doubt be much amused if you say that this is what you're looking for. Perhaps directions would be better – the Old Market is on the north side of ĐL Ham Nghi, between Đ Ton That Dam and Đ Ho Tung Mau.

Ben Thanh Market (Map 4) Ben Thanh Market, or Cho Ben Thanh, and the surrounding streets are the city's liveliest, most bustling market areas. Everything commonly eaten, worn or used by local residents is available here: vegetables, fruits, meat, spices, biscuits, sweets, tobacco, clothing, conical hats, travel bags, backpacks, household items, hardware and so forth. The tourism market has not been overlooked: stalls carry lacquerware and other handicraft items. The legendary slogan of US country stores applies equally well here: 'If we don't have it, you don't need it.' There are also food stalls that sell inexpensive meals. A surprisingly large number of vendors here understand basic English.

Ben Thanh Market is in the city centre, 700 metres south-west of the Rex Hotel at the intersection of ĐL Le Loi, ĐL Ham Nghi, ĐL Tran Hung Dao and Đ Le Lai. Known to the French as the Halles Centrales, it was built in 1914 out of reinforced concrete. It covers an area of 14,000 sq m; the central cupola is 28m in diameter. The

JOHN BORTHWICK

The belfry of Ben Thanh Market has become one of the symbols of Ho Chi Minh City.

main entrance, with its belfry and clock, has become a symbol of Ho Chi Minh City.

Opposite the belfry, in the centre of the traffic roundabout, is an equestrian statue of Tran Nguyen Hai, the first person in Vietnam to use courier pigeons. At the base, on a pillar, is a small white bust of Quach Thi Trang, a Buddhist woman killed during antigovernment protests in 1963.

Tan Dinh Market (Map 2) Though not a top priority, this large indoor market is worth a look if you are checking out the Tan Dinh Church or Le Van Tam Park (north of the city centre). It stocks the usual selection of food and household wares, and there are plenty of street stalls in the area where you can grab a bite to eat.

Binh Tay Market (Map 5) Binh Tay Market (Cho Binh Tay) is Cholon's main marketplace. Actually, it's technically not in Cholon proper, but about one block away, in District 6. Much of the business here is wholesale. Binh Tay Market is on ĐL Hau Giang, about 1km south-west of Đ Chau Van Liem.

Andong Market (Map 5) Cholon's other indoor market, Andong, is very close to the intersection of ĐL Tran Phu and ĐL An Duong Vuong. This market is four storeys tall and is packed with shops. The upmarket Caesar Hotel (a foreign joint venture) is built right into the ground floor of the marketplace. The 1st floor has heaps of clothing – the latest pumps from Paris, Shiseido make-up from Tokyo, counterfeit designer jeans from the sweatshop next door – and just about everything else imaginable. The basement is a gourmet's delight of small restaurants – a perfect place to pig out on a shoestring.

Excursions

There are times when you simply need to get away from the whining motorcycles, throngs of people and heavy-duty commercialism that give Ho Chi Minh City its robust character. Amazingly, for all its sound and fury, refugees from this urban chaos don't have to go far to find serenity and sanity. There are plenty of one-day journeys that will bring you to rural places seemingly untouched by the heart attack pace of city living. The only problem is that public transport to most of them is virtually nonexistent. A hired car, shared with others, is the best option.

Many of the cafes in the Pham Ngu Lao area run combined full-day tours to the Cu Chi tunnels and Caodai Great Temple, for as little as US$4. Organised tours are also available from travel agencies and hotels.

CU CHI TUNNELS

The town of Cu Chi is now a district of greater Ho Chi Minh City, with a population of 200,000 people. At first glance, there is little evidence here to indicate the heavy fighting, bombing and destruction that went on in Cu Chi during the Vietnam (American) War. To see what went on, you have to dig deeper – underground.

The tunnel network of Cu Chi became legendary during the 1960s for its role in facilitating Viet Cong (VC) control of a large rural area only 30km to 40km from Ho Chi Minh City. At its height, the tunnel system stretched from the South Vietnamese capital to the Cambodian border; in the district of Cu Chi alone, there were over 250km of tunnels. The network, parts of which were several storeys deep, included innumerable

RICHARD I'ANSON

Motorcycle-mad Ho Chi Minh City soon gives way to the timeless, stately pace of rural Vietnam.

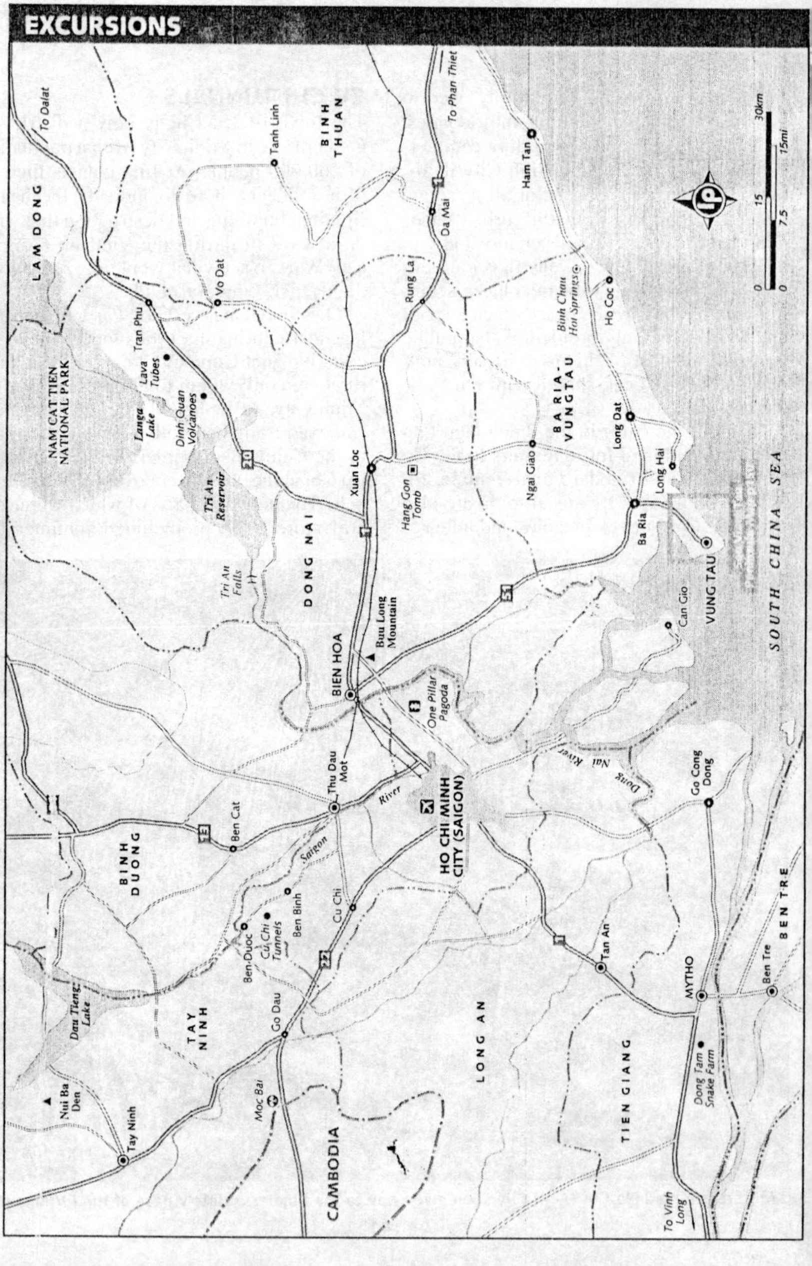

EXCURSIONS

To Dalat
LAM DONG
NAM CAT TIEN NATIONAL PARK
Langa Lake
Lava Tubes
Tran Phu
Dinh Quan Volcanoes
Tri An Reservoir
Tri An Falls
Vo Dat
Tanh Linh
BINH THUAN
To Phan Thiet
Ham Tan
Da Mai
Rung La
Xuan Loc
Hang Gon Tomb
DONG NAI
Ngai Giao
BARIA-VUNGTAU
Binh Chau Hot Springs
Ho Coc
Long Dat
Long Hai
Ba Ria
VUNG TAU
Can Gio
SOUTH CHINA SEA
Buu Long Mountain
BIEN HOA
One Pillar Pagoda
Thu Dau Mot
Saigon River
Dong Nai River
HO CHI MINH CITY (SAIGON)
Go Cong Dong
Ben Cat
BINH DUONG
Ben Binh
Cu Chi
Cu Chi Tunnels
Ben Duoc
Dau Tieng Lake
TAY NINH
Go Dau
Nui Ba Den
Tay Ninh
Moc Bai
CAMBODIA
LONG AN
Tan An
TIEN GIANG
MYTHO
Dong Tam Snake Farm
Ben Tre
BEN TRE
To Vinh Long
0 15 30km
0 7.5 15mi

trapdoors, specially constructed living areas, storage facilities, weapons factories, field hospitals, command centres and kitchens.

The tunnels made possible coordination between VC-controlled enclaves isolated from each other by South Vietnamese and US land and air operations. They also allowed the guerrillas to mount surprise attacks wherever the tunnels went – even within the perimeters of the US military base at Dong Du – and to disappear into hidden trapdoors without a trace. After ground operations against the tunnels claimed large numbers of casualties and proved ineffective, the Americans resorted to carpet bombing, eventually turning Cu Chi's 420 sq km into a moonscape.

Today, Cu Chi has become a pilgrimage site for school children, Communist Party cadres and foreign tourists. Parts of this remarkable tunnel network – enlarged and upgraded versions of the real thing – are open to the public. The unadulterated tunnels, though not actually closed to tourists, are hard to get to and are rarely visited. There are numerous war cemeteries all around Cu Chi, though tour groups don't usually stop at these except on special request.

Presently, two of the tunnel sites are open to visitors. One is near Ben Binh and the other is at Ben Duoc.

Ben Binh Tunnels

This small, renovated section of the tunnel system is near the village of Ben Binh. In one of the classrooms of the visitors' centre, a large map shows the extent of the network.

The section of the tunnel system presently open to visitors is a few hundred metres south of the visitors' centre. The tunnels are about 1.2m high and 80cm across. A knocked-out M-48 tank and a bomb crater are near the exit, which is in a reafforested eucalyptus grove.

Entry to the tunnel site, which is now controlled by Saigon Tourist, costs US$4 for foreigners, but is free for Vietnamese nationals.

Ben Duoc Tunnels

These are not the genuine tunnels, but a fully fledged reconstruction for the benefit of tourists. The emphasis here is more on fun and fantasy: tourists are given the chance to imagine what it was like to be a guerrilla. At this site there is even the opportunity to fire an M-16, AK-47 or Russian carbine rifle. This costs US$1 per bullet. It's recommended that you wear hearing protection. Saigon Tourist has talked of dressing the place up with heroic statues of VC guerrillas.

Admission to the Ben Duoc tunnels costs US$4.

Cu Chi War History Museum

This museum is not actually at the tunnel sites, but rather just off the main highway in the central area of the town of Cu Chi. Sad to say, the Cu Chi War History Museum (Nha Truyen Thong Huyen Cu Chi) is rather disappointing and gets few visitors. It's a small museum where almost all explanations are in Vietnamese.

The exhibits have a severe propaganda bias. There is a collection of gruesome photos showing severely wounded or dead civilians after being attacked by US bombs or burned with napalm. A painting on the wall shows US soldiers armed with rifles being attacked by Vietnamese peasants armed only with sticks. A sign near the photos formerly read (in Vietnamese) 'American conquest and crimes', but this was changed in 1995 to read 'enemy conquest and crimes'. Apparently, some effort is being made to tone down the rhetoric in anticipation of receiving more US visitors.

One wall of the museum contains a long list of names, all VC guerrillas killed in the Cu Chi area. An adjacent room displays recent photos of prosperous farms and factories, an effort to show the benefits of Vietnam's socialist revolution. There is also an odd collection of pottery and lacquerware with no explanations attached. In the lobby near the entrance is a statue of Ho Chi Minh with his right arm raised, waving hello.

Admission costs US$1 for foreigners.

Getting There & Away

Cu Chi is a district which covers a large area, parts of which are as close as 30km to

Ho Chi Minh City. The Cu Chi War History Museum is the closest place to the city, but the Ben Binh and Ben Duoc tunnels are about 50km and 70km from central Saigon by highway. There is a back road which cuts the drive time down, though it means driving on bumpy dirt roads.

Bus Buses from Ho Chi Minh City to Tay Ninh leave from the Tay Ninh Bus Station (Ben Xe Tay Ninh) in Tan Binh District and Mien Tay Bus Station in An Lac. All buses to Tay Ninh pass though Cu Chi town, but getting from the town of Cu Chi to the tunnels by public transport is difficult.

Car Hiring a car in Ho Chi Minh City and just driving out to Cu Chi is not all that expensive, especially if the cost is split by several people. A visit to the Cu Chi tunnel complex can easily be combined with a stop at the headquarters of the Caodai sect in Tay Ninh. A car for an all-day excursion to both should cost about US$40.

TAY NINH

Tay Ninh serves as the headquarters of one of Vietnam's most interesting indigenous religions, Caodaism.

The Tay Ninh region was also, during the period of tension between Cambodia and Vietnam in the late 1970s, the scene of raids by the Khmer Rouge, during which horrific atrocities were committed against the civilian population. Several cemeteries around Tay Ninh are stark reminders of these grisly acts.

Caodai Holy See

The Caodai Great Temple at the sect's Holy See is one of the most striking structures in Vietnam. Built between 1933 and 1955, it is a rococo extravaganza combining the architectural idiosyncrasies of a French church, a Chinese pagoda, the Tiger Balm Gardens and Madame Tussaud's Wax Museum. As in all Caodai temples, above the altar there is the divine eye, which became the religion's official symbol after the sect's founder Ngo Minh Chieu saw it in a vision. Americans often comment that it looks like the symbol found on the back of a US$1 bill.

All Caodai lands were confiscated by the new Communist government, and four members of the sect were executed in 1979. But in 1985 the Holy See and some 400 temples were returned to Caodai control. Though Caodaism is strongest in Tay Ninh Province and the Mekong Delta, temples can be found throughout southern and central Vietnam. Today, perhaps 2% of Vietnamese are followers of Caodaism.

Caodai temples observe four daily ceremonies, which are held at 6 am, noon, 6 pm and midnight. Visitors from Ho Chi Minh City usually try to arrive on time to witness the noon ceremony.

Information

Tourist Office Tay Ninh Tourist (☎ 822 376) is presently in the Hoa Binh Hotel on Đ 30/4. The staff here have plans to introduce tours to nearby Dau Tieng Reservoir, complete with boat trips and optional waterskiing.

Long Hoa Market

Long Hoa Market is several kilometres south of the Caodai Holy See complex and open from 5 am to about 6 pm daily. Before reunification, the Caodai sect had the right to collect taxes from the merchants here.

Places to Stay

The main place in town is the ***Hoa Binh Hotel*** *(☎ 822 376)* on Đ 30/4. Rooms with fan only are US$8, but most rooms are aircon and are priced from US$11 to US$22. The hotel is about 5km from the Caodai Great Temple.

The other alternative is the ***Anh Dao Hotel*** *(☎ 827 306)* on Đ 30/4, 500m west of the Hoa Binh Hotel. Twin rooms here cost US$15 to US$20; the better rooms (ie, cheaper and quieter) are in the rear.

Places to Eat

Nha Hang Diem Thuy *(☎ 827 318)* on Đ 30/4 is a great restaurant with low prices. Giant crayfish *(tom can)* are one of their specialities, and, although not cheap, cost only a third of what you'd pay in Ho Chi Minh City.

The ***Hoang Yen Restaurant*** is one kilometre north of the Tay Ninh market, just

GREG ELMS
The Divine Eye of Caodai

GREG ELMS
Casting a net at Bien Hoa

GREG ELMS
The extravagant interior of the Caodai Great Temple, Tay Ninh...

KRAIG LIEB
...is matched only by the ostentation of its exterior.

GREG ELMS
One fish 'to go', Bien Hoa

JOHN BANAGAN

Conical hats and baseball caps, Mekong Delta

JOHN BANAGAN

A day's catch being hung out to dry, Vung Tau.

RICHARD I'ANSON

Cu Chi: land of the tunnels. During the American War, bombing reduced it to a moonscape.

Caodai Religion

Caodaism was an attempt to create the ideal religion through the fusion of the secular and religious philosophies of the East and West. The result is a colourful and eclectic potpourri of the religious philosophies popularly practised in Vietnam during the early 20th century – Buddhism, Confucianism, Taoism, Christianity and Islam – together with sprinklings of native Vietnamese animism and Western humanism.

Caodaism was founded by the mystic Ngo Minh Chieu (born 1878), a civil servant who was widely published inside and outside of Vietnam. He became active in seances, where his presence was said to greatly improve the quality of communication with the spirits. Around 1919, he began to receive a series of revelations in which the tenets of Caodai doctrine were set forth. Most of the sacred literature of Caodaism consists of messages communicated to Caodai leaders by spirits during seances held between 1925 and 1929. Since 1927, only the official seances held at Tay Ninh have been considered reliable and divinely ordained by the Caodai hierarchy.

Spirits who have been in touch with the Caodai include deceased Caodai leaders, patriots, heroes, philosophers, poets, political leaders and warriors. Westerners include Joan of Arc, René Descartes, William Shakespeare (who hasn't been heard from since 1935), Louis Pasteur and Vladimir Lenin. One very frequent contact, Victor Hugo, was posthumously named the chief spirit of foreign missionary works.

Within a year of its founding, the group had 26,000 followers. By the mid-1950s, one in eight southern Vietnamese was a Caodai. The sect established a virtually independent feudal state in Tay Ninh Province and retained enormous influence in local affairs until the Communist victory in 1975.

near the river, is , considered by locals to be the best in town. Right on the river next to the bridge is the government-owned ***Festival Restaurant***, which has great ambience – though the food is not spectacular.

Getting There & Away

Buses from Ho Chi Minh City to Tay Ninh leave from the Tay Ninh bus station (Ben Xe Tay Ninh) in Tan Binh District and Mien Tay bus station in An Lac.

Tay Ninh is on National Highway 22 (Quoc Lo 22), 96km from Ho Chi Minh City. The road passes through Trang Bang, where the famous news photo of a severely burned naked girl, screaming and running, was taken during an US napalm attack. There are several Caodai temples along National Highway 22, including one, under construction in 1975, that was heavily damaged by the VC.

An easy way to get to Tay Ninh is by taxi. Perhaps the best thing to do is to visit it on a day trip that includes a stop in Cu Chi. An all-day round trip to both places should cost about US$40.

NUI BA DEN

Nui Ba Den (Black Lady Mountain), 15km north-east of Tay Ninh town, rises 850m above the surrounding countryside. Over the centuries, Nui Ba Den has served as a shrine for various peoples of the area, including the Khmer, Chams, Vietnamese and Chinese. There are several cave temples on the mountain.

Nui Ba Den was used as a staging ground by both the Viet Minh and the VC and was the scene of fierce fighting during the wars with France and the USA. At one time, there was a US Army fire base and relay station at the summit of the mountain, which was set up after the mountain had been defoliated and heavily bombed by US aircraft.

The name Black Lady Mountain is derived from the legend of Huong, a young woman who married her true love despite the advances of a wealthy mandarin. While her husband was away doing military service, she would visit a magical statue of Buddha at the summit of the mountain. One day, Huong was attacked by kidnappers, but preferring death to dishonour she threw herself off a cliff. She reappeared in the visions of a monk living on the mountain, who told her story.

The hike from the base of the mountain to the main temple complex and back takes about 1½ hours. Although steep in parts, it's not a difficult walk. At the base of the mountain, you'll have to fend off the usual crowd of very persistent kids selling tourist junk, lottery tickets and chewing gum – they'll pursue you up the mountain but you can easily outpace them if you wear running shoes and don't carry a heavy bag. Things are much more relaxed around the temple complex, where there are only a few stands selling snacks and drinks and the vendors are not pushy. A walk to the summit and back takes about six hours.

If you prefer not to walk, there is a system of 120 cable cars taking tourists from the main gate up the mountain. The cable car is the kind that never stops: you have to jump in and out quickly. However, there are guards to help you to enter and disembark. Tickets cost US$1.60 each way. The entrance fee to the area is US$0.80.

Places to Stay

About 500m past the main entrance gate are eight A-frame bungalows, where double rooms can be rented for US$8 to US$12.

ONE PILLAR PAGODA

The official name of this interesting place is Nam Thien Nhat Tru, but everyone calls it the One Pillar Pagoda of Thu Duc (Chua Mot Cot Thu Duc).

The pagoda is modelled after Hanoi's One Pillar Pagoda, though the two structures do not look identical. Hanoi's original pagoda was built in the 9th century, but was destroyed by the French. It was rebuilt by the Vietnamese in 1954. (Ho Chi Minh City's version was constructed in 1958.)

When Vietnam was partitioned in 1954, Buddhist monks and Catholic priests wisely fled south so that they could avoid persecution and continue practising their religion. One monk from Hanoi who came south in 1954 was Thich Tri Dung. Shortly after arrival in Ho Chi Minh City, Thich petitioned the South Vietnamese government for permission to construct a replica of Hanoi's famous One Pillar Pagoda. President Diem, a Catholic with little tolerance for Buddhist clergy, denied him permission. Nevertheless, Thich and his supporters raised the funds and built the pagoda. Ordered to tear down the temple, the monks refused even though threatened with imprisonment for not complying. The government's dispute with the monks reached a stand-off – a stalemate that lasted until 1963.

In the current political atmosphere, Vietnamese history books say that the One Pillar Pagoda afterwards served as a base for Viet Cong guerrillas disguised as clergy. Certainly, at this pagoda – and others – VC cadres did pose as poor peasants willing to donate their labour to Buddhism. This provided them with a convenient cover in Saigon, where they conducted secret activities (holding political indoctrination meetings, smuggling weapons, planting bombs etc) at night. However, since most monks then (and now) were divorced from politics, it's doubtful that they had any idea just to what extent they were being used by the VC, and it's unlikely they offered their protection wittingly.

During the war, the One Pillar Pagoda of Thu Duc was in possession of an extremely valuable plaque, said to weigh 612kg. After liberation, the government took it for 'safekeeping' and brought it to Hanoi. None of the monks alive today can say just where it is. There is speculation that the government sold it to overseas collectors, but this cannot be confirmed.

The One Pillar Pagoda (☎ 896 0780) is in the Thu Duc District, about 15km east of central Saigon. The official address is 1/91 Đ Nguyen Du. Tours to the pagoda are rare, so most likely you'll have to visit by rented motorcycle or car.

BIEN HOA

Bien Hoa is on the east bank of the Dong Hai River, 32km north-east of Ho Chi Minh City. It's now the capital of Dong Nai Province.

Bien Hoa has the distinction of being the place to claim the very first US casualties in the Vietnam War – in July 1959, two

American 'advisors' were killed here during a VC raid.

Pagodas & Temples

Buu Son Temple The most famous religious site in Bien Hoa is Buu Son Temple, which houses a Cham statue of Vishnu dating from the 15th century. The four-armed figure, carved in granite, was erected on the orders of a Cham prince who conquered the region. When the area reverted to Khmer control, the statue was hidden in a tree trunk, where it remained until rediscovered in the 18th century by Vietnamese farmers, who built a temple for it. Buu Son Temple is in Binh Thuoc village, 1.5km from town and 150m from the river bank.

Thanh Long Pagoda Ornately decorated Thanh Long Pagoda is in Binh Thuoc village, about 300m from the Bien Hoa train station.

Dai Giac Pagoda Dai Giac Pagoda is near Bien Hoa on an island not far from the railroad bridge. It is claimed to be at least 150 years old.

Buu Phong Pagoda Buu Phong Pagoda, with its numerous granite statues, stands on top of a hill of blue granite 7km from Bien Hoa. The pagoda was built on the site of an earlier Cham or Khmer temple on the orders of Emperor Gia Long.

Getting There & Away

There is a four-lane highway from Ho Chi Minh City to Bien Hoa, a distance of 32km.

TRI AN FALLS

Tri An Falls are an 8m-high and 30m-wide cascade on the Be River (Song Be). They are especially awesome in the late autumn, when the river's flow is at its peak. Tri An Falls are in Song Be Province, 36km from Bien Hoa and 68km from Ho Chi Minh City (via Thu Dau Mot).

Farther upstream from Tri An Falls is Tri An Reservoir (Ho Tri An). This large artificial lake, which is fed from the forest highlands around Dalat, was created by the Tri An Dam.

CAN GIO

The name Can Gio denotes both a small village (sometimes called Duyen Hai) by the sea and the Can Gio District of Ho Chi Minh City. Can Gio District is the largest in Ho Chi Minh City and consists entirely of swampy delta islands at the mouth of the Nha Be River.

As you would expect in a river delta, the beach consists of hard-packed mud rather than the fluffy white sand that sun worshippers crave. Furthermore, the beach sits in an exposed position and is lashed by strong winds. For these reasons, Can Gio gets few visitors and the beach remains entirely undeveloped.

Before you scratch Can Gio off your list of places to visit, however, it's worth knowing that the island does have a wild beauty of its own. The land here is only about 2m above sea level and the island is basically one big mangrove swamp. Unlike the rest of Ho Chi Minh City, overpopulation is hardly a problem here.

Can Gio Market

Can Gio does have a large market, made conspicuous by some rather powerful odours. Seafood and salt are definitely the local specialities. The vegetables, rice and fruit are all imported by boat from Ho Chi Minh City.

Caodai Temple

Though much smaller than the Caodai Great Temple at Tay Ninh, Can Gio can boast a Caodai temple of its own. The temple is near the market and is easy to find.

War Memorial & Cemetery

Adjacent to the shrimp hatchery is a large and conspicuous War Memorial and Cemetery (Nghia Trang Liet Si Rung Sac). Like all such sites in Vietnam, the praise for bravery and patriotism goes entirely to the winning side and there is nothing said about the losers. Indeed, all of the former war cemeteries containing remains of South Vietnamese soldiers were bulldozed after liberation, a fact that still causes much bitterness.

The War Memorial and Cemetery is 2km from Can Gio Market.

Shrimp Hatchery

The Coastal Fishery Development Corporation (COFIDEC) is a large company that has sewn up much of the shrimp-breeding industry in Can Gio. Two varieties of shrimp – black tiger and white shrimp – are bred here.

COFIDEC has its operational headquarters close to the War Memorial in Can Gio, but the shrimp breeding ponds stretch out for several kilometres along the beachfront.

The staff at COFIDEC are friendly and not opposed to your poking around a bit, but please don't interfere with their operations. Foreigners will only continue to be welcomed here if they tread lightly.

Beach

The southern side of the island faces the sea, creating a beachfront nearly 10km long. Unfortunately, a good deal of it is inaccessible because it's been fenced off by shrimp farmers and clam diggers. Nevertheless, there is a point about 4km west of the Can Gio Market where a dirt road turns off the main highway to Ho Chi Minh City and leads to the beach.

The surface of the beach is as hard as concrete and it is possible to drive a motorcycle on it. However, this is not recommended as it damages the local ecology. While the beach may seem dead at first glance, it swarms with life just below the surface, as the breathing holes in the mud suggest. You can hear the crunch of tiny clam shells as you stroll along the surface. The water here is extremely shallow and you can walk far from shore, but take care – you can be sure that there is a good deal of inhospitable and well-armed sea life in these shallow waters. Stingrays, stonefish and sea urchins are just some of the xenophobic marine residents who can, and will, retaliate if you step on them.

The hills of the Vung Tau peninsula are easily visible on a clear day. If you're inclined, you should also be able to see the offshore oil-drilling platforms.

Places to Stay

Most visitors do Can Gio as a day trip, and for good reason – the two hotels in town are total dumps. Moreover, both are usually full, so you need to call ahead if you intend to stay.

The small ***Duyen Hai Hotel*** *(☎ 874 0246)* has a fresh-water tank, which means you don't have to bathe in sea water. The water is brought in from Ho Chi Minh City by ship, so perhaps this partially justifies paying for the accommodation. The toilets, a short walk from the main building, are built on stilts over a canal, which might just reduce your enthusiasm for eating Can Gio clams. Foreigners are charged US$8 to stay in this shack.

A second option, the larger ***Guesthouse 30/4*** *(☎ 874 3022)*, is not much better. Rates are US$6 to US$8 for fan rooms, or US$12 with air-con.

The hotels are about 4km from the main beach area.

Places to Eat

There are a few stalls around the market near the fishing port, but one look at the level of sanitation can eliminate your appetite without your needing to eat anything at all.

That said, Can Gio boasts one remarkably good restaurant, with an extensive menu. In fact, it's so good that Saigonese in the know come to Can Gio for no other reason than to eat here. The place you want is the ***Duyen Hai Restaurant***, which is a stone's throw from the Duyen Hai Hotel. Unlike the hotel, the restaurant is good value.

There is one solitary food and drink stall next to the beach. Basically, all they have on the menu is Coca-Cola and instant noodles, but it beats starving. It might be prudent to bring some bottled water with you on the odd chance the stall is closed.

Getting There & Away

Car & Motorcycle Can Gio is about 60km from central Saigon, and the fastest way to make the journey is by motorcycle. Travel time is approximately three hours.

Cars can also make the journey, but this is much slower. The reason is that you need to make two ferry crossings. The large ferries that can accommodate cars are infrequent, averaging about one every 1½ hours. By contrast, small boats make these crossings every few minutes, shuttling passengers and motorcycles. These small boats are so cheap that you could even charter one, if need be.

The first ferry crossing is 15km from Ho Chi Minh City, at Binh Khanh (Cat Lai), a former US Navy base. Small ferry boats cost about US$0.25 for a motorcycle and two passengers. Cars must wait for the large ferry, which runs about once every 30 minutes, and there is usually a long queue of vehicles.

About 3km beyond Dan Xay is a right-hand turn-off to Lam Vien Can Gio (a mangrove nature reserve). There are a lot of monkeys in the forest, and in lieu of an entrance fee many buy food for the monkeys (corn, potatoes, bananas etc) from the staff. Beware of your belongings: the monkeys can become very aggressive, especially if you are not friendly with them.

The second ferry, which is less frequent, is 42km from Ho Chi Minh City and connects the two tiny villages of Dan Xay (closer to Ho Chi Minh City) and Hao Vo (on Can Gio Island). Motorcycle riders can take a small ferry which costs around US$0.35 and runs about once every 10 to 15 minutes. The car ferry is much less frequent, but there is a posted schedule.

Boat There is one boat daily between Can Gio and Ho Chi Minh City. From either direction, the boat departs at approximately 5 to 6 am and takes six hours for the journey.

There is also a small boat between Can Gio and Vung Tau. Departure from Can Gio is at 5 am, arriving in Vung Tau at 8 am. The boat departs Vung Tau about noon, arriving in Can Gio three hours later. Occasionally, there is a later boat which leaves Can Gio at around 2 pm – inquire locally.

In Can Gio, you catch boats at the shipyards, which are built on an inlet 2km west of the Can Gio Market. In Ho Chi Minh City, you get the boat at Thu Thiem, the pier opposite the Riverside Hotel (Map 3). In Vung Tau, you catch the boats from the beachfront market area, just over the road from the Grand Hotel.

VUNG TAU

Vung Tau, known under the French as Cap St Jacques (it was so named by Portuguese mariners in honour of their patron saint), is a beach resort on the South China Sea, 128km (by road) south-east of Ho Chi Minh City.

Vung Tau's beaches are easily reached from Ho Chi Minh City and have thus long been a favourite of the Saigonese elite, ever since French colonists first began coming here around 1890. However, they are not Vietnam's nicest by any stretch of the imagination, in large part because the city has cut down most of the palm trees in order to widen the roads.

Seaside areas near Vung Tau are dotted with the villas of the pre-1975 elite, now converted to guesthouses and restaurants for the post-1975 elite. In addition to sunning on the seashore and sipping sodas in nearby cafes, visitors to this city of 100,000 people can cycle around, or climb up, Vung Tau Peninsula's two mountains. There are also a number of interesting religious sites around town, including several pagodas and a huge standing figure of Jesus presiding over the South China Sea.

Vung Tau became briefly famous to the world in 1973, when the last US combat troops in Vietnam left here by ship.

Vung Tau is heavily commercialised by Vietnamese standards and seems to be getting more so all the time. Despite this and a few other negative points, there is still plenty of sand, sun, surf, good food, draft beer and even a few budding discos. It's a party town and – for traffic-weary Saigonese – a welcome change of pace.

Orientation

The triangular Vung Tau Peninsula juts into the South China Sea near the mouth of the Saigon River. Sewage flowing down the river from Ho Chi Minh City is a considerable source of pollution – Vung Tau's four beaches are none too clean. Pollution from offshore drilling is another problem.

Ben Da fishing village is in the north-west area of the peninsula. In the north-east is most of Vung Tau's industry and the airport.

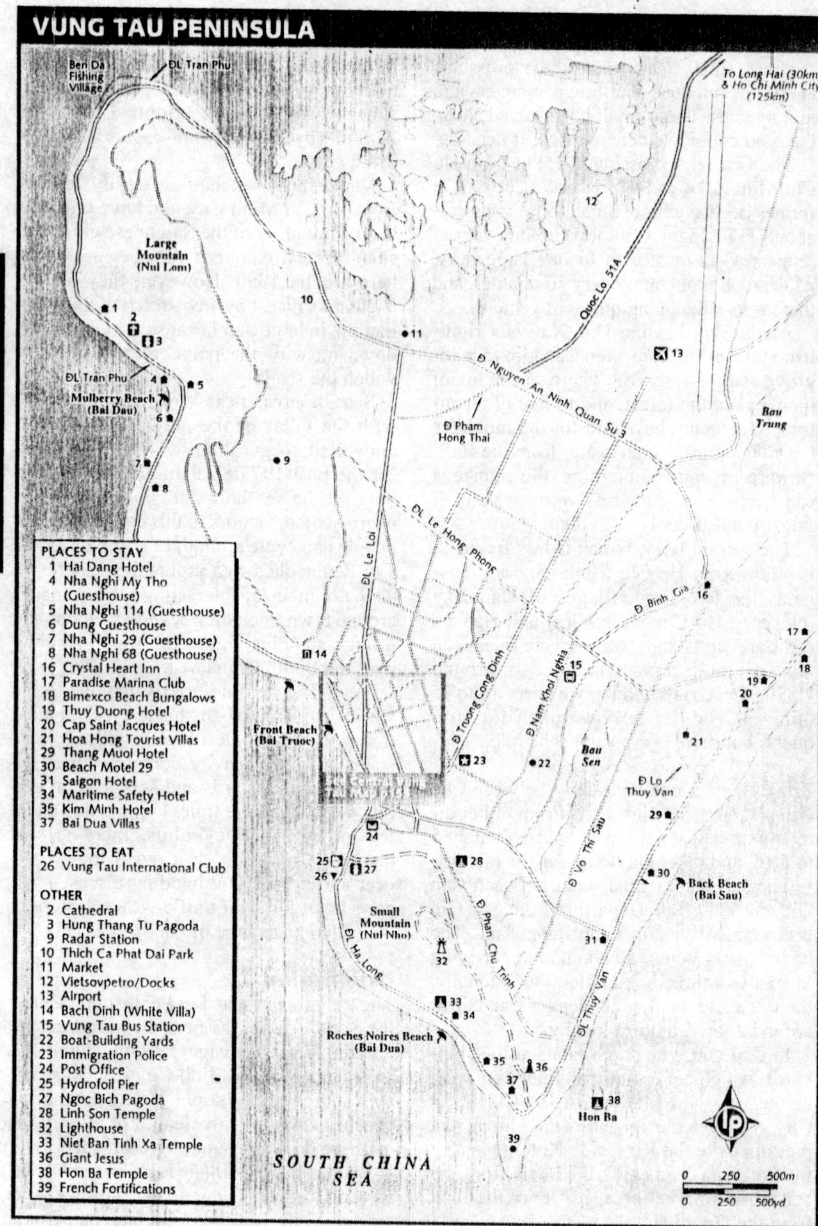
VUNG TAU PENINSULA
Ben Da Fishing Village
ĐL Tran Phu
To Long Hai (30km) & Ho Chi Minh City (125km)
Large Mountain (Nui Lon)
Quoc Lo 51A
Đ Nguyen An Ninh Quan Su 3
Đ Pham Hong Thai
Bau Trung
Mulberry Beach (Bai Dau)
ĐL Le Loi
ĐL Le Hong Phong
Đ Binh Gia
Đ Truong Cong Dinh
Đ Nam Khoi Nghia
Front Beach (Bai Truoc)
Bau Sen
Đ Lo Thuy Van
Đ Vo Thi Sau
Back Beach (Bai Sau)
Small Mountain (Nui Nho)
Đ Phan Chu Trinh
ĐL Ha Long
ĐL Thuy Van
Roches Noires Beach (Bai Dua)
Hon Ba
SOUTH CHINA SEA
0 250 500m
0 250 500yd
PLACES TO STAY
1 Hai Dang Hotel
4 Nha Nghi My Tho (Guesthouse)
5 Nha Nghi 114 (Guesthouse)
6 Dung Guesthouse
7 Nha Nghi 29 (Guesthouse)
8 Nha Nghi 68 (Guesthouse)
16 Crystal Heart Inn
17 Paradise Marina Club
18 Bimexco Beach Bungalows
19 Thuy Duong Hotel
20 Cap Saint Jacques Hotel
21 Hoa Hong Tourist Villas
29 Thang Muoi Hotel
30 Beach Motel 29
31 Saigon Hotel
34 Maritime Safety Hotel
35 Kim Minh Hotel
37 Bai Dua Villas
PLACES TO EAT
26 Vung Tau International Club
OTHER
2 Cathedral
3 Hung Thang Tu Pagoda
9 Radar Station
10 Thich Ca Phat Dai Park
11 Market
12 Vietsovpetro/Docks
13 Airport
14 Bach Dinh (White Villa)
15 Vung Tau Bus Station
22 Boat-Building Yards
23 Immigration Police
24 Post Office
25 Hydrofoil Pier
27 Ngoc Bich Pagoda
28 Linh Son Temple
32 Lighthouse
33 Niet Ban Tinh Xa Temple
36 Giant Jesus
38 Hon Ba Temple
39 French Fortifications

Money

Vietcombank (☎ 859874), or Ngan Hang Ngoai Thuong Viet Nam, is at 27–29 Đ Tran Hung Dao.

Beaches

Back Beach The main bathing area on the peninsula is Back Beach (also called Bai Sau or Thuy Van Beach), an 8km stretch of sun, sand and tourists. Unfortunately, it's also the ugliest stretch of beach in Vung Tau, thanks largely to crass commercialisation. Basically, this is land of concrete, car parks, hotels and cafes.

Front Beach Front Beach (also called Bai Truoc or Thuy Duong Beach), borders on the centre of town. The trees (a rarity in Vung Tau) make it reasonably attractive, though the beach itself has become eroded and polluted. Shady ĐL Quang Trung, lined with kiosks, runs along Front Beach. Early in the morning, local fishing boats moor here to unload the night's catch and clean the nets. The workers row themselves between boats or to the beach in *thung chai* – gigantic round wicker baskets sealed with pitch. Watch out for kids around the kiosks along Front Beach. Some may try to pick your pockets or snatch a bag.

Mulberry Beach Mulberry Beach (Bai Dau), a quiet, coconut-palm-lined stretch of coastline, is probably the most scenic spot in the Vung Tau area – because it hasn't been overdeveloped.

The beach stretches around a small bay nestled beneath the verdant, western slopes of Large Mountain (Nui Lon). The only real problem with Mulberry Beach is that there isn't a lot of sand – it's rocky with only a few small sandy coves and the water is not exactly pristine. Nevertheless, Mulberry Beach's many cheap guesthouses attract low-budget backpackers. It would be our first choice for a relaxing holiday in Vung Tau.

The large and unusual outdoor cathedral at Mulberry Beach is very photogenic and a major drawcard for Vietnamese tourists.

Mulberry Beach is 3km from the city centre along ĐL Tran Phu. The best way to get there is by bicycle or motorcycle.

On a clear day you can look out into the distance from Mulberry Beach and see Can Gio, a low-lying palm-fringed island.

There is a daily boat from Vung Tau's Front Beach to Can Gio (see the Can Gio section earlier in this chapter for details).

Roches Noires Beach Roches Noires Beach (Bai Dua) is a small, rocky beach about 2km south of the town centre on ĐL Ha Long. This is a great place to watch the sun setting over the South China Sea. Road widening has made it treeless and new hotels are continually being built.

Pagodas & Temples

Hon Ba Temple Hon Ba Temple (Chua Hon Ba) is on a tiny island just south of Back Beach. It can be reached on foot at low tide.

Niet Ban Tinh Xa Niet Ban Tinh Xa, one of the largest Buddhist temples in Vietnam, is on the western side of Small Mountain (Nui Nho). Built in 1971, it is famous for its 5000kg bronze bell, a huge reclining Buddha and intricate mosaic work.

Thich Ca Phat Dai Park

Thich Ca Phat Dai, a must-see site for domestic tourists, is a hillside park of monumental Buddhist statuary built in the early 1960s. Inside the main gate and to the right is a row of small souvenir kiosks selling, among other things, inexpensive items made of seashells and coral. Above the kiosks, shaded paths lead to several large white cement Buddhas, a giant lotus blossom, and many smaller figures of people and animals.

The park is on the eastern side of Large Mountain, at 25 ĐL Tran Phu, and it's open from 6 am to 6 pm. To get there from the town centre, take ĐL Le Loi north, almost to the end, and turn left on to ĐL Tran Phu.

Lighthouse

The 360-degree view of the entire hammerhead-shaped peninsula from the lighthouse *(hai dang)* is truly spectacular, especially at sunset. The lighthouse was built in 1910 and sits atop Small Mountain. The concrete passage from the tower to the building next

Popular with local tourists: Thich Ca Phat Dai Park's Buddhist statuary, constructed in the 1960s

to it was constructed by the French as a response to Viet Minh attacks. A 1939 French guidebook warns visitors that photography is not permitted from here and, unfortunately, this is still the case over half a century and four regimes later.

The narrow paved road that ascends Small Mountain to the lighthouse intersects ĐL Ha Long 150m south-west of the post office. The grade is quite mild and could be bicycled. There is also a dirt road to the lighthouse from near Back Beach.

Giant Jesus

An enormous, Rio de Janeiro-style figure of Jesus (Thanh Gioc), gazing out across the South China Sea with his arms outstretched, can be seen from the southern end of Small Mountain.

The 30m-high Giant Jesus statue was constructed in 1974 on the site of an old lighthouse built by the French a century before. The statue can be reached on foot by a path that heads up the hill from a point just south of Back Beach. The path circles around to approach the figure from the back.

Bach Dinh

Bach Dinh, the White Villa (Villa Blanche in French), is a former royal residence set amid frangipanis and bougainvilleas on a lushly forested hillside overlooking the sea. It is an ideal place to sit, relax and contemplate.

Bach Dinh was built in 1909 as a retreat for French governor Paul Doumer. It later became a summer palace for Vietnamese royalty. King Thanh Thai was kept here for a while under house arrest before being shipped off to the island of Réunion to endure hard labour. From the late 1960s to the early 1970s, the building was a part-time pleasure palace for South Vietnamese president Thieu.

The mansion itself is emphatically French in its ornamentation, which includes colourful mosaics and Roman-style busts set into the exterior walls. Inside, there is an exhibit of old Chinese (Qing Dynasty) pottery salvaged from an 18th century shipwreck near Con Dao Island.

The main entrance to the park surrounding Bach Dinh is just north of Front Beach, at 12 DL Tran Phu. It is open from 6 am to 9 pm; admission is US$1.20.

Boat-Building Yards

New wooden fishing craft are built at a location which – oddly enough – is over a kilometre from the nearest water. The boat yards are on D Nam Ky Khoi Nghia, 500m south of Vung Tau bus station.

Golf Course

The Paradise Marina Club (see Places to Stay, this section) does not have a marina, but it does have an international standard 27-hole golf course. For nonmembers, green fees are a trifling US$97 per day. Membership costs US$20,000, but then green fees are reduced to just US$12 per day. At these rates, becoming a member will pay off – provided you play golf here more than 235 times.

Small Mountain Circuit

The 6km circuit around Small Mountain (elevation 197m), known to the French as *le tour de la Petite Corniche*, begins at the post office and continues on ĐL Ha Long along the rocky coastline. ĐL Ha Long passes **Ngoc Bich Pagoda** (which is built in the style of Hanoi's famous One Pillar Pagoda), Roches Noires Beach and a number of villas before reaching the tip of the Vung Tau Peninsula. The promontory, reached through a traditional gate, was once guarded by French naval guns, whose re-enforced concrete **emplacements** remain, slowly crumbling in the salt air.

Đ Phan Boi Chau goes from the southern end of Back Beach into town along the eastern base of Small Mountain, passing century-old **Linh Son Temple**, which contains a Buddha of pre-Angkorian Khmer origin.

Large Mountain Circuit

The 10km circuit around Large Mountain (elevation 520m) passes seaside villas, Mulberry Beach, the homes of poor families living in old French fortifications and a number of quarries where boulders blown out of the hillside by dynamite are made into gravel by workers using sledgehammers. Blasting sometimes closes the road for a few hours. At the northern tip of Large Mountain is **Ben Da fishing village**. The village is notable for its large church and bad roads. From here a road leads up and along the spine of the hill to the old **radar installation** *(rada)*.

On the eastern side of Large Mountain, which faces tidal marshes and the giant cranes of the Vietsovpetro docks, is Thich Ca Phat Dai park.

Places to Stay

During holidays, Vung Tau's hotels are usually booked out. Aside from price, the main consideration is finding a place at the beach you most prefer.

Back Beach Cheapest is ***Beach Motel 29*** *(☎ 853 481, 29 ĐL Thuy Van)*. Weekday prices are US$5 to US$10 with fan only, rising to US$14 to US$18 with air-con.

At the northern end of Back Beach are the ***Bimexco Beach Bungalows*** *(☎ 859 916)*. The cheapest rooms, with shared bath, are US$10. Rooms with air-con and bath range from US$15 to US$25.

The ***Thuy Duong Hotel*** *(☎ 852 6354)* on ĐL Thuy Van, is an attractive place. Its brochure advertises 'massage – sauna with the skilled technicians'! Rooms cost between US$28 and US$55.

Close to the beach is the ***Saigon Hotel*** *(☎ 852 317, 72 ĐL Thuy Van)*. Only the old building, where rooms are US$12 to US$38, has sea views; in the new wing rooms are US$25.

Thang Muoi Hotel *(☎ 852 665 or 859 876, 4–6 ĐL Thuy Van)* boasts an alluring garden. Doubles with fan/air-con cost US$11/23.

Nearby, on Ngoc Tuoc Hill, are the ***Hoa Hong Tourist Villas*** *(☎ 852 633, fax 859 262)* with self-contained, condo-style villas for US$20 and US$25.

The long-awaited ***Paradise Marina Club*** *(☎ 859 687, fax 859 695)* should be open soon. Eventually, the complex will have 1500 rooms! Facilities include a golf course (for details, see earlier this chapter), a swimming pool and tennis courts.

The ***Crystal Heart Inn*** *(☎ 854 043, fax 854 044, 143–145 Đ Binh Gia)* is its own little condo-village. Air-con rooms with rattan furnishings cost US$20 to US$40.

Front Beach One of the few cheap places in this neighbourhood is the ***Thang Long Hotel*** *(☎ 852 175, 45 Đ Thong Nhat)*. Doubles with fan are US$10 to US$15. Air-con will set you back US$15 to US$20.

Also cheap, the ***Truong Son Hotel*** *(☎ 859 864, fax 852 452)*, on Đ Phan Ding Phong, charges US$14 for air-con doubles.

The ***Song Huong Hotel*** *(☎ 852 491, fax 859 862, 10 Đ Truong Vinh Ky)* was once a dormitory for Russian experts (luckily, it's been renovated since then). Twins are US$17 to US$36.

Don't confuse the foregoing with the very similarly named ***Song Hong Hotel*** *(☎ 852 137, fax 852 452, 12 Đ Hoang Dieu)*, where twins with air-con and bath cost US$24 to US$27.

The ***Pacific Hotel*** *(☎ 859 522, fax 853 391, 4 ĐL Le Loi)* is a clean and modern place. Room rates depend on whether or not you get a sea view. The price range here is US$15 to US$35.

The ***Sea Breeze Hotel*** *(☎ 852 392, fax 859 856, 11 Đ Nguyen Trai)*, which also serves as an office for express buses to Ho Chi Minh City, charges from US$35 to US$60.

The ***Grand Hotel*** *(☎ 856 164, fax 859 878, 26 ĐL Quang Trung)* has a grand location just opposite the beach. The hotel proudly boasts a souvenir shop, steam bath, disco and Thai massage facilities. Singles with fan and attached cold bath are US$15, while twins with air-con are US$20 to US$46.

The ***Royal Hotel's*** *(☎ 859 852, fax 859 851, 48 ĐL Quang Trung)* glossy pamphlet promises that it is 'where the sunkissed beaches and cool sea breeze bring you into the exciting world of deep crystal blue sea'. Thoroughly air-con rooms cost US$40 to US$120.

Mulberry Beach There are dozens of cheap guesthouses *(nha nghi)* in former private villas along Mulberry Beach. The relative cheapness is not because Mulberry Beach is an unattractive place (indeed, it's the opposite), but because the lack of a white-sand beach and other tourist amusements makes this a relative backwater.

Most of the guesthouses have rooms with fans and communal bathrooms, and cost US$15 or less, but several upmarket places have air-con and baths.

The ***Hai Dang Hotel*** *(☎ 858 536, 194 ĐL Tran Phu)* is one of the larger Mulberry Beach hotels. Rooms with fan/air-con cost US$10/20. The five room guesthouse just next door charges US$6 to US$9.

Nha Nghi My Tho *(☎ 832 035, 47 ĐL Tran Phu)* has a rooftop terrace overlooking the beach. A light, airy room with ceiling fan and beach view will cost you US$8 per person.

Nha Nghi 114 *(☎ 832 023, 114 ĐL Tran Phu)* charges US$12 for livable twins.

The appropriately named ***Dung Guesthouse*** *(☎ 836 010, 31 ĐL Tran* Phu) costs US$7 and US$8 for basic twin rooms.

Nha Nghi 29 *(73 ĐL Tran Phu)* is right on the seafront. It's a large, good-looking place and is recommended. Rooms with air-con cost US$14.

Nha Nghi 68, at 68 ĐL Tran Phu, has doubles/triples for US$5/10.

Roches Noires Beach This is a new development area – the small guesthouses have been demolished recently and new tourist pleasure palaces are under construction. The first one to open its doors is the ***Kim Minh Hotel*** *(☎ 856 192, fax 856 439, 60A ĐL Ha Long)*. Rooms cost US$35 to US$95. There is a karaoke and disco.

The ***Maritime Safety Hotel*** *(☎ 856 357, fax 856 360, 110 ĐL Ha Long)* has rooms from US$30 to US$45.

The ***Bai Dua Villas*** *(☎ 856 285, fax 856281, 22 ĐL Ha Long)*, a 'village of villas', charges US$15 to US$35.

Places to Eat

Back Beach The northern end of Back Beach has excellent cheap cafes hidden among the few remaining palm trees.

Front Beach The kiosks lining the beach do cheap noodle dishes. Opposite the kiosks on Front Beach is ***The Frenchie Restaurant***, at 26 ĐL Quang Trung, which does fine French food.

For excellent seafood, try ***Huong Bien Restaurant*** at the south cornor of Đ Duy Tan and Đ Tran Hung Dao. Hotels with restaurants include the Grand, Palace and the Pacific.

Mulberry Beach Mulberry Beach chips in with numerous seaside restaurants. The specialty is, no surprise, seafood.

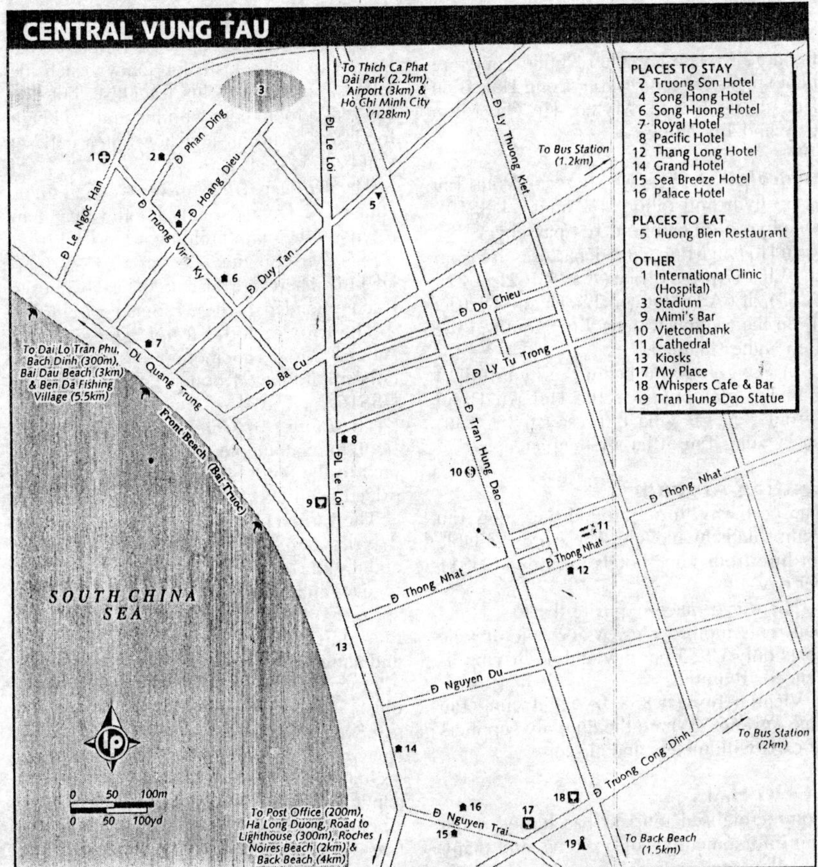

Roches Noires Beach The *Vung Tau International Club* has good food and a sweeping view of the sea.

Entertainment

Bars favoured by expats and local trendies that get moving in the evening include ***My Place*** *(☎ 856 028, 14 Đ Nguyen Trai)*, ***Whispers Cafe & Bar*** *(☎ 856 762, 438 Đ Truong Cong Dinh)*, ***Chi Chi's Bar*** *(☎ 853 948, 236 Đ Bacu)* and the popular ***Mimi's Bar*** on ĐL Le Loi.

The Grand Hotel has a disco and karaoke lounge operating from 7 pm until midnight.

Getting There & Away

Bus The most conveniently located minibuses to Vung Tau depart from the front of the Saigon Hotel on Đ Dong Du, near the Saigon Central Mosque. Departures occur approximately once every 15 minutes between 6 am and 6 pm. The 128km trip takes two hours and costs US$4. To return from Vung Tau, there are minibus stops at the petrol station and the Sea Breeze Hotel.

Large public air-con buses depart from Ho Chi Minh City's Van Thanh bus station (Ben Xe Van Thanh).

Vung Tau bus station (Ben Xe Khach Vung Tau) is about 1.5km from the city centre at 52 Đ Nam Ky Khoi Nghia. There are nonexpress buses to Baria, Long Hai, Bien Hoa, Long Khanh, Mytho, Ho Chi Minh City and Tay Ninh.

Hydrofoil The best way to reach Vung Tau is by hydrofoil (about 1¼ hours; US$10). One hydrofoil can hold 124 passengers.

In Ho Chi Minh City, departures are from the Vina Express office (☎ 822 4621 or 825 3888), at 6A Đ Nguyen Tat Thanh, District 4, on the Saigon River a little south of the Ben Nghe Channel.

In Vung Tau you board the hydrofoil at Cau Da pier opposite the Hai Au Hotel (Front Beach). Vina Express (☎ 856 530) has a Vung Tau office by the pier.

Getting Around

The best way to get around the Vung Tau Peninsula is by bicycle. These are available for hire from some hotels for around US$1 per day.

There is a place opposite the Rex Hotel that rents motorcycles. A 50cc motorcycle costs only US$5 per day and no driving licence is required.

Vicaren Taxi (☎ 858 485) and Vung Tau Taxi (☎ 856 565) are the duopoly suppliers of cabs with meters and air-con.

LONG HAI

Commercialised tourism has turned Vung Tau into something of a circus, and many travellers crave a less developed seaside retreat. As a result, backpackers are increasingly heading to Long Hai, 30km north-east of Vung Tau, and backpacker cafes can organise tours here. The western end of the beach is where fishing boats moor and is therefore none too clean. However, the east end is attractive, with a reasonable amount of white sand and palm trees.

Places to Stay

The ***Huong Bien Hotel*** *(☎ 868 430)* offers five beach bungalows with two rooms in each. Most rooms have fan and cold bath, and cost US$8. With air-con it's US$13.

The ***Palace Hotel*** *(☎ 868 364)* was originally built to accommodate Emperor Bao Dai, who had a taste for fancy beachside villas. Bao Dai lost his franchise, but you can rent a room here with fan and cold bath for US$8. Air-con and hot water will set you back US$11.

The ***Military Guesthouse*** *(☎ 868 316)*, or Nha Nghi Quan Doi, is good value. Fan rooms in the main building are priced from US$5. Air-con ups the tab to US$10 to US$14. There are also two beach houses (recommended!) where rooms cost US$7.

The Soviet-style ***Rang Dong Hotel*** *(☎ 868 356)* is memorable chiefly for its noisy karaoke. Rooms cost US$10 to US$16.

The ***Long Hai Hotel*** *(☎ 868 312)* is difficult to recommend. For starters, the beach next to the hotel is rather dirty. Rooms are priced from US$18 to US$25.

The ***Thuy Duong Tourist Resort*** *(☎ 886 215, fax 886 210)* is in Phuoc Hai village, about 4km from Long Hai. The beach here is nice, and it's easy to continue to the hot springs at Binh Chau. There are eight types of rooms, including bungalows, cottages and suites, ranging from US$15 to US$80.

Long Hai's finest accommodation is at the plush ***Anoasis Beach Resort*** *(☎ 868227, fax 868229, @ anoasisresort@hcm.vnn.vn, www.anoasisresort.com.vn)*, a charming and secluded haven boasting a private beach, gigantic swimming pool and two tennis courts. Anoasis features 27 luxury bungalows and two fully-outfitted villas (yes, with spa baths). Cottage bungalows rent for US$104, 'family bungalows' from US$126 to US$155. The palatial 'ocean villa' – with kitchenette, terrace and spa – rents for US$248.

Getting There & Away

There are some Long Hai–Ho Chi Minh City buses, though not many. Getting from Vung Tau to Long Hai is more problematic – you may have to rent a motorcycle and drive yourself. Indeed, this is what most travellers do.

Motorcycle-taxi drivers hang around all the likely tourist spots and will repeatedly offer you a ride, whether you want one or not.

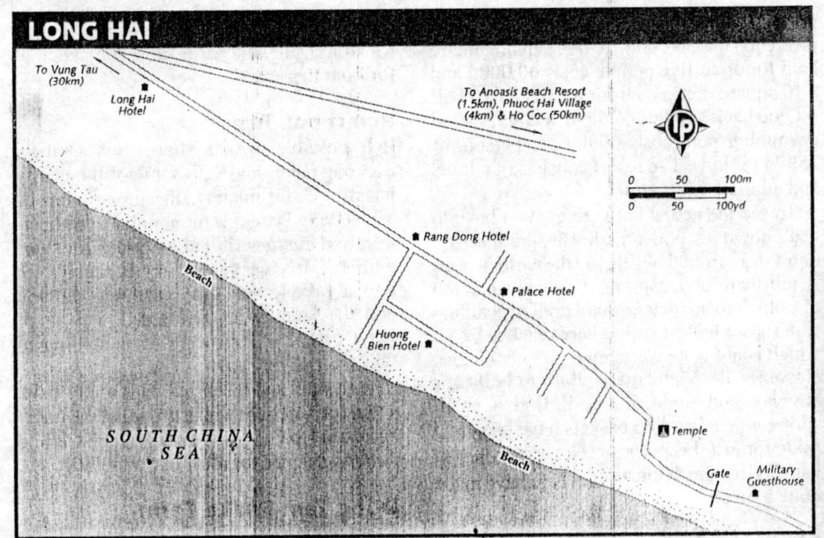

HO COC BEACH

About 50km north-east of Long Hai is the remote but beautiful Ho Coc Beach. It's still a very undeveloped area, though weekends bring out crowds of Vietnamese tourists. There are two accommodation choices right at the beach. ***Khu Du Lich Bien Ho Coc*** *(☎ 878175, fax 871130)* consists of five little wooden A-frame bungalows which rent for US$7. Each bungalow has an attached bath with cold water. The adjoining ***restaurant*** serves good seafood. Just down the beach about 50m south is ***Hang Duong Ho Coc*** *(☎ 878145, fax 874146)*, which has 11 cosy wooden cottages set back about 100m from the beach. Rooms cost US$8 and have attached bath (cold water only). There is also one larger cottage on the beach. Beds in the first floor room, which sleeps five people, rent for US$4 per person. The upstairs single room rents for US$6.

Getting There & Away

Public transport can be a little difficult, mainly because there isn't any. Some of the budget cafes in Ho Chi Minh City offer appealing day and overnight trips to Ho Coc. This also makes for a good (but very long) day trip on a motorcycle.

HAM TAN

Ham Tan is the new name for this place, but many locals still call it by its former name, Binh Tuy. It's a pleasantly secluded beach 30km north of Binh Chau Hot Springs. There are a couple of small hotels here, but visitors remain infrequent.

BINH CHAU HOT SPRINGS

About 60km north-east of Long Hai is Binh Chau Hot Springs, Suoi Nuoc Nong Binh Chau (☎ 871 130). There is a small resort here and tacky commercialisation is blessedly absent. The resort is in a compound 6km north of the village of Binh Chau. There is an admission fee of 6000d.

The main drawing card is the outdoor hot spring baths. There are 11 private baths for rent, each on its own covered wooden platform, complete with a small changing room. The baths range from 37° to 40°C, and the minerals in the water are said to be beneficial to your bones, muscles and skin, and also to improve blood circulation and mental disorders! The baths come in different sizes and prices. A three sqare metre bath for two people rents for 36,000d, a five square metre bath for up to five people costs 60,000d and a 10 square metre bath for a party of 10 will set you back 96,000d. A dip in a large, shared swimming pool costs 6000d per person, or 2500d for kids. The resort consists of a hotel and adjoining restaurant.

To see the actual hot springs, you have to walk down a wooden path. Be sure that you don't stray from the paths, as the earthen crust is thin here and you could conceivably fall through into an underground pool of scalding water! The hottest spring here reaches 82°C, which is not quite warm enough to boil eggs. However, the Vietnamese all try to boil eggs anyway and, indeed, you'll find a small spring where bamboo baskets have been laid aside for just this purpose. The eggshells and half-boiled eggs lying around here have made quite a mess.

Places to Stay

If you want to spend the night, the only choice is ***Hotel-Restaurant Cumi*** *(☎ 871 131)*. There is a main hotel, as well as some bungalows and a tree house with shared bath only costing US$8. Fan rooms in the hotel cost US$9, and with air-con you'll pay US$12 to US$16.

Getting There & Away

There is a sealed highway all the way to the hot springs, yet no public transport. You'll need a motorcycle or car. If you choose the latter, perhaps you can find some travellers to share the expense.

MYTHO

Mytho, the capital of Tien Giang Province, is a quiet place 90 minutes by car from Ho Chi Minh City. The town is in the lush Mekong Delta and is the closest place to go for boat trips on the river.

Riverboat Trips

It is possible to take short cruises on the Mekong River and visit some of the nearby islands. Unfortunately, the government of Tien Giang Province monopolises this business and charges ridiculous prices for short journeys. It's bad value, but you cannot hire a local private boat – doing so may get you and the boat owner arrested. For a bit of extra cash, the locals are often willing to take the risk anyway.

A cheaper and easier option is to pre-book a tour (privately or with a group) at the travel agents in Ho Chi Minh City (see the Getting Around chapter for a list of possibilities).

Dong Tam Snake Farm

There is a snake farm at Dong Tam, which is about 10km west from Mytho towards Vinh Long. Most of the snakes raised here are pythons and cobras. The snakes are raised for a variety of purposes: for eating, for their skins and for the purpose of producing snake antivenins. Admission costs US$1.

Vinh Trang Pagoda

Vinh Trang Pagoda, in Mytho, is a beautiful and well-maintained sanctuary. The charitable monks here provide a home to orphans and handicapped and other needy children.

The pagoda is about 1km from the city centre, at 60A Đ Nguyen Trung Truc. To get there, take the bridge across the river (at Đ Nguyen Trai) and continue for about a kilometre. The entrance to the sanctuary is on the right-hand side of the building as you approach it from the ornate gate.

Language

The Vietnamese language (Kinh) is a fusion of Mon-Khmer, Tai and Chinese elements. For centuries, the Vietnamese language was written in standard Chinese characters. The Latin-based *quoc ngu* script, in wide use since WW I, was developed in the 17th century by Alexandre de Rhodes (see the boxed aside).

The most widely spoken foreign languages in Vietnam are English, French and Chinese (Cantonese and Mandarin), more or less in that order. Many of the older Saigonese who speak fluent English learned it while working with the Americans during the Vietnam War. These days, almost everyone has a desire to learn English.

The Vietnamese treat every syllable as an independent word, so 'Saigon' gets spelled 'Sai Gon' and 'Vietnam' is written as 'Viet Nam'.

The words and phrases listed in this chapter should help provide you with the basics. If you want a more in depth guide to Vietnamese get a copy of Lonely Planet's *Vietnamese phrasebook*. Also available is Lonely Planet's *Vietnamese audio pack*, companion to the phrasebook, and available on CD or cassette.

Alexandre de Rhodes

One of the most illustrious of the early missionaries was the brilliant French Jesuit scholar Alexandre de Rhodes (1591-1660). Rhodes first preached in Vietnamese only six months after arriving in the country in 1627, and he is most recognised for his work in devising *quoc ngu*, the Latin-based phonetic alphabet in which Vietnamese is written to this day. By replacing Chinese characters with quoc ngu, de Rhodes facilitated the propagation of the gospel to a wide audience.

Over the course of his long career, de Rhodes flitted back and forth between Hanoi, Macau, Rome and Paris, seeking support and funding for his missionary activities and battling both Portuguese colonial opposition and the intractable Vatican bureaucracy. In 1645, he was sentenced to death for illegally entering Vietnam to proselytise, but was expelled instead; two of the priests with him were beheaded.

For his contributions, Alexandre de Rhodes gained the highest respect from the Vietnamese (in the south, anyway), who called him *cha caá* (father). A memorial statue of Rhodes stands in central Saigon.

Pronunciation

Most of the names of the letters of the quoc ngu alphabet are pronounced like the letters of the French alphabet. Dictionaries are alphabetised as in English except that each vowel/tone combination is treated as a different letter. The consonants of the Romanised Vietnamese alphabet are pronounced more or less as they are in English with a few exceptions, and Vietnamese makes no use of the Roman letters 'f', 'j', 'w' and 'z'.

c	as an unaspirated 'k'
đ	(with crossbar) a hard 'd' as in 'do'
d	(without crossbar) as the 'y' in 'yes'
gi-	as 'y'
kh-	as the 'ch' in German *buch*

ng-	as the '-nga-' in 'long ago'
nh-	as the 'ni' in 'onion'
ph-	as the 'f' in 'far'
r	as 'r'
s	as 'sh'
tr-	as 'tr'
th-	a strongly aspirated 't'
x	like an 's'
-ch	like a 'k'
-ng	as the 'ng' in 'long' but with the lips closed
-nh	as the 'ng' in 'sing'

Tones

The hardest part for westerners in mastering Vietnamese is learning to differentiate between the tones. There are six tones in spoken Vietnamese. Thus, every syllable in Vietnamese can be pronounced six different ways. For example, depending on the tones, the word *ma* can be read to mean 'ghost', 'but', 'mother', 'rice seedling', 'tomb' or 'horse'.

In written form the six tones of spoken Vietnamese are indicated by the use of five diacritical marks (the first tone is left unmarked). These should not be confused with the four other diacritical marks used to indicate special consonants, such as the crossbar in **đ**.

The following examples show the six different tone representations:

Tone Name	Example	
dấu ngang	*ma*	'ghost'
dấu sắc	*má*	'mother'
dấu huyền	*mà*	'but'
dấu nặng	*mạ*	'rice seedling'
dấu hỏi	*mả*	'tomb'
dấu ngã	*mã*	'horse'

A visual representation looks something like this:

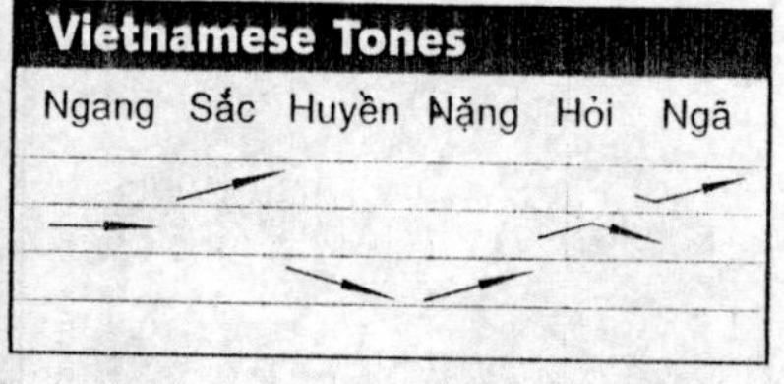

You should also be aware that there are major differences between northern, central and southern Vietnamese. Foreign students who learn Vietnamese in Hanoi and then move to Saigon to find work (or vice versa) have been dismayed to discover that they cannot communicate. The language spoken in the north is considered 'Queen's Vietnamese', while central and southern dialects have a harsher sound to them.

Proper Names

Most Vietnamese names consist of a family name, a middle name and a given name, in that order. Thus, if Henry David Thoreau had been Vietnamese, he would have been named Thoreau David Henry. He would have been addressed as Mr Henry – people are called by their given name, but to do so without the title Mr, Mrs or Miss is considered as expressing either intimacy or arrogance of the sort a superior would use with an inferior.

In Vietnamese, Mr is *Ong* if the man is of your grandparents' generation, *Bac* if he is of your parents' age, *Chu* if he is younger than your parents and *Anh* if he is in his teens or early 20s. Mrs is *Ba* if the woman is of your grandparents' age and *Bac* if she is of your parents' generation or younger. Miss is *Chi* or *Em* unless the woman is very young, in which case *Co* might be more appropriate. Other titles of respect are for a Buddhist monk *(Thay)*, Buddhist nun *(Ba)*, Catholic priest *(Cha)* and Catholic nun *(Co)*.

There are 300 or so family names in use in Vietnam, the most common of which is Nguyen (pronounced something like 'nwyen'). About half of all Vietnamese have the surname Nguyen!

Pronouns

I	*tôi*
you (to an older man)	*(các) ông*
you (to an older woman)	*(các) bà*
you (to a man of your own age)	*(các) anh*

you (to a woman your own age) — *(các) chi*
he — *cậu đó/anh đó*
she — *chị đó/anh đó*
we — *chúng tôi*
they — *họ*

Greetings & Civilities

Hello. — *Xin chào.*
How are you? — *Có khoẻ không?*
Fine, thank you. — *Khoẻ, cám ơn.*
Good night. — *Chúc ngủ ngon.*
Excuse me. (often used before questions) — *Xin lỗi.*
Thank you. — *Cám ơn.*
Thank you very much. — *Cám ơn rất nhiều.*
Yes. — *Dạ.*
No. — *Không.*

Useful Words & Phrases

change money — *đổi tiền*
come — *đến*
give — *cho*
fast — *mau*
slow — *chậm*
man — *nam*
woman — *nữ*
understand — *hiểu*

I don't understand. — *Tôi không hiểu.*
I need ... — *Tôi cần ...*

Small Talk

What's your name? — *Tên là gì?*
My name is ... — *Tên tôi là ...*
I like ... — *Tôi thích ...*
I don't like ... — *Tôi không thích ...*
I want ... — *Tôi muốn ...*
I don't want ... — *Tôi không muốn ...*

Getting Around

What time does the first bus leave? — *Chuyến xe buýt sớm nhất chạy lúc mấy giờ?*
What time does the last bus leave? — *Chuyến xe buýt cuối cùng sẽ chạy lúc mấy giờ?*
How many kilometres to ...? — *Cách xa bao nhiêu ki-lô-mét ...?*
How long does the journey take? — *Chuyến đi sẽ mất bao lâu?*
I want to go to ... — *Tôi muốn đi ...*
What time does it arrive? — *Mấy giờ đến?*
Go. — *Đi.*
hire a car — *muốn xe hơi*
bus — *xe buýt*
bus station — *bến xe*
cyclo (pedicab) — *xe xích lô*
map — *bản đồ*
railway station — *ga xe lửa*
receipt — *biên lai*
sleeping berth — *giường ngủ*
timetable — *thời biểu*
train — *xe lửa*

Around Town

office — *văn phòng*
post office — *bưu điện*
restaurant — *nhà hàng*
telephone — *điện thoại*
tourism — *du lịch*

boulevard — *đại lộ*
bridge — *cầu*
highway — *xa lộ*
island — *đảo*
mountain — *núi*
National Highway 1 — *Quốc Lộ 1*
river — *sông*
square (in a city) — *công viên*
street — *đường/phố*

north — *bắc*
south — *nam*
east — *đông*
west — *tây*

Accommodation

hotel — *khách sạn*
guest house — *nhà khách*

Where is there a (cheap) hotel? — *Ở đâu có khách sạn (rẻ tiền)?*
How much does a room cost? — *Giá một phòng là bao nhiêu?*
I'd like a cheap room. — *Tôi thích một phòng loại rẻ.*

Emergencies

Help!	*Cửu tôi với!*
I'm sick.	*Tôi bị đau*
Please call a doctor.	*Làm ơn gọi bác sĩ.*
Please take me to the hospital.	*Làm ơn đưa tôi bệnh viện.*
Thief!	*Cướp, cắp!*
Pickpocket!	*Móc túi!*
police	*công an*
immigration police station	*phòng quản lý người nước ngoài*

I need to leave at (5) o'clock tomorrow morning.	*Tôi phải đi lúc (năm) giờ sáng mai.*
air-conditioning	*máy lạnh*
bathroom	*phòng tắm*
blanket	*mền*
fan	*quạt máy*
hot water	*nước nóng*
laundry	*giặt ủi*
mosquito net	*mùng*
reception	*tiếp tân*
room	*phòng*
room key	*chìa khóa phòng*
1st-class room	*phòng loại 1*
2nd-class room	*phòng loại 2*
sheet	*ra trãi giường*
toilet	*nhà vệ sinh*
toilet paper	*giấy vệ sinh*
towel	*khăn tắm*

Shopping

I'd like to buy ...	*Tôi muốn mua ...*
How much is this?	*Cái này giá bao nhiêu?*
I want to pay in dong.	*Tôi muốn trả bằng tiền Việt Nam.*

buy	*mua*
sell	*bán*
cheap	*rẻ tiền*
expensive	*mắc tiền*
very expensive	*mắc quá*
market	*chợ*
mosquito coils	*nhang chống muỗi*
insect repellent	*thuốc chống muỗi*
sanitary pads	*băng vệ sinh*

Time, Days & Numbers

evening	*chiều*
now	*bây giờ*
today	*hôm nay*
tomorrow	*ngày mai*

Monday	*Thứ hai*
Tuesday	*Thứ ba*
Wednesday	*Thứ tư*
Thursday	*Thứ năm*
Friday	*Thứ sáu*
Saturday	*Thứ bảy*
Sunday	*Chủ nhật*

1	*một*
2	*hai*
3	*ba*
4	*bốn*
5	*năm*
6	*sáu*
7	*bảy*
8	*tám*
9	*chín*
10	*mười*
11	*mười một*
19	*mười chín*
20	*hai mươi*
21	*hai mươi mốt*
22	*hai mươi hai*
30	*ba mươi*
90	*chín mươi*
100	*một trăm*
200	*hai trăm*
900	*chín trăm*
1000	*một ngàn*
10,000	*mười ngàn*

one million	*một triệu*
two million	*hai triệu*

first	*thứ nhất*
second	*thứ hai*

Health

dentist	*nha sĩ*
doctor	*bác sĩ*
hospital	*bệnh viện*
pharmacy	*nhà thuốc tây*

backache	*đau lưng*
diarrhoea	*ăa chảy*

dizziness	*chóng mặt*
fever	*cảm/cúm*
headache	*nhức đầu*
malaria	*sốt rét*
stomachache	*đau bụng*
toothache	*nhức răng*
vomiting	*ói/mửa*

FOOD

Breakfast

pancake	*bánh xèo ngọt*
banana pancake	*bánh chuối*
pineapple pancake	*bánh khóm*
papaya pancake	*bánh đu đủ*
orange pancake	*bánh cam*
plain pancake	*bánh không nhân*
bread with ...	*bánh mì ...*
omelette	*trứng chiên*
fried eggs	*trứng ốp la*
butter	*bơ*
butter & jam	*bơ mứt*
jam	*mứt*
cheese	*phomai*
butter & cheese	*bơ phomát*
butter & honey	*bơ mật ong*
combination sandwich	*săn huýt*

Lunch & Dinner

noodles & rice noodles	*mì, hủ tíu*
beef noodle soup	*hủ tíu bò*
chicken noodle soup	*hủ tíu gà*
vegetarian noodle soup	*mì rau/mì chay*
duck, bamboo shoot noodle soup	*bún măng*
potatoes	*khoai tây*
french fries	*khoai chiên*
fried potato & tomato	*khoai xào cà chua*
fried potato & butter	*khoai chiên bơ*
fried dishes	*các món xào*
fried noodle with chicken	*mì xào gà/hủ tíu xào gà*
fried noodle with beef	*mì xào bò/hủ tíu xào bò*
mixed fried noodle	*mì xào thập cẩm*
chicken	*gà*
roasted chicken	*gà quay/gà rô-ti*
chicken salad	*gà xeù phay*
fried chicken in mushroom sauce	*gà sốt nấm*
batter fried chicken	*gà tẩm bột rán/chiên*
fried chicken with lemon sauce	*gà rán/chiên sốt chanh*
curried chicken	*gà cà-ri*
pork	*lợn/heo*
skewered-grilled pork	*chả lợn xiên nướng/ chả heo nướng*
sweet & sour fried pork	*lợn xào chua ngọt/ heo xào chua ngọt*
roasted pork	*heo quay*
grilled pork	*thịt lợn nướng xả/ heo nướng xả*
beef	*thịt bò*
beefsteak	*bít tết*
skewered grilled beef	*bò xiên nướng*
spicy beef	*bò xào sả ớt*
fried beef with pineapple	*bò xào khóm*
fried beef with garlic	*bò xào tỏi*
grilled beef with ginger	*bò nướng gừng*
rare beef with vinegar	*bò nhúng giấm*
hot pot (hot & sour soup)	*lẩu*
beef hot pot	*lẩu bò*
eel hot pot	*lẩu lươn*
fish hot pot	*lẩu cá*
combination hot pot	*lẩu thập cẩm*
spring roll	*chả giò*
meat spring rolls	*chả giò*
vegetarian spring rolls	*chả giò chay*
sour spring rolls	*nem chua*
pigeon	*chim bồ câu*
roasted pigeon	*bồ câu quay*
fried pigeon in mushroom sauce	*bồ câu xào nấm sốt*

soup	*súp*
chicken soup	*súp gà*
eel soup	*súp lươn*
combination soup	*súp thập cẩm*
maize soup	*súp bắp*
vegetarian soup	*súp rau*
fish	*cá*
grilled fish with sugarcane	*chả cá bao mía*
fried fish in tomato sauce	*cá rán/chiên sốt cà*
sweet & sour fried fish	*cá sốt chua ngọt*
fried fish with lemon	*cá rán/chiên chanh*
fried fish with mushrooms	*cá xào hành nấm rơm*
steamed fish with ginger	*cá hấp gừng*
boiled fish	*cá luộc*
grilled fish	*cá nướng*
steamed fish in beer	*cá hấp bia*
shrimp/prawns	*tôm*
sweet & sour fried shrimp	*tôm xào chua ngọt*
fried shrimp with mushrooms	*tôm xào nấm*
grilled shrimp with sugarcane	*chạo tôm*
batter fried shrimp	*tôm tẩm bột/ tôm hỏa tiễn*
steamed shrimp in beer	*tôm hấp bia*
crab	*cua*
salted fried crab	*cua rang muối*
crab with chopped meat	*cua nhồi thịt*
steamed crab in beer	*cua hấp bia*
squid	*mực*
fried squid	*mực chiên*
fried squid with mushrooms	*mực xào nấm*
fried squid with pineapple	*mực xào khóm*
squid in sweet & sour sauce	*mực xào chua ngọt*

eel	*lươn*
fried eel with chopped meat	*lươn cuốn thịt rán/chiên*
fried eel with mushrooms	*lươn xào nấm*
simmered eel	*lươn um*
snail	*ốc*
spicy snail	*ốc xào sả ớt*
fried snail with pineapple	*ốc xào khóm*
fried snail with tofu & bananas	*ốc xào đậu phu (đậu hủ) chuối xanh*
vegetarian	*các món chay*
I'm a vegetarian.	*Tôi là người ăn chay.*
fried noodles with vegetable	*mì/hủ tíu xào rau*
vegetarian noodle soup	*mì/hủ tíu nấu rau*
fried vegetables	*rau xào*
boiled vegetables	*rau luộc*
vegetables	*rau*
fried vegetables	*rau xào*
boiled vegetables	*rau luộc*
sour vegetable	*dưa chua*
fried bean sprouts	*giá xào*
vegetable soup (large bowl)	*canh rau*
salad	*rau sa lát*
fried vegetable with mushrooms	*rau cải xào nấm*
tofu	*đậu phụ/đậu hủ*
fried tofu with chopped meat	*thòt nhồi đậu phụ/ đậu hủ*
fried tofu with tomato sauce	*đậu phụ/đậu hủ sốt cà*
fried tofu with vegetable	*đậu phụ/đậu hủ xào*
rice	*cơm*
steamed rice	*cơm trắng*
mixed fried rice	*cơm chiên*
rice porridge	*cháo*
specialities	*đặc sản*
lobster	*con tôm hùm*
frog	*con ếch*
oyster	*con sò*

bat	*con dơi*
cobra	*rắn hổ*
gecko	*con tắc kè/kỳ nhơng/ kỳ đà*
goat	*con dê*
pangolin	*con trúc/tê tê*
porcupine	*con nhím*
python	*con trăn*
small hornless deer	*con nai tơ*
turtle	*con rùa*
venison	*thịt nai*
wild pig	*con heo rừng*

Fruit

fruit	*trái cây*
apple	*trái bơm*
apricot	*trái lê*
avocado	*trái bơ*
banana	*trái chuối*
coconut	*trái dừa*
custard apple	*trái mãng cầu*
durian	*trái sầu riêng*
grapes	*trái nho*
green dragon fruit	*trái thanh long*
guava	*trái ổi*
jackfruit	*trái mít*
jujube (Chinese date)	*trái táo ta*
lemon	*trái chanh*
longan	*trái nhãn*
lychee	*trái vải*
mandarin orange	*trái quýt*
mangosteen	*trái măng cụt*
orange	*trái cam*
papaya	*trái đu đủ*
peach	*trái đào*
persimmon	*trái hồng xiêm*
pineapple	*trái khóm/trái dứa*
plum	*trái mận/trái mơ*
pomelo	*trái bưởi*
rambutan	*trái chôm chôm*
starfruit	*trái khế*
strawberry	*trái dâu*
tangerine	*trái quýt*
three seed cherry	*trái sê-ri*
water apple	*trái mận*
watermelon	*trái dưa hấu*
fruit salad	*trái cây các loại*
yoghurt	*da-ua*
mixed fruit cocktail	*cóc-tai hoa quả*

Condiments

pepper	*tiêu xay*
salt	*muối*
sugar	*đường*
ice	*đá*
hot pepper	*ớt trái*
fresh chillis	*ớt*
soy sauce	*nước tường*
fish sauce	*nước mắm*

DRINKS

coffee	*cà phê*
hot black coffee	*cà phê đen nóng*
hot milk coffee	*cà phê sữa nóng*
iced black coffee	*cà phê đá*
iced milk coffee	*cà phê sữa đá*
tea	*trà*
hot black tea	*trà nóng*
hot milk black tea	*trà pha sữa*
hot honey black tea	*trà pha mật*
chocolate milk	*cacao sữa*
hot chocolate	*cacao nóng*
iced chocolate	*cacao đá*
hot milk	*sữa nóng*
iced milk	*sữa đá*
fruit juice	*nước quả/nước trái cây*
hot lemon juice	*chanh nóng*
iced lemon juice	*chanh đá*
hot orange juice	*cam nóng*
iced orange juice	*cam đá*
pure orange juice	*cam vắt*
fruit shake	*sinh tố/trái cây xay*
banana shake	*nước chuối xay*
milk & banana shake	*nước chuối sữa xay*
orange-banana shake	*nước cam/chuối xay*
papaya shake	*nước đu đủ xay*
pineapple shake	*khóm xay*
mixed fruit shake	*sinh tố tổng hợp/ nước thập cẩm xay*
mango shake	*nước xoài xay*
mineral water	*nước suối*
lemon mineral water	*suối chanh*
spring water (large/small)	*nước suối chai (lớn/nhỏ)*

beer	*bia*
333 beer	*bia 333*
BGI beer	*bia BGI*
Carlsberg beer	*bia Carlsberg*
Chinese beer	*bia Trung Quốc*
Halida beer	*bia Halida*
Heineken beer	*bia Heineken*
Mastel beer	*bia Amstel*
San Miguel beer	*bia San Miguel*
Tiger beer	*bia Tiger*
Tiger (large bottle)	*bia Tiger (chai to)*
tinned soft drinks	*thức uống đóng hộp*
Coke	*Coca Cola*
Pepsi	*Pepsi Cola*
7 Up	*7 Up*
tinned orange juice	*cam hộp*
soda water & lemon	*soda chanh*
soda water, lemon & sugar	*soda chanh đường*

Glossary

ao dai – national dress of Vietnamese women and (rarely) men

bang – congregation (in the Chinese community)
bo doi – North Vietnamese (Communist) troops who occupied Ho Chi Minh City in 1975
buu dien – post office

Caodai – indigenous Vietnamese religious sect
Celadon – a type of Chinese porcelain, with a greyish-green glaze
Champa – Hindu kingdom dating from the late 2nd century AD
Chams – the people of Champa
cho – market
Cochinchina – the southern part of Vietnam during the French-colonial era
cyclo – pedicab or bicycle rickshaw (from French)

doi moi – economic renovation, restructuring

Funan – see *Oc-Eo*

ghe – long, narrow rowboat

Hoa – ethnic Chinese
Honda om – motorcycle taxi
huyen – rural district

Indochina – Vietnam, Cambodia and Laos. The name derives from the influence of Indian and Chinese cultures on the region.

khach san – hotel
Khmer – ethnic Cambodians

Liberation – the 1975 invasion and takeover of South Vietnam by the North Vietnamese; referred to by most foreigners as 'reunification'

nha hang – restaurant
nha khach – hotel or guesthouse
nha nghi – guesthouse
nha thuoc – pharmacy
nha tro – dormitory
NLF – National Liberation Front; official name for the Viet Cong
NVA – North Vietnamese Army

Oc-Eo – Indianised kingdom (also called Funan) of southern Vietnam from 1st to 6th centuries

pagoda – traditionally, an eight-sided Buddhist tower, but in Vietnam the word is commonly used to denote a temple

quan – urban district
quoc ngu – Latin-based phonetic alphabet in which Vietnamese is written

rap – cinema
roi nuoc – water puppetry

Tam Giao – Vietnam's 'triple religion'
tay balo – backpacker (literally, 'foreigner with backpack')
Tet – the Vietnamese lunar new year

VAT – Value Added Tax (currently 10%)
VC – Viet Cong; Vietnamese Communists
Viet Kieu – Overseas Vietnamese
Viet Minh – League for the Independence of Vietnam, a nationalistic movement which fought the Japanese and French but later, under the influence of Ho Chi Minh, became Communist-dominated

xe lam – three-wheeled motorised vehicle, from 'Lambretta'

LONELY PLANET

Guides by Region

Lonely Planet is known worldwide for publishing practical, reliable and no-nonsense travel information in our guides and on our Web site. The Lonely Planet list covers just about every accessible part of the world. Currently there are 16 series: Travel guides, Shoestring guides, Condensed guides, Phrasebooks, Read This First, Healthy Travel, Walking guides, Cycling guides, Watching Wildlife guides, Pisces Diving & Snorkeling guides, City Maps, Road Atlases, Out to Eat, World Food, Journeys travel literature and Pictorials.

AFRICA Africa on a shoestring • Cairo • Cape Town • Cape Town City Map • East Africa • Egypt • Egyptian Arabic phrasebook • Ethiopia, Eritrea & Djibouti • Ethiopian (Amharic) phrasebook • The Gambia & Senegal • Healthy Travel Africa • Kenya • Malawi • Morocco • Moroccan Arabic phrasebook • Mozambique • Read This First: Africa • South Africa, Lesotho & Swaziland • Southern Africa • Southern Africa Road Atlas • Swahili phrasebook • Tanzania, Zanzibar & Pemba • Trekking in East Africa • Tunisia • Watching Wildlife East Africa • Watching Wildlife Southern Africa • West Africa • World Food Morocco • Zimbabwe, Botswana & Namibia
Travel Literature: Mali Blues: Traveling to an African Beat • The Rainbird: A Central African Journey • Songs to an African Sunset: A Zimbabwean Story

AUSTRALIA & THE PACIFIC Auckland • Australia • Australian phrasebook • Australia Road Atlas • Bushwalking in Australia •Cycling New Zealand • Fiji • Fijian phrasebook • Healthy Travel Australia, NZ and the Pacific • Islands of Australia's Great Barrier Reef • Melbourne • Melbourne City Map • Micronesia • New Caledonia • New South Wales & the ACT • New Zealand • Northern Territory • Outback Australia • Out to Eat – Melbourne • Out to Eat – Sydney • Papua New Guinea • Pidgin phrasebook • Queensland • Rarotonga & the Cook Islands • Samoa • Solomon Islands • South Australia • South Pacific • South Pacific phrasebook • Sydney • Sydney City Map • Sydney Condensed • Tahiti & French Polynesia • Tasmania • Tonga • Tramping in New Zealand • Vanuatu • Victoria • Watching Wildlife Australia • Western Australia
Travel Literature: Islands in the Clouds: Travels in the Highlands of New Guinea • Kiwi Tracks: A New Zealand Journey • Sean & David's Long Drive

CENTRAL AMERICA & THE CARIBBEAN Bahamas, Turks & Caicos • Baja California • Bermuda • Central America on a shoestring • Costa Rica • Costa Rica Spanish phrasebook • Cuba • Dominican Republic & Haiti • Eastern Caribbean • Guatemala • Guatemala, Belize & Yucatán: La Ruta Maya • Healthy Travel Central & South America • Jamaica • Mexico • Mexico City • Panama • Puerto Rico • Read This First: Central & South America • World Food Mexico • Yucatán
Travel Literature: Green Dreams: Travels in Central America

EUROPE Amsterdam • Amsterdam City Map • Amsterdam Condensed • Andalucía • Austria • Baltic States phrasebook • Barcelona • Barcelona City Map • Berlin • Berlin City Map • Britain • British phrasebook • Brussels, Bruges & Antwerp • Budapest • Budapest City Map • Canary Islands • Central Europe • Central Europe phrasebook • Corfu & the Ionians • Corsica • Crete • Crete Condensed • Croatia • Cycling Britain • Cycling France • Cyprus • Czech & Slovak Republics • Denmark • Dublin • Dublin City Map • Eastern Europe • Eastern Europe phrasebook • Edinburgh • Estonia, Latvia & Lithuania • Europe on a shoestring • Finland • Florence • France • Frankfurt Condensed • French phrasebook • Georgia, Armenia & Azerbaijan • Germany • German phrasebook • Greece • Greek Islands • Greek phrasebook • Hungary • Iceland, Greenland & the Faroe Islands • Ireland • Istanbul • Italian phrasebook • Italy • Krakow • Lisbon • The Loire • London • London City Map • London Condensed • Madrid • Malta • Mediterranean Europe • Mediterranean Europe phrasebook • Moscow • Munich • Norway • Out to Eat – London • Paris • Paris City Map • Paris Condensed • Poland • Portugal • Portuguese phrasebook • Prague • Prague City Map • Provence & the Côte d'Azur • Read This First: Europe • Romania & Moldova • Rome • Russia, Ukraine & Belarus • Russian phrasebook • Scandinavian & Baltic Europe • Scandinavian Europe phrasebook • Scotland • Sicily • Slovenia • South-West France • Spain • Spanish phrasebook • St Petersburg • St Petersburg City Map • Sweden • Switzerland • Trekking in Spain • Tuscany • Ukrainian phrasebook • Venice • Vienna • Walking in Britain • Walking in France • Walking in Ireland • Walking in Italy • Walking in Spain • Walking in Switzerland • Western Europe • Western Europe phrasebook • World Food France • World Food Ireland • World Food Italy • World Food Spain
Travel Literature: Love and War in the Apennines • The Olive Grove: Travels in Greece • On the Shores of the Mediterranean • Round Ireland in Low Gear • A Small Place in Italy

INDIAN SUBCONTINENT Bangladesh • Bengali phrasebook • Bhutan • Delhi • Goa • Healthy Travel Asia & India • Hindi & Urdu phrasebook • India • Indian Himalaya • Karakoram Highway • Kerala • Mumbai

Mail Order

Lonely Planet products are distributed worldwide. They are also available by mail order from Lonely Planet, so if you have difficulty finding a title please write to us. North and South American residents should write to 150 Linden St, Oakland, CA 94607, USA; European and African residents should write to 10a Spring Place, London NW5 3BH, UK; and residents of other countries to Locked Bag 1, Footscray, Victoria 3011, Australia.

(Bombay) • Nepal • Nepali phrasebook • Pakistan • Rajasthan • Read This First: Asia & India • South India • Sri Lanka • Sri Lanka phrasebook • Tibet • Tibetan phrasebook • Trekking in the Indian Himalaya • Trekking in the Karakoram & Hindukush • Trekking in the Nepal Himalaya
Travel Literature: The Age of Kali: Indian Travels and Encounters • Hello Goodnight: A Life of Goa • In Rajasthan • A Season in Heaven: True Tales from the Road to Kathmandu • Shopping for Buddhas • A Short Walk in the Hindu Kush • Slowly Down the Ganges

ISLANDS OF THE INDIAN OCEAN Madagascar & Comoros • Maldives • Mauritius, Réunion & Seychelles

MIDDLE EAST & CENTRAL ASIA Bahrain, Kuwait & Qatar • Central Asia • Central Asia phrasebook • Dubai • Hebrew phrasebook • Iran • Israel & the Palestinian Territories • Istanbul • Istanbul City Map • Istanbul to Cairo on a shoestring • Jerusalem • Jerusalem City Map • Jordan • Lebanon • Middle East • Oman & the United Arab Emirates • Syria • Turkey • Turkish phrasebook • World Food Turkey • Yemen
Travel Literature: Black on Black: Iran Revisited • The Gates of Damascus • Kingdom of the Film Stars: Journey into Jordan

NORTH AMERICA Alaska • Boston • Boston City Map • California & Nevada • California Condensed • Canada • Chicago • Chicago City Map • Deep South • Florida • Hawaii • Hiking in Alaska • Hiking in the USA • Honolulu • Las Vegas • Los Angeles • Miami • Miami City Map • New England • New Orleans • New York City • New York City City Map • New York City Condensed • New York, New Jersey & Pennsylvania • Oahu • Out to Eat – San Francisco • Pacific Northwest • Puerto Rico • Rocky Mountains • San Francisco • San Francisco City Map • Seattle • Southwest • Texas • USA • USA phrasebook • Vancouver • Virginia & the Capital Region • Washington, DC City Map • World Food Deep South, USA
Travel Literature: Caught Inside: A Surfer's Year on the California Coast • Drive Thru America

NORTH-EAST ASIA Beijing • Cantonese phrasebook • China • Hiking in Japan • Hong Kong • Hong Kong City Map • Hong Kong Condensed • Hong Kong, Macau & Guangzhou • Japan • Japanese phrasebook • Korea • Korean phrasebook • Kyoto • Mandarin phrasebook • Mongolia • Mongolian phrasebook • Seoul • South-West China • Taiwan • Tokyo
Travel Literature: In Xanadu: A Quest • Lost Japan

SOUTH AMERICA Argentina, Uruguay & Paraguay • Bolivia • Brazil • Brazilian phrasebook • Buenos Aires • Chile & Easter Island • Colombia • Ecuador & the Galapagos Islands • Healthy Travel Central & South America • Latin American Spanish phrasebook • Peru • Quechua phrasebook • Read This First: Central & South America • Rio de Janeiro • Rio de Janeiro City Map • Santiago • South America on a shoestring • Trekking in the Patagonian Andes • Venezuela
Travel Literature: Full Circle: A South American Journey

SOUTH-EAST ASIA Bali & Lombok • Bangkok • Bangkok City Map • Burmese phrasebook • Cambodia • Hanoi • Healthy Travel Asia & India • Hill Tribes phrasebook • Ho Chi Minh City • Indonesia • Indonesian phrasebook • Indonesia's Eastern Islands • Jakarta • Java • Lao phrasebook • Laos • Malay phrasebook • Malaysia, Singapore & Brunei • Myanmar (Burma) • Philippines • Pilipino (Tagalog) phrasebook • Read This First: Asia & India • Singapore • Singapore City Map • South-East Asia on a shoestring • South-East Asia phrasebook • Thailand • Thailand's Islands & Beaches • Thailand, Vietnam, Laos & Cambodia Road Atlas • Thai phrasebook • Vietnam • Vietnamese phrasebook • World Food Thailand • World Food Vietnam

ALSO AVAILABLE: Antarctica • The Arctic • The Blue Man: Tales of Travel, Love and Coffee • Brief Encounters: Stories of Love, Sex & Travel • Chasing Rickshaws • The Last Grain Race • Lonely Planet Unpacked • Not the Only Planet: Science Fiction Travel Stories • On the Edge: Extreme Travel • Sacred India • Travel with Children • Travel Photography: A Guide to Taking Better Pictures

LONELY PLANET

You already know that Lonely Planet produces more than this one guidebook, but you might not be aware of the other products we have on this region. Here is a selection of titles that you may want to check out as well:

Hanoi
ISBN 0 86442 799 9
US$14.95 • UK£8.99 • 110FF

Vietnamese phrasebook
ISBN 0 86442 661 5
US$7.99 • UK£4.50 • 49FF

Vietnam
ISBN 1 86450 189 8
US$19.99 • UK£12.99 • 149FF

Thailand, Vietnam, Laos & Cambodia Road Atlas
ISBN 1 86450 102 2
US$14.99 • UK£8.99 • 109FF

Healthy Travel Asia & India
ISBN 1 86450 051 4
US$5.95 • UK£3.99 • 39FF

Read This First: Asia & India
ISBN 1 86450 049 2
US$14.99 • UK£8.99 • 99FF

Available wherever books are sold

Index

Text

Boxed Text

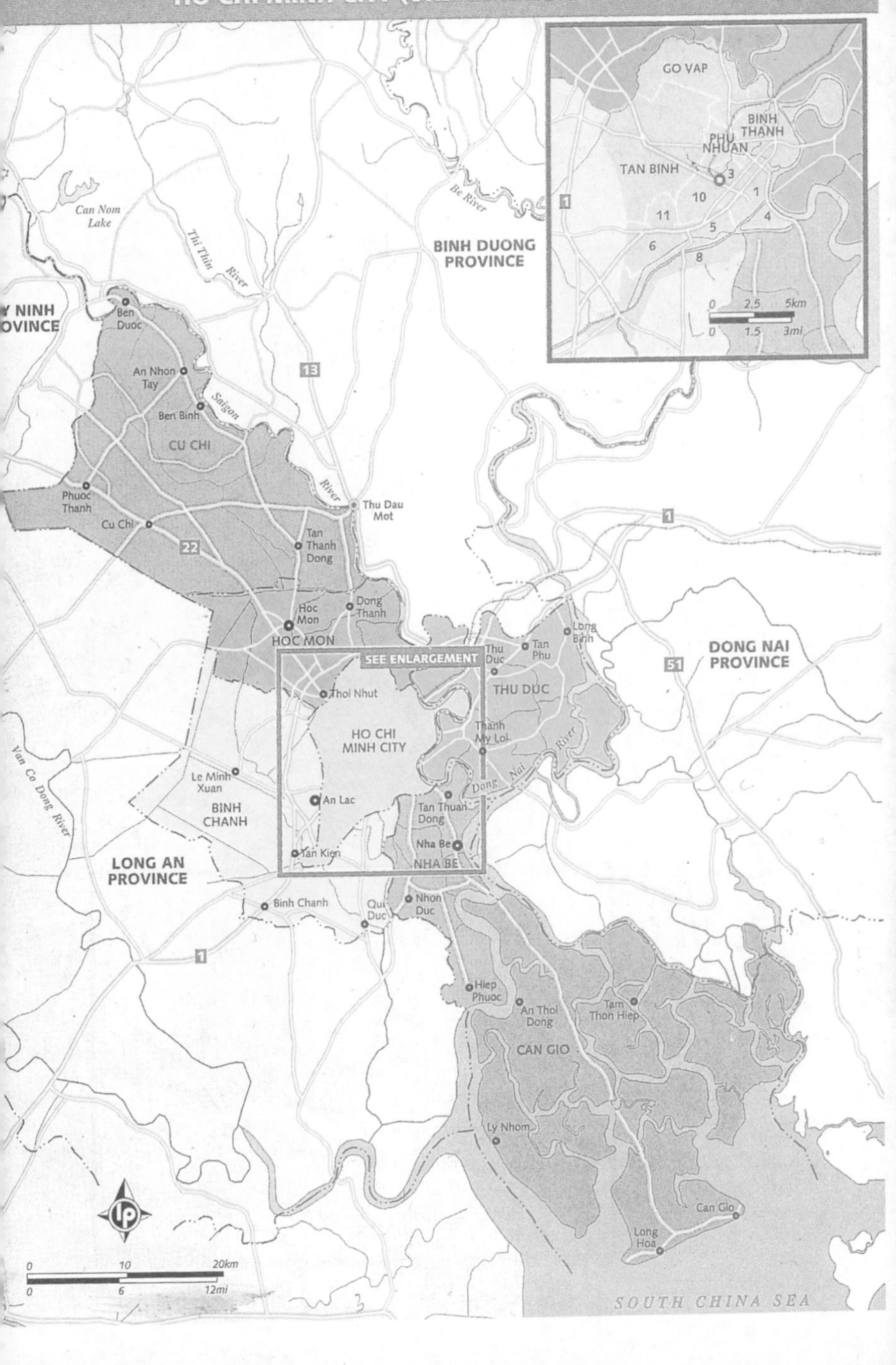
GO VAP
BINH THANH
PHU NHUAN
TAN BINH
3
10
1
11
5
4
6
8
1
0 2.5 5km
0 1.5 3mi
Can Nom Lake
Thi Thin River
Be River
BINH DUONG PROVINCE
TAY NINH PROVINCE
Ben Duoc
An Nhon Tay
Ben Binh
Saigon River
CU CHI
13
Phuoc Thanh
Cu Chi
22
Thu Dau Mot
Tan Thanh Dong
1
Hoc Mon
Dong Thanh
HOC MON
Thu Duc
Tan Phu
Long Binh
SEE ENLARGEMENT
DONG NAI PROVINCE
51
THU DUC
Thoi Nhut
HO CHI MINH CITY
Thanh My Loi
Dong Nai River
Van Co Dong River
Le Minh Xuan
BINH CHANH
An Lac
Tan Thuan Dong
Nha Be
NHA BE
Tan Kien
LONG AN PROVINCE
Binh Chanh
Qui Duc
Nhon Duc
1
Hiep Phuoc
An Thoi Dong
Tam Thon Hiep
CAN GIO
Ly Nhom
Can Gio
Long Hoa
0 10 20km
0 6 12mi
SOUTH CHINA SEA

To Cu Chi & Tay Ninh (90km)
Đ Cach Mang Tam
Runway
Terminal
Gia Dinh Park
Đ Nguyen Kiem
Đ Nguyen Thai Son
Phu Nhuan District
Đ Cong Hoa
ĐL Hoang Van Thu
Đ Cach Mang Thang Tam
ĐL Hoang Van Thu
Đ Le Van Sy
Đ Nguyen Van Troi
Tan Binh District
Đ Tran Quoc Thao
Huong Lo 14
Đ Au Co
Đ Ly Thuong Kiet
Le Thi Rieng Park
Đ Cach Mang Thang Tam
Saigon Train Station
Huong Lo 2
Đ To Hien Thanh
District 10
Ho Ky Hoa Park
Đ Dien Bien Phu
Huong Lo 14
Đ Lac Long Quan
Đ Le Dai Hanh
Phu Tho Race Track
Đ Nguyen Tri Phuong
Đ Binh Thoi
ĐL Ly Thai To
Đ Tran Binh Trong
Dam Sen Lake
Đ Ngo Gia Tu
District 5
District 11
Đ 3 Thang 2
Đ Tan Hoa
ĐL Nguyen Chi Thanh
ĐL Hung Vuong
ĐL An Duong Vuong
Đ Hung Vuong
ĐL Tran Hung Dao
Đ Ba Hom
Đ Minh Phung
ĐL Tran Hung Dao
Đ Ben Ham Tu
Đ Hung Vuong
To Mien Tay Bus Station & the Mekong Delta
ĐL Hau Giang
See Map 5 – Cholon
Đ Binh Tien
Đ Tran Van Kieu
Đ Pham The Hien
District 8
1
2
3
4
5
6
7
8
9
10
11
12
13
14
23
24
25
29
30
31
32
33
34

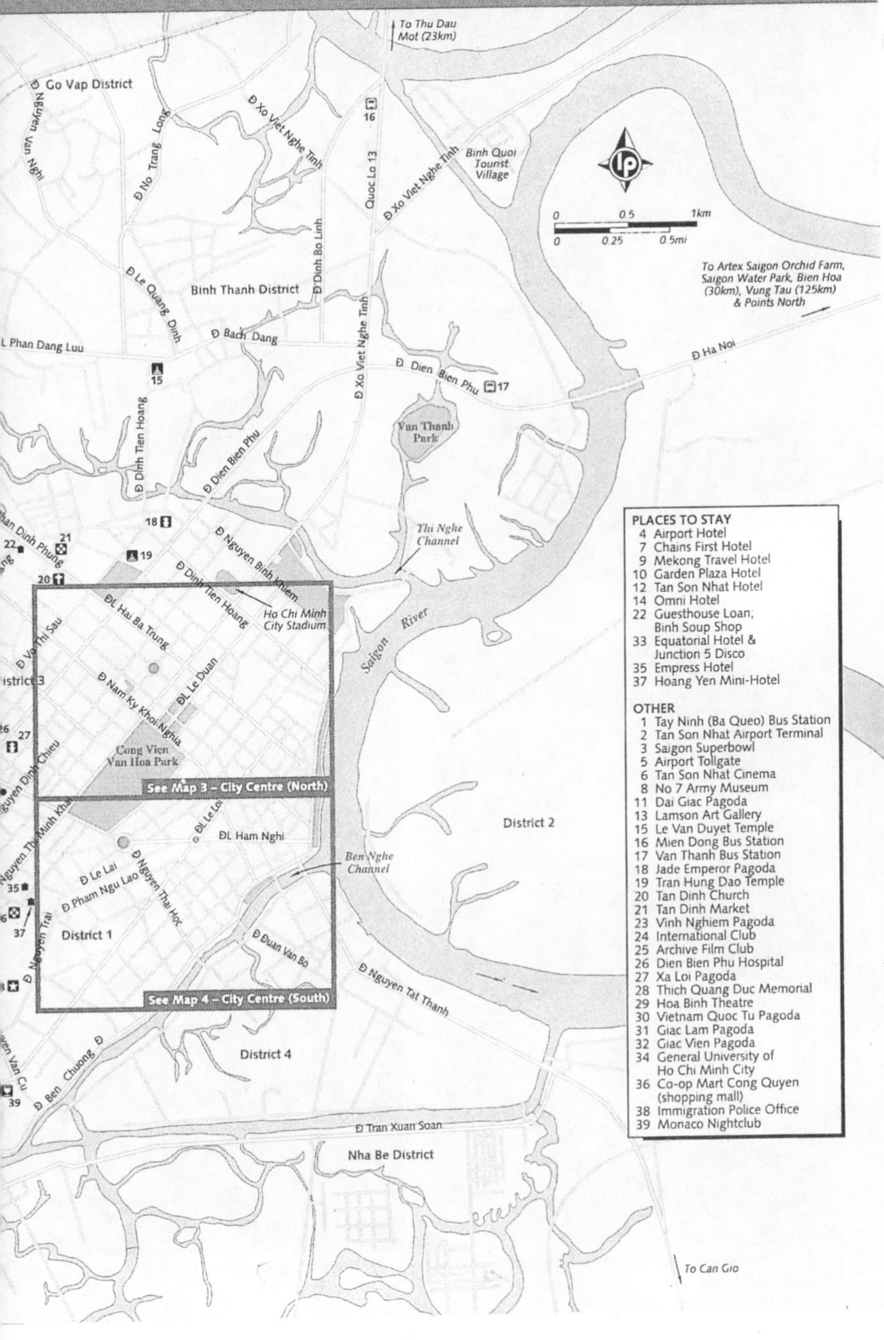

PLACES TO STAY
4 Airport Hotel
7 Chains First Hotel
9 Mekong Travel Hotel
10 Garden Plaza Hotel
12 Tan Son Nhat Hotel
14 Omni Hotel
22 Guesthouse Loan; Binh Soup Shop
33 Equatorial Hotel & Junction 5 Disco
35 Empress Hotel
37 Hoang Yen Mini-Hotel

OTHER
1 Tay Ninh (Ba Queo) Bus Station
2 Tan Son Nhat Airport Terminal
3 Saigon Superbowl
5 Airport Tollgate
6 Tan Son Nhat Cinema
8 No 7 Army Museum
11 Dai Giac Pagoda
13 Lamson Art Gallery
15 Le Van Duyet Temple
16 Mien Dong Bus Station
17 Van Thanh Bus Station
18 Jade Emperor Pagoda
19 Tran Hung Dao Temple
20 Tan Dinh Church
21 Tan Dinh Market
23 Vinh Nghiem Pagoda
24 International Club
25 Archive Film Club
26 Dien Bien Phu Hospital
27 Xa Loi Pagoda
28 Thich Quang Duc Memorial
29 Hoa Binh Theatre
30 Vietnam Quoc Tu Pagoda
31 Giac Lam Pagoda
32 Giac Vien Pagoda
34 General University of Ho Chi Minh City
36 Co-op Mart Cong Quyen (shopping mall)
38 Immigration Police Office
39 Monaco Nightclub

MASON FLORENCE

Wherever you look, there's construction going on.

JOHN BANAGAN

13th-century warrior Tran Hung Dao, Vung Tau

PHIL WEYMOUTH

Saigon's mercantile instinct is unsuppressible.

Cookie jars

ERIC L WHEATER

A scoop of 'kem' is a welcome treat.

PHIL WEYMOUTH

A couple of hours out of town

JOHN BORTHWICK

War-flavoured souvenirs at the Dan Sinh Market

ERIC L WHEATER

Incence coils, Chinese pagoda

NICK WELLMAN

Le Van Tam Park
Đ Mac Dinh Chi
Đ Phung Khac Khoan
Đ Vo Thi Sau
Đ Nguyen Van Thu
ĐL Hai Ba Trung
Đ Nguyen Dinh Chieu
Đ Dien Bien Phu
Đ Pham Ngoc Thach
Đ Vo Van Thanh
Đ Pasteur
Đ Nam Ky Khoi Nghia
Đ Dong Khoi
Đ Le Qui Don
Đ Ngo Thoi Nhiem
Đ Tran Quoc Thao
District 3
Đ Nguyen Dinh Chieu
Đ Vo Van Thanh
Đ Nguyen Thi Minh Khai
ĐL Le Duan
Đ Troung Dinh
Cong Vien Van Hoa Park
Đ Ba Huyen Thanh Quan
Đ Huyen Tran Cong Chua
Đ Vo Van Thanh
Đ Tran Quoc Thao
Đ Cach Mang Thang Tam
1
2
3
4
5
6
7
8
9
10
11
12
29
30
31
32
33
34
35
36
37
38
39
40
171
172

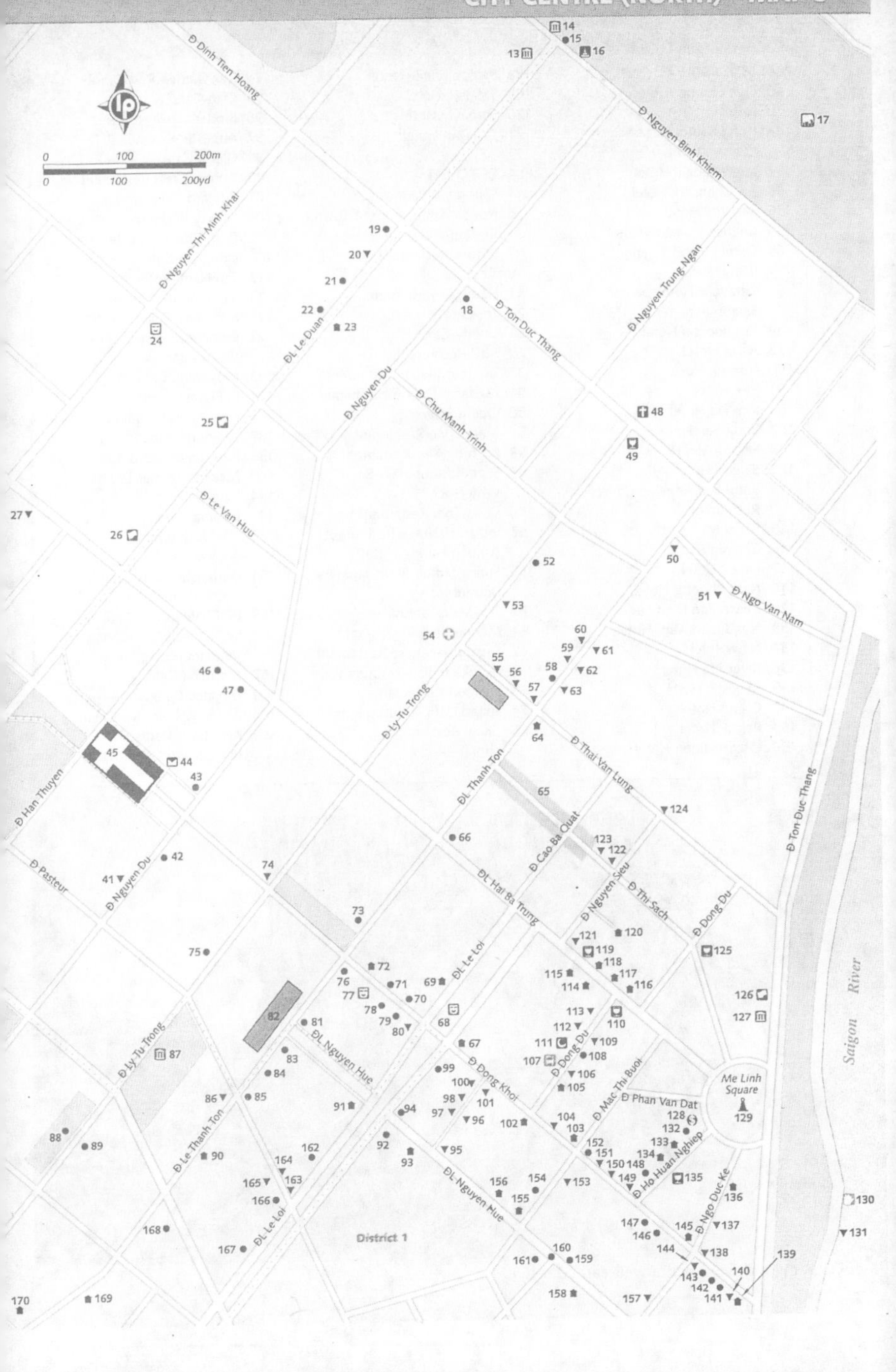

0
100
200m
0
100
200yd
Đ Dinh Tien Hoang
Đ Nguyen Binh Khiem
Đ Nguyen Thi Minh Khai
ĐL Le Duan
Đ Nguyen Du
Đ Ton Duc Thang
Đ Nguyen Trung Ngan
Đ Chu Manh Trinh
Đ Le Van Huu
Đ Ngo Van Nam
Đ Ly Tu Trong
ĐL Thanh Ton
Đ Thai Van Lung
Đ Han Thuyen
Đ Pasteur
Đ Nguyen Du
Đ Cao Ba Quat
ĐL Hai Ba Trung
Đ Nguyen Sieu
Đ Thi Sach
Đ Dong Du
Đ Ton Duc Thang
ĐL Le Loi
ĐL Nguyen Hue
Đ Dong Khoi
Đ Dong Du
Đ Mac Thi Buoi
Đ Phan Van Dat
Me Linh Square
Đ Ho Huan Nghiep
Đ Ngo Duc Ke
Đ Ly Tu Trong
Đ Le Thanh Ton
ĐL Le Loi
ĐL Nguyen Hue
District 1
Saigon River
13
14
15
16
17
18
19
20
21
22
23
24
25
26
27
41
42
43
44
45
46
47
48
49
50
51
52
53
54
55
56
57
58
59
60
61
62
63
64
65
66
67
68
69
70
71
72
73
74
75
76
77
78
79
80
81
82
83
84
85
86
87
88
89
90
91
92
93
94
95
96
97
98
99
100
101
102
103
104
105
106
107
108
109
110
111
112
113
114
115
116
117
118
119
120
121
122
123
124
125
126
127
128
129
130
131
132
133
134
135
136
137
138
139
140
141
142
143
144
145
146
147
148
149
150
151
152
153
154
155
156
157
158
159
160
161
162
163
164
165
166
167
168
169
170

CITY CENTRE (NORTH)

PLACES TO STAY

10 Que Huong (Liberty) Hotel
23 Hotel Sofitel Plaza Saigon; L'Elysee Jazz Bar
32 International Hotel
33 Sol Chancery Hotel
36 Bao Yen Hotel
39 Chancery Saigon Hotel
65 Orchid Hotel; Sheridan's Irish House
67 Caravelle Hotel; Saigon Saigon Bar
69 Continental Hotel
72 Asian Hotel
90 Norfolk Hotel
91 Rex Hotel
93 Kim Do Hotel
102 Bong Sen Hotel
103 Huong Sen Hotel
105 Saigon Hotel
114 Bong Sen Annexe; Ca Noi Restaurant
115 Hotel 69
116 Chuson Hotel
117 Fimex Hotel
118 Nam Phuong Hotel
120 Khach San Dien Luc
133 Nga Quan Mini-Hotel
134 New Hotel
136 Riverside Hotel
139 Majestic Hotel
145 Grand Hotel
155 Palace Hotel
156 Oscar Saigon Hotel
158 Saigon Prince Hotel
169 Tan Loc Hotel
170 Embassy Hotel
171 Tao Dan Hotel

PLACES TO EAT

1 Ristorante Pendolasco
5 Noodle Shop; Ancient Town Restaurant
7 L'Etoile Restaurant
8 Tib Cafe
11 Han Han Restaurant
20 Tin Cafe
27 Goody Cafe
29 ABC Restaurant
37 Tandoor Indian Restaurant
41 Madame Dai's Bibliotheque
50 Opera Saigon
51 Mandarine Restaurant
53 Bo Tung Xeo Restaurant
55 Sapa Restaurant & Bar; Why Not?
56 Chao Thai Restaurant
57 Indian Heritage Restaurant & Xuan Huong Hotel
59 Spring Hotel; A-Un Japanese Restaurant
60 Tex-Mex Cantina
61 Marine Club Restaurant
62 Sagano Japanese Restaurant
63 Ashoka Indian Restaurant
65 Seafood Restaurants
74 Spago Cafe & Restaurant
80 Givral Restaurant; Rap Dong Khoi
86 Rex Garden Restaurant
95 Ciao Cafe
96 Brodard Delicatessen
97 Augustin Restaurant
98 Globo Cafe
100 Lemon Grass Restaurant
101 Brodard Cafe
104 Liberty Restaurant
106 Com Chay 39 Restaurant
108 Dong Du Cafe
112 Tan Nam Restaurant
113 Sari Indo Restaurant
121 Kem Bach Dang (ice cream)
122 Camargue Restaurant & Vasco's Bar
123 Mogambo Cafe
124 Bi Bi Restaurant
131 Floating Restaurants
137 La Fourchette Restaurant
138 Restaurants 19 & 13
140 Maxim's Dinner Theatre
144 Paris Deli
149 Paloma Cafe
150 Cool Restaurant; Bookazine
151 Gartenstadt Restaurant; Authentique Interiors
153 PL Chateau Coffee Shop; Le Tonneau Spirits Shop; Vietnam House
157 Montana Cafe
163 Monaco Cafe
164 Baskin Robbins Ice Cream
165 Kem Bach Dang (Ice Cream)

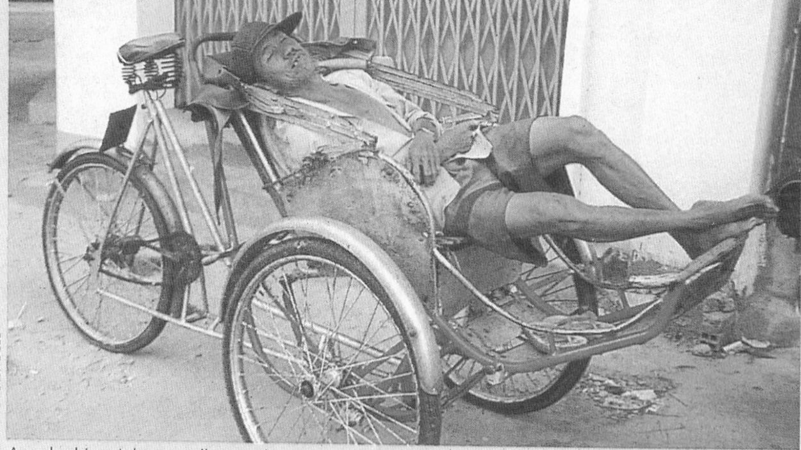

CRAIG PERSHOUSE

A cyclo driver takes a well-earned rest.

OTHER

2 Nha Ao Dai Tailor
3 Pasteur Institute
4 Si Hoang 2 Ao Dai Tailor
6 Ho Chi Minh City Association of Fine Arts
9 Laos Consulate
12 Cambodian Consulate
13 Ho Chi Minh Military Museum
14 History Museum
15 Main Zoo Gate
16 Temple of King Hung Vuong
17 Zoo & Botanical Garden
18 Saigon Trade Center; Panorama Restaurant; Singapore Airlines; Panorama 33
19 The Home Zone; Vidotour
21 Nguyen Freres Antique Shop
22 Viet My Bookshop (Stern's Books)
24 Ben Thanh Theatre
25 US Consulate; Former US Embassy
26 French Consulate
28 Hazzard Disco
30 War Remnants Museum
31 Xuan Gallery
34 Nha Van Hoa Lao Dong (Ballroom)
35 Tao Dan Photocopy
38 Vinh Loi Gallery
40 Reunification Palace
42 AEA Clinic; Thai Airways
43 EMS, UPS, Airbourne Express (courier services)
44 Central Post Office
45 Notre Dame Cathedral
46 VMS Mobi-Fone
47 Customs Office
48 Phao Co Church
49 No 5 Ly Tu Trong
52 Duc Minh Art Gallery
54 Hospital
58 Made in Vietnam (shop)
66 Saigon Art Frame
68 Municipal Theatre
70 Vietcombank Currency Exchange
71 Tu Do Gallery
73 Chi Linh Coffee Shop
75 Si Hoang Ao Dai Tailor
76 Saigon Tourist
77 Mang Non Theatre; Rap Mang Non Cinema
78 Hieu Sach Xuan Thue Bookstore
79 Vietnam Silk
81 Vietnam Airlines
82 People's Committee (Hôtel de Ville)
83 Kieu Giang Embroidery Shop
84 Kim Phuong Embroidery Shop
85 Federal Express
87 Museum of Ho Chi Minh City
88 City Court House
89 Municipal Library
92 Tax Department Store
94 Duty Free Shop
99 Foreign Currency Exchange Desk 59
107 Unofficial Bus Stop
109 Celadon Green; Indochine House
110 Hien & Bob's Place; Wild West
111 Saigon Central Mosque; Indian Canteen
119 Cafe 58
125 Apocalypse Now Bar
126 Australian Consulate
127 Ton Duc Thang Museum
128 ANZ Bank
129 Tran Hung Dao Statue
130 Ferries across Saigon River & to Mekong Delta
132 Ben Thanh Tourist
135 Tropical Rainforest Disco
141 Vietsilk
142 Precious Qui
143 Nam Kha Silk Collection
146 Heritage Arts & Crafts
147 Saigon Tourist Art Gallery
148 Tiem Sach Bookshop; Bo Gia Cafe
152 Cathay Pacific Airways
154 Khai Silk
159 Fahasa Bookshop
160 Clock Tower
161 Sun Wah Tower; Japan Airlines
162 East Meets West Shop
166 Kem Bach Dang
167 Saigon Bookstore
168 Saigon Intershop & Minimart
172 Conservatory of Music

PHIL WEYMOUTH

Water puppetry came originally from the north.

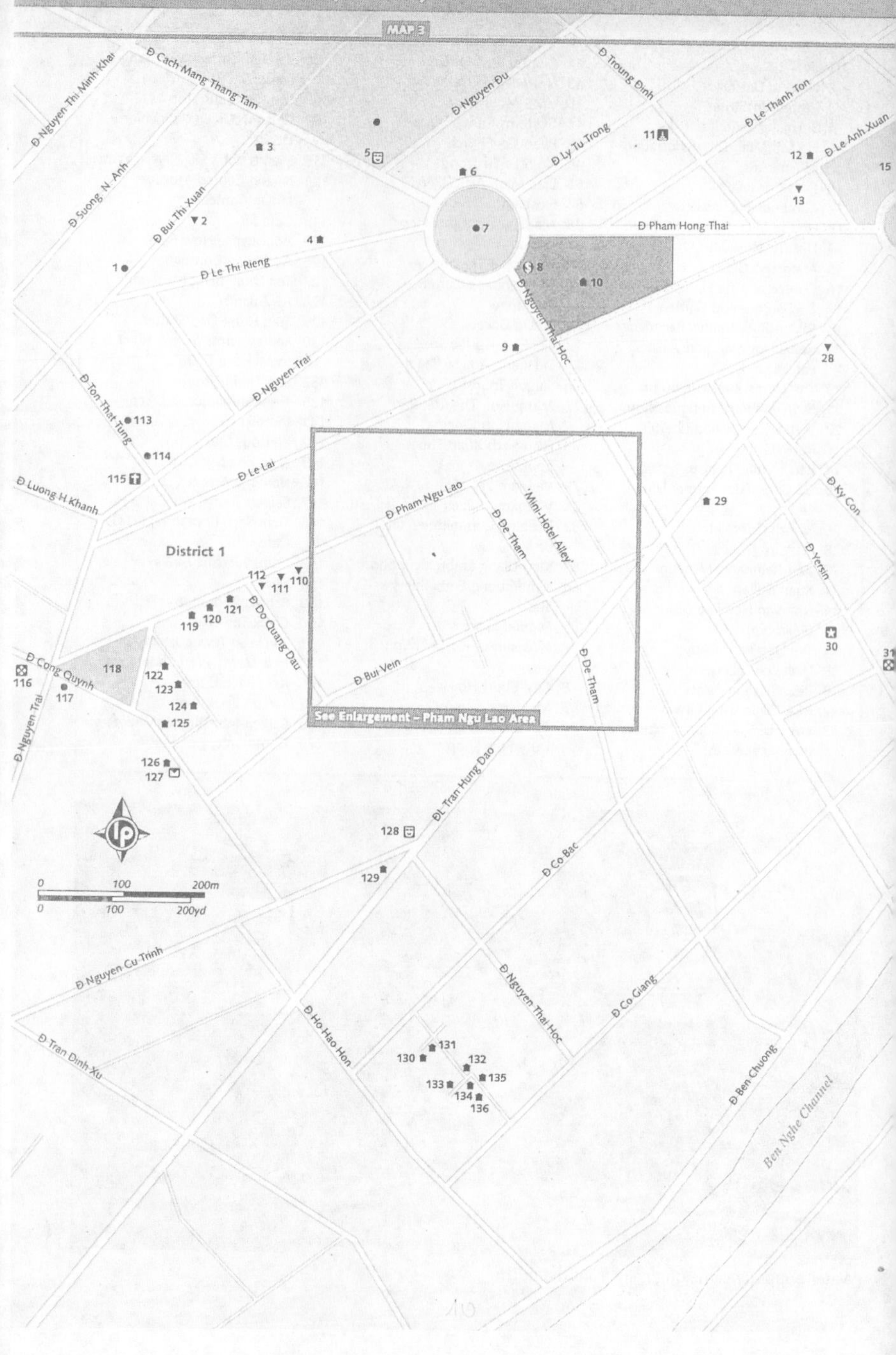
MAP 3
Đ Nguyen Thi Minh Khai
Đ Cach Mang Thang Tam
Đ Nguyen Du
Đ Truong Dinh
Đ Le Thanh Ton
Đ Le Anh Xuan
Đ Suong N. Anh
Đ Bui Thi Xuan
Đ Ly Tu Trong
Đ Pham Hong Thai
Đ Le Thi Rieng
Đ Nguyen Thai Hoc
Đ Nguyen Trai
Đ Ton That Tung
Đ Le Lai
Đ Luong H Khanh
District 1
Đ Pham Ngu Lao
Đ De Tham
'Mini-Hotel Alley'
Đ Ky Con
Đ Yersin
Đ Do Quang Dau
Đ Cong Quynh
Đ Bui Vein
Đ De Tham
See Enlargement – Pham Ngu Lao Area
Đ Nguyen Trai
ĐL Tran Hung Dao
Đ Co Bac
0 100 200m
0 100 200yd
Đ Nguyen Cu Trinh
Đ Nguyen Thai Hoc
Đ Co Giang
Đ Ho Hao Hon
Đ Tran Dinh Xu
Đ Ben Chuong
Ben Nghe Channel
1 2 3 4 5 6 7 8 9 10 11 12 13 15
28 29 30 31
110 111 112 113 114 115 116 117 118 119 120 121 122 123 124 125 126 127 128 129
130 131 132 133 134 135 136

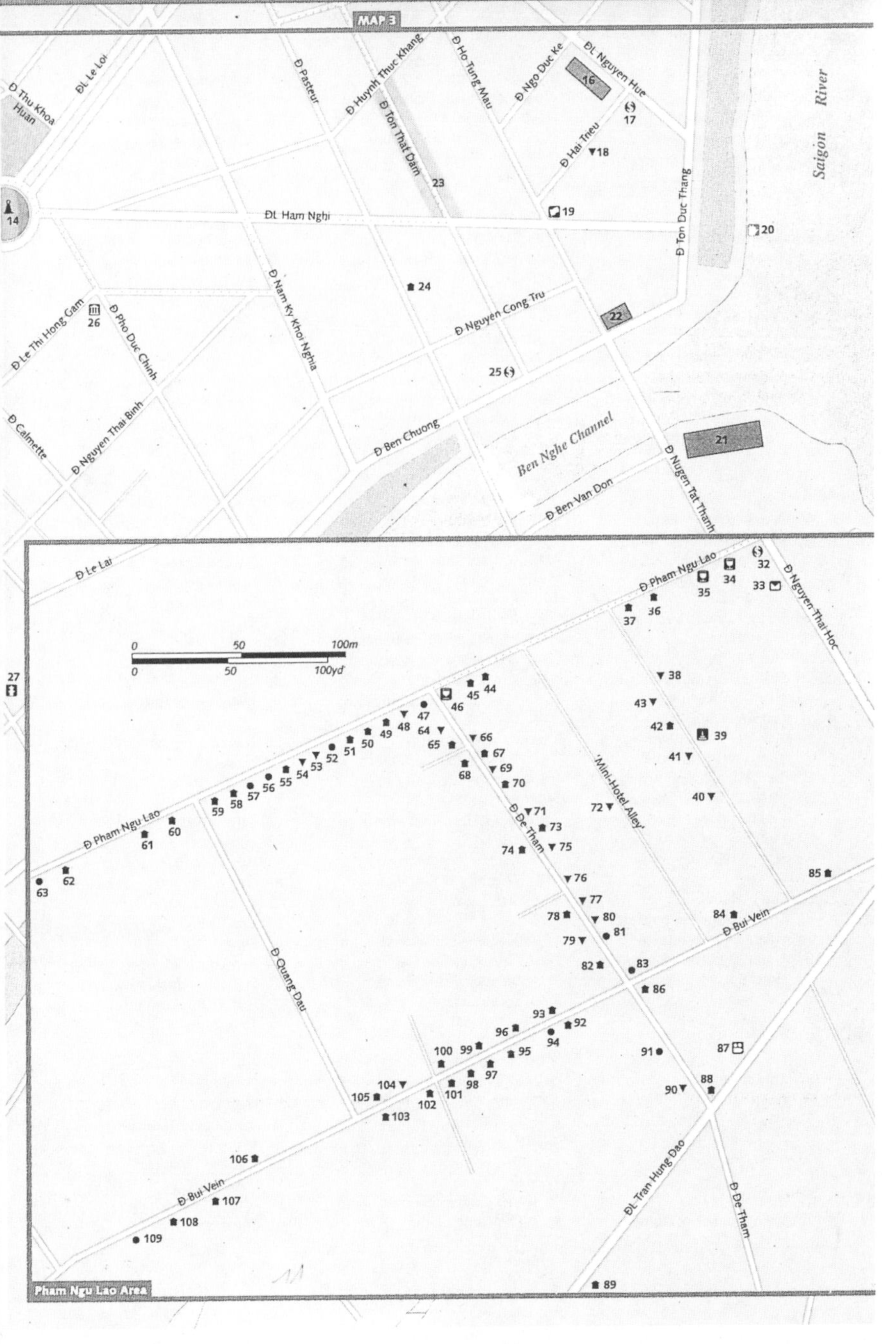

MAP 3
Đ Thu Khoa Huan
ĐL Le Loi
Đ Pasteur
Đ Huynh Thuc Khang
Đ Ton That Dam
Đ Ho Tung Mau
Đ Ngo Duc Ke
ĐL Nguyen Hue
Đ Hai Trieu
Saigon River
ĐL Ham Nghi
Đ Ton Duc Thang
Đ Nam Ky Khoi Nghia
Đ Le Thi Hong Gam
Đ Pho Duc Chinh
Đ Nguyen Cong Tru
Đ Calmette
Đ Nguyen Thai Binh
Đ Ben Chuong
Ben Nghe Channel
Đ Nugen Tat Thanh
Đ Ben Van Don
Đ Le Lai
Đ Pham Ngu Lao
Đ Nguyen Thai Hoc
0 50 100m
0 50 100yd
Đ De Tham
'Mini-Hotel Alley'
Đ Quang Dau
Đ Bui Vein
ĐL Tran Hung Dao
Pham Ngu Lao Area

CITY CENTRE (SOUTH)

PLACES TO STAY
3 Rang Dong Hotel
4 Oriole Hotel
5 Saigon Royal Hotel
9 Palace Saigon Hotel
10 New World Hotel; Catwalk Night Club; Saxophone Lounge
12 Galaxy Hotel
24 Rose Hotel
29 Mercure Hotel
36 Le Le Hotel
37 Giant Dragon Hotel
42 Linh Linh Hotel
44 Liberty 3 Hotel
45 Saigon Commercial Centre (Under Construction)
49 Tan Thanh Thanh Hotel
50 Mai Phai Hotel
51 Hotel 211; Guns & Roses Bar
55 Ocean Hotel
58 Hanh Hoa Hotel
59 Liberty 4 Hotel
60 Hotel 269; Anh Khoa Bookshop
61 Vien Dong Hotel & Cheers Nightclub
62 Tan Kim Long Hotel
65 Le Le 2 (Vinh) Guesthouse
67 Peace Hotel
68 Hotel 265
70 Hoang Anh Mini-Hotel
73 Ngoc Dang Hotel; Lan Anh Hotel
74 Anh Dao Guesthouse
78 Thanh Ngi Guesthouse
82 Tan Thanh & Thanh Tam Hotel; Cua Hang Mat Kinh Optical Shop
84 Vuong Hoa Guesthouse
85 Hong Kong Mini-Hotel
86 Quyen Thanh Hotel
88 The A Hotel
89 The Windsor Saigon Hotel; Four Seasons Restaurant
92 Phuong Hoang Mini-Hotel
93 Hotel 64; Minh Phuc Guesthouse
95 Hong Quyen Hotel
96 Phuong Lan Guesthouse; Linh Thu Guesthouse
97 Vu Chau Hotel
98 Guesthouse 41
99 Huy Doc Hotel; Hai Ha Mini-Hotel
100 Van Trang Hotel; Hai Duong Hotel
101 Hotel Hong Loi
102 Minh Chau Guesthouse
103 Thanh Guesthouse
105 96 Guesthouse
106 Hop Thanh Guesthouse
107 Guesthouse 97
108 Tuan Anh Guesthouse
119 Tan Kim Long Hotel
120 Hai Son Hotel
121 Bau Chau Hotel
122 Coco Loco Guesthouse
123 Nhat Thai Hotel
124 My Man Mini-Hotel
125 Tuan Anh Hotel
126 Hotel 127
129 Metropole Hotel
130 Minh Guesthouse
131 Kim Loan Guesthouse
132 Guesthouse Thanh
133 Ngoc Hue Guesthouse
134 Bich Hong Guesthouse
135 Miss Loi's Guesthouse
136 Xuan Thu Guesthouse

PLACES TO EAT
2 Annie's Pizza
13 Bavaria Restaurant
18 Urvashi Restaurant
28 Tin Nghia Vegetarian Restaurant
38 Margherita Restaurant
40 Penny Lane Russian BBQ
41 Zen Vegetarian Restaurant
43 Bodhi Tree 1 & 2 Vegetarian Restaurants
48 Lotus Cafe
53 Cafe 215
54 Trang Indian Restaurant
64 Saigon Cafe
66 Bin Cafe
69 Kim Cafe & Tour Booking Office
71 Cappuccino Restaurant
72 Thuong Chi Restaurant
75 Sinh Cafe & Booking Office
76 Sasa Cafe
77 Sunshine Indian Restaurant
79 Cafe 333; Good Morning Vietnam Bar-Restaurant
80 Lucky Cafe; An Do Indian Restaurant
90 Cafe Van (The Sandwich Box)
104 Pho Bo Noodle Shop
110 Kim's Cafe & Bar
111 Linh Cafe
112 Song Bao Bakery

OTHER
1 Viet Quang Internet Service
7 Phu Dong Statue
8 HSBC
11 Mariamman Hindu Temple
14 Tran Nguyen Hai Statue
15 Ben Thanh Market
16 Courthouse
17 Bangkok Bank
19 Former US Embassy
20 Bach Dang Wharf; Vung Tau Hydrofoil; Saigon Water Park Ferry; Small Boats for Hire
21 Ho Chi Minh Museum
22 Treasury Building
23 Old Market; Huynh Thuc Khang Street Market
25 Vietcombank
26 Fine Arts Museum; Blue Space; Nhat Le & Lac Hong Galleries
27 Phung Son Tu Pagoda
30 Yersin Police Station
31 Dan Sinh (War Surplus) Market
32 Sacombank
33 Post Office; Saigon Net Internet Service
34 Bia Hoi
35 Long Phi Bar
39 Chua An Lac Temple
46 Allez Boo Bar
47 Fiditourist & Vietcombank Currency Exchange
52 Nam Duong Travel Agency
56 Photo Nhu
57 Sapa 2
63 Saigon Railways Tourist Company; Bar Rolling Stones
81 Saigon Net Internet Service
83 Quyen Thanh Hotel
87 Cong Nhan Cinema
91 Sapa 3
94 Ben Thanh Tourist; Sinhbalo Adventures
109 Duc Thanh Coffee & Tea Shop
113 Ann Tours
114 Huy Hoang Tailor Shop
115 Huyen Si Cathedral
116 Hanoi Mart Supermarket
117 Vietnamese Traditional Massage Institute
118 Thai Binh Market
127 Post Office
128 Nha Hat Cai Luong Theatre

GREG ELMS

A party of revellers assembles before the photogenic Hôtel de Ville (People's Committee Building).

PHIL WEYMOUTH

The vaulted interior of the Central Post Office, completed 1891, central Saigon

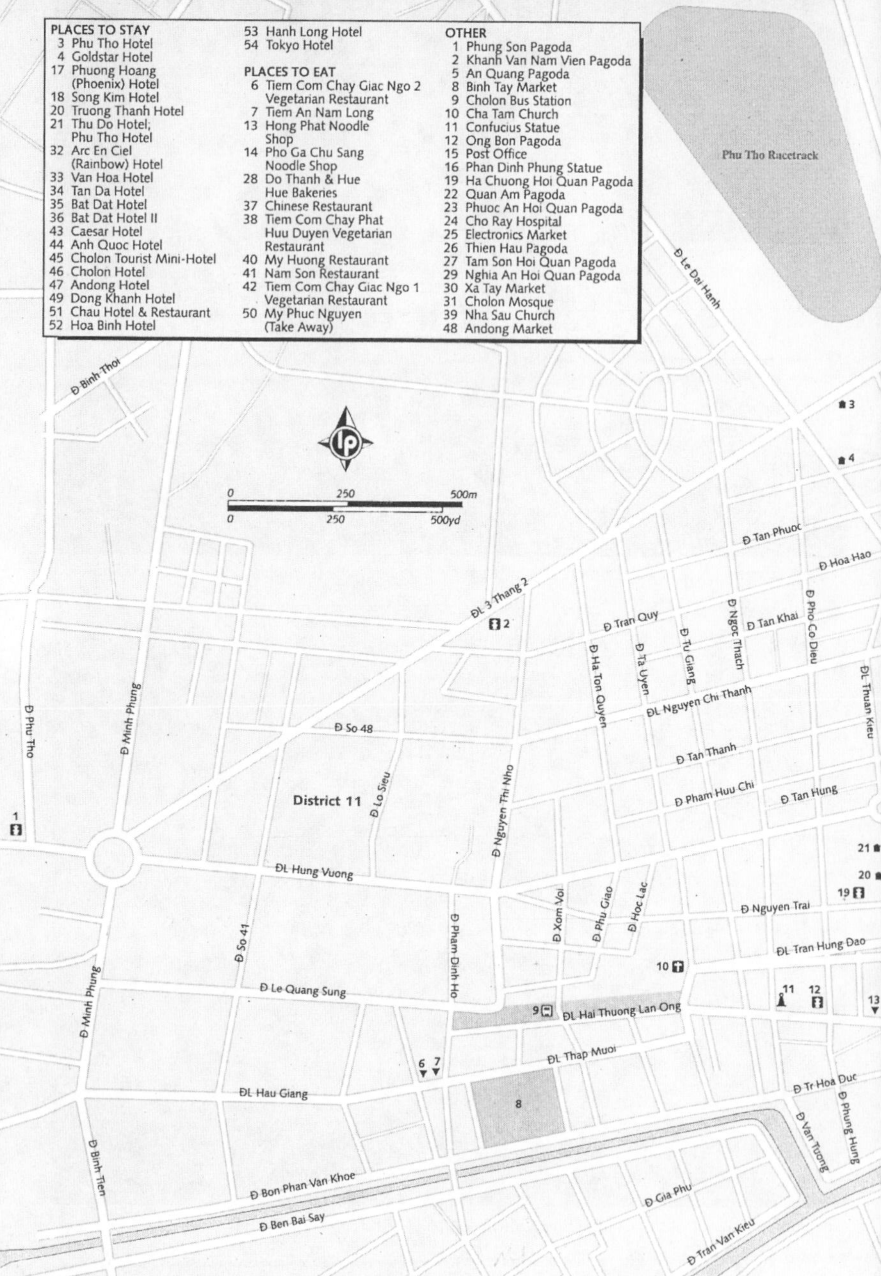
PLACES TO STAY
3 Phu Tho Hotel
4 Goldstar Hotel
17 Phuong Hoang (Phoenix) Hotel
18 Song Kim Hotel
20 Truong Thanh Hotel
21 Thu Do Hotel; Phu Tho Hotel
32 Arc En Ciel (Rainbow) Hotel
33 Van Hoa Hotel
34 Tan Da Hotel
35 Bat Dat Hotel
36 Bat Dat Hotel II
43 Caesar Hotel
44 Anh Quoc Hotel
45 Cholon Tourist Mini-Hotel
46 Cholon Hotel
47 Andong Hotel
49 Dong Khanh Hotel
51 Chau Hotel & Restaurant
52 Hoa Binh Hotel
53 Hanh Long Hotel
54 Tokyo Hotel
PLACES TO EAT
6 Tiem Com Chay Giac Ngo 2 Vegetarian Restaurant
7 Tiem An Nam Long
13 Hong Phat Noodle Shop
14 Pho Ga Chu Sang Noodle Shop
28 Do Thanh & Hue Hue Bakeries
37 Chinese Restaurant
38 Tiem Com Chay Phat Huu Duyen Vegetarian Restaurant
40 My Huong Restaurant
41 Nam Son Restaurant
42 Tiem Com Chay Giac Ngo 1 Vegetarian Restaurant
50 My Phuc Nguyen (Take Away)
OTHER
1 Phung Son Pagoda
2 Khanh Van Nam Vien Pagoda
5 An Quang Pagoda
8 Binh Tay Market
9 Cholon Bus Station
10 Cha Tam Church
11 Confucius Statue
12 Ong Bon Pagoda
15 Post Office
16 Phan Dinh Phung Statue
19 Ha Chuong Hoi Quan Pagoda
22 Quan Am Pagoda
23 Phuoc An Hoi Quan Pagoda
24 Cho Ray Hospital
25 Electronics Market
26 Thien Hau Pagoda
27 Tam Son Hoi Quan Pagoda
29 Nghia An Hoi Quan Pagoda
30 Xa Tay Market
31 Cholon Mosque
39 Nha Sau Church
48 Andong Market
Phu Tho Racetrack
Đ Le Dai Hanh
Đ Binh Thoi
0 250 500m
0 250 500yd
Đ Tan Phuoc
Đ Hoa Hao
ĐL 3 Thang 2
Đ Tran Quy
Đ Ngoc Thach
Đ Pho Co Dieu
Đ Tan Khai
Đ Tu Giang
Đ Ta Uyen
Đ Ha Ton Quyen
ĐL Thuan Kieu
ĐL Nguyen Chi Thanh
Đ Phu Tho
Đ Minh Phung
Đ So 48
Đ Tan Thanh
Đ Pham Huu Chi
Đ Tan Hung
District 11
Đ Lo Sieu
Đ Nguyen Thi Nho
ĐL Hung Vuong
Đ Xom Voi
Đ Phu Giao
Đ Hoc Lac
Đ Nguyen Trai
ĐL Tran Hung Dao
Đ So 41
Đ Pham Dinh Ho
Đ Le Quang Sung
ĐL Hai Thuong Lan Ong
ĐL Thap Muoi
ĐL Hau Giang
Đ Tr Hoa Duc
Đ Van Tuong
Đ Phung Hung
Đ Binh Tien
Đ Bon Phan Van Khoe
Đ Ben Bai Say
Đ Gia Phu
Đ Tran Van Kieu